The Namibian War
of Independence,
1966–1989

The Namibian War of Independence, 1966–1989

Diplomatic, Economic and Military Campaigns

RICHARD DALE

McFarland & Company, Inc., Publishers
Jefferson, North Carolina

All maps are public domain and can be found at
http//ian.macky.net/pat/map/country.html

LIBRARY OF CONGRESS CATALOGUING-IN-PUBLICATION DATA

Dale, Richard, 1932– author.
The Namibian war of independence, 1966–1989 : diplomatic, economic and military campaigns / Richard Dale.
    p.   cm.
Includes bibliographical references and index.

ISBN 978-0-7864-9659-4 (softcover : acid free paper) ∞
ISBN 978-1-4766-1807-4 (ebook)

1. Namibia—History—1946–1990.
2. Namibia—History—Autonomy and independence movements.
3. Namibia—Politics and government—1946–1990.
4. Decolonization—Namibia.   I. Title.
DT1645.D35 2014   968.8103—dc23   2014037037

BRITISH LIBRARY CATALOGUING DATA ARE AVAILABLE

© 2014 Richard Dale. All rights reserved

No part of this book may be reproduced or transmitted in any form or by any means, electronic or mechanical, including photocopying or recording, or by any information storage and retrieval system, without permission in writing from the publisher.

On the cover: Acacia tree next to a sand dune © 2014 iStock/Thinkstock

Printed in the United States of America

*McFarland & Company, Inc., Publishers
Box 611, Jefferson, North Carolina 28640
www.mcfarlandpub.com*

For Doris

Table of Contents

Acknowledgments viii
Abbreviations and Acronyms xi
Preface 1
Maps 6
Introduction 13

Part I: The Diplomatic Campaigns
CHAPTER ONE: The Diplomacy of Resistance   25
CHAPTER TWO: The Diplomacy of Controlled Change   37

Part II: The Economic Campaigns
CHAPTER THREE: Waging Economic Warfare   53
CHAPTER FOUR: No Easy Target   62

Part III: The Military Campaigns
CHAPTER FIVE: The War for the Colonial Spoils   73
CHAPTER SIX: South Africa's Bush War   92

Part IV: The Residue of the Campaigns
CHAPTER SEVEN: The Art of Bending   111
CHAPTER EIGHT: Conclusions   121

Appendix: The United Nations and Namibia 133
Chapter Notes 139
Bibliography 173
Index 195

Acknowledgments

This research is the result of an enormous amount of cooperation and assistance from a wide array of individuals and institutions that, together, constitute what has been termed the invisible college. My interest in Southern Africa began in 1957, when I wrote my master's thesis on Namibia and the United Nations at The Ohio State University. That led to further research on this topic for my doctoral dissertation at Princeton University in 1962, and in the summer of 1964 I was able to begin a study of Afrikaans at the University of California at Los Angeles thanks to a National Defense Foreign Language Fellowship. While a faculty member of the Department of Political Science at Southern Illinois University I had the pleasure of listening to speakers Ambassador Donald McHenry and Assistant Secretary of State for African Affairs Herman Cohen, both of whom were involved in United States policy toward Namibia.

Under the aegis of the Department of State program for overseas visitors, my wife Doris and I had houseguests from Namibia, the journalist Clive Cowley and the political scientist Gerhard K.H. Tötemeyer. In 1984–1985 I served as a visiting faculty member in the U.S. Army's foreign area officer program at Fort Bragg, North Carolina. One of the recent graduates of that program, Lt. Col. Kenneth Crabtree, and a Foreign Service Officer, Dennis Keogh, had been killed by a car bomb in Oshakati, Namibia, on 15 April 1984. One of the classrooms used in the foreign area officer program was named in memory of Lt. Col. Crabtree, while Mr. Keogh's photograph is displayed in the U.S. Embassy in Windhoek. That experience at Ft. Bragg, my prior 1957–1959 service as an enlisted man in the Third Infantry Division in the United States and West Germany, and several years of teaching a course in comparative civil-military politics at Southern Illinois University accounts for the considerable attention devoted to the military aspects of the Namibian war of independence.

I am especially grateful for the time, care and effort that Gary F. Baines, Christo B. Botha, Christopher C. Saunders, and Gerhard K. H. Tötemeyer took to read and to suggest improvements in the first draft of the manuscript as well as to send me additional materials. Quite a number of university and institute libraries and their librarians have been most accommodating, especially the African Studies Center (Leiden), the Africa Institute of South Africa (Pretoria), Arizona State University Hayden Library (Tempe), the Basler Afrika Bibliographien (Basel), the Center for Research Libraries (Chicago), the

Institute for Contemporary History of the University of the Free State (Bloemfontein), the Institute for Strategic Studies of University of Pretoria, the Namibia Scientific Society (Windhoek), the National Archives of Namibia (Windhoek), the National Library of Namibia (Windhoek), the Parliamentary Library of Namibia (Windhoek), the Scottsdale, Arizona Public Library System, the South African Department of Defense Documentation Center (Pretoria), the South African Institute of International Affairs Library (Braamfontein), the South African Institute of Race Relations Library (Braamfontein), Southern Illinois University at Carbondale Morris Library, the State Library (Pretoria and Cape Town), the University of Cape Town Library (Rondebosch), the University of Wisconsin–Madison Library, the Stellenbosch University Law School Library, and the University of the Witwatersrand Cullen Library (Braamfontein).

In particular, I am most obliged to the following persons for providing information, materials, and bibliographic assistance: Ms. Constance Adamson (Stauffer Library, Queen's University), Ms. Carol Archibald (Historical Collection, Cullen Library, University of the Witwatersrand), Mr. Jacob Astley (University of Central Oklahoma), the late Professor Leo Barnard (University of the Free State), Mr. Erik Blumer (South African Consulate General, Chicago), Professor Tilman Dedering (University of South Africa), Mrs. Ingrid Demasius (Namibia Scientific Society), Mrs. Elmien de Weerdt (University of South Africa Library), Dr. Tanya du Plessis (University of Johannesburg–Rand Afrikaans University), Professor C. John R. Dugard (University of the Witwatersrand School of Law), Warrant Officer Paul J. Els (South African Defense Force, retired), Professor Deon F .S. Fourie (University of South Africa), Ms. Karen Fung (Stanford University Library), Dr. Jan-Bart Gewald (African Studies Center, Leiden), Professor Robert J. Gordon (University of Vermont), Ms. Sally A. Harper (University of Namibia), Mrs. Melinda Heese (J.S. Gericke Library, Stellenbosch University), Dr. David Henige (University of Wisconsin–Madison Library), Dr. Dag Henrichsen (Basel Afrika Bibliographien), Mr. Werner Hillebrecht (National Archives of Namibia), Dr. Terence McNamee (Royal United Services Institute for Defense and Security Studies, London), Mr. Graham Hopwood (Institute for Public Policy Research, Windhoek), Ms. Louise Jooste (South African National Defense Force Documentation Directorate, Pretoria), Mr. F. Jochen Kutzner (National Archives of Namibia), Dr. Peter Limb (Michigan State University), Mrs. Jewell Koopman (Alan Paton Center, University of KwaZulu-Natal, Pietermaritzburg), Dr. Henning Melber (Dag Hammarskjöld Foundation, Uppsala), Dr. Thomas Ohlson (Uppsala University), Ms. Latifa Omar (University of Cape Town), Ms. Michele Pickover (Historical Collection, Cullen Library, University of the Witwatersrand), Dr. Paul B. Rich (University of Cambridge), Professor Annette Seegers (University of Cape Town), Mr. Tor Sellström (Swedish International Development Authority), Ms. Mary-Lynn Suttie (University of South Africa Library), Professor S. Susanna Visser (Northwest University, Potchefstroom campus), General Chris Thirion (South African Defense Force, retired), Mrs. Hester van den Berg (Institute for Contemporary History, University of the Free State), Mrs. Amanda Wortmann (Africa Institute of South Africa Library), Professor André Wessels (University of the Free State), Dr. Thomas D. Young (U.S. Naval Postgraduate School), and Mrs. Jenifer Zies (Scottsdale Public Library).

During my visits to Namibia and South Africa, several persons were most hospitable to me and to my wife Doris, and they were able to arrange meetings and interviews for me. I am especially grateful to the late Professor Leo Barnard, Mrs. Cathy Blatt (Windhoek), Mr. Clive Cowley (Windhoek), Professor André du Pisani (University of Namibia), Ms. Louise Jooste, Mrs. Johanna C. F. Schoeman (Windhoek), Professor Annette Seegers, the late Mr. Eric B. Stander (Pretoria), Professor Gerhard Tötemeyer, and Dr. Paul S. van der Merwe (Otjiwarongo, Namibia). Over the course of my career in the Department of Political Science at Southern Illinois University at Carbondale, I was fortunate to have received grants from the American Philosophical Society, the Earhart Foundation, and the Inter-University Seminar on Armed Forces and Society to support some of my research work on Southern Africa. My departmental colleagues in Carbondale were always generous with their time and counsel, and the Department as well as the University Office of Research Development kindly arranged for me to have graduate research assistants, released research time, and university funding for my Southern African research projects. Dr. Dan L. Seiters and Mr. James D. Simons of the Southern Illinois University Press went to great lengths to provide exceptionally helpful advice on the intricacies of the book-publishing world. I have dedicated this book to my wife Doris with gratitude for her counsel, skills, and patience. She went overseas with me and was involved in ever so many of the research tasks and trips.

Abbreviations and Acronyms

Currency
N$ — (Namibian) dollars
R — (South African) Rand

Governmental and International Organization Materials and Terms

CIVPOL — Police element of UNTAG
CRS — Congressional Research Service
DGASLS — Department of Governmental Affairs, Section Liaison Services
doc. — document
GPr — Government Printer
ICJ — International Court of Justice
ICJPOAD, *Legal Consequences* — International Court of Justice. Pleadings, Oral Arguments Documents, *Legal Consequences for States of the Continued Presence of South Africa in Namibia (South West Africa) Notwithstanding Security Council Resolution 276 (1970)*
ICJPOAD, *South West Africa Cases* — International Court of Justice. Pleadings, Oral Arguments, Documents, *South West Africa Cases (Ethiopia v. South Africa; Liberia v. South Africa)*
ICJRJAOO, *Admissibility* — International Court of Justice. Reports of Judgments, Advisory Opinions, and Orders, *Admissibility of Hearings of Petitioners by the Committee on South West Africa: Advisory Opinion of June 1st, 1956*
ICJRJAOO, *Legal Consequences* — International Court of Justice. Reports of Judgments, Advisory Opinions, and Orders, *Legal Consequences for States of the Continued Presences of South Africa in Namibia (South West Africa) Notwithstanding Security Council Resolution 276 (1970): Advisory Opinion of 21 June 1971*
ICJRJAOO, *Preliminary Objections* — International Court of Justice. Reports of Judgments, Advisory, Opinions, and Orders, *South West Africa Cases (Ethiopia v. South Africa; Liberia v. South Africa): Preliminary Objections*
MP(s) — Member(s) of Parliament
NAN — National Archives of Namibia
NMFA — Namibia. Ministry of Foreign Affairs
NPNA, *Debates* — Namibia. Parliament. National Assembly, *Debates*
OAU — Organization of African Unity
para(s). — paragraph(s)
PMC — Permanent Mandates Commission (of the League of Nations)
PRO — Public Records Office
res. — resolution
SADFA — South Africa. Department of Foreign Affairs
SAP, *Debates* — South Africa. Parliament, *Debates*
SAPHA, *Debates* — South Africa. Parliament. House of Assembly, *Debates*
SAPS, *Debates* — South Africa. Parliament. Senate, *Debates*
SIDA — Swedish International Development Authority

SRM — Summary Records of Meetings
SWALAVP — South West Africa. Legislative Assembly, *Votes and Proceedings*
TRCSA, *Report* — Truth and Reconciliation Commission of South Africa, *Report*
UN — United Nations
UNCN — United Nations Council for Namibia
UNDPI — United Nations Department of Public Information
UNESCO — United Nations Educational, Scientific, and Cultural Organization
UNGA — United Nations General Assembly
UNGAOR — United Nations General Assembly Official Records
UNIN — United Nations Institute for Namibia
UNSC — United Nations Security Council
UNTAG — United Nations Transition Assistance Group
USAWCSSI — United States Army War College Strategic Studies Institute
USCHRCFA — United States Congress. House of Representatives. Committee on Foreign Affairs
USCSCJ — United States Congress. Senate. Committee on the Judiciary
USGPO — United States Government Printing Office
WB — World Bank
YUN — Yearbook(s) of the United Nations

Journals and Yearbooks

AA — *African Affairs*
AAASPS — *Annals of the American Academy of Social and Political Science*
AFS — *Armed Forces and Society*
AHR — *African Historical Review*
AI — *Africa Insight*
AJIL — *American Journal of International Law*
APSR — *The American Political Science Review*
AQ — *Africa Quarterly*
AR — *Africa Report*
BNR — *Botswana Notes and Records*
BYIL — *British Yearbook of International Law*
CeD — *Cultures et Développment*
CQ — *Conflict Quarterly*
CRSN — *Canadian Review of Studies in Nationalism*
CSP — *Contemporary Security Policy*
CSSH — *Comparative Studies in Society and History*
CSt — *Comparative Strategy*
CYIL — *Canadian Yearbook of International Law*
DA — *Defense Analysis*
FPRSA — *Focus on Political Repression in Southern Africa*
HRQ — *Human Rights Quarterly*
IA — *International Affairs*
IFLAJ — *International Federation of Library Associations and Institutions Journal*
IOr — *International Organization*
IP — *International Peacekeeping*
ISP — *International Studies Perspectives*
ISQ — *International Studies Quarterly*
ISSUPB — Institute of Strategic Studies, University of Pretoria, *Bulletin*
ISSUPSR — Institute of Strategic Studies, University of Pretoria, *Strategic Review*
ISSUPSRSA — Institute of Strategic Studies, University of Pretoria, *Strategic Review for Southern Africa*
JAH — *Journal of African History*
JCAS — *Journal of Contemporary African Studies*
JCH — *Journal for Contemporary History*
JCR — *Journal of Conflict Resolution*
JCS — *Journal of Conflict Studies*
JES — *Journal of European Studies*
JMAS — *The Journal of Modern African Studies*
JNS — *Journal of Namibian Studies*
JSAS — *Journal of Southern African Studies*
LJIL — *Leiden Journal of International Law*
MHJ — *Military History Journal*
MOPJSADF — *Militaria: Official Professional Journal of the SADF*
MR — *Military Review*
NEP — *Nationalism and Ethnic Politics*
PG — *Political Geography*
PHR — *Pacific Historical Review*
PJUSAWC — *Parameters: Journal of the U.S. Army War College*
POMSADF — *Paratus: Official Magazine of the SADF*
PS — *Plural Societies*
PSAJPS — *Politikon: South African Journal of Political Science/Studies*
PSQ — *Political Science Quarterly*

RdC — *Recueil des Cours: Collected Courses of the Hague* — Academy of International Law
SA — *Die Suid-Afrikaan*
SAD — *South African Digest*
SAHJ — *South African Historical Journal*
SAI — *South Africa International*
SAIIAIAB — South African Institute of International Affairs International Affairs *Bulletin*
SAIRRRRN — South African Institute of Race Relations, *Race Relations News*
SAJIA — *South African Journal of International Affairs*
SAR — *Southern Africa Report*
SARc — *Southern Africa Record*
SAYIL — *South African Yearbook of International Law*
SJSAAS — *Safundi: The Journal of South African and American Studies*
SM — *Scientia Miitaria*
SWAPSSQ — *The Southwestern Political and Social Science Quarterly*
SWI — *Small Wars and Insurgencies*
TAF — *TransAfrica Forum*
TE — *The Economist*
TF — *The Forum*
TNt — *The Nation*
WoP — *World Politics*
WPSAS — *Working Papers in Southern African Studies*

Military Terms

ALN — Army of National Liberation
CCB — Civilian Cooperation Bureau
COIN — counterinsurgency
FAPLA — People's Armed Forces for the Liberation of Angola
NDF — Namibia Defense Force
PLAN — People's Liberation Army of Namibia
POW(s) — Prisoner(s) of War
SAAF — South African Air Force
SADF — South African Defense Force
SAP — South African Police
SWATF — South West Africa Territorial Force
UDF — Union (of South Africa) Defense Force
WHAM — winning hearts and minds
ZANLA — Zimbabwe National Liberation Army

ZIPRA — Zimbabwe People's Revolutionary Army

Newspapers

CSM — *Christian Science Monitor* (Boston)
CT — *Cape Times* (Cape Town)
FM — *Financial Mail* (Johannesburg)
NE — *New Era* (Windhoek)
NYT — *New York Times* (New York)
ST — *Sunday Times* (Johannesburg)
STr — *Sunday Tribune* (Durban)
TH — *The Herald* (Harare)
TN — *The Namibian* (Windhoek)
TO — *The Observer* (London)
TS — *The Star* (Johannesburg)
WA — *Windhoek Advertiser* (Windhoek)
WeA — *Weekend Argus* (Cape Town)
WM — *Weekly Mail* (Johannesburg)

Non-Governmental Organizations, Professional Associations, and Institutions

AAAS — American Academy of Arts and Sciences
AB — Africa Bureau
ABI — Arnold Bergstraesser-Institut
AEI — African-European Institute
ANC — African National Congress
APSA — American Political Science Association
ASA — African Studies Association
ASC — African Studies Center
BI — The Brookings Institution
CAN — Church Action on Namibia
CCN — Council of Churches in Namibia
CFR — Council on Foreign Relations
CIIR — The Catholic Institute for International Relations
CJAM — City of Johannesburg Africana Museum
CUASRC — Cornell University Africana Studies and Research Center
DUCAS — Dalhousie University Center for African Studies
EIN — Ecumenical Institute for Namibia
EISA — Electoral Institute of Southern Africa

FAA — Foreign Affairs Association
FF — Ford Foundation
FLN — National Liberation Front
FNLA — National Front for the Liberation of Angola
FPA — Foreign Policy Association
HAZ — Historical Association of Zimbabwe
IComJ — International Commission of Jurists
IDAFSA — International Defense and Aid Fund for Southern Africa
IDASA — Institute for a Democratic South Africa
IDRC — International Development Research Center
IPS — Institute for Policy Studies
ISSUP — Institute of Strategic Studies, University of Pretoria
JF — The Johnson Foundation
KAS — Konrad-Adenauer-Stiftung
LRRI — Labor Resource and Research Institute
LSMIC — Liberation Support Movement Information Center
MPLA — Popular Movement for the Liberation of Angola
NAI — Nordic Africa Institute
NAM — Non-Aligned Movement
NATO — North Atlantic Treaty Organization
NCC — Namibia Communications Center
NDIIA — National Democratic Institute for International Affairs
NEPRU — Namibian Economic Policy Research Unit
NID — Namibia Institute for Democracy
NSC — Namibia Support Committee
NUNW — National Union of Namibian Workers
OPO — Ovamboland People's Organization
OUCISAP — Ohio University Center for International Studies, Africa Program
PAC — Pan Africanist Congress of South Africa
PC — Pax Christi
PEACEC — People's Education, Assistance, and Counseling for Empowerment Center
RANDC — RAND Corporation
SAIIA — South African Institute of International Affairs
SAIRR — South African Institute of Race Relations
SAIS — School of Advanced International Studies, The Johns Hopkins University
SG — Society for Geography
SWANU — South West Africa National Union
SWAPO — South West Africa People's Organization
UBDPS — University of Bradford, Department of Peace Studies
UDSSFGSIS — University of Denver, The Social Science Foundation and Graduate School of International Studies
UNITA — National Union for the Total Independence of Angola
UNNISER — University of Namibia, Namibian Institute for Social and Economic Research
UPA — Union of Angolan Peoples
UUDEH — Uppsala University, Department of Economic History
UUDG — Uppsala University, Department of Government
UUPCR — Uppsala University, Department of Peace and Conflict Research
UWCCSAS — University of the Western Cape, Centre for Southern African Studies
ZANU — Zimbabwe African National Union
ZAPU — Zimbabwe African People's Union

Preface

It is exhausting to scroll through the fifty-one pages of entries listed under the subject heading Namibia in the e-library catalogue of Michigan State University, which has one of the more impressive collections of Namibiana in the United States.[1] Partly as a response to that, this study attempts not only to incorporate the considerable body of literature that emerged during the independence era but also to consider the aftereffects of the 1966–1989 war of independence. Although a considerable amount of material has been destroyed,[2] researchers are still being denied access to certain of the remaining military archival files.[3] Archival records of the activities of the South West African Police counterinsurgency unit known as *Koevoet* (meaning crowbar in Afrikaans) have disappeared, apparently on purpose.[4] Finally, not all the official records bearing on the conduct of South African foreign policy have been turned over to the South African archives.[5]

Some of the postwar literature that is available draws upon recently declassified archival material, particularly in South Africa, Portugal,[6] Cuba,[7] Germany,[8] France,[9] and Russia,[10] as well as upon the personal accounts of both Namibian civilians and soldiers involved in that war and their opponents in the South African Defense Force (SADF).[11] The National Archives of Namibia in Windhoek has been involved in collecting, organizing, and publicizing the vast range of written and oral records concerning this war and earlier twentieth century anticolonial episodes and movements. This is the focus of the Archives of the Anti-Colonial Resistance and the Liberation Struggle Project (AACRLS), which began in 2001.[12] However, the archives of the principal Namibian nationalist organization, the South West African People's Organization, remain closed.[13]

My particular approach to analyzing the course and significance of the Namibian war of independence includes four complementary perspectives. First, I examine the independence war (1966–1989) within the larger context of the post–World War II decolonization. In 1960, the United Nations General Assembly declared colonialism anathema and urged its rapid termination.[14] It took almost thirty years after that *pronunciamento* for colonial South West Africa to become an independent Namibia on 21 March 1990. Surely, this was an egregious example of *une décolonisation retardée,* as one recent book called it.[15] A noted Canadian political scientist used the apposite phrase "belated decolonisation."[16] Much earlier, the United Nations General Assembly drew attention to the "delay [in] the decolonization process in Namibia."[17] One British scholar has indicated that decolonization is a rather recent term[18] and that this concept often entails somewhat different definitions, for example, by Suret-Canale,[19] Crawford,[20] and Srivastava.[21] Nevertheless, it enjoys wide currency within the academic and political worlds.

The 1966–1989 conflict has been known by several different names, which stress different facets of the war, according to its geographical location or its declared purposes. From a geographical perspective it has been designated as a border war.[22] This particular phrasing, especially the term border, used in South African circles, suggests any number of metaphors and lacks precision.[23] A second term is frontier war,[24] with an added variation for the geographical terrain, namely, a bush war.[25] Three other labels draw attention to the goal of the war, namely, liberation war.[26] Variants of this appellation are liberation struggle and armed liberation war[27] as well as armed liberation struggle.[28] Yet another designation is decolonization war.[29] Strictly speaking, Anthony Clayton does not even mention Namibia in his book *The Wars of French Decolonization*, but, *mutatis mutandis*, the text certainly fits the Namibian war. At the end of his book he uses the term "colonial wars" to encompass these wars, implying that the two terms are synonymous.[30] Similarly, Anthony Low has employed the phrase colonial wars.[31] Finally, there is the designation war of independence, a rather uncommon designation mainly applied to the eighteenth century war between the future United States and the United Kingdom.[32] However, the British apparently used this term, while the Americans chose to call it the American Revolution.[33] This term is discussed further in the Introduction.

Secondly, I analyze the independence war in a sectoral or topical fashion employing three rubrics: diplomatic, economic, and military. These three sectors are analytically separate but mesh with one another, creating an empirical overlap. For instance, there are diplomatic, economic, and military facets to the creation and maintenance of bilateral and multilateral arms embargoes against South Africa, and also to the various types of support offered to the Namibian African nationalists. Such overlap is evident in the exceptionally helpful inventory that five RAND Corporation researchers have developed.[34] Two chapters are allocated to each of the three sectors, one for each antagonist, the Namibian African nationalists (chapters One, Three, and Five) on the one hand, and the South African government (chapters Two, Four, and Six) on the other hand.

Thirdly, in addition to these six sectoral chapters, I have included an introduction providing general background and explaining the concepts appearing throughout the book, and a penultimate chapter (Chapter Seven), assessing the human and material costs incurred and the changes brought about by the war. Moreover, Chapter Seven briefly discusses "the politics of memory" in Namibia in which "nations memorialize their own suffering, but not what they inflict on others."[35] Justine Hunter has explored the relevance of this topic to the aftermath of the war in Namibia.[36] Chapter Seven thus attempts to create a before-and-after study of this particular armed decolonization,[37] with special attention to those Namibian diplomatic, economic, and military considerations that arose in pre-independence Namibia.

In the fourth place, this study divides the various topical (diplomatic, economic, and military) chapters into sections to facilitate the use of various examples drawn from other nations to indicate that the pattern of the Namibian war has several parallels with other small scale wars and wars of decolonization. Strictly speaking, the analysis does not rigorously compare the Namibian war with all other decolonization wars, a term that is a slight variant of the one used in the title of Clayton's *The Wars of French Decolonization*. My analysis does not entail what has been termed cross-case comparisons, but rather it tends to be within-case analysis.[38] Two apposite examples of cross-case comparisons that include South Africa are Thomas G. Weiss, David Cortright, George A. Lopez, and Larry Minear[39] as well as that undertaken by Gary F. Baines.[40] Examples of the within-case approach are the works of Thomas H. Henriksen,[41] Kenneth W. Grundy,[42] Graeme Callister,[43] and Elena Torreguitar.[44] There are a few genuine comparative analyses of decolonization, for example, by Grimal,[45] whose study neglects the Portuguese empire. That omission can be covered by the work of Kenneth R. Maxwell.[46] Tony Smith[47] and David B. Abernethy[48] have published remarkably astute comparative works. Such studies rarely ever cover the American decolonization of the Philippines, which merits only a meager three paragraphs in M. Crawford Young's magisterial work, *The African State in Comparative Perspective*.[49] Much of the literature on decolonization tends to be configurative rather than comparative, that is, parallel studies that do not cross back and forth between systems, searching for similarities and differences to develop explanations and hypotheses.[50] There is clearly an equal need for more comparative studies of national liberation movements, such as the South West Africa People's Organization (SWAPO).[51]

At this point, I wish to emphasize what is not covered in this book. Insofar as humanly possible, I have attempted to avoid the polemics that characterize much of the writing on the war. In terms of actual subject matter, I have concentrated on the diplomatic, economic, and military aspects of the war, realizing that there are other topics and other approaches. Consequently, my primary focus concerns what James H. Mittelman has termed legal decolonization, while the secondary goal explores some of the considerations involved in what he called effective decolonization.[52] The former type of decolonization, which usually precedes the latter type, has sometimes been given the pejorative term of flag independence.[53] His distinction between these two types of decolonization parallels that made by Robert H. Jackson and Carl G. Rosberg regarding juridical and empirical statehood, noted at the beginning of Chapter One.[54] Roughly the same distinction seems implicit in R. A. Alkindele's observation that "African diplomacy in world politics has sought to restore human dignity by finally burying colonialism, and by rehabilitating Africans from racial humiliation and the tyranny of poverty, disease, and underdevelopment."[55]

Chapter Seven considers some of the burdens facing Namibia as it moves beyond legal independence, sometimes with external assistance, to achieve a greater degree of effective decolonization. Because there are already several excellent works covering the often delicate bilateral and multilateral negotiations leading to the international approval of the final stages of Namibian decolonization, such as those by Geldenhuys,[56] Zartman,[57] Jabri,[58] Davies,[59] and Vergau,[60] there is no pressing need to recapitulate all the narratives and analyses of the sequential diplomatic maneuvers and agreements culminating in the achievement of independence for Namibia on 21 March 1990.

Similarly, I have concentrated on those international economic sanctions directed against the South African defense establishment and industry because they link together the economic and military aspects of my inquiry. To keep the research manageable, I have considered just those non-military economic sanctions that are clearly linked to Namibia. There is an abundance of solid works on the full range of other public as well as private sector sanctions directed against South Africa (which might subsume Namibia, but which nevertheless treat it in a cursory fashion), for example, those by Keith Ovenden and Tony Cole,[61] Trevor Bell,[62] Kenneth A. Rodman,[63] and Neta C. Crawford and Audie J. Klotz.[64]

Moreover, I have chosen to avoid what Albert Grundlingh called "the 'drum and trumpet' school of military history"[65] that provides more narrative and detail than analysis and context. There are an ample number of these studies, which focus primarily on the Namibian (and Angolan) campaigns of the South African Defense Force (SADF). This school of writing relies heavily on narrative and often goes into great detail, as exemplified by Helmoed-Römer Heitman's *South African Armed Forces*[66] and his *War in Angola: The Final South African Phase*,[67] and only minimally on its subaltern South West Africa Territorial Force (SWATF). I have only uncovered one publication dealing with the SWATF, and it is neither scholarly nor analytical, namely, P. H. R. Snyman, *Beeld van die SWA Gebiedsmag* (The Image of the Territorial Force).[68]

Unfortunately the same cannot be said of the People's Liberation Army of Namibia (PLAN), which has yet to generate much significant military or historical interest. Presumably the acquisition of more archival material, ample research funding, the interest of the faculty and students of the University of Namibia, and the support and legitimation of the leadership elements of the Namibia Defense Force (NDF) will lead to greater, well documented, and focused research studies and publications in this neglected area. So far I have been able to locate only two academic works on this topic, namely, those by Guy Lamb[69] and Nengovhela J. Livhiwani.[70] Although usually written in a narrative style, they provide a wealth of detail, some of which has heuristic and comparative value. Indeed, at least one recent comparative study of insurgency (which included Namibia) was pitched at such a high level of generalization and quantification that it yielded very little material that would help position the Namibian war of independence into a larger framework.[71]

In addition, I have not covered the full range of international and transnational organizations, such as the Non-Aligned Movement, which A.W. Singham and Shirley Hume[72] as well as Suresh C. Saxena[73] have briefly explored. Ronald Dreyer has devoted some attention to the Afro-Asian Peoples Solidarity Organization,[74] while Christopher C. Saunders[75] and George W. Shepherd, Jr.,[76] have investigated several of the many non-governmental support groups in Western nations that mobilized resources and lobbied parliamentarians and administrators to benefit Namibian nationalists. Allan D. Cooper has explored those groups devoted to blocking the activities of those South African businesses (and often transnational business firms) that benefit from trade with or investment in Namibia and that are perceived to be hostile to the Namibian nationalists.[77] The activities of these special groups often treated Namibia as part of a larger anti-apartheid focus[78] and they could be regarded, in Donald R. Culverson's felicitous phrase, as the "conscience constituency."[79] I have been selective, rather than exhaustive, in approaching this facet of the research, which reflects the interaction between the traditional state-centric view and the more recent one termed the multi-centric world that transcends the limits of sovereignty so that it is more correct to think of two worlds of world politics.[80] This theme has been applied to the South African case by the Swedish sociologist Håkan Thörn in his *Anti-Apartheid and the Emergence of a Global Society*.[81] Although it contains only two references to Namibia[82] and several more to decolonization,[83] nevertheless, it is one of the few really sophisticated and theoretically elegant analyses of anti-apartheid in a larger, more complex milieu.

What, then, are the six fundamental questions that I seek to answer in this book? At the most basic level, there are two comprehensive questions: first, why was the decolonization of Namibia so protracted? This is hardly a novel question; it was raised earlier with regard to Portuguese Africa.[84] Nevertheless, such a standard question certainly facilitates comparative analysis. Second, how was this decolonization internationalized? Horace Campbell has attempted to answer this question.[85] This subsequently leads now to two supplementary questions: third, were there any features of this decolonization process that were exhibited in other decolonization wars, and fourth, were there any that appeared to be unique to Namibia? Turning to each of the protagonists, there are two equally compelling queries: fifth, what repertoires did the Namibian nationalists use to secure their goals and sixth, how did the South African regime attempt to challenge those goals with a competing vision or with what Thomas Henriksen called a counterideology[86] for the future of Namibia? This signifies that the conflict can be interpreted as one of vision versus alternative vision and force versus counterforce. How did these two opponents mesh their diplomatic, economic, and military capabilities in this war and what were, in the words of Prosser Gifford and William R. Louis, "the consequences of decolonization"[87] in terms of these three sectors, primarily for Namibia and secondarily for South Africa? The final chapter (Chapter Eight) is devoted to answering these six questions.

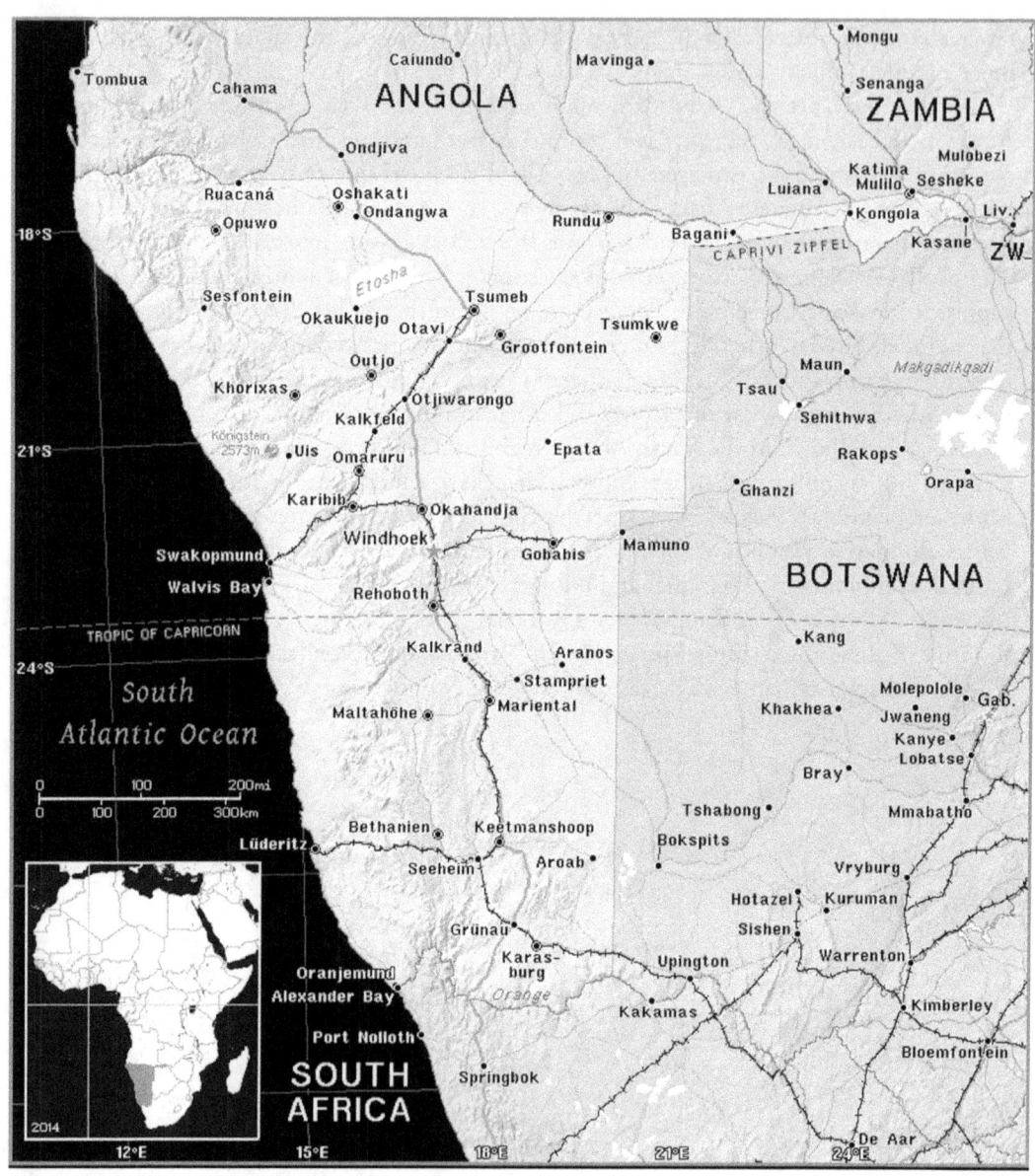

Namibia

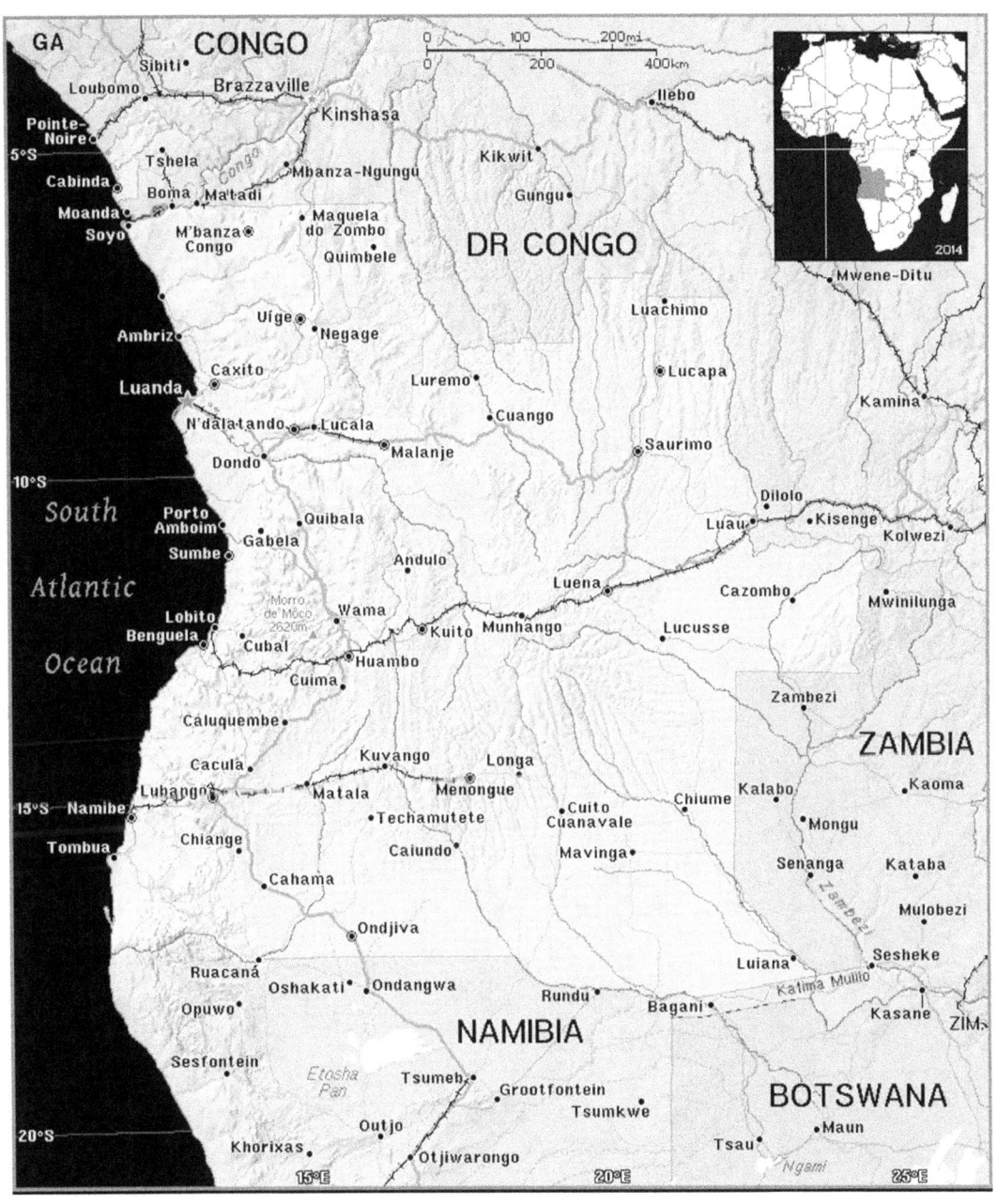

Angola

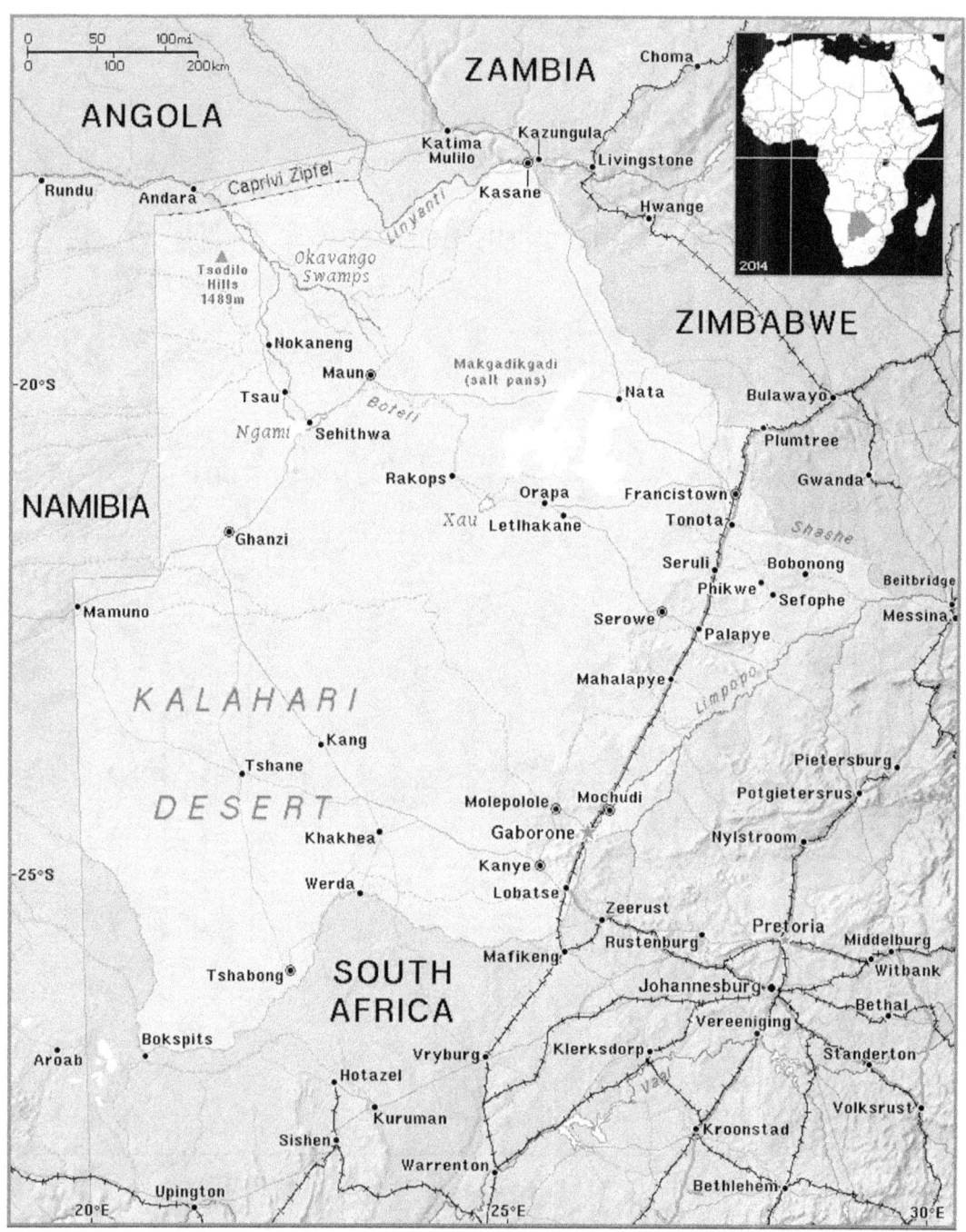

Botswana

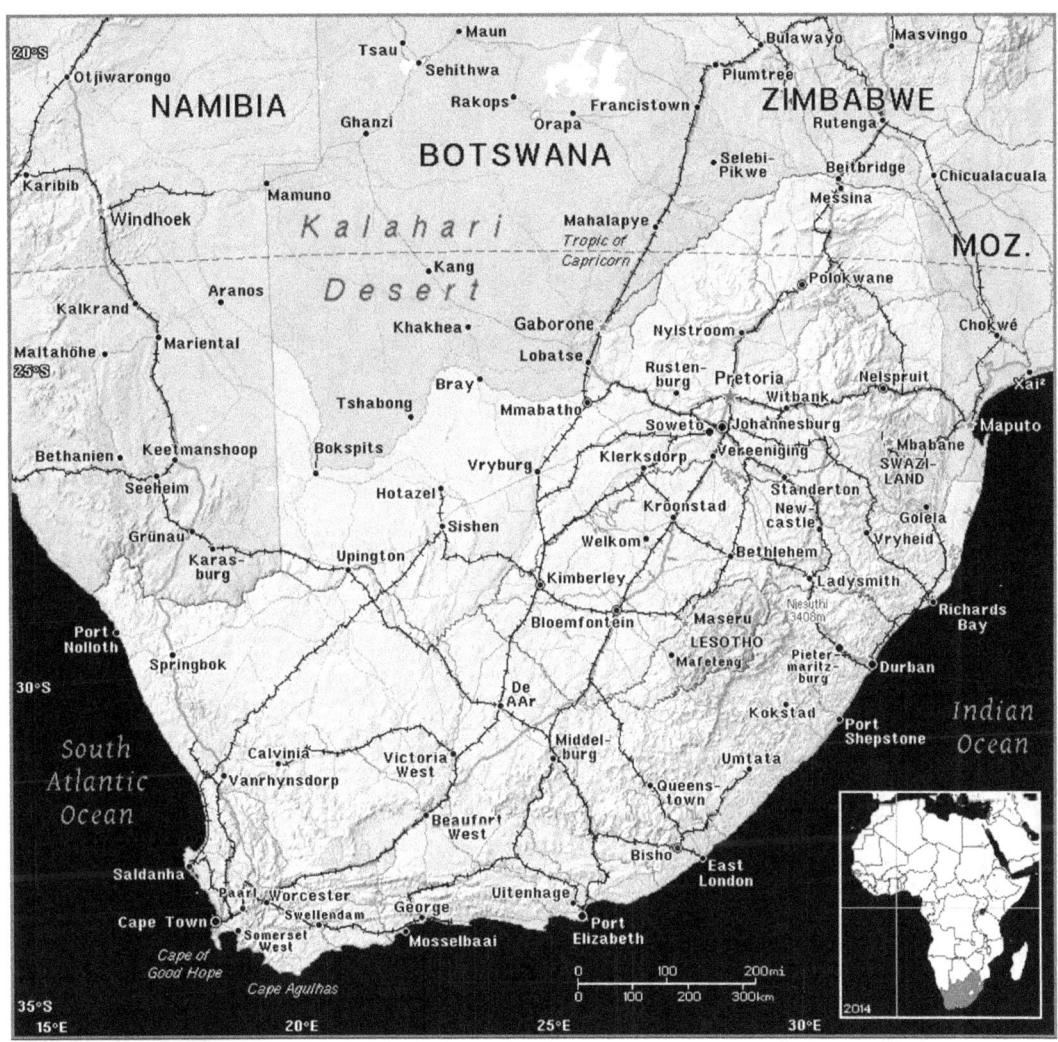

South Africa

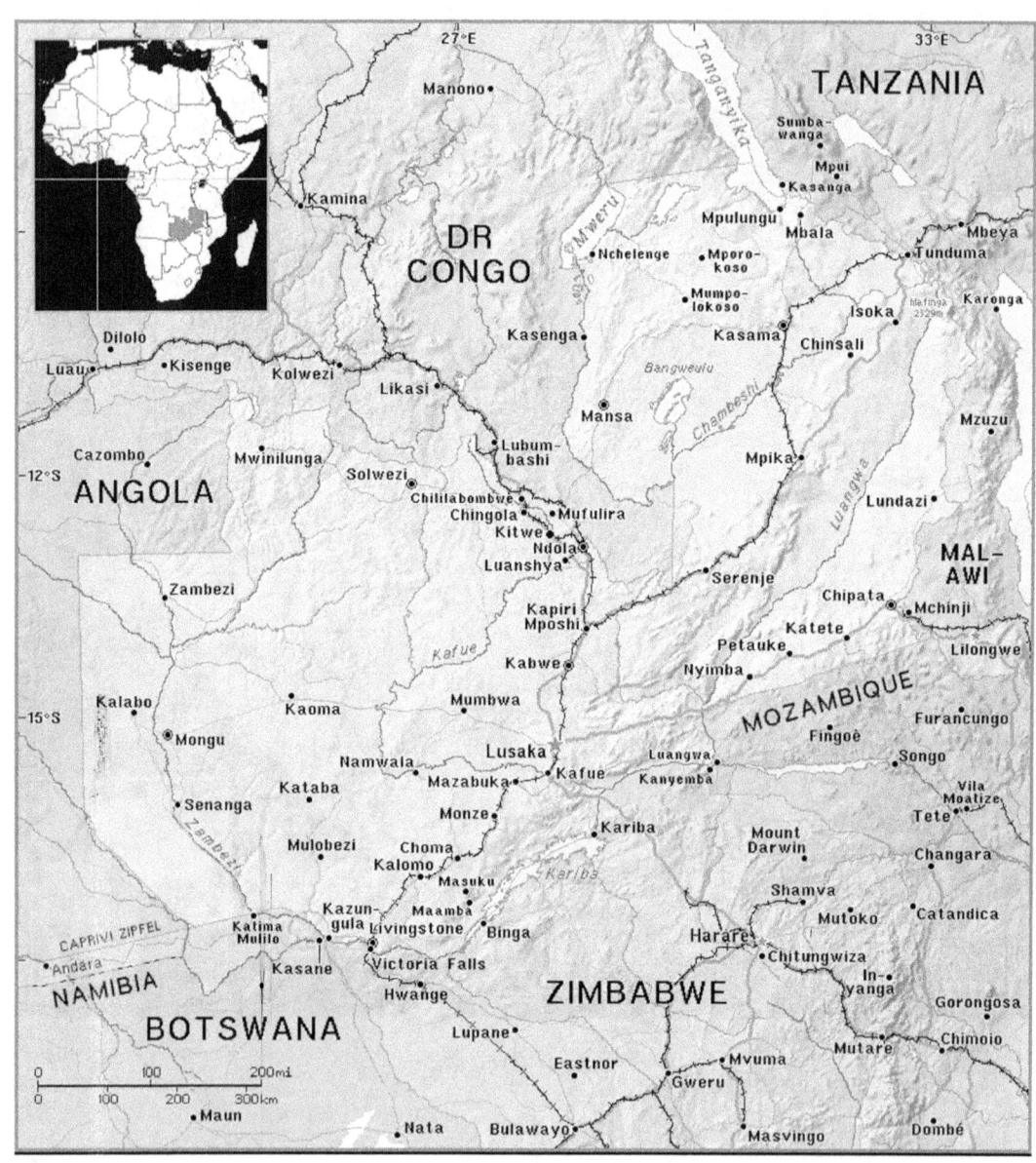

Zambia

Zimbabwe

Introduction

The Namibian war of independence began in August 1966 and lasted until April 1989. This appellation of the Namibian war of independence is a relatively new description. The earliest reference to this particular phrase I have found dates back only to 1983.[1] It appeared in print four years later,[2] and the same phrasing appears on the website list of historic small wars conflicts in Africa compiled by the U.S. Marine Corps Small Wars Center of Excellence.[3] By now, this phrase seems to be accepted in South African military literature.[4] Although this war was only one of Africa's many wars, it was one of the most complex and multifaceted journeys to independence in the last century.[5] According to two sources, this conflict cost the lives of between 12,500[6] and 25,000 people.[7] However, neither author furnished the original sources for these two estimates.

It has merited considerable attention, both in the popular press and scholarly literature and in Western, African, and other Third World diplomatic circles. Calling the conflict the Namibian war of independence is meant to draw attention to the end result of the armed conflict and does not imply that the military engagements took place only in Namibia. Indeed, Angola turned out to be a battleground involving armed forces of Angola, Cuba, and South Africa as well as guerrilla and subaltern forces from Namibia and Angola.[8] The dispute over the international status of Namibia involved a total of five United Nations General Assembly committees and subcommittees, one hundred and sixty-two General Assembly resolutions, thirty-seven Security Council resolutions, seven special United Nations visiting missions, five International Court of Justice opinions, and thirty separate United Nations organizations.[9] This war ran up an expense account at the United Nations in terms of its personnel and resources, and it gave rise to a fairly extensive peacekeeping and nation-building United Nations mission in 1989–1990. In what seemed like a counter-intuitive manner, the Canadian scholar, Lauren Dobell, lamented in 1998 that "there is relatively little written of an academic nature concerning the liberation struggle in Namibia or its likely legacy."[10] She seems, however, to have underestimated the productivity of a wide range of academics who have produced an array of scholarly conference papers, articles, theses, dissertations, and books on Namibia noted in the preface.

At the outset, there needs to be clarification about the name of the future nation of Namibia. South West Africa was the name of the territory after it was conquered from

Germany in 1915, and the South African Government used that name until 1990. This book explores three special, interrelated aspects of that lengthy war that involved fifty different nations as donors of goods and services to one protagonist or another.[11] The African nationalists began using the term Namibia as a counter symbol suggesting independence for the territory under African majority rule, a practice followed in other parts of Africa. Although the United Nations General Assembly accepted the replacement of the term South West Africa by Namibia in 1968,[12] SWAPO never changed its name to NAPO (Namibian African People's Organization) or NPO (Namibian People's Organization). It merely added "of Namibia" after SWAPO. The name SWAPO was not changed, but consciously retained, after independence.[13] Even so, the term NAPO (thus replacing the term South West by Namibia) has been suggested as a more accurate and modern appellation.[14] In 1990, there was a name change, so it is now termed SWAPO of Namibia.[15]

The most visible and the best-reported side of the war has been the diplomatic one. A second facet of the war concerns the economics of decolonizing Namibia, which includes some elements of world politics in terms of transnational corporations and economic sanctions as well as external funding for the insurgent organization. Finally, there is the ebb and flow of insurgency, counterinsurgency, and conventional warfare that involved the armed forces of South Africa, Angola, Cuba, and the principal Namibian liberation group, the South West Africa People's Organization (SWAPO) of Namibia, and the armed forces of UNITA (National Union for the Total Liberation of Angola).

The first and third (diplomatic and military) of these three facets appear in Dobell's path breaking work[16] as well as in an official SWAPO history of their liberation movement.[17] I have chosen to sidestep the other portion of the triad used by Dobell and SWAPO, namely, political[18] or political mobilization,[19] and included economic factors because they suffuse both the diplomatic and military policies. In terms of the level of analysis[20] or research frameworks,[21] the diplomatic, economic, and military factors operate at the local, regional, and world (or transnational) levels. Ronald Dreyer has published an erudite example of the regional approach to analyzing Namibian decolonization,[22] while Mordechai Tamarakin has applied the level of analysis to what he portrays as a conflict system in his magisterial work on Zimbabwe.[23] The diplomatic, economic, and military approaches can equally be incorporated into a more heuristically sophisticated framework that Joseph Nye, Jr. has recently developed. He visualizes the field of world politics as "a three-dimensional chess game in which one can win only by playing vertically as well as horizontally." The three dimensions are military issues, interstate economic issues, and transnational issues arrayed on the top, middle, and bottom boards, respectively.[24]

To grasp the scale and complexities of the independence war it is necessary to focus on each of these three (diplomatic, economic, and military) features not only separately but also in conjunction with the other companion features. The triad I have selected incorporates two of the three components that Sam Nujoma, the first president of Namibia, used to describe the war. His selection included political, diplomatic, and military.[25] In a rather early work, the American scholar Baron F. Barnett identified four facets, namely, political, economic, psychological, and military, one more than I have selected.[26] In addition, two of the three components I have chosen are found in the work of South African political scientist Guy Lamb, who has characterized SWAPO's strategy as a combination of military and diplomatic campaigns, along with "domestic resistance and protest."[27]

Concerning another example of an independence war, Alistair Horne has suggested that the Algerian War of 1954–1962 subsumed seven different wars simultaneously, although he did not cluster the seven by sectors, as I have done, but instead used the term "planes."[28]

My enquiry will entail an analysis of the strategies and tactics of the protagonists: the South African Government, on the one hand, and SWAPO, on the other hand, within a larger comparative framework covering decolonization which lends itself to significant generalizations. This approach acknowledges Professor Singer's advice to refrain from producing works that "amount to little more than an ever-growing potpourri of discrete, disparate, non-comparable, and isolated bits of information or extremely low-level generalizations."[29] From this perspective, I regard Neta C. Crawford's *Argument and Change in World Politics* as the most theoretically elegant and rigorous work that I have yet encountered that analyzed much of the dispute/war over Namibia. SWAPO and the South African regime battled for over twenty years to establish the future configuration of Namibia and its place in southern Africa, the continent, and the remainder of the world. At the end of this study, I consider the residue or impediments of each of these three factors in the context of the challenges facing postcolonial Namibia. This record is an integral part of the contending memories (including memory management) about the war that intrude into Namibian civil society and political discourse.

The Diplomatic Campaigns

At its most basic, the war of independence was preeminently a war of symbols, with each side drawing from what the Israeli political scientist Yossi Shain has called their "symbolic arsenal."[30] This war was fought at a time when there was a profound change in the symbols, political discourse, and norms surrounding decolonization as a feature of international politics. Considering the post–1945 displacement of the colonial idea and its structures by its antithesis, decolonization, it is appropriate to regard Namibia's exceptionally lengthy, costly, and sometimes sanguinary journey to independence as an example, *par excellence*, of delayed and armed decolonization. The South African regime did not accept this normative shift in favor of decolonization favored by most other Western colonial powers, for it operated from the premise that the benefits of continued control of the territory outweighed the costs of retention. This is the nub of the argument that Robert H. Jackson has advanced.[31] Professor Gary F. Baines, a South African historian at Rhodes University averred that "retired SADF generals tend to claim that Namibian independence was always part of their agenda — but it was an independence on their own terms, one in which SWAPO would not come to monopolize power."[32] Along with two other colonial holdouts, Portugal and Rhodesia, South Africa could be characterized as an authoritarian regime that presumably would decolonize at a far slower rate than would democratic regimes.[33] Prohibitive economic costs, geographical overextension (into Angola), and military stalemates are three explanations offered for the end of the 1966–1989 Namibian war and the subsequent independence of Namibia in 1990.[34]

Two of the fundamental symbols that both parties manipulated in the diplomatic battle were legitimacy and self-determination. Legitimacy indeed features in the literature on twentieth century insurgency. For example, one finds this concept in studies by

Hough,[35] Lomperis,[36] Wright,[37] Prisk,[38] and Burns.[39] Indeed, what one analyst termed "the legitimacy war" is an integral part of an insurgency.[40] "The concept of legitimacy," as Peter Novick wrote in his study of Vichy and post–World II France, "is an extremely slippery one, resting ... on largely intangible factors."[41] "Legitimacy," as Samuel P. Huntington also cautioned, "is a mushy concept that political analysts do well to avoid."[42] Even so, he proceeds to mention it innumerable times in the text (but not in the index) of his classic study of the transition from authoritarian to democratic political systems. Yossi Shain also draws attention to the perils of the concept in his comparative work on political exiles, preferring instead to employ the terms loyalty and recognition.[43] Finally, I. William Zartman cautions that "Of all the broad concepts associated with independence ... the most elusive is legitimacy."[44]

One of the reasons for this elusiveness is what Deborah Posel has termed the "contradictory standards of legitimacy."[45] To minimize any conceptual ambiguity, I have used the term legitimacy with caution throughout this work. Indeed, it helps to note several distinctions about the use of this seemingly protean concept. Lawrence S. Finkelstein has shown that legitimacy serves not only as an end but also as a means.[46] Moreover, Shain and Tamarakin distinguish between external and internal legitimacy,[47] while Huntington refers to external and international legitimacy.[48] This foreign-domestic dichotomy is helpful, provided one understands that one type of legitimacy can spill over into, and reinforce, the other; they are not altogether mutually exclusive. Each represents a type of conceptual equity, rather than conceptual fungibility. The acquisition of one can facilitate the subsequent attainment of the other.

Regrettably this does not end the ambiguity. As this study shows, legitimacy can be not only an end in itself but also a means to other public goods or diplomatic entitlements.[49] In this sense, it is similar to a credit rating. Francis Fukuyama has indicated that "Some have compared legitimacy to a kind of cash reserve,"[50] but unfortunately he does not specify who those "some" are. Moreover, Shain (in a different context) refers to international creditors in his study of exile politics.[51] There is still another distinction between political and moral legitimacy that comes into play in the discourse over insurgency, and the discussion goes on to include five indicators of legitimacy that analysts can employ to assess the outcome of the conflict.[52]

Legitimacy, moreover, is a dynamic concept, as suggested by the noun delegitimization and by the commonly used phrase legitimacy deflation, often found in the literature explaining military coups, especially in the Third World.[53] A complementary phrase implying some sort of minimum standard is legitimacy deficit.[54] It has the verb forms (to legitimize and to delegitimize) that denote the idea of bestowal and withdrawal.[55] Moreover, there can be a return to legitimacy, as indicated by yet another verb, to relegitimate.[56] This, in turn, leads to two crucial questions: who (or which actor[s]) undertakes the task? And what are the criteria for awarding or retracting legitimacy? About two decades after the founding of the United Nations, Inis L. Claude, Jr. drew attention to what he regarded as a significant function of the United Nations, namely, collective legitimation.[57]

Such a concept, as J. Leo Cefkin has shown, is very apropos for the study of decolonization in Namibia.[58] Somewhat later, a Namibian political scientist, André du Pisani, drew upon the concept of legitimacy as a motif in analyzing the course of the dispute over the international status of the territory.[59] During the diplomatic battle over the future of Namibia, African international organizations, such as the Organization of African Unity, and ententes, such as the Front Line States (of Angola, Botswana, Mozambique, Tanzania, Zambia, and then Zimbabwe) and the Western Contact Group (of Canada, France, the Federal Republic of Germany, the United Kingdom, and the United States), performed this task as well as various United Nations bodies. Indeed, "To read international politics without paying attention to the competition over legitimacy," wrote one student of the United Nations, "would leave one with no way to comprehend such common acts as saving face, offering justifications, using symbols, and being in a position of authority."[60]

Within the context of the United Nations, the concept contains subjective and perceptual attributes, including internalization,[61] so that one can speak about "legitimacy language," "the politics of legitimation," as well as "the contestation over legitimacy," "legitimating strategy," and the "reinterpretation of legitimacy."[62] It applies, argues Hurd, to "particular decisions, processes, or individuals."[63]

Although the criteria for operational definitions of legitimacy are not always explicit and are only infrequently quantifiable,[64] they certainly include several of the varieties of legitimacy that Huntington has developed. His four categories of regime legitimacy, ideological legitimacy, performance legitimacy, and procedural legitimacy seem to capture much of the political dynamics in the Namibian war of independence. As the war wound on, two other categories would tap other aspects of the conflict; I choose to call them territorial legitimacy and constitutive legitimacy. What is the meaning and significance of each of the six types? In his *Third Wave* study, Huntington presents regime legitimacy in terms of a standard classification of political systems according to the number and type of ruler(s), namely, one-party, personal, military, and racial (where South Africa is singled out).[65] Ideological legitimacy in his view, suggests a deep commitment to a concrete, identifiable body of political beliefs and praxis, such as communism (the example he uses).[66] If one were to interpret the system of apartheid in South Africa (which was applied in Namibia) as an ideology, rather than, say, as a system of political mythology[67] or even Afrikaner civil religion,[68] then presumably ideological legitimacy would apply to the Namibian war of independence.

Performance legitimacy is less arcane and derives from the achievement of certain quantifiable goals, such as the delivery of material goods and services, or the avoidance of national humiliation, such as the loss of a war. Government is a provider and is judged accordingly.[69] This measure can readily be applied to the South African governance of Namibia, particularly in terms of the notions of international stewardship implied in the League of Nations mandate agreement for the territory. From this perspective, Robert L. Bradford has written a landmark study of Namibia.[70] Procedural legitimacy appears, in Huntington's schema, to apply to what might loosely be called the package of civil liberties, especially those connected with the exercise of the franchise, and it lends itself to international monitoring.[71]

Territorial legitimacy is linked with the concept of self-determination (which will be examined shortly) and applies to competing versions of political geography. It lies at the heart of the dispute over the South African policy of separate development and defines the frontiers of the political kingdom. Recently, Pierre Englebert has probed the relationship between various aspects of legitimacy and the capacity of African states for economic growth and performance.⁷² In the course of his statistically grounded exploration, he draws upon two facets of territorial legitimacy, namely horizontal and vertical legitimacy; the former is his term,⁷³ while Kaveli J. Holsti coined the latter term.⁷⁴ Vertical legitimacy concerns "the presence of a consensus on the content of the social contract" among the residents of a given state, whereas horizontal legitimacy focuses on "an agreement about who participates in the [social] contract negotiations. It establishes a link between the population and territory of a state."⁷⁵ My emphasis on territorial legitimacy deals with political fragmentation and consolidation and entails observations about the legitimacy of the African ethnic homelands in Namibia (which were patterned after those in South Africa).

Constitutive legitimacy also has close ties with self-determination, for it involves the nature of the self in the phrase self-determination. In the parlance of the U.S. constitution, it concerns the nature of "we, the people." It comes into play when SWAPO, for example, is regarded as the "authentic representative" of the people of Namibia, which was the case with its recognition by the United Nations General Assembly in resolution 3111 (XXVIII) of 12 December 1973. This status was elevated to a monopoly when, in General Assembly resolution 31/146 of 20 December 1976, SWAPO was declared to the "sole and authentic" representative of these people, a move which one senior United Nations official later regarded as the canonization of SWAPO, especially vis-à-vis other Namibian political parties.⁷⁶ The United Nations, in turn, acted as the international patron for the 1989 elections to the Constituent Assembly, which drafted the constitution of the soon to be independent Namibia. Just which groups were authentic (and constituted what Shain called "the nation to come"⁷⁷) was a nettlesome and disputed question,⁷⁸ particularly when it came to the diplomatic and political hegemony of SWAPO.

The other symbol manipulated on the diplomatic battlefield was self-determination, an equally opaque and ambiguous concept. Such a term was closely linked to the discourse of anti-colonialism, especially after the First World War, when President Woodrow Wilson utilized it in his political rhetoric regarding the peace settlement, as Erez Manela has so clearly demonstrated.⁷⁹ In his nuanced analysis of this critical and often confusing concept in the context of decolonization, Robert H. Jackson contended that self-determination became an element in the language and normative construction of decolonization.⁸⁰ Indeed, Manela contended that "the language of self-determination could be used to challenge the relationships between race, civilization, and sovereignty that underlay the prewar international order."⁸¹ In the context of decolonization, self-determination was legitimized in such a way as to endorse a war of liberation.⁸²

It thus fits in well with what Huntington termed procedural legitimacy. Process, not necessarily outcome, is the focus of attention. Indeed, as a South African political scientist observed, "Self-determination is not opposed by non- or anti-self determination but by alternative interpretations of it."⁸³ Even though the concept was marred by an absence of "logical limits,"⁸⁴ self-determination was an integral, albeit implicit, component of the United Nations trusteeship idea, and the General Assembly began to link it to self-government or independence for the trust territories. None of the preambular or operative paragraphs of United Nations General Assembly resolution 1064 (XI) of 26 February 1957 explicitly referred to self-determination. Yet preambular paragraph three drew attention to the General Assembly's consideration since 1952 of explicit deadlines for achieving self-government or independence in such territories. Three years later the General Assembly invoked the concept in its well-known "Declaration on the Granting of Independence to Colonial Countries and Peoples,"[85] which became a doctrinal talisman for global anti-colonial forces and groups.[86]

The 1960 declaration contained a significant qualification to the achievement of independence that was to surface often in the conflict over the mode and timing of Namibian independence, namely, it strongly endorsed the notion of territorial integrity and castigated any attempt to undermine this integrity.[87] This notion of territorial integrity was central to South African policy regarding the implementation of separate development (that is, the creation of ethnic homelands) and the subsequent incorporation of Walvis Bay into the Cape Province. Self-determination appealed to both protagonists in the Namibian war, and both invoked it to sanctify their version of political correctness. The future first prime minister of Namibia, Hage G. Geingob, observed that "when South Africa speaks of self-determination, it means determination based on ethnic lines, and when it speaks of independence, it means bantustans."[88] Yet the South African authorities were lax or inattentive when it came to implementing the concept, failing to anticipate those steps that might make the concept appealing to potentially skeptical audiences outside South Africa and Namibia. The South African Ambassador to the United States, Dr. Willem C. Naudé, unsuccessfully tried to use this concept with reference to South African policy in the Transkei when dealing with the Kennedy Administration.[89]

Benyamin Neuberger has examined the application of self-determination to postcolonial Africa, indicating the range of its application, the circumstances in which it is modified or rejected, and the other concepts with which it competes. With regard to southern Africa, the difficulties are principally two. First, which self does the determining?[90] This can shade off into an ancillary question of who is an African and who is not (a type of authenticity problem). In South Africa, for instance, both African and Afrikaner regard themselves as authentic African, which heightens the tension.[91] This would also hold true for Namibia, although for a time there was a question about the status of the German-speaking community in Namibia, which claimed political rights from both Germany and South Africa. A number of them were interned in the Second World War, yet they were politically rehabilitated after the Malan Government was ushered into power in South Africa in 1948.[92] The largesse later included granting pensions to those German-speaking whites who had served in the German armed forces in Namibia prior to 1920.[93]

Secondly, the South Africans practiced what Neuberger has called "other-determination,"[94] that is, they decided for others who were not part of the polity, namely, the non-whites. Although there may be an element of hyperbole in this, his assessment is basically correct insofar as the Africans in Namibia were not consulted about the mechanics and rules of determination, particularly in a plebiscite held under the Smuts Government in 1945. Moreover, the South African perception of the self and of the other were at loggerheads with the African nationalist perception, reflecting the political culture and mythology of apartheid. For the white South Africans the self was the single individual whose opinion was counted in the one person, one vote fashion, whereas the other was the collectivity, the tribe or ethnic group that was not disaggregated into individuals. This was reflected in the way in which African votes were recorded in the 1945 plebiscite in Namibia, on the one hand, and white votes in the 1960 in South Africa and Namibia regarding the change from the Union to the Republic of South Africa, on the other hand. The tribal notables cast bloc votes for their charges in the former exercise (thus obviating the need for voter registration),[95] while individual white voters in South Africa and Namibia cast their votes as single citizens in the latter exercise.[96]

For the African nationalists, then, the nation was indivisible, while for the South African regime there was no single nation, but a cluster of nations for the others, and one for themselves. Critics have pointed out that, to be consistent, the white community should be divided, in turn, into the various language groups.[97] This not only highlights the specious nature of the separate development model (as validated by self-determination, so the South Africans hoped) but also reveals a deeper question that has troubled the Afrikaners ever since their defeat in 1902 by the British. Afrikaner nationalism itself was divided over the issue of who constituted the white people (the body politic or, more broadly, the nation) in South Africa. Was that group (the South Africa nation) to consist only of Afrikaners or was it to include assimilated English-speaking whites? How were the two language groups to relate to one another? In an equal fashion? Eventually the Afrikaners acquired political dominance, although the English-speaking group maintained their economic hegemony.

The Economic Campaigns

Even though the war for Namibia was waged on a symbolic battlefield, with each contestant attempting to manipulate symbols to advance its cause and (if possible) to undermine that of its opponent, the battle was indeed waged in the workplace and in the boardroom. Economic grievances and anxieties became grist for the international mill, involving mobilization of followers and appeals to patrons of various stripes. The focal points became the asymmetry of wealth and of the distribution of that wealth. Economic exploitation and maldistribution of goods served to galvanize the Africans of Namibia, who found ever so little to inherit in the land of their birth. There are four significant elements of the economic battlefield: patterns of land distribution, the migrant labor system, ownership of natural resources, and international economic sanctions.

The first core element of the economic battle for Namibia was the acquisition of African land by the whites by means that now would be regarded as demonstrably unethical and reprehensible.[98] The South African government was the stimulus for the preferential pattern of land distribution to white inhabitants who lived in, or moved to, Namibia[99]; it was also generous to veterans of the Second World War with regard to farm acquisition.[100] The British[101] and Portuguese[102] metropoles at one time briefly had notions of buying out their settler communities, and the American ambassador to Portugal in the middle of the 1960s, Admiral George Anderson, made this suggestion. However, there is no documentation for this American proposal nor are there any indications which Portuguese African territories were covered in the suggestion.

In the case of Namibia, there are no indications that Pretoria would shrink the size of their white population in Namibia. As the amounts of land diminished, Africans were crowded into rural areas that usually contained a single ethnic group. This system of reserves can be traced back to the German era in Namibia, and not only did the South

Africans continue it but also it formed the basis for the subsequent policy of separate development. In general, the Africans were forced to accept the least desirable land in the territory, on the one hand, and they received little, if any, financial or technical assistance to become or to aspire to be efficient, affluent farmers or ranchers, on the other hand. African concepts of land tenure, moreover, differed from those used by the white farmers, whose farming practices were based upon individual, capitalist notions regarding ownership and collateral. It became common, therefore, to describe the economy of Namibia as a bifurcated one, with subsistence or traditional agriculture and commercial agriculture. This characterization represented differential access to agricultural resources as well as divergent modes of ownership and production.

Migrant labor is the second basic element in the Namibian economic battlefield, although it is not unique to Namibia and is found throughout southern Africa. Robert J. Gordon[103] as well as Gillian and Suzanne Cronje[104] have carefully examined this topic. The migrant labor system rests upon the debatable assumption that the African worker is anchored in the countryside in the traditional economic system (subsistence agriculture) and periodically commutes from that bucolic environment to the commercial or industrial sector for brief periods of time to supplement his income from agricultural pursuits. Thus the worker is not a permanent stakeholder in the modern sectors of the economy. The most visible manifestation of this truncated life is the prohibition against residing near the workplace with one's family and the need to live in a barracks-type housing compound.

In light of the constraints upon individual land ownership, the need for large tracts of land to sustain viable animal husbandry in this arid country, as well as the sunken costs of drilling wells and fencing to maintain a modest ranch,[105] it is no surprise that the African has to journey to the factories, farms, and households of the white community to sustain himself and his family. Taxation, if nothing else, acts as a powerful incentive to participate in the migrant labor system which undercuts the Africans' earlier mode of earning a living by grazing his flocks, supplemented by hunting and small-scale crop farming.[106] The parallels with Botswana (which sends its migrant laborers primarily to South Africa) are all too apparent.[107]

What is particularly striking about the system of migrant labor in Namibia is the pronounced asymmetry between employer and employee, which is reinforced by the racial divide. The system is one that is employer dominant, and hence it can be regarded as a buyers' market, an oligopsony. This oligopsony is quite visible in the form of a labor supplier known (earlier) as the South West Africa Native Labor Association (SWANLA). This organization operated in the catchment area of Ovamboland, an African reserve in northern Namibia that became the first ethnic polity (known colloquially as a Bantustan) under the system of separate development.[108] At the more ad hoc level, African prisoners were sometimes assigned as laborers to white employers under the provisions of the vagrancy laws.[109] The indignities of the migrant labor system, especially its effect upon African family life and upon the workers' perception[110] of their relative powerlessness to bargain with their employers in any collective and efficacious fashion, were a powerful recruiting tool for African nationalist groups, particularly those that were able to operate among the Ovambo people. Moreover, because of the movement between the homestead and the work site, the laborers could act as a human transmission belt of new values, aspirations, and norms that sustained the political mobilization process. Political awareness could not be geographically encapsulated by the migrant labor system.

Transnational corporations were the third component of the economic battlefield, for they could serve as pressure points for local activists and for nongovernmental organizations in the Western boardrooms of these corporations. Many of the Third World members of the United Nations General Assembly regarded these corporations as the bugbear of international politics and capitalism.[111] They were, in the phrasing of the American political scientist James N. Rosenau, sovereignty-free actors,[112] which made them all the more slippery and difficult to bring to heel. In the Namibian case, the battle was over what I call anticipatory sovereignty and the application of that sovereignty. This means that full sovereignty would operate in a post-colonial Namibia and that prior to independence sovereignty is latent, rather than manifest. Even though anticipatory sovereignty resembles the term suspended sovereignty that Quincy Wright has utilized,[113] it serves to complement Lauren Dobell's notion of SWAPO as a government-in-waiting.[114] The League of Nations mandate system was characterized by uncertainty over the nature and locus of sovereignty over the mandated territories, a topic that was particularly germane to Namibia. The League of Nations Permanent Mandates Commission, a group of nongovernmental experts appointed to serve as monitors regarding the administration of the mandated territories, took strong exception to South African juridical claims of sovereignty over Namibia.[115] Such claims could well have been intended for domestic consumption, given the jingoistic tenor of remarks made about South African control over Namibia in the South African House of Assembly and Senate.[116]

Following the decision of the International Court of Justice that neither Ethiopia nor Liberia had sufficient material national interests involved in the administration of Namibia to question the quality of South Africa's stewardship of Namibia, the General Assembly of the United Nations declared, in its resolution 2145 (XXI) of 27 October 1966, that South Africa had no recognized international rights to continue to rule Namibia. Thus the United Nations acquired rights of administration as an international steward. The General Assembly, in essence, determined that South African rule had failed the test of performance legitimacy, even though the International Court narrowly declined to rule on the merits of the case (which entailed allegations of South African violations of the principles contained in the mandate agreement). Thereafter, the United Nations became the *de jure* authority for Namibia until the territory became an internationally recognized state.

This authority, in effect, was subcontracted to the United Nations Council for Namibia by virtue of General Assembly resolution 2248 (S-V) of 19 May 1967. This council became the international shadow government of the territory, even though it had no physical presence in Namibia, where South Africa exercised de facto control. Drawing upon an earlier General Assembly resolution (1803 [XVII] of 14 December 1962), which claimed that the natural resources of a given state are public goods belonging to the citizens of that state, the council declared in 1974 that the Namibians owned the natural resources of their state. Consequently, only they could legitimate contracts with transnational corporations for the exploration, exploitation, and processing of those natural resources. The council, to all intents and purposes, recognized the sovereignty of the Namibians over their own natural resources even though they were in no position to enforce that sovereignty. Anticipating the advent of independence, the council gave notice that those who contracted for the exploitation of those resources without the permission of the council (as the agent of the shadow government) would be liable for any penalties that the future, independent government might impose for such illegal behavior.[117] Such a declaration, provided it became incorporated into the municipal law of member states of the United Nations, could lay the foundation for legal action at the level of the nation-state against those who defied the council.

This is closely connected with the fourth element of the economic battleground, the imposition (and avoidance) of international economic sanctions. Of the four separate economic battlegrounds, this is the most imprecise in terms of geographic location because it shades into the larger anti-apartheid campaign against the metropole of South Africa. That is, some of the economic sanctions were not specifically applicable to Namibia but instead involved the larger South African domain (including Namibia). Furthermore, the application of such sanctions had profound ramifications in terms of the military battleground, which was graphically illustrated by the logistical constraints under which the South African Air Force operated in northern Namibia and southern Angola against their Angolan and Cuban foes.

The Military Campaigns

There is not a clear-cut demarcation between the economic and the military battlegrounds when it came to defense budgeting and manpower allocation, for the South African state was drawing upon limited financial and human resources. Moreover, such overlap characterizes the diplomatic and military battlefields when it comes to analyzing the case that SWAPO made for the legitimacy of the war in (and north of) Namibia. These nationalists turned outward to seek legitimation for their war of independence, drawing upon universal norms to validate their call to arms and to enlist the diplomatic, economic, and military support of their international patrons.[118] As was true for the Zimbabwean nationalists, they were involved in a patron-client relationship with their regional and extra-regional sponsors.[119]

Both contestants developed overarching worldviews to explain and reproach the actions of their opponents as well as to explain the propriety of their own conduct; these views tended to be Manichean and to place the battle within a wider, global contest for power and prestige. Each side had its ideological mentors and its symbolic arsenals, as Yossi Shain called them.[120] They would utilize these arsenals to firm up their support at home, to widen their circle of patrons, and to denigrate or delegitimate their foe, expecting that their skilled manipulation of symbols would generate material or diplomatic support. From the military point of view, each needed weapons, ammunition, manpower, transportation or access to and from the field of battle, rear echelon areas, communications and intelligence networks, command and control procedures, some degree of doctrinal coherence, rules of engagement, routine channels for coordination with the civilian leadership, and mechanisms for rapidly revising techniques and reforming institutions and practices to reflect changes in and lessons learned on the battlefield. Although one high-ranking South African officer termed the Namibian war "the corporal's war,"[121] perhaps it would be prudent to regard it as a "small war," which places it in a larger, comparative context. Roger Beaumont has explored the small wars topic,[122] while the United States Marine Corps Small Wars Center of Excellence of Quantico, Virginia maintains a website that facilitates further research on this topic.[123]

There was an array of costs connected with the war of independence, not all of which are quantifiable. Raymond Copson examines a full range of such costs and benefits without establishing a precise cost-benefit ratio.[124] The human costs involved casualties for both sides, with the insurgents suffering higher losses, although in such wars there is good reason to question the statistics involved, either because of the temptation of the combatants to inflate the numbers in war communiqués or the non-comparability of the methodology or assumptions used in compiling the data.[125] One needs to maintain a certain amount of skepticism regarding the veracity of numbers cited in terms of guerrilla war operations.[126] Such computations need to take account of war-related non-combatant civilian deaths, such as those involving land mines[127] (which were a prominent feature of the Mozambiquan war of independence and the civil war in Angola[128]). This type of warfare would tend to spill over onto African villagers given the shifting boundaries of the battlefield.

An ancillary human cost was the manpower involved on both sides, although here again there are difficulties in estimating numbers, especially for the insurgents in the People's Liberation Army of Namibia (PLAN), the military component of SWAPO. Unlike their opponents in the SADF (South African Defense Force) or SWATF (South West Africa Territorial Force), members of PLAN were more self-selective and not subject to legally enforceable conscription. There were no white soldiers in PLAN, and some African Namibians were coerced to join PLAN.[129] Moreover, a number of Namibian Africans volunteered to serve in the ethnically distinct components of the counterinsurgency forces, and in the latter stages of the war both African and white Namibian men were liable for military service.[130] Thus the war was not a sharply divided racial war, but one characterized by some degree of crosscutting racial and ethnic cleavages. To a large extent, it was, as one South African military journalist described it, a "political war."[131]

PART I: THE DIPLOMATIC CAMPAIGNS

Chapter One

The Diplomacy of Resistance[1]

Following the end of the Second World War, the literature of international politics was enriched by data and questions about the former colonies of western European states. Such an inclusion marked a major shift in the emphasis in this literature that has added an economic dimension as well as a strategic Cold War one. Thus it was commonplace to refer to a north-south split as well as an east-west divide, and the literature of comparative politics, in turn, began to be organized in terms of First, Second, and Third World studies. Among historians and political scientists the study of decolonization complemented this interest in Third World phenomena, much of which was channeled into a further field of political and economic development as an adjunct of foreign aid planning.

Following the rush of decolonization, the membership of the United Nations increased and many of its newer members pushed to refashion some of the United Nations' agenda. These changes prompted scholars to reassess the political changes wrought by decolonization, and they suggested that many of these new states lacked several of the attributes previously associated with viable statehood. They contended that although such new states enjoyed juridical statehood, they fell short of empirical statehood. They employed the neologism quasi-states to demonstrate the hiatus between juridical and empirical statehood. The international system, they argued, created and sustained these states.[2] Robert H. Jackson credits Hedley Bull and Adam Watson with the first use of the term "quasi-states."[3] Along the same lines, South African political scientist Deon J. Geldenhuys drew attention to a fascinating aspect of international politics that concerns this study. His investigation of several pariah states (including South Africa) has shown the existence of what he called *ersatz* embassies, that is, diplomatic outposts of countergovernments or governments-in-exile.[4] Christopher Clapham has called these diplomatic posts shadow embassies.[5] In the case of minority-ruled South Africa, for example, Professor Geldenhuys observed that the African National Congress was far better represented overseas than the South African Government ever was.[6] His term complements the notion of international legitimacy for regime opponents or, alternatively, delegitimation for the pariah regime.[7]

From Petitioners to *Ersatz* Diplomats

At the beginning of the twentieth century, when Germany had begun to establish itself as a colonial power, the Africans of Namibia had no direct or indirect representation in the administration that ruled over them following their defeat in war. Under the circumstances, they could expect little, if any, access to the local or imperial authorities. Only the missionaries seemed concerned about their welfare, and even that was debatable. The German residents in Namibia only belatedly were granted limited powers of self-governance by the Berlin government. In the Reichstag, however, members of the Social Democratic Party questioned the quality of the colonial system, pointing out cases of maladministration. Yet they hardly regarded the Africans of Namibia as members of their constituency; these Africans had no overseas patrons. Helmut Stoecker and Peter Sebald consider such handicaps in their thoughtful analysis of the "Enemies of the Colonial Idea."[8]

Although the South African Government authorities made an inventory of German colonial malfeasance in Namibia (known as the Blue Book) once Prime Minister Louis Botha's Government had responded to the British request to seize the territory at the outset of the First World War, later the South African regime attempted a rapprochement (known as the London Agreement) with the Weimar Republic to engage the members of the local German community in the process of limited territorial self-government. The inclusion of the German residents in the Namibian body politic was begun by Prime Minister Jan C. Smuts and completed by his successor, Prime Minister James B. M. Hertzog, who subsequently repudiated the Namibian Blue Book. It is only fairly recently that historians of Namibia have taken a careful exegesis of this critical Blue Book.[9]

Once limited self-government was established in the territory, the Africans had only the most minimal representation by others who were supposed to be acquainted with their needs. The Africans were allocated neither elected nor appointive seats in the twenty-four member Legislative Assembly. Of the eight persons serving on the Advisory Council (comparable to the cabinet), only one member served as a spokesman for the unenfranchised Africans, and the Administrator of South West Africa appointed that person.[10] This arrangement was essentially compatible with Professor Neuberger's notion of other-determination mentioned in chapter one. The Africans were outside the political system, whereas the London Agreement had placed the Germans within that system. Indeed, "South African administrators," noted one American historian, "worked to convert South West Africa into the archetypal settler colony."[11] This meant that the mandated territory "was to be turned ... into a 'white man's country.'"[12]

During the League of Nations era, the Africans in Namibia were not much better off. Even though historians William R. Louis,[13] Robert C. Eils,[14] and Wolfe W. Schmokel[15] have carefully demonstrated that the British had excoriated the German colonial record as part of their wartime colonial aims, the League of Nations mandates system operated in such a way that it posed no real threat to the legitimacy of western colonial rule.[16] The League was predominately a European intergovernmental organization with European norms and values, and its Permanent Mandates Commission consisted of members from predominately colonial states, with two exceptions, namely, Sweden and Norway,[17] both of which had cordial relations with SWAPO during the United Nations era. Once Germany joined the League of Nations, two of its nationals served on the Permanent Mandates Commission.[18] Although one of the commissioners was Japanese, there were no black commissioners from League states, such as Haiti, Ethiopia, or Liberia. The League of Nations rejected the Haitian proposal for such a commissioner.[19]

Here again the Africans had little opportunity to articulate their views because written petitions to the commission were transmitted through the mandatory power, on the one hand, and oral petitions were not permitted, on the other hand.[20] During its tenure the Permanent Mandates Commission received a total of sixty-four written petitions from Namibia, none of which came from African petitioners.[21] If members of the Rehoboth mixed-race group are also considered Africans, then this statement needs to be corrected.[22] The petitioning process began in 1925 with Jacobus Beukes, a member of the Rehoboth community, who continued petitioning even through the United Nations; he has been described as "a pioneer in the political awakening of Namibians."[23] As Professor Tilman Dedering has suggested, this exercise in petitioning in the League era can be regarded as a forerunner of a much broader based and persistent Namibian effort in the United Nations, which was much more hospitable to African complaints and aspirations.[24] Although it was a highly circumscribed privilege, petitioning could be regarded as a poor surrogate for exclusion from the Legislative Assembly of the territory, which was restricted to white membership.[25] This exclusionary policy did not escape the notice of the United Nations,[26] but it persisted until independence.

After the United Nations General Assembly had denied its request to incorporate Namibia, the South African Government provided for the representation of the territory in the bicameral parliament in Cape Town. Once again, the German element of the white population was reintegrated into the Namibian polity following their backsliding during the era of the Third Reich and the Second World War. But the Africans were only indirectly represented in the Namibian delegation in the South African parliament. One of the Senators from Namibia was expected to look after their interests. There were ten representatives — six of whom served in the House of Assembly (as Members of Parliament [MPs]) and the other four in the Senate. These six Namibian MPs, together with the members of the Namibian Legislative Assembly, elected two senators. The Governor-General (and later the State President) appointed the remaining two senators. One of the two appointed senators was responsible for the needs of the Africans.[27] This was a clear illustration of what the Australian political scientist David Goldsworthy called "vicarious representation."[28]

This paternalistic pattern continued into the early years of the United Nations, where the Anglican priest, the Reverend Michael Scott, served as the spokesman for the Africans of Namibia. It was not until November 1949 that he appeared before the Fourth (Trusteeship) Committee of the General Assembly to discuss conditions in the territory. The South African diplomats were annoyed and indicated their displeasure by staying away from the meeting. They were concerned that the petitioner's presence was setting a precedent.[29] Ton J. M. Zuijdwijk has provided a detailed analysis of the petitioning process regarding Namibia at the United Nations,[30] while Christopher C. Saunders[31] and Roger S. Clark[32] have carefully examined the Rev. Scott's work. His petitioning was indeed a notable departure from the rules utilized by the League of Nations Permanent Mandates Commission, but then, as Judge Sir Gerald Fitzmaurice of the International Court of Justice has shown, the United Nations trusteeship system was far less attentive to the concerns of administering states than the League mandates system and far more cordial to non-administering states and to the inhabitants of the trust territories.[33]

Nearly seven years after the Rev. Michael Scott addressed the Fourth Committee, the International Court of Justice (ICJ) handed down an advisory opinion that permitted the Committee on South West Africa to grant petitioners an audience,[34] thereby enabling the Namibians to move further way from the system of surrogate representation which was all they had known. In 1956, Mr. Mburumba Kerina was the first Namibian to serve as a petitioner before the United Nations.[35] Thereafter, Namibians themselves became the petitioners before the United Nations, and the number of petitions from Namibia jumped from one in 1946 to 120 in 1960.[36] This, in a way, marked the beginning of an *ersatz* diplomatic corps, although the Pretoria Government described them as "professional petitioners."[37] Nevertheless, they laid the foundation for what Lauren Dobell aptly termed SWAPO's "quasi-diplomatic missions worldwide."[38] According to the future deputy foreign minister of Namibia, in 1970, SWAPO created a Department of Foreign Affairs, and by the time Namibia became independent in 1990, there were a total of twenty-seven different missions, twelve of which were in Africa, eleven in Eastern and Western Europe, two in Asia, two in the Western hemisphere, one in Australia, and one at the United Nations.[39]

By the late 1950s, there was an increasing tendency not only to question the performance legitimacy of South Africa in Namibia but also to anticipate the weakening of the resolve of the western colonial states to stem the anticolonial tide throughout much of the world. Some of the newly independent states began to cluster together through continental or global meetings or organizations, with the result that their leaders and political elites developed a network of personal contacts and a repertoire of anti-colonial ideas, slogans, and catchwords. The Afro-Asian Conference held in Bandung, Indonesia in 1955, coupled with the pan–African conference system, which had its roots in the early twentieth century, provided a suitable platform for the display of rhetorical solidarity as well as opportunities to forge alliances among newly emergent states and nationalist movements.

In addition, the anti-colonial bloc was instrumental in shifting the accountability and control mechanisms contained in the United Nations trusteeship system over into the wider realm of the non–self-governing territories. They were unable to enlarge the trusteeship system, which rested upon the voluntary transfer of former League of Nations mandated territories to the United Nations system. Until the colonial powers chose to shift their own, rather than mandated, territories to the trusteeship system, there was little opportunity for the opponents of colonial rule to help dismantle colonial regimes. Consequently, they improved the machinery that offered ample scope for their anti-colonial talents. Thus, the residual system for the oversight of non–self-governing territories attracted their attention and talents. This is not to imply that such nations were single interest nations, with a total fixation on the elimination of colonialism. Rather, it means that reducing the number of colonial territories by turning them into independent states (and therefore future members of the United Nations) was a salient, and a high priority, issue for these new states.

A second path these anti-colonial states pursued in addition to the reorganization of oversight mechanisms for colonial territories was to change the rules of engagement for the battle against colonial rule. Drawing upon the collective legitimizing capabilities of the United Nations, they in effect started a type of bankruptcy proceedings against the entire colonial enterprise.[40] They condemned the colonial estate, declaring it to be illegitimate in General Assembly resolution 1514 (XV) of 14 December 1960. So significant was this resolution that the American political scientist Rupert Emerson regarded it "as almost an amendment to the [United Nations] Charter."[41] There was also a shift at this time in the position of the African bloc in the United Nations regarding the future international status of Namibia. Their delegates moved from supporting trusteeship for the territory to backing independence, which was a much stronger position.[42] Particularly within the General Assembly, when one reads the text of the numerous resolutions concerning Namibia, one finds considerable repetition, as well as predictability, of the anti-colonial themes in the preambular and operational parts of the various resolutions. This apparent tendency to redundancy was a common and rational diplomatic maneuver within the United Nations, where the aim was to create layers of precedent in hopes that they might later be transmuted into commonly accepted principles of international law.[43] Others, such as Robert E. Riggs, dissent from this view.[44]

Nevertheless the African nationalists within Namibia were not in a secure enough organizational position to be able to take maximum advantage of the change in international climate supportive of their anti-colonial mission. They were dependent upon the resources and patronage of sympathetic African and Eastern bloc states in the United Nations. This was a period of growth and organizational transformation of African political consciousness into an effective, authentic voice for a wide range of Namibians, many of whom lacked a pan-ethnic perspective. The challenge was to develop a nationalist agenda, symbols, and goals, to draw attention to protest behavior in the past to bolster self-confidence, to define and demonize the enemy, to win friends, particularly in other African states and territories, and to acquire powerful international patrons. In so doing, particularly in terms of the United Nations, they were able to utilize what Lawrence S. Finkelstein has termed "the leverage of legitimacy"[45] to secure, enlarge, and institutionalize access to the material resources needed for decolonization.

Transnational Theologians

One of the provisions in the League of Nations mandate agreement concerned the right of access of missionaries to the territory, which amounted to a type of theological open door policy.[46] The Germans had sent missionaries to the territory in the nineteenth century when there was what two well-known historians dubbed the "spiritual scramble for Africa."[47] Although they have sometimes been charged with being the cat's-paw of the colonial powers and of being quite paternalistic, if not downright racist, in their relations with their flock, these clergymen constituted a very significant interest group in the colonial environment.[48] Their importance rested not so much in the number of their converts or in the size of their congregations but rather upon their links to their counterparts and benefactors in the metropole.

Even though the missionaries of the Protestant Rhenish Missionary Society were probably the leading critics of German military policy during the suppression of both the Herero and Nama rebellions from 1904 to 1907, they had little success in dealing with the Berlin authorities to secure more humane treatment of Herero and Nama prisoners of war. Yet they were the only group of whites in the territory to provide any humanitarian assistance to those Herero and Nama who suffered grievously in the aftermath of their rebellion against the German regime from 1904 to 1907.[49] Recently Casper W. Erichsen has carefully documented this horrific treatment.[50]

In the Namibian case, one can argue that they formed a remarkable transnational network of protest that the South African authorities would not able to bend to their will. These theologians, moreover, complemented the work of the African nationalists in aggregating and articulating grievances within the country and then confronting the South African governors about the redress of these grievances. The classic case concerned the 30 June 1971 open letter of Bishop Leonard Auala and Pastor Paulus Gowaseb of the Evangelical Lutheran Ovambo-Kavango Church and the Evangelical Lutheran Church in Namibia (Rhenish Mission Church), respectively, to South African Prime Minister Vorster regarding the 1971 advisory opinion of the International Court of Justice and their complaint that South Africa was abridging the human rights of their fellow Namibians.[51] Of course, they were able to publicize these grievances as well. At a much later stage in the evolution of the war, church groups overseas operated their own information and communication services, such as the Namibia Communications Center, which began operating in London in 1984,[52] as well as supplying unofficial observers for the internationally supervised transition to independence in 1989–1990.[53]

Indeed, the late Reverend Michael Scott, an Anglican priest, was the first petitioner before the United Nations, and he took up the cudgels on behalf of the Namibians. He worked closely with Regent Tshekedi Khama of Botswana, who in turn had befriended Chief Hosea Kutako, leader of the exile Herero community in Botswana. In due course, Namibian petitioners took over from the Rev. Scott and presented their own case, while the Anglican priest became more involved in metropolitan-based activities, including the founding of the Africa Bureau in London.[54] That organization was one of the clusters of liberal and left-of-center groups based in London that attempted to influence British policy in southern Africa and that cultivated a number of prominent intellectuals and Labor Party MPs.[55]

The contention here is not that many of the churches acted as spokespersons for the Namibians. Rather, in a society which is as highly Christianized as Namibia, with estimates of church membership varying from 80 to 97 per cent of the populace,[56] church organizations and spokesmen have been able to supplement or to reinforce the activities of the African nationalists, especially SWAPO. They provide a significant link to economic support groups in the western world, groups that functioned as solidarity organizations.

Self-Determination and Symbolic Warfare

An integral part of the Namibian nationalist lexicon was the well-known term of self-determination, which often appears in the popular and academic discourse over the fate and future of the League of Nations mandated territory. It is also an integral part of the twentieth century rhetoric of anti-colonialism and decolonization, and ironically enough spokesmen of the white minority government of South Africa had no qualms about appropriating this term for their political vocabulary. "Politics," claimed a deputy minister in the parliament of newly independent Namibia, "concerns perceptions."[57] As John Barratt, director of the South African Institute of International Affairs, incisively pointed out, two different geographical names have been used for the territory, namely, South West Africa, on the one hand, and Namibia, on the other hand. Each term carried emotional and political baggage, reflecting the ideals and preferences of the protagonists. Self-determination was an integral part of both sets of baggage. From the Namibian perspective, "self-determination is a right for the people of Namibia as a whole, whereas South West Africans maintain that each *group* of the population has that right (as does the National Party of South Africa), fearing domination by one group which could yield majority voting power."[58] The white community also wanted to ensure its control over its own customary geographical domain.[59]

The term self-determination, however, never appeared in the fifty-seven United Nations General Assembly resolutions on Namibia passed in the 1946–1960 period. The term trusteeship, however, appeared on seventeen of these resolutions, while the phrase independence appeared only once, at the end of this period.[60] This was a period characterized by attempts to persuade South Africa to transform Namibia from a League of Nations mandate into a United Nations Trust Territory, considerable sparring with South Africa, and frustration, ending with the initiation (by Ethiopia and Liberia, both former League of Nations members) of an International Court of Justice case against South Africa.

During the 1961–1966 period of the marathon court case, there were nineteen United Nations General Assembly resolutions dealing with Namibia, three of which mentioned self-determination, none of which dealt with trusteeship, and six of which were concerned with independence. It was only in 1961 that independence was mentioned as a goal for Namibia.[61] This long lag (1946–1960) without any reference to independence in the General Assembly resolutions on Namibia can, in part, be accounted for by the introduction of a classic General Assembly resolution excoriating the colonial condition and calling for independence for colonies. The title of the 14 December 1960 resolution (no. 1514 [XV]) was "Declaration on the Granting of Independence to Colonial Countries and Peoples," and operative paragraph two of the resolution specifically referred to self-determination. This particular resolution could well be considered an indication that an international regime of decolonization was being created.[62] Indeed, it rejected the arrangements made at the 1945 San Francisco United Nations Conference on International Organization for the handling of trust territories as well as non–self-governing territories and it amounted to "a *de facto* revision of the [United Nations] Charter."[63]

Symbolic warfare, which grew to be increasingly significant as the international regime of decolonization became securely entrenched in the General Assembly, was characterized by the nearly predictable annual repetition of prior General Assembly resolutions dealing with Namibia, and by resolutions (which tended to use formulaic and catechismal language) castigating the South African metropole, those nations that provided weaponry to South Africa,[64] and an array of transnational or multinational corporations that the diplomatic friends of Namibia regarded as financial backers of the apartheid regime.[65] Parallel with these resolutions, there were twenty-three other General Assembly resolutions from 1967

(UNGA res. 2288 [XXII] of 7 December 1967) to 1989 (UNGA res. 44/84 of 11 December 1989) castigating foreign economic interests involved in Namibia and other territories for being impediments to decolonization. This was a predictable, annual event. John P. Powelson has carefully evaluated the role of these corporations in developing nations.[66]

At the more positive level, the General Assembly continued to use the lexicon of self-determination, independence, and legitimacy in the thirty-two resolutions on Namibia that it passed from 1967 until 1976, when it recognized SWAPO as the "sole and authentic" representative of the Namibian people.[67] Nineteen of these resolutions referred to self-determination, twenty-two to independence, and thirteen to legitimacy.[68] Roughly the same pattern emerged in the subsequent period of SWAPO hegemony (1977–1989). Of the twenty-one General Assembly resolutions passed during these years, seventeen mentioned self-determination, seventeen drew attention to independence, and thirteen referred to legitimacy.[69]

In addition, from 1970 (UNGA res. 2649 [XXV]) until 1989 (UNGA res. 44/79) the General Assembly passed at least one resolution each year expressly concerned with self-determination, and in some cases there were two (1982–1985) and three (1985–1989) resolutions annually on this topic. This verbal offensive was designed to undercut and thereby weaken the South African government's support system, while the verbal defensive was to enhance the diplomatic prestige and economic resources of SWAPO. Indeed, this was a graphic example of what James H. Mittelman has dubbed "collective decolonization."[70] African delegations to the United Nations were able to employ three types of influence tactics to advance their decolonization agenda, namely, persuasion, isolation, and confrontation.[71] At a later date, the General Assembly would legitimize SWAPO, first by describing it as "the authentic representative of the Namibian people,"[72] and subsequently upgrading its status to "the sole and authentic representative of the Namibian people."[73] Along with this monopoly recognition, the General Assembly bestowed General Observer status on SWAPO.[74] The General Assembly privileged SWAPO's access to a range of United Nations bodies,[75] and subsequently interpreted the concept of self-determination in such a way as to legitimize SWAPO's resort to arms against the Pretoria regime.[76]

Thus, much of the activity in the United Nations over the status of Namibia can be subsumed under the rubric of the ceaseless battle for tangible and intangible resources between the antagonists, with the Namibian nationalists and their diplomatic allies utilizing what could be characterized as the diplomacy of shame against South Africa and its supporters.[77] It might also be termed "the politics of hyperbole" in the United Nations.[78] Nevertheless, this was not a transient phenomenon that South Africa and its supporters could ignore for long, for the UN Security Council began to incorporate the language of self-determination, independence, and legitimacy into some of its resolutions concerning Namibia.[79] Like President Theodore Roosevelt's West African aphorism, the Security Council would "speak softly and carry a big stick"—the stick of economic sanctions.[80]

Cultivating Friends

One of the principal structural challenges facing Namibian Africans who had become politicized during the earlier period of their lives was the system of white dominance practiced in the territory not only by the German officials and residents but also by their South African successors. In particular, these Namibians were accorded minimal, if any, dignity, modest, if not marginal, educations, and demeaning work conditions. Such constraints made it difficult for them to visualize alternative and positive futures and to communicate these visions and aspirations throughout the territory to other Namibians except through the literate Africans. Oral communications and travel to and from work sites, such as those involved in regimented migrant labor system, would be the characteristic experience of these Namibians. Literacy and organizational skills were at a premium. Travel opportunities, other than family visits and extended labor experience, were few in number. Legal travel beyond the territory for higher education required both funding and travel documents. Some Namibians apparently were able to attend South African schools during the mandate era, and these privileged few subsequently became members of the Namibian intelligentsia.[81] However, the number of such privileged students is not known.[82] No Namibian African could appear in person before the Permanent Mandates Commission of the League of Nations because oral petitioning was not part of the Commission's operating procedure. To use Albert Hirschman's classic phrasing, both vote and exit were the prerogative of the white regime in Namibia.[83] Thus, Namibian Africans could neither participate meaningfully in their own governance nor easily opt out of the prevailing system of omnipresent white privilege.

There were only a few windows of opportunity for the development of what might be thought of as African protonationalism under the League of Nations era. One of the earliest was the link to the U.S.-based Marcus Garvey movement through the Herero people[84] and, in southern coastal Namibia, through labor unions in the fish canneries.[85] Neither experience produced any lasting tangible results nor generated a great deal of publicity, even though there was a fanciful impression among some Namibians that the Garvey movement would provide some overseas help from Afro-Americans.[86] Far greater publicity was generated overseas in the League of Nations Permanent Mandates Commission by the South African use of military force to suppress the revolts of the Bondelswarts group of Nama people in southern Namibia[87] and of the Rehoboth community south of Windhoek.[88]

Although the containment of these two revolts detracted from South Africa's international prestige as a mandatory power, they brought no material or non-material benefits for those who were suppressed. Nevertheless, such displays of armed force could form part of the chronicle of white South African rigidity and obtuseness which would be political grist for the mills of Namibian African nationalist publicists and intellectual entrepreneurs. Like the Americans a century and a half earlier, who realized the symbolic import of the Boston massacre[89] and of the attitude of King George III regarding the thirteen American colonies, the Namibian African nationalists had an ample number of grievances to air.

The petitioning process took on much greater significance in the post–World War II period, as exemplified by the creation of the United Nations. Indeed the Namibians benefited from the efforts of Tshekedi Khama, the Bamangwato traditional leader in the neighboring Bechuanaland Protectorate (now Botswana), where there was a Herero as well as a Nama[90] diaspora. Tshekedi notified the British government of his (and his fellow chiefs') opposition to the South African proposal that the United Nations should legitimate the incorporation of Namibia, fearing that this would make it easier for the South Africans subsequently to absorb the Bechuanaland Protectorate,[91] which the South African constitution permitted, assuming the United Kingdom assented to such a move. Concern about the territorial absorption of the Bechuanaland Protectorate by South Africa had been a long-standing irritant between these two neighbors.[92]

Beginning in 1946, the evanescent links to the Afro-American community that the Namibian followers of Marcus Garvey hoped might bring relief in the early 1920s became more concrete with the activities of the non-racial American Council on African Affairs. However, the leftward drift of the Council, along with growing McCarthyite anti-communist sentiments, helped to scuttle that organization in the mid–1950s.[93] Thereafter, the American Committee on Africa, founded in 1953, continued the interest in, and support for, Namibian African nationalists.[94] Such a connection was especially valuable because of the location of the United Nations in New York, which became one of the central foci of Namibian external nationalism.

Challenging South African Legitimacy

Even with a slowly growing number of friends, the Namibian nationalists were not able to accomplish much in the United Nations other than constant petitioning, especially within the framework of the Fourth (Trusteeship) Committee of the General Assembly. This was a slow process and, one that differed markedly from the practice in the Geneva-based League of Nations Permanent Mandates Commission, which forbade such a practice. It took an advisory opinion of the International Court of Justice (in 1956) to institutionalize that right within the United Nations. In a sense, that advisory opinion allowed the Namibian petitioners a seat at the table in the United Nations, but they needed more leverage and traction to win more friends and positively influence key delegations. Perhaps that access to the table could be designed as protobargaining—a necessary, but not sufficient condition. Although an earlier advisory opinion of the International Court (in 1950) on the international status of the territory dramatically brought the future of the Namibian mandate to the attention of various voting blocs within the General Assembly, the matter did not directly involve the Security Council until 1968, when considerations of power and armed insurgency began to obtrude alongside the perennial anti-colonial rhetoric. The Security Council called upon the South African regime to terminate the Pretoria terrorism trial (*State versus Tuhadeleni and others*), to release the defendants, and to return them to Namibia.[95] The United Nations Institute for Namibia has provided a detailed synopsis of the Council's involvement in the future of Namibia.[96]

This 1968 Security Council pronouncement on the Tuhadeleni case was an indication of Finkelstein's notion of "the leverage of legitimacy" referred to earlier in this chapter. Equally, it could be seen as an instance of international delegitimation of South African legal practices of counterinsurgency, and it was a logical consequence of the General Assembly's revocation of South Africa's mandate for the territory embodied in its 1966 resolution and the corresponding United Nations assumption of *de jure*, but hardly *de facto*, responsibility for the territory.[97] These two actions by United Nations General Assembly and Security Council in 1966 and 1968, respectively, certainly undercut any South African claims to legitimacy in its administration of the territory.

Admittedly, it changed very little in the daily operation of the South African officials in the territory, for they commanded the *de facto* power, but it put the Pretoria regime on the defensive in the field of shifting international norms with respect to decolonization. Their rule was henceforth delegitimated by important international bodies. The General Assembly, where African delegations could muster more voting strength than in the Security Council,[98] went still further in delegitimizing the Pretoria regime by expelling the South African delegation from the floor of the General Assembly.[99] However, South Africa kept its permanent mission to the United Nations in New York as a listening post, a place to circulate information, and an opportunity to make significant contacts. Yet, the regime maintained a discreet silence about this presence with respect to members of its own parliament.[100] The General Assembly further asserted that the South African regime was "illegitimate,"[101] and it criminalized its racial policy of apartheid.[102] This would cover the situation in Namibia, where the prevailing system was aptly designated as "apartheid by proxy."[103]

A United Nations Presence and Non-Economic Sanctions

At this point, the question arises: what clout was there in this delegitimation of the South Africans and the General Assembly's legitimation of the Namibians' claim for independence?[104] Was it merely rhetoric that the major powers and South Africa could safely ignore? The answer would be probably yes, in the short term, but no in the long term. Beginning in the 1950s, France and the United Kingdom, two of the most significant colonial powers, managed to divest themselves of their sub–Saharan and North African colonies without much prolonged violence, although there were several significant exceptions (Algeria, Kenya, and Southern Rhodesia). The ease with which these two powers managed their decolonization policies can be accounted for, in part, by competent planning and by the enunciation of values for the people of the metropole that appealed as well to those of the colonies. That is, there was no major disjunction between the values that the metropolitan and the colonial peoples held, and this enabled the colonial people to insist that they also share in the metropolitan values.

An interesting, heuristic example of this congruence of metropolitan-colonial values, although taken from the eighteenth century, is the way in which Benjamin Franklin felt himself to be thoroughly British throughout most of his life. It was only later when autocratic changes in the British rule of the American colonies violated his sense of proper British behavior that he reacted by reinventing himself as an American and subsequently became thoroughly estranged from his son William, who served as the royal governor of New Jersey.[105] Other than France and the United Kingdom, the only other Western European nations with sub–Saharan African possessions after the Second World War were Belgium and Portugal, and the imperial exit of the former was precipitous and that of the latter truculent, sanguinary, and prolonged. There was little reason to expect that most Angolans, Mozambicans, and Guineans found much to admire or emulate in the authoritarian Portuguese system, notwithstanding the assimilationist rhetoric of the Salazar regime. *A fortiori*, the Namibians could not envision any future within the larger South African polity in which they could aspire to be anything other than subalterns, at best.

Indeed, they could not use South African ideals as ideological leverage against the South Africans to achieve any sort of parity with the dominant South Africans. There was no dialogue over shared values or aspirations.

At the very least, the United Nations General Assembly had made it abundantly clear to various attentive publics throughout the world that it found South African colonial concepts and practices in Namibia anathema. Yet, the skeptics could regard these pronouncements as little more than a house of rhetorical cards. What to do? Until the final run-up to the 1989 Constituent Assembly elections held under the aegis of UNTAG (the United Nations Transition Assistance Group) the United Nations had not established any visible presence in the territory, other than the temporary rare visit of some senior UN officials who were invited by the Pretoria authorities.[106] The South African Government denied entry to the members of the United Nations Council for South West Africa in 1961 and 1968.[107] However, Martti Ahtissaari, the future special representative of the Secretary-General, briefly visited Namibia in 1978.[108] The UN General Assembly had authorized an on-going UN presence in the territory as early as 1967, but the South African regime was in no mood to cooperate.[109] Indeed, during the era of the League of Nations Permanent Mandates Commission (PMC), visiting missions to the various mandated territories were not part and parcel of the mandates system. If a PMC member wished to visit such a territory he or she did so at his or her own expense,[110] and there is a record of such a personal visit to Namibia in 1935 by Marquis Theodoli, the Italian member of the PMC.[111] Prime Minister Hertzog invited the Marquis Theodoli to visit the territory.[112] Only with the coming of the UN trusteeship system were visiting missions authorized (to trust territories).[113]

Unable to establish itself in the territory, the UN continued to investigate conditions in the territory, drawing upon data supplied by petitioners and specialists and upon data gleaned from a wide range of official and unofficial sources. It thus assumed research as well as publicity functions. In addition, it positioned itself in Lusaka, Zambia through the United Nations Institute for Namibia, which trained (refugee) Namibians for future posts in an independent Namibia — as possible shadow civil servants — and also became a think tank for developing policy proposals and options for majority-ruled Namibia.[114] The General Assembly authorized establishment of this institute, which was to be financed through the UN Fund for Namibia.[115] Hage G. Geingob, the director of the Institute from 1975 to 1989, became the first prime minister of independent Namibia.[116]

Chapter Two

The Diplomacy of Controlled Change[1]

South Africa the Supervisor

South Africa's international standing reached its zenith during the era of the League of Nations and did not return until the 1990s with the advent of the Mandela Government, which inaugurated an era of widespread regional, continental, and international respectability and legitimacy. The nub of the Namibian problem was that South Africa wished to act as its own supervisor for the task of international stewardship. I aver that the reason for this policy is essentially domestic, rather than international. With a changing international milieu, South African political leaders had reason to be anxious about external supervision of the mandate for Namibia. For these leaders, the League of Nations, a Eurocentric organization, was a relatively friendly group, most of whose members shared unspoken assumptions about the colonial system and who believed in what Gary Wasserman has called "the rectitude of the imperial mission."[2]

A crucial component of South African foreign policy was the defense of the established domestic order, which was, as Gwendolen M. Carter so aptly described it, the politics of inequality.[3] The pursuit of such a policy, particularly as the National Party stalwarts envisioned it, entailed a certain consistency of treatment of non-whites throughout South Africa and its domains in southern Africa. There was little dispute over the general principle, however, for, as Prime Minister Smuts expressed it as World War II drew to a close, "There are certain things in regard to which we in South Africa are all agreed, all parties, all sections, except those who are completely out of their minds, and that is that it is our firm policy and resolution to maintain the European civilization in South Africa, to maintain it and to perpetuate it in every possible way."[4] At the time South Africa joined the United Nations in 1945, there was relatively little African nationalist activity in bordering areas of Namibia, Botswana, Swaziland, Lesotho, and Southern Rhodesia; only in South Africa had African nationalism developed a coherent philosophy and a devoted constituency that spanned a range of ethnic groups.

After the end of the First World War, the Smuts Government (1919–1924) had unsuccessfully attempted to persuade the whites of neighboring Zimbabwe to merge their country with South Africa. The Hertzog Government was anxious to have the United Kingdom transfer the High Commission Territories (Botswana, Lesotho, Swaziland) to it, and its successor governments continued to request that transfer well into the 1950s. In the case of Namibia, the Smuts Government assured the whites of South Africa that Pretoria had sufficient control over the territory that it did not need to take the additional step of annexing it.[5] The League of Nations Permanent Mandates Commission took umbrage with this type of assertion, but they could do little about it except to publicize and decry it.

The United Nations, however, was another matter. Its trusteeship system included a number of powers that were lacking in the League mandates system, and it was these powers that enabled the United Nations to become a much more effective supervisor of the anticipated demise of colonial rule. Such supervision would, in time, certainly corrode South African control over Namibia. Fred E. Bishop contended that were Namibia to become a United Nations trust territory that institutional change would jeopardize the system of white paramountcy in South Africa itself.[6] This was unacceptable to the South African establishment if only to protect its own white constituency. This white bonding relationship between these neighbors became more obvious to observers as the Namibian war of independence wore on.[7] Expressed slightly differently, Robert I. Rotberg claimed that "Namibia is a proxy issue."[8] The respected Namibian political scientist André du Pisani underscored the strength of this bond between the two neighboring racial oligarchies, observing that "the majority of whites in South West Africa came to regard politics as a mere extension of white politics in South Africa."[9]

Moreover, the thought of two different, probably competing, policies for non-whites was anathema to the South African authorities. As Dr. Heinrich Vedder, a distinguished German missionary in Namibia, explained in the South African Senate, apartheid was nothing new in Namibia The Germans had implemented it early in the twentieth century.[10] Implementing divergent racial policies flew in the face of twentieth century South African history, which was marked by an attempt to secure a uniform policy toward non-whites. The first civilian administrator of the mandated territory, Gysbert R. Hofmeyr, indicated to General Smuts that "Native policy in South West Africa ... is part and parcel of the native policy ... of South Africa[.]"[11] Three decades later, the South African Minister of External Affairs explained that "The Government's standpoint is that the colour policy applied here [in South Africa] ought also, in broad terms, to be the policy applied in South West Africa."[12] American and British researchers, Richard Dale[13] and Christopher A. Ford,[14] have explored this congruence of African policy between Namibia and South Africa. This *idée fixe* of white South Africans concerning political primacy, as the South African political scientist Robert Schrire has pointed out, entails the politics of "power, privilege, and prejudice."[15] The application of this policy of white paramountcy throughout the South African domains seems similar to what the American political scientist Tony Smith termed the French "colonial consensus" regarding Algeria[16]; these shared outlooks and perceptions made the task of decolonization a difficult and threatening one.

To minimize such a threat, the Pretoria regime in effect named itself as the supervisor of its international obligations. What it wanted to avoid was the intrusive effects of the trusteeship system on the internal South African and Namibian balance of racial power, so it avoided any actions that could reasonably be interpreted as recognizing the tenets of the international supervision of the mandate[17] or international accountability for its administration of the territory.[18]

Other-Determination and Symbolic Warfare

As representatives of a system that embodied a set of norms that were slowly being challenged in the United Nations and other international fora, the South African authorities and their delegates to the United Nations utilized a range of tactics and employed conceptual weapons to blunt their critics. One of the earliest stratagems was to invoke the concept of self-determination to legitimize their policy in Namibia. In its earliest form, it complemented the British attempt to undercut the moral underpinnings of German colonial rule. The allegation, which the Germans called the colonial guilt lie,[19] was that Germany had forfeited any right to participate in the work of colonizing non-western peoples because of its maladministration as well as its cruelty toward and inhuman treatment of its wards, particularly (but not exclusively) in Namibia. Such criticism was predicated on the "rectitude of the imperial mission," of course. The Germans, in turn, alleged that British colonial rule was hardly exemplary and defended their record in Namibia.[20]

Although the matter of German fitness to undertake the imperial mission was quietly dismissed later when the German Weimar republic was reintegrated into the international community,[21] the South Africans dutifully queried the Africans of Namibia about their colonial preferences. Even though the referendum could be thought of as an exercise in what Professor Neuberger called other-determination,[22] it entailed no international monitoring. It was deficient on other procedural or methodological counts as well.[23] The Germans, in turn, argued that the Africans in their erstwhile colonies had not really been consulted about their future status, so that the Allies were not serious about the concept of self-determination that many associated with President Wilson.[24]

It appears that Prime Minister Smuts chose to ignore the advice that Prime Minister Winston Churchill had proffered him in 1943 and again in 1944, namely, to proceed with the annexation of the territory.[25] Later, when it prepared its case for the incorporation of Namibia into South Africa for presentation to the United Nations General Assembly in 1946, the Smuts Government again dusted off the concept of self-determination and used a plebiscite among the Africans.[26] This concept had never appeared in the text of the Covenant of the League of Nations that provided for the mandates system, but it was later incorporated in the United Nations Charter.[27] Although the plebiscites arranged during the League of Nations era precluded the option of independence for the territory in question, there was still an element of international oversight regarding the conduct of the plebiscite.[28] Although they may not be equivalents, the notions of plebiscite and self-determination have been closely linked in practice.[29] "The resort to [an] internationally supervised plebiscite," as Professor Crawford has observed, "is perhaps the best example of the institutionalization of the principle of self-determination."[30] Yet the South African regime repeated the same mistake it had made earlier: there was no international monitoring of the plebiscite.

Given the racial and political structure of its own system of governance (and public relations techniques), it is doubtful that the South African delegation to the United Nations could have succeeded in convincing the majority of the United Nations General Assembly members of the cogency of its arguments regarding self-determination for its mandated territory. In the Paris Peace Conference a quarter of a century earlier, there were no black members of the South African delegation to contribute to the discourse.[31]

Once again, in 1946, there was no significant change in the racial composition of the South African delegation. Yet a quarter century later, three non-whites (one each from the South African Colored and Indian communities, and the Transkei government) were added to the South African delegation in the subordinate role of observers.[32] This was not the first time that South Africa had included an African in its delegation to an international event. An African chief was a member of the two-man South African delegation attending the centenary celebration of Liberian independence in Monrovia in 1947.[33]

In 1946 the senior Native Commissioner for Ovamboland, Major C. H. L. (Cocky) Hahn, was included on an *ad hoc* basis as a consultant on the plebiscite.[34] He came from one of the oldest missionary and pioneering families in the territory and had an established reputation as an administrator and ethnologist in Ovamboland.[35] A second Native Commissioner from the territory, H. J. Allen, also served on the South African delegation.[36] The Pretoria diplomats, however, did not include any members of the all-white Legislative Assembly of the territory who could make their own case for self-determination as expressed in two separate resolutions of that legislature.[37] Indeed, the Assembly had formally asked the territorial Administrator to request the Pretoria government to include one of their members, Mr. J. P. de M. Niehaus of the United National South West Party, in the South African delegation.[38] Seven years later, however, the United Nations General Assembly endorsed the idea of having "indigenous representatives" form part of the United Nations delegations of those states that administered non–self-governing territories[39] South Africa ignored this suggestion which doubtless would have been an affront to the members of the Legislative Assembly.

Added to the traditional nature of their United Nations delegation, the South African regime did not present an unassailable case regarding the transparency and thoroughness of the plebiscite among the African inhabitants of the territory even though they distributed ten thousand copies of their glossy publication *South West Africa and the Union of South Africa*, with every United Nations General Assembly delegation receiving a copy.[40] The position of the white community on the future of the territory, though, seemed to be of little interest to other United Nations delegations and, as was anticipated,[41] was consequently ignored. The central focus was on the overwhelming majority of the inhabitants, the Africans (who were not present). Consequently, the South African case for incorporation was contingent upon the broader issue of the acceptability of its racial policies not only to white audiences overseas but also to African ones.[42] Essentially, there were three principal flaws in the design and administration of the South African–sponsored plebiscite that was intended to buttress the South African delegation's case for incorporation of the territory.

First, and most obvious, was the absence of either officially or unofficially sanctioned observer groups or individuals during the conduct of the plebiscite. Indeed, the Smuts Government refused the Johannesburg-based South African Institute of Race Relations permission to send representatives to monitor the plebiscite.[43] This was a public relations blunder of the first magnitude for it precluded the possibility of creating favorable stakeholders in the plebiscite administration, especially the various national delegations to the United Nations who formed a critical audience.[44] The distinguished student of African colonial administration, Lord Hailey, who had been a member of the Permanent Mandates Commission from 1936 to 1939,[45] had been invited by Prime Minister Smuts to visit the territory, but his visit took place after the plebiscite was completed. Therefore he had no first hand observations about the plebiscite, and he made no mention of it either in his report to Prime Minister Smuts or when interviewed by the South African press.[46] The South African Government did not ask for his opinion of the plebiscite. He was, however, asked about his views by the British Government, which apparently misconstrued his carefully guarded statements, with the result that he seems to have tacitly approved of the referendum. That was sufficient for the London authorities, and the United Kingdom delegation was the only one in the United Nations to have supported the South Africans on this matter.[47] Privately, however, some British officials expressed concern about the absence of international monitors, yet the desire to show support for the Smuts regime prevailed, especially after the Prime Minister had warned his British counterparts that failure to support the South African position might increase South African pressure for the incorporation of the contiguous High Commission Territories.[48]

Secondly, the process was not transparent. Indeed, current published sources at the time suggest a considerable reticence on the part of South African officialdom to disclose how the plebiscite was being conducted.[49] The idea for such a consultation has been traced back to 1943, when Prime Minister Smuts consulted with Colonel Petrus I. Hoogenhout, the administrator of the territory, about conducting such an exercise.[50] The consultation, which was administered secretly; this has since been confirmed by scholars who have consulted the Namibian archives.[51] The referendum began in December 1945 and lasted until April 1946.[52]

Thirdly, there were several technical flaws in the plebiscite which commentators as well as various United Nations delegates spotted and which, consequently, undermined its political credibility, if not its legitimacy. Possibly these shortcomings could have been reduced or even eliminated had the Pretoria authorities sought expert advice on the design and implementation of plebiscites; there certainly was no lack of such expertise in the international community on this topic.[53] It seems that no such efforts were made to do, and one can perhaps assume that failure to do so might well have a reflection of domestic political considerations. The National Party Opposition had introduced a motion in the House of Assembly on 26 February 1946 urging the Smuts United Party Government to incorporate the territory with any delay. The most forceful and articulate Opposition spokesmen in the debate was Mr. Eric Louw, who earlier had served as the South African delegate to meetings of the League of Nations Permanent Mandates Commission and who was later to become South African foreign minister.[54] One of the principal foreign policy differences separating Government and Opposition on Namibian policy centered on how much attention to pay to international opinion, with the Government anxious to seek international approbation, while the Opposition was much more attentive to domestic considerations.[55]

The plebiscite contained primarily three technical flaws, namely, the framing of the question, the severe time constraints, and the manner in which the Africans' opinions were tabulated. Overriding these three deficiencies was an internal contradiction or paradox contained in holding the plebiscite. If, as the United Nations General Assembly stipulated in its resolution rejecting the South African case, the Africans were not yet politically mature enough at that time to express a considered opinion on the incorporation,[56] then why would the South African government even consider consulting them?[57] Political maturity and voter competence were not defined in any objective, quantifiable way, so that fourteen years later the United Nations General Assembly, in its classic pronouncement on self-determination and decolonization in 1966, indicated that lack of political experience was not an acceptable excuse to defer the granting of independence.[58] This generalized policy statement, as part of the delegitimation of colonial rule, contrasted sharply with the one it assumed in 1946 with respect to the African majority in Namibia.[59]

Turning to the technical shortcomings of the plebiscite, the first imperfection is the nature of the electorate consulted. Who was charged with making decisions or choices? What was the nature of the self that was determining its future status? It was not single Africans but collectivities under their traditional leaders who were consulted so that the sum of the various collectivities were collated, group by group.[60] Essentially the same group (rather than individual) approach in a subsequent polling of the Africans after the United Nations General Assembly rejected the South African request for incorporation in 1946. The data on the second consultation (which yielded essentially the same positive responses favoring incorporation) are quite sparse.[61] Indeed, children were included in the count.[62] In the case of Ovamboland, for example, it appears that the tally included women, who traditionally were excluded from tribal decision-making. This obviously inflated the size of the vote.[63] Moreover, the traditional African leaders, holding remunerative positions within the traditional system operated by the Windhoek government, were hardly impartial agents; they did not recuse themselves from their duties.[64] All of this changed, as independence became a reality. Individuals, not collectivities, voted, and the minimum voting age was eighteen.[65] Admittedly, under the new dispensation, Namibians were voting for individual candidates, running under political party labels, rather than for the future status of their country. The difference in issues or choices, however, does alter the drastic shift in the definition of a voter over nearly half a century.

A second deficiency in the plebiscite concerns the nature of the choices involved. The low level of formal education among most of the Africans persisted well into the 1989 independence elections monitored by the United Nations Transition Assistance Group (UNTAG).[66] In 1989, roughly 60 per cent of Namibians were estimated to be illiterate.[67] Even if this impediment is taken into consideration, the pros and cons of the choices put to the people in 1945–1946 were not carefully spelled out, namely, incorporation or participation in the United Nations trusteeship system. Indeed, no representative of the United Nations could put the case for trusteeship to these Africans, Independence for the territory was not even considered an option at that time.[68] This may well have been a result of the phrasing of, as well as conventional wisdom at that time about, the terms of the League of Nations class C mandate for Namibia.[69] There was little attention paid to this option, although the League of Nations mandate system was mentioned in the prepared text, which had been approved by the Administrator of the territory. In the third place, although the consultation of the various African groupings by various native commissioners was spread out over a five-month period, the Africans had ever so little time to make their actual decision on the future of their country, namely, they decided on the same day that they heard the native commissioner read his address. One day is hardly sufficient to make such a momentous choice without much opportunity to engage in serious discourse.[70]

Despite the rejection of the mechanics of the 1945–1946 plebiscite among the Africans by the United Nations General Assembly in 1946, the South African regime continued to expend political capital promoting the concept of self-determination to legitimate the theory and practice of African administration in the territory. On 17 September 1947, the South African delegation to the United Nations notified the secretary-general of the United Nations that it consulted with the Africans of Namibia once again, explaining to them that the United Nations had rejected the notion of incorporation. When asked whether they would change their preferences, the overwhelming majority (193,400 out of the 258,900 who were consulted[71]) still opted for incorporation. The South Africans, however, did not describe this procedure as a plebiscite; it was termed "deliberations" at several "meetings."[72] Furthermore, the representatives of the white community reiterated their wish for incorporation by passing a resolution in the Legislative Assembly on 7 May 1947.[73]

Self-government for Africans and white minority rule were not necessarily antipodes within the cosmology of apartheid, which was subsequently verbally segued into separate development. Some of the self-determination aspect of this theoretical construct can be traced to the outcome of the Second Anglo-Boer War (1899–1902) in which the two Afrikaner republics were defeated, lost their independence, and were subsequently absorbed into the Union of South Africa. The Afrikaner republics sent a delegation to the Paris Peace Conference to attempt to reestablish their independence from Britain. In short, they wished to avail themselves of Wilsonian self-determination in order to return to their 1899 status.[74] Consequently, the Afrikaner leadership, which was institutionalized within the National Party, especially after the 1948 South African general election, took the position, at least rhetorically, that they would grant others (the Africans) what the Afrikaners cherished and claimed for themselves. Self-determination, in this sense, could be co-opted in the service of separate development, at least at the symbolic level. An equally attractive feature, as Ithiel de Sola Pool and his fellow researchers have asserted, is the significant links between the symbols of self-determination and democracy.[75] Although it formed part of the political lexicon for the whites that applied it to themselves,[76] in practice, as Joseph Lelyveld has observed, "'white self-determination' is impossible without [white] supremacy."[77] Given the general symmetry between South Africa's policy towards Africans in both the metropole and in Namibia that was acknowledged as early as 1923,[78] the South African regime became involved in the creation of various reserves or homelands for Africans (as well as the Rehoboth people[79]) in Namibia that reflected the Panglossian ethnic and political engineering goals of the policy of grand apartheid. Prime Minister Dr. Hendrik F. Verwoerd visualized apartheid on a sweeping basis with the whole of South Africa being segmented into African homelands and a white core, with eventual independence for the African homelands.[80] This policy was enunciated in the Odendaal Report of 1964, which was the master plan for territorial apartheid, with separate areas for separate African groups and with an evolving political framework for each group. It was grounded upon the primacy of African subnationalism, rather than pan- or trans-ethnic nationalism and was the policy of choice for the privileged Namibian white minority (which, in turn, was divided into three language groups of German-, English-, and Afrikaans-speakers). The report also reaffirmed the South African commitment to, and interpretation of, self-determination for the territory.[81] When the enabling legislation (the Development of Self-Government for Native Nations in South West Africa

Bill) was introduced into the South African Parliament in 1968, the talisman was again self-determination for the Namibian Africans granted on a local, territorial base, one ethnic group at a time. While introducing the second reading debate on this bill in the House of Assembly, Mr. M. C. Botha, the Minister of Bantu Administration and Development, averred that "The Native nations of South West Africa ... are, like every nation all over the world, entitled to ... self-determination, and this Government is intent on assisting them to attain as much as they can in this respect."[82] Indeed, the South African regime considered its creation of these mini-nations (often termed Bantustans by their detractors) as an exercise in decolonization as well as semantic sleight-of-hand.[83]

Although South Africa might be said to have emerged victorious with the 1966 (technical) non-decision of the International Court of Justice in the case brought against it by both Ethiopia and Liberia, the question of the international validity of South African policy applied to Namibia was mooted. The majority of the members of the United Nations General Assembly were sufficiently appalled by what they perceived to be the Court's bias in favor of South Africa, and they arranged the termination of the League of Nations mandate for the territory. In addition, they shifted the responsibility for the administration of the territory from South Africa to the United Nations.[84] Subsequently, the United Nations Security Council concurred in these decisions to wrest the mandate from South Africa and to make the United Nations the new governor of Namibia.[85] Despite the United Nations' insistence that South Africa vacate the territory,[86] South Africa continued to exercise *de facto* power in Namibia, which meant that the territorial changes envisioned in the Odendaal Plan were being effected.

Subsequently, the United Nations once again turned to the International Court of Justice for yet another advisory opinion. This time what was at stake was the validity of what amounted to an eviction notice to South Africa as well as a tacit assessment of the propriety of South Africa's separate development project.[87] What is noteworthy about the case at The Hague is the South African attempt to win the Court's endorsement of yet another plebiscite among the inhabitants. This plebiscite proposal, which would test whether Namibians wished South African or United Nations rule, represented a slight improvement on the 1945–1946 one for it did permit a degree of international supervision, which South Africa would grant to the Court.[88] A well-known Namibian expert on African politics in the territory advised the South African legal team at The Hague to drop the idea of a plebiscite, but they disregarded his counsel,[89] and the Court dismissed the proposal.[90] In January 1972, South African Prime Minister B. J. Vorster withdrew the offer of a plebiscite.[91]

What is particularly interesting about the plebiscite offer, however, is that both the (opposition) Progressive Party and the United Party went on record as supporting the Prime Minister on this proposal.[92] This was the last time that the Pretoria regime sought to utilize the self-determination concept contained within a plebiscite proposal for Namibia that probably would not stand up to international scrutiny. Nevertheless, one highly respected South African legal scholar, Professor John Dugard, suggested that a carefully constructed, administered, and supervised plebiscite involving both South Africa and the United Nations would be a satisfactory exercise in self-determination.[93] Moreover, Mr. Theo-Ben Gurirab, who became SWAPO's secretary of foreign affairs in 1989 and the first foreign minister of Namibia in 1990, indicated in 1974 that SWAPO might be willing to agree to an international plebiscite that met several international standards and that had the appropriate international safeguards. The operative words were international, safeguards, and standards.[94] In retrospect, some of these revised plebiscite ideas in 1973–1974 seemed to have reappeared in the norms surrounding the 1989 elections for the Constituent Assembly held under the auspices of the United Nations Transition Assistance Group. (UNTAG).

Pursuant to operative paragraph five of UN Security Council resolution 319 (1972) of 1 August 1972, the UN Secretary-General dispatched the Swiss diplomat Alfred M. Escher to visit South Africa and Namibia to explore how self-determination might be applied to the territory. Self-determination was expressly mentioned in operative paragraphs two and four of this Security Council resolution. In addition to holding seventy-four private meetings (from which the South African authorities were excluded) with a range of Namibians, he also met with Prime Minister Vorster during his visit to Namibia and South Africa, which took place from 8 October until 3 November 1972.[95] There was no meeting of minds between the Secretary-General's representative and the Prime Minister with respect to the precise meaning of self-determination, which remained as elusive as ever.[96] The same divergence in interpretation of this term had been evident in Secretary-General Waldheim's discussions with Prime Minister Vorster in March 1972.[97] This is a notable example of the maxim that "one of the politician's arts is the deliberate use of ambiguous language."[98]

André du Pisani's notion of controlled change (the title of this chapter) encapsulates the South African attempt to appropriate the language of its opponents, especially the term decolonization. Yet Pretoria's cognitive map of decolonization was based upon earlier South African policies and preferences, some of which lent themselves to obfuscation, as well as upon later fears and perceptions. Social and geographical engineering as well as paternalism characterized its decolonization efforts and rhetoric.

Following the 1948 general election in South Africa which ushered the National Party into a dominant political position, South Africa shifted from its policy of racial segregation to one of apartheid, which was much more ideologically coherent and which created a small bureaucratic empire to administer the new dispensation. Neither system rejected white dominance and both were attempts to garner white electoral support and to manage the socioeconomic changes accompanying industrialization.[99] Pretoria's slightly Micawberish policy for Namibia was to forge ahead with the geographical aspects of apartheid (or separate development as it was later called),[100] thereby creating various ethnic fiefdoms that afforded possibilities for patronage and employment for some Africans. These were termed second tier authorities.[101]

Moreover, the South Africans attempted to fashion a newer polity by arranging a territory-wide conference in Windhoek to explore paths to independence and to draft a constitution for the future state. This was referred to as the Turnhalle Conference (named after a former German gymnasium), which lasted from 1975 to 1977. However, it was organized very much along separate development lines, with participation based upon delegations representing racial and ethnic groupings.[102] The conference forbade the participation of political parties and overruled the suggestion of an academic adviser to the National Party, Professor Gerhard Tötemeyer of Stellenbosch University, that SWAPO be invited to attend.[103] This meant that the conference was unrepresentative of the whole country and attracted the white community and pliant, co-opted Africans. Indeed, it turned out that this was an exercise in political theater, with the African delegates subjected to some degree of discreet handling by the white managers and advisers, although they enjoyed a range of perquisites unknown to the average African. The delegates were required to take a pledge of secrecy about the proceedings and no written record of the discussions was published.[104]

The Turnhalle Conference produced a rather tepid bill of rights, proclaimed that the country should be independent by the end of 1978, and that an interim government should rule the country until that time.[105] After the conference ended, the Windhoek regime undertook a program of cosmetic administrative reform which did away with what has been termed petty apartheid, reinforced the powers of the senior executive of the territory (now called the Administrator-General rather than just Administrator), and returned some mostly inconsequential responsibilities that Pretoria previously had acquired from the territorial government. Moreover, the territory lost its representation in the South African Parliament. None of the really vital government departments, such as foreign affairs, finance, and defense, were transferred and stayed in Pretoria.[106] These constitutional arrangements met with the approval of the white electorate in a 17 May 1977 referendum that was restricted to Namibian citizens and to 30,000 South African civil servants in the territory; it excluded the 10,000 German citizens living in the territory.[107]

Thereafter, South African–sponsored decolonization efforts in Namibia were grounded in a complex web of jurisdictions and authorities that effectively doled out packets of power among white supporters and homeland-based African clients, with the most significant packet reserved to the white electorate. From the white perspective, there was a need to create a South West African, rather than a South African identity, which was not helped by the presence of so many South African civil servants in the territory. Moreover, there was feeling that these South West Africans no longer wanted to think of their country as a colony of South Africa. As the presiding officer of the Turnhalle Conference, Mr. Dirk F. Mudge stressed the need for such a new identity.[108] Nevertheless, this cognitive, perceptual shift was ironically parallel to the SWAPO goal of a pan-ethnic identity for the inhabitants of a refashioned nation to be called Namibia. The South West African perception and the subsequent territorial constitutional engineering throughout the 1970s and 1980s were manifestly deficient in international legitimacy.[109]

Monopolizing Legitimacy

In the context of the Namibian war of independence, the South African regime devoted considerable effort to defending the legitimacy not only of the Pretoria regime itself but also of its rule in Windhoek. It denigrated any form of, or pretense to, legitimacy that its Namibian opponents and their supporters claimed. The challenge regarding the legitimacy of South African control over Namibia can be traced back to the early days of the League of Nations mandate period, when the issue of sovereignty arose. Were the mandatory powers sovereign over their mandated territories? Because Namibia was termed a class C mandate, at the bottom of the triadic political scale (with A being the highest level and B the mid-level), some regarded it as nearly annexed or incorporated territory.[110]

The issue of sovereignty was a contentious one for the Permanent Mandates Commission, which reminded the South African regime that it was not sovereign over the territory.[111] Nevertheless, South Africa was able to claim sufficient internal sovereignty to secure a conviction of high treason in the 1924 classic case of *Rex v. Christian*.[112] Indeed, the Permanent Mandates Commission did not consider the ramifications of this case, which did not address the complementary issue of external sovereignty.[113] The case, however, was noted in the South African Parliament.[114]

Once the war began in 1966, the South African Parliament exerted its political and judicial dominance in the territory through the passage of the 1967 Terrorism Act, which was one of the principal weapons used to prosecute those who challenged the hegemony of the South African state. By conducting the first terrorism trial against Namibian defendants in Pretoria, rather than in Namibia, the regime sent an outward and visible signal of its control over the territory.[115] This 1967 act was made retroactive to 1962.[116] Although the issue of high treason was not the centerpiece of the 1967 legislation, the Terrorism Act did include the same penalty as high treason, namely, the death penalty.[117]

The first terrorism trial (*State v. Tuhadeleni and others*) occasioned rebukes from both the United Nations General Assembly and Security Council,[118] but it did not end in any death sentences. Indeed, the Prime Minister B. J. Vorster cautioned presiding judge Ludorf on the need to avoid such sentences.[119] Apparently, only in one case did the state apply the death penalty to a captured deserter from a SWAPO military base in Angola; he was not acting under the authority of SWAPO and was found guilty of murdering four civilians in Namibia.[120] Throughout the Namibian war era, the South African regime never really defined what it meant by the noun or adjective 'terrorist.' This suggests the power of lexical ambiguity.

Subnational and Real Estate Diplomacy

After Namibia was transferred to South African administration as a mandated territory under the aegis of the League of Nations, the Permanent Mandates Commission not only took exception to occasional South African claims to sovereignty over the territory[121] but also expressed its concern over the South African practice of subcontracting the administration of a portion of the territory (the eastern portion of the Caprivi Zipfel or Strip) to the British authorities in the contiguous Bechuanaland Protectorate.[122] This occurred from 1921 until 1929. From 1929 to 1939 this part of the Caprivi Strip was under the jurisdiction of the Administrator of Namibia, then it became the responsibility of the South African Minister of Native Affairs until 1978 when its administration reverted to Namibia. This administrative reshuffling also attracted international attention during the written and oral proceedings of the International Court of Justice in its 1966 advisory opinion on the South West Africa cases.[123] Even though Walvis Bay had been a British (and subsequently South African) enclave in Namibia that was an extraterritorial portion of the Cape Province, it was treated as though it were an integral part of Namibia. Lynn Berat provides a meticulous analysis of the relationship between Walvis Bay and Namibia in the 1884–1977 period.[124]

These two examples suggest that during the League of Nations era Namibian territorial integrity was altered, if only temporarily, to suit budget constraints or to enhance administrative efficiencies.[125] Once the United Nations began to deal with the international status of the territory and realized that the South African regime had increasingly developed its own divergent agenda for the future of Namibia, a United Nations good offices committee (composed of an American, a Brazilian, and a Briton) attempted unsuccessfully to resolve the conflict in 1958. This committee proposed to resolve the conflict by separating Namibia into two portions, the northern portion (where the bulk of the Africans resided) to come under international trusteeship system and the southern one (where the whites were located) to be incorporated into South Africa.[126] The Minister of External Affairs, Mr. Eric Louw, discussed the partition idea with the Prime Minister and his Cabinet.[127] This 1958 partition idea apparently was grounded on a similar idea that the British Anti-Slavery Society had advanced in its petition to the *Ad Hoc* Committee on South West Africa in 1951.[128] The Anti-Slavery Society proposal apparently was never considered.[129] Nevertheless, the United Nations forwarded this document to South Africa, indicating that this was the procedure used by the League of Nations.[130] The United Nations General Assembly rejected the good offices committee proposal for a divided Namibia in 1958.[131]

As the dispute over the future of the territory wore on, one of the emerging themes of the majority of the General Assembly membership dealt with the territorial integrity of Namibia. Above and beyond the perennial concern with institutionalized racial inequality was a manifest hostility to territorial fragmentation[132] as proposed in the 1964 Report of the Commission of Inquiry into South West Africa Affairs (headed by the Administrator of the Transvaal, Mr. Frans H. Odendaal), which the Pretoria regime regarded as a genuine application of the precepts of self-determination.[133]

To the extent that the Africans of Namibia shared this interpretation of self-determination, it would facilitate government allocation of socioeconomic and political power into "penny packets"[134] and would privilege African subnationalism at the expense of African nationalism. A disaggregated African nationalism would allow scope for coalition building, just as it has in other parts of the world at various times, and for developing clusters of counter-power.[135] For a short period the South African planners of the redesigned political map of Namibia even went so far as to visualize independence for the various ethnic homelands, but this idea was subsequently dropped.[136] However, this notion was put into effect with a few of the South African homelands under the separate development design, but not one of the newly independent states ever received any international recognition. Nevertheless, the South African regime developed an entire diplomatic repertoire to deal with such former homelands.[137]

One of the more graphic examples of this juggling with real estate and subnationalism was the trial balloon floated in late 1974 (after the 25 April 1974 *coup d'état* in Portugal) by Mr. Jannie de Wet, who served as the Commissioner-General for the Indigenous Peoples of South West Africa. He suggested, in an interview with a Johannesburg newspaper correspondent, that the northern Namibian homeland of Ovamboland be territorially linked up with the corresponding Ovambo ethnic region of southern Angola to form a greater Ovamboland which could be granted independence. Although considered an exercise in applied self-determination, this time there would be no suggestion about the use of a plebiscite among the inhabitants.

Although this new ethnically exclusive territory could become independent, it was clearly to be linked to the remainder of Namibia and these ties would very likely replicate those that South Africa forged with its own ethnic enclaves, such as the Transkei which was granted independence in 1976 — an independence no state other than South Africa recognized. The Commissioner-General did not suggest why the Ovambos of Angola would find a pan–Ovambo mini-state wedged between Namibia and Angola an attractive real estate offer. It appeared as though the cabinet of Ovamboland was considering the idea, but indications were that neither the United Nations nor those African political parties in Namibia opposing territorial fragmentation would accept this proposal. Indeed, the Pretoria regime did not endorse the de Wet proposal, and it faded into political oblivion.[138] Roland Dreyer has provided a thoughtful analysis of the greater Ovamboland proposal.[139]

The greater Ovamboland proposal was essentially an ethnic application of self-determination which would shrink the size of a potential SWAPO domain (by encapsulating its Ovambo supporters in one unit) and the large remainder of the territory in another unit where separate development would prevail and the white community could more readily and easily rule, free from potential, feared Ovambo domination.[140] Of the three political parties in Angola (MPLA, FNLA, and UNITA), only UNITA expressed an interest in the idea, although this was transient, while the MPLA was hostile to the idea, and the FNLA's position was ambiguous.[141]

South Africa: Friend of the West

There are three particular facets involved in South Africa's information diplomacy with respect to Namibia in particular and also with regard to South Africa itself. These are the messages, the messengers, and the audiences, and all three are interconnected, preferably in a cost-effective manner, to maximize the number of its friends and to minimize or neutralize the number and/or effectiveness of its foes, some of whom termed the South African effort "The Great White Hoax."[142] With the passage of time, the principal concern was to thwart its opponents' goal of isolating South Africa in a range of sectors. In brief, it was to check a multi-faceted campaign of sanctions launched by a wide range of nations and international organizations.

During the League of Nations era both the messengers and audiences were basically restricted to elites in the South African diplomatic corps[143] and in the League of Nations Permanent Mandates Commission (PMC) and its staff in Geneva. Although the Commission members found the Pretoria regime truculent at times (when the annual mandates reports were examined and discussed by the Commission and the accredited South African representative),[144] the South Africans were usually comfortable in the League setting[145] (and were elected to leadership positions in the League Assembly[146]). "The PMC," noted one American historian, "was not anti-imperialist; if anything, it was seeking to rehabilitate (and not to discredit) imperialism."[147]

Even though the South Africans took a remarkably principled and courageous stand on the maintenance of sanctions against Italy during the Italo-Ethiopian War,[148] the League never seriously and continuously challenged the colonial system and its reliance upon white paramountcy. The Haitian delegate to the League, Mr. Dantès Bellegrade, however, was influential in focusing the League Assembly's attention on the Bondelswarts rebellion in 1922. Although two Pan-African Congresses had recommended the appointment of a black member of the PMC, this did not happen even though Mr. Bellegrade's name had been suggested for such a position.[149] Recent scholarship, however, has challenged the conventional wisdom that the mandates system precluded the option of eventual independence for Namibia.[150]

The major South Africa message on Namibia at this time could be termed a colonial technocratic one which concentrated on running a more administratively and financially efficient system of colonial rule which, to use Robert Schrire's alliterative phrasing, protected the "power, privilege, and prejudice" of the white Namibian and South African electorate[151] while employing the rhetoric of stewardship embodied in the "sacred trust of civilization" phrasing of the mandates system. There was embarrassment over the rapid repression of two revolts between the Bondelswarts segment of the Nama group[152] and the inhabitants of the more privileged mixed-race group living in Rehoboth.[153] After the advent of National Socialism in Germany in 1933, South Africa added a minor message regarding Namibia, aimed at two audiences: the decision-makers in Berlin and the German-speaking white residents of Namibia. This message indicated that South Africa intended to retain control over Namibia, preferably by incorporating it (presumably with the approval of the appropriate League of Nations organizations), and that it would not permit Namibia to revert to German control as part of a larger plan to rectify the colonial settlement at Versailles.[154]

After the Second World War, the South African Government made a serious effort to cultivate a wider circle of friends, particularly within the context of the United Nations, where it faced challenges not only with respect to the future of Namibia but also with regard to its traditional practice of white minority rule, including the issue of its treatment of those who had emigrated to South Africa from India. The rejection by the United Nations General Assembly in 1946 of its request to incorporate Namibia (which was elaborately orchestrated and presented using the familiar symbol of self-determination as well as sophisticated brochures and the prestige of Prime Minister Smuts himself) was a stunning setback and left Prime Minister Smuts quite disillusioned. He recognized that the issue of racial discrimination and equality had a deleterious impact on the effectiveness of South Africa in the United Nations.[155]

With the growth of a professional South African foreign service, created in 1927 as a result of Prime Minister Hertozog's Government concern for providing credible evidence of South Africa's independent diplomatic space relative to the United Kingdom, there was a lagged creation of an information service. This service dates back to 1938, when the South African High Commission in London included a press officer; the next such appointment followed four years later in the United States. By 1946 South Africa had created a State Information Office, and the Dr. Daniel F. Malan's Government appointed Wentzel C. du Plessis to head that office in 1948, and he subsequently served as high commissioner to Canada, ambassador to the United States, and then administrator of South West Africa (1963–1968) during the early years of the Namibian war of independence. Beginning in 1958, the State Information Office became the responsibility of the Department of External Affairs.[156]

In light of its limited resources and the nature of its electoral clientele, it chose to concentrate its attention on those states which offered it ample opportunities for trade, foreign investment, preferred immigrants, and patrons to come to its diplomatic and military aid. North America and Western Europe seemed to offer the optimal rate of return on such an investment of time, personnel, and funds. Anti-communism — in word and deed — was a key element in securing access to the corridors of Western power, and the newly-elected Malan Government burnished its credentials by the passage of the Suppression of Communism Act in 1950 and followed that by closing down the Soviet consulate in South Africa (which was established in 1942) in 1956.[157] I have found no documentary evidence that there was a Communist Party in Namibia, and Christopher Saunders seemed to have implied that this was indeed the case.[158] The 1950 statute (and its amendments) covered a very wide range of behavior that the regime perceived and labeled as communist, so the authorities were legally well equipped to throttle anti-regime activities in Namibia. Per Strand has provided an exceeding insightful analysis of the role of socialism, both scientific and non-scientific, in SWAPO's domestic and foreign policy rhetoric and policy.[159] Currently there is a Communist Party of Namibia, which failed to elect any member of the National Assembly in the 2009 general election and lost its deposit in the 2009 presidential election.[160]

This anti-communist stance, which was not exclusive to the Afrikaner nationalists but also appealed to Prime Minister Smuts, dates back to the 1922 Rand revolt and subsequently provided part of the doctrinal basis for the total onslaught policy enunciated by the P. W. Botha regime.[161] The Pretoria regime also expended some of its political and financial capital when it provided South African Air Force pilots for the operation of the Berlin airlift[162] and for combat duty in the Korean War.[163] Such gestures could be interpreted as diverting Western attention from the National Party policy of neutrality in, if not outright hostility to, the Second World War.[164] They could also function as acquiring anti-communist credentials for future diplomatic and military largesse from Western powers.[165] South African political and military leadership sought closer multilateral defense ties with the metropoles of Western colonial powers in order to protect itself from communist military aggression which would sooner or later undermine the basic racial hierarchy within South Africa, but the effort turned out to be a chimerical one. Geoffrey R. Berridge[166] and Frederik J. Nöthling[167] have thoroughly explored and documented this topic in their archival-based studies. Anxiety about extraterritorial encroachment on the core of white paramountcy, especially when linked to the arming of Africans, was a particularly Afrikaner nationalist preoccupation which had been clearly articulated by an earlier Afrikaner Minister of Defence, Oswald Pirow, in 1933, so the notion of a buffer zone or the need for external, Western patrons is of long-standing origin.[168] Indeed, the white South Africans perceived the developed Western nations as the location of "…their spiritual homeland."[169]

Western nations, especially those with colonial possessions, were an obvious audience for Pretoria's anti-communist message, which became a more elaborate one, stressing the importance of South Africa to the West in terms of its strategic mineral resources and its crucial geographical position, bordering both the South Atlantic and Pacific Oceans. The American political scientist William J. Foltz has undertaken a thoughtful reappraisal of the South African claims on this subject.[170] However, this type of strategic argument resonated with the U.S. Naval War College authorities.[171] At a less visible level, the South African intelligence apparatus developed links with it American and British counterparts,[172] and the South Africans publicized the occasional capture (and subsequent exchange) of Soviet spies operating in their country[173] as well as focusing upon weaponry that the Soviets supplied to several guerrilla organizations.[174] The Cold War context of its message would presumably trump other less attractive features of the South African political landscape, such as the highly visible and increasingly systematic system of white paramountcy, which generated growing hostility within certain segments of these Western nations as well as non–Western states. Martin A. Sovik, Assistant Director of the Office of Governmental Affairs of the Lutheran Council in the United States, provided an exegesis and analysis of the South African Cold War message with particular emphasis upon Namibia in his 1985 Congressional testimony.[175]

Just as the anti-apartheid non-governmental organizations carried on their advocacy networks,[176] so the private sector in South Africa created a counter-lobby known as the South Africa Foundation, which drew its principal support from the leadership of the business community, along with other white South African notables who were not currently members of the Government. It attempted to bridge the Afrikaans-speaking v. English-speaking gap between the two white communities in South Africa (and also in Namibia) by also recruiting prominent English-speakers as members, which added to the nonpartisan image it was trying to create. The amply funded Foundation focused its attention on Western overseas elites, especially those from the business world, which were not known to be demonstrably anti–South African. In 1984, the Foundation hosted six members of the U.S. House of Representatives and one member of the U.S. Senate.[177]

The Foundation's preferred mode of operation was customized travel within South Africa or Namibia for its overseas guests, who were also treated to specially designed private seminars where the discourse was confidential and open. Such a format put the visitors at ease, and they often returned home to create greater goodwill for South Africa particularly among their influential peers, who had access to well positioned decision-makers.[178] These contacts and relaxed style of persuasion supplemented the more traditional and transparent operations of the government information service, and they could be used to emphasize the economic and defense (as a manifestation of its anti-communist commitment in the Cold War) strengths which merited closer cooperation and greater rates of foreign investment. The South African government did utilize American lobbyists and public relations firms and paid them handsomely for their services.[179]

PART II: THE ECONOMIC CAMPAIGNS

Chapter Three

Waging Economic Warfare[1]

Carrots, Sticks and a Helping Hand

In their pioneering work on sanctions and South Africa,[2] the American political scientists Neta C. Crawford and Audie Klotz have deepened our understanding of the complexities, ambiguities, and utilities of sanctions, especially as they applied to South Africa (and perforce Namibia), and they have ventured beyond the customary realm of economic sanctions. In this chapter, I consider the matter of economic sanctions, having covered the diplomatic sanctions in previous chapters, but I also move somewhat beyond their admirable models[3] to consider the converse of their concerns. Not only did the protagonists engage one another in battles of economic warfare — sanctions for the one side and counter-sanctions or sanctions evasion for the other side — but also they sought out sources of assistance such as moral or normative, theological, financial, military, political, and legal support, as well as assistance in the areas of information retrieval and dissemination. One part of this could aptly be designated a "transnational anti-apartheid support network," to use Scott Thomas' phrase.[4] It was, in brief, a multidimensional zero sum game, with rewards offset by losses, involving corresponding trade-offs. Who supported whom with what resources would be an apt characterization, as suggested by the title of Harold D. Lasswell's classic book on politics.[5]

One of the more striking aspects of SWAPO's war against the Pretoria regime is that the funding was essentially from external patrons, which distinguishes this organization from its Algerian counterpart, the National Liberation Front (FLN). The FLN was able to draw upon the financial resources of expatriate Algerian workers in France by means of what was termed the (Francis) Jeanson Network that arranged to transport those funds from France to banks in Switzerland. This network involved some three thousand French sympathizers in this underground transit system. Much of the funds were used to purchase arms for the ALN (the FLN's military wing), and there has been no record of the disposition of the remaining funds. The French security service uncovered a number of operatives, and the French government put eighteen French citizens, who did not include the leader, Francis Jeanson, and six Algerians on trial.[6] Similarly, the Palestinians, in their 1937–1939 rebellion, used a system of rural taxation to fund their uprising in this British mandated territory.[7]

According to Article IV.A. (4) of its 1976 constitution, SWAPO did have membership dues, consisting of an initial payment (of R1.00), for which a receipt would be given, and monthly payments (of R0.50) thereafter, so that a single membership would entail an expenditure of R7.00 for the initial year and R6.00 per annum thereafter. That fee apparently applied to all members, both in Namibia and in exile.[8] In addition, Article IX.G. (4)—(5), and (7) of that constitution noted that SWAPO had a national treasurer who was responsible for district, regional, and national finances.[9] Although the dues structure would provide something tangible to SWAPO members, making them stakeholders in a larger nationalist enterprise, it is doubtful whether the sum total of membership fees would generate very substantial funds for internal and external operations, including the prosecution of a guerrilla warfare. Given the ubiquity of the security police with their informer network as well as the pitifully small wages of the Namibians, especially those involved in contract labor, it would be challenging not only to collect the membership dues but also to bank them except outside the country. All of this suggests the need for external beneficence. SWAPO sought to "borrow power from the developed countries," as Professor I. William Zartman phrased it, to take advantage of "their resources of persuasion and coercion."[10]

Undermining Military Logistics

Once SWAPO committed itself to battle against the South African regime on 26 August 1966, it selected the customary weapon that militarily weak commonly use in a revolutionary war, namely, guerrilla warfare.[11] Charles Maechling, Jr., has distinguished between guerrilla war and revolutionary war, indicating that "the injection of ideology into guerrilla operations transforms partisan warfare into revolutionary war."[12] The term partisan warfare, he noted, is a far older one than guerrilla warfare, which dates back only to the resistance to the French invasion of Spain at the time of Napoleon.[13]

Although the central goal of such combat was political control of the population, rather than of the territory, the guerrilla forces faced a well armed, technologically sophisticated foe sustained by the resources of an industrialized economy.[14] Indeed its foe has been termed "the apartheid war machine."[15] Conducting a guerrilla campaign against the South African military and police forces was a daunting challenge to SWAPO, and one obvious way of diluting the strength of its military and police opponents was to diminish, if not terminate, the flow of internationally-based economic resources needed by the SADF and the SAP (South African Police) operating in Namibia.

The task of mobilizing international support for applying militarily-related economic sanctions against South Africa was a challenging one for SWAPO and its diplomatic allies in the United Nations, although beginning in the 1970s it was able to point to two international achievements to marshal support for its position. First, it was able to point to its own legitimated position as the sole, authentic representative of the Namibian people, according to two United Nations General Assembly resolutions.[16] In addition, the General Assembly granted it observer status in the General Assembly and in international conferences held under the aegis of the General Assembly.[17] The United Nations Security Council, which had veto power over sanctions resolutions, granted no such privileges to SWAPO.[18]

The second achievement concerned the Organization of African Unity (OAU), which functioned as a gatekeeper for national liberation groups. This organization was also an observer in the General Assembly upon an earlier recognition.[19] By 1974, there was a nexus involving General Assembly–approved observers, the OAU, and national liberation movements.[20] The OAU, through its Liberation Committee based in Dar es Salaam, Tanzania, provided a modicum of financial assistance to those liberation groups it recognized.[21] However, SWAPO leaders were upset about the meager arms assistance that the OAU Liberation Committee provided.[22] Although the OAU reflected the African nations' desire to maximize their influence in global affairs and to express their extreme displeasure with white minority regimes, not every nation contributed to the liberation fund, thus creating a free rider problem for the organization.[23] Franz Ansprenger has provided data on the financial contributions to the Liberation Committee for the 1963–1973 period.[24]

According to the personal recollection of the first Prime Minister of Namibia, Hage H. Geingob, the African diplomats eased the passageway for SWAPO representatives at the United Nations through their contact networks.[25] Moreover, the United Nations, through its Council for Namibia, provided the necessary funding for SWAPO to have an office in New York.[26] Lynn Berat added that the Council, in turn, represented SWAPO in several international organizations as a non-voting observer.[27] SWAPO drew compound interest from its OAU recognition as the sole representative of the Namibian people The OAU granted exclusive recognition to SWAPO in 1965.[28] Moreover, SWAPO could point to the delegitimation of the South African presence in Namibia by both the International Court of Justice (in an advisory opinion)[29] and the United Nations Security Council.[30] Given the nature of the South African economic interests and investments of the Western permanent membership of the Security Council *vis-à-vis* the General Assembly, it was an easier task to persuade the non–Western members of the General Assembly (who tended to have fewer vested interests in South Africa) to undermine the economic underpinnings of the South African military and police establishment.

Even though I refer to the South African military and police establishment, it needs to be emphasized that this establishment functioned in both South Africa and in Namibia, whereas SWAPO engaged both South African police and army units in Namibia (and Angola) rather than in South Africa. Thus, PLAN had mainly one theater of operations, whereas the SADF/SAP continuously functioned in two theaters (and projected its presence to a range of Southern African nations, including Angola and Zambia). Consequently, it made no strategic or tactical sense for SWAPO to treat the SADF/SAP as two distinct units, one in Namibia and the other in metropolitan South Africa, and to impose sanctions merely on the those forces stationed in, or assigned to, Namibia. Force rotation was an essential attribute of the SADF/SAP *modus operandi*. The case, therefore, had to be made against the entire military and police forces, resident and non-resident, which, in turn, would allow for a widening of the international campaign to include African nationalist groups in South Africa.

The United Nations as Benefactor

One of the more significant aspects of the Namibian War of Independence is the financial backing of the two protagonists in what amounted, at least originally, to an asymmetrical conflict in which there was a marked imbalance in access to economic resources. Lauren Dobell claimed that, when examined from a *per capita* perspective, SWAPO received more "financial, material, moral and diplomatic resources" than any other Southern African liberation movement. Yet she provided no numerical and comparative data to support this claim.[31] On the one hand, the United Nations served as a diplomatic forum for both the South African regime and the Namibian nationalists to seek and encourage supporters as well as to castigate each other and to undermine the supporters of their opponents. On the other hand, it became one of the financial patrons of SWAPO over the course of time. This reflected not only the growing ranks (and majority status) of African and Asian states within the United Nations, especially within the General Assembly but also the salience of anti-colonial rhetoric and actions to these new members.[32] Moreover, the top two leadership roles in the important Fourth (Trusteeship) Committee of the General Assembly — the chairmen and vice-chairmen — more often than not went to delegates from former colonies.[33] This committee met more often than any other General Assembly committee, and it attracted top delegates from the anti-colonial states.[34] Furthermore, the plenary sessions of General Assembly adopted the overwhelming majority of the Fourth Committee draft resolutions without making any changes.[35] As the era of decolonization advanced within the General Assembly, so too did the palpable UN support of SWAPO which had acquired a hegemonic position as well as observer status within the General Assembly. It had no important nationalist rivals.

The Pretoria regime found this incremental policy appalling, charging that the United Nations was no longer an impartial organization,[36] and, as I point out in Chapter Six, the South African authorities used their political leverage to terminate the financial support that the United Nations provided SWAPO during the run-up to Namibian independence in 1989. This remonstrance did not mean, however, that the South Africans adopted a neutral financial stance in the 1989 Constituent Assembly elections. Far from it. They provided ample slush funds to anti–SWAPO political parties competing in that crucial election. I examine this topic later in Chapter Six. Just how much financial aid the United Nations provided SWAPO is a question that has not been definitively answered so far because the sources tend to be scattered, on the one hand, and because the data sometimes need to be disaggregated, on the other hand.

For example, there is a sixteen-page, undated South African mimeographed document titled "United Nations Assistance to SWAPO" which covers the year 1981.[37] Presumably, there would have been companion documents for other years, perhaps located in the South African and/or Namibian national archives. There are also some hints in the answer to parliamentary questions in the South African House of Assembly *Debates*[38] but there seems to be no consistent, annual, transparent coverage of this matter enabling one to track disaggregated patterns of expenditure. For instance, Margaret P. Karns gave a figure of $260,400 as "UN direct aid to SWAPO in 1978–79." However, she provided no source for this datum and did not explain what the term "direct aid" meant or even how it was computed.[39] Similarly, Jan C. Heunis asserted that the United Nations supported SWAPO with annual amounts of R 20 million, but he did not clarify his sources or the years involved.[40] What is readily available, though, are the United Nations contributions to the UN Fund for Namibia contained in the text of various General Assembly resolutions. These contributions are listed in table six.

With Some Ecclesiastical Assistance

SWAPO emissaries cultivated a wide array of financial patrons outside of the United Nations to defray the expenses of their organization, and most of these patrons were members of a global web of anti-apartheid interest groups that focused on Namibia and on South Africa (and usually on other white-ruled Southern African nations as well). Nina Drolsum has termed these non-governmental groups (NGOs) solidarity organizations,[41] while Mark Israel referred to some of the politically active expatriate South Africans in Britain as "international solidarity lobbyists."[42] Gretchen Bauer used the term "solidarity literature" to cover the writings of these groups.[43] Their principal tasks were to mobilize subnational, national, and transnational support for the liberation movements and, conversely, against the South African and other Southern African minority-ruled regimes. Characteristically, they demonstrated a strong strain of humanitarian concern, which was often theologically grounded, and did not countenance any direct military aid to SWAPO, preferring instead to allocate their resources to benign, non-violent pursuits. Within North America and Western Europe, the solidarity organizations tended to cluster at the center-left and left of the political spectrum.

Historically, the missionaries had a significant presence in Southern Africa, and, as noted in Chapter One, the League of Nations mandate agreement for Namibia specifically guaranteed access to, and freedom of movement for, missionaries.[44] "Political relations between religious societies and the colonial state," wrote the Rhodes Scholar Nils O. Oermann, "were largely dependent on the co-operation or conflicts of individuals who never behaved solely according to a pro–African or pro–German pattern, but changed their mind, words or deeds depending on the political interests involved."[45] Even though they sometimes acted in complicity with colonial regimes, particularly with the German one in Namibia, the historian Isabel V. Hull contended that the German Protestant missionaries there were "the best informed and most outspoken critics" of German military policy regarding the suppression of the Herero revolt.[46]

However, some individual missionaries and churches broke out of the conservative fold to befriend the Namibian nationalists and their cause. The Finnish Lutheran church provides an apposite case study of the shift in the views of the metropolitan hierarchy and its representatives in northern Namibia.[47] The Anglican priest, the Rev. Michael Scott, was probably the earliest champion of the nationalists and has been honored in post-independence Namibia by having both a Namibian archival oral history project and a Windhoek street named in his memory. Foreign missionaries whose activities threatened the prevailing order in Namibia were frequently deported,[48] local clergymen and church workers were harassed,[49] and some church properties were destroyed.[50] Africans, in turn, began to assume greater leadership roles and authority within their own churches, thus demonstrating that they were significant elements within the Namibian political environment.[51] Especially was this the case when the Namibian clergy began to speak and act within the context of contemporary liberation theology, which covered considerations of moral and state legitimacy.[52] According to Anglican Bishop James Kauluma, who was the President of the Council of Churches in Namibia, there was a "chaplaincy program" in the Angolan SWAPO camps for refugees.[53] The German cleric, Siegfried Groth, has provided limited data on this point.[54] Unlike the insurgents in Zimbabwe,[55] I have discovered no evidence that any traditional religious leaders, usually termed spirit mediums in Zimbabwe, ever supported SWAPO.

There was a mutual dependence between Namibian clergy (and foreign missionaries), on the one hand, and their opposite numbers in Western Europe and North America, on the other hand. The local clergy served as both conduits of information for the overseas solidarity organizations and channels of distribution of goods and services (including symbolic and moral support) for their parishioners and others relevant to SWAPO goals, while the overseas groups provided funds and, in some instances, volunteers. The overseas organizations, moreover, assisted in the mobilization of their attentive laity, as illustrated by the Lutherans, who have had an abiding missionary presence (for a century), as well as interest in Namibia. In 1976, for example, SWAPO representatives, the United Nations Commissioner for Namibia, prominent Lutherans, representatives of other denominations, academic notables, lawyers, and representatives of the U.S. government attended a conference on Namibia co-sponsored by Lutherans.[56] In addition, a prominent Lutheran spokesman appeared before a Congressional subcommittee dealing with human rights in Namibia in early 1985.[57] The Lutherans have the highest proportion of communicants in Namibia, with fifty-seven percent of the total population in a nation that claims that ninety per cent of its people are Christians.[58] As one American Lutheran spokesman suggested, in a U.S. House of Representatives subcommittee hearing, "on any given Sunday, more Lutherans attend church in Namibia than in Norway."[59] The denomination, in turn, is linked at the international level to the Lutheran World Federation, which assisted in the creation of the Council of Churches in Namibia (CCN). Subsequently, the CCN linked up with the wider World Council of Churches.[60]

At the national ecumenical level, the CCN was deeply involved in the Namibian civil society and became closely, perhaps too closely, identified, with SWAPO.[61] Such a relationship between the Namibian churches and SWAPO, argued one British scholar, meant that these churches appeared to lose some of their "potential to act as a moral watchdog."[62] The British Council of Churches (BCC) and Colin Winter, a British Anglican priest who had been expelled from Namibia in 1972 by the South African authorities,[63] did, however, demonstrate concern about SWAPO's treatment of renegade members, particularly Andreas Shipangna. Shipanga, however, claimed "[Bishop] Winter never risked his close relationship with SWAPO by speaking out publicly about our plight."[64] The bishop as well as the BCC drew attention to SWAPO's subsequent behavior in the case of those who were imprisoned in its Angola camps, alleging that they were South African agents. Such intrusion annoyed some in SWAPO,[65] who also expressed their displeasure and anger at those Namibians and their outspoken German Lutheran pastor, the Rev. Siegfried Groth, who publicized the case of those detainees.[66] Not unexpectedly, the SADF Military Intelligence was covertly involved in the publication of a volume dealing with the detainees,[67] although the SADF and the detainees themselves had divergent political and moral agendas.

Those Britons involved in church-related groups sometimes felt that Namibia was neglected in the larger anti-apartheid scheme of things, and it was no small matter to develop a modicum of interest in the matter among the British public.[68] It was consequently important to develop a communications network to disseminate news reports about the country and the effects of South African rule there and go beyond, for example, the conference on Namibia held at Oxford University in March, 1966 chaired by Olaf Palme, who later became the Prime Minister of Sweden.[69] By 1984 the Namibia Communications Center (NCC) was opened in London, with funding from a wide range of European and North American church organizations. Its director was an American Anglican cleric, the Rev. John Evenson.[70]

Two other institutions, with varying support from governments and church groups, supplemented the work on the NCC. The first, the Catholic Institute of International Relations (CIIR) in London, was able to sponsor a series of monographs on the future of Namibia by a British scholar, Richard Moorsom, who later headed the Namibian Economic Policy Unit in Windhoek. However, the focus of the CIIR was not restricted to Namibia.[71] The second, the International Aid and Defense Fund for Southern Africa (IDAFSA), as Al Cook has shown, was much more active in the Southern African field, publishing monographs as well as issuing a news service, covering print and broadcast media sources from a variety of nations.[72] As a newspaper and radio broadcast file it had few equals, and recently its clipping files have been placed on microfiche and indexed as well for scholarly use. Both the Sterling Library at Yale University[73] and the Institute of Commonwealth Studies of the University of London have copies.[74]

In addition, the IDAFSA provided funds for reimbursing South African lawyers who were instrumental in defending thirty-seven Namibian nationalists in the sensational 1967 Pretoria trial of *The State v. Eliaser Tuhadeleni and Others*, although the funding was elaborately and successfully concealed to protect the defense attorneys who could not accept any funds from the IDAFSA, which was a banned organization. Such an infraction could result in a ten-year imprisonment under the terms of the 1960 Unlawful Organizations Act.[75] Legal assistance to these Namibian detainees was also funded by the Lawyers Committee for Civil Rights under Law, based in Washington D.C.[76]

At the theological level, considerable effort was devoted to matters of legitimacy, thus reinforcing the work of the SWAPO diplomatic corps, particularly in the United Nations. The daunting task was to challenge any claims the South African regime might make as to its legitimacy as a Christian state,[77] given the importance the Afrikaner elites placed upon the divine legitimacy of their state.[78] To announce that the policy of apartheid was theological heresy[79] was a goal that complemented efforts in the political and international legal realms to deny legitimacy to the minority-ruled South African state and Namibia. The optimal aim would be to shift loyalties and resources from a delegitimated to a legitimated (soon-to-be) regime, a theological variant perhaps of the well-known counterinsurgency doctrine of winning (both domestic and foreign) hearts and minds.

Church bodies, both Protestant and Catholic, in South Africa probed the question of the moral and theological foundations of the apartheid state (upon which a raft of questions dealing with proper civic duties and responsibilities rested), and the South African Council of Churches (SACC) decided that the apartheid state had no legitimacy, with the South African Catholic Bishops' Conference leaning in the same way, but falling short of giving as definitive answer as the SACC.[80] Moreover, both sets of theologians considered the application of sanctions[81] as well the appropriateness of the just war doctrine,[82] a topic that cropped up years later in the South African Truth and Reconciliation Commission hearings. Janet Cherry has examined this discourse with regard to the African National Congress (ANC),[83] which, *mutatis mutandis*, would also apply to SWAPO and its PLAN. Indeed one Namibian cabinet member (the Minister of Fisheries and Marine Resources) claimed that SWAPO had fought a "just war" against South Africa, which was engaged in "an unjust war against the Namibian people."[84]

In addition to claiming that the South African presence in Namibia was devoid of legitimacy, the clergy aggregated and articulated grievances of the Africans in Namibia regarding the commission of atrocities by the SADF.[85] On occasion the clergy were able to arrange legal aid for African defendants on trial. This moral remonstrance, which reinforced the work of the Namibian petitioners and representatives at the United Nations, was linked with an ability to facilitate communication among their predominantly dispersed and rural flock.[86] Beginning in 1983, thanks to their British church connections, the Namibians were able to have an annual Namibian Prayer Day in Britain, and subsequently church memorial services in London in 1988 and 1989 as well as in Manchester in 1989 to commemorate those killed during the 4 May 1978 SADF raid on Cassinga, in Angola.[87] This symbolic gesture regarding Cassinga probably ranks as high, or nearly as high, as the public esteem granted years later by the first independence regime to those members of the People's Liberation Army of Namibia (PLAN) who fought at Ongulumbashe on 16 August 1966. Probably the most exhaustive and carefully written monograph that tends to reflect the SWAPO perspective on this controversial topic is Annemarie Heywood.[88] SWAPO regarded the matter as an attack on a refugee camp, whereas the SADF considered it as an attack on a PLAN base.[89] South African historians Leo Barnard[90] and Gary Baines[91] have examined this attack from different perspectives. The "politics of memory"[92] is certainly no small part of nation building.

The Nordic Connection

One of the most significant group of benefactors for SWAPO was the Nordic cluster of nations, whose beneficence has recently been fully documented in archival-based accounts published by the Nordic Africa Institute in Uppsala, Sweden. Although there are five Nordic states (Denmark, Finland, Iceland, Norway, and Sweden), the Nordic Africa Institute studies excluded Iceland because of its insignificant participation in this Southern African issue area.[93] A number of themes characterize the financial patronage of the Nordic states regarding the war of independence in Namibia. The most obvious is that three (Denmark, Iceland, and Norway) of these states were members of the North Atlantic Treaty Organization (NATO), while the other two (Finland and Sweden) were non-aligned, which infused the Namibian independence war with Cold War considerations, particularly because of Portugal. Portugal, a NATO member, was heavily involved in counterinsurgency wars in West Africa (in Guinea-Bissau and the Cape Verde islands) as well as in Southern Africa, and its paramountcy in Angola until 1974 was a crucial geopolitical aspect of the Namibian war.

Both Finland's and Sweden's foreign policy establishment were very attentive to demonstrating their independence from either the Western or the Eastern bloc, on the one hand, and in staying very close to what they regarded as the dictates of international law, particularly in terms of United Nations' actions regarding Namibia, on the other hand.[94] The Swedes had greater latitude than the Finns (who became members of the

United Nations only in 1955) in terms of neutrality *vis-à-vis* the Soviet Union, and the former were rather vocal in their denunciation of the United States role in the Vietnam War. Such opposition established Sweden's foreign policy *bona fides* with African nationalist elites in Southern Africa. From 1970 until 1990, according to Ulla Beckman's analysis, the Swedish authorities provided a total of about $10.3 million (671 million Swedish krona) in direct aid to SWAPO.[95] In the case of Norway, official direct aid to SWAPO from 1974 until 1990 amounted to roughly $3.6 million (225 million kroner).[96] Finnish direct aid to SWAPO for the 1974–1987 period amounted to about $3.5 million (15. 4 million markka).[97]

Such a neutral stance, from the Swedish perspective, signaled to the African nationalists that the Eastern bloc had no corner on the market with respect to sympathy and assistance for Southern African decolonization. The African nationalists did not need to limit their quest for assistance to the East, thus adding to the plurality of aid donors (and undercutting the monopoly position of any other patrons). However, a second major theme in the Nordic policy for these nationalist movements was that of demonstrable non-violence. The nationalists would have to search elsewhere for their weapons. Although such a stance could serve to deflect any charges, say, by South Africa, that these nations were arming the insurgents, the matter was more complex and more nuanced. Just as those who favored ever tighter military sanctions against South Africa were quick to point out the opaqueness of the line separating civilian from military supplies — equipment with dual civil-military uses — the Swedes, for instance, went to some lengths to draw up criteria for aid to refugees from Southern African minority regimes that would maintain the sometimes invisible wall separating military from non-military supplies. Inescapably, there was no invariant rule particularly with respect to food, clothing, and transportation, items that civilians needed just as much as guerrilla forces do. The SWAPO leadership understood these normative policy constraints and framed their requests accordingly.[98] There was certainly an element of economic fungibility at work here.

Still another, third, common Nordic theme was the engagement of civil society in the policy process from two perspectives. Although it involved only small numbers of persons, the Nordic states sent experts termed "solidarity workers" to provide services and transfer skills to residents of refugee camps, thereby providing visible evidence to at least some Namibians of the donors' sense of commitment to the goal of decolonization.[99] At the domestic level, away from Southern Africa, a wide range of non-governmental organizations became involved in various solidarity tasks throughout the country, directly involving school children, trade union members, and university students. As was true with the anti-apartheid movement in the United States[100] and in Canada,[101] subnational governments initiated economic measures against South Africa in concert with, or in lieu of, sanctions enacted at the national level.[102]

Yet a fourth characteristic of Nordic policy regarding Southern African decolonization was the conscious attempt to develop complementary, if not always congruent, policies at the regional level, thus providing greater diplomatic leverage and political visibility for Nordic foreign policy positions as well as making optimal allocation of their economic resources. Coordination and complementarity, rather than conflict, characterized the policy of the foreign ministries' approach designated in 1978 as the Joint Nordic Program of Action against Apartheid.[103]

Chapter Four

No Easy Target[1]

The Supply and Manufacture of Arms

Once South Africa left the Commonwealth of Nations in 1961, its armed forces were sufficiently impressive to deter any immediate attack by any African majority-ruled state on the continent, provided such states had no extra-continental military allies willing to commit forces, funds, and equipment. Those who thought of regime change prudently avoided a direct confrontation with that military machine and operated in such a way as to weaken the South African Defense Force (SADF) without engaging in armed combat. The repertoire of the opponents was rather straightforward, consisting of economic and psychological techniques that would limit the mobility and the morale of the force and deprive it of a steady flow of appropriate weapons and technology, along with the ability to maintain and monitor the military system. Pressures on the SADF system would be primarily externally applied bilaterally or multilaterally, but in retrospect there has been no evidence adduced so far that South Africa's opponents even attempted to subvert or co-opt the officer corps, thus depriving the white-ruled state of the loyalty of its military leadership. As the SADF became increasingly the province of the Afrikaners,[2] there was little political space in which to conduct such (clandestine) ethnic manipulation, and the Afrikaner military elite tended to cohere rather well despite any doctrinal or strategic differences they may have had.

Three common ways to weaken the economic underpinnings of a military force would be to immobilize it, to deprive it of weapons, and to prevent it from either matching or surpassing the technological sophistication of its actual or potential opponents. In short, the goal is to place the military of the target state at a disadvantage, impairing its ability to wage war, and reducing its chances of winning. To immobilize the SADF, then, would require the massive, continuous, and nearly foolproof interdiction of the supply of externally acquired fuel for its vehicles and aircraft, thereby impairing its tactical mobility and ability to engage in training maneuvers. Because of South Africa's natural endowment of coal reserves, and its widespread railways network adapted to coal, the logical fuel supply to interrupt would be petroleum. Optimally, little or no advance notice of such a sanction should be made lest the target name have time to take evasive action, thereby attenuating the effect of the economic offensive. Moreover, oil sanctions, arms sanctions, and measures to diminish military technology transfer should be orchestrated in such a way that they cascade against the target state, allowing little or no time for a counteroffensive.

This, briefly, was the tripartite challenge facing the civil and military elite and their (sometimes covert) friends and allies. In meeting this challenge, the civil and military managers enjoyed one very substantial advantage *vis-à-vis* most of its detractors, namely, the increasingly thick shroud of secrecy surrounding their work. Following South Africa's departure from the Commonwealth of Nations in 1961, the British Government acted to minimize the cost of South Africa in a wide range of areas, including defense. Indeed, a secret understanding between the United Kingdom and South Africa was reached in 1961 to continue the sale of arms to South Africa, albeit with some minor exclusions.[3] Although the United Kingdom had been the traditional supplier of armaments for the various branches of the SADF, particularly for the South African Navy (which had close ties with the Royal Navy),[4] the South African forces began to widen the range of their purchases to include four other patrons: the United States, France, Italy, and Israel.[5] Although the South Africans made full use of their anti-communist arguments that resonated with several types of American audiences,[6] they had no guaranteed and continual access to American weapons due to the 1963 American embargo on arms sale. Although the American ambassador to the UN, Adlai Stevenson, announced the existence of this embargo in the UN Security Council on 2 August 1963, the embargo did not go into effect until the end of 1963.[7] The initial United Nations voluntary embargo began on 7 August 1963[8] and fourteen years later, on 4 November 1977, acting in accordance with chapter seven of the UN Charter, it shifted to a mandatory embargo.[9] The growing sensitivity of policymakers to the concerns of increasingly vocal African diplomats in the United Nations facilitated such changes.[10] However, what is striking about the Cold War perspective and rhetoric is that the western states imposing the arms embargo did not adopt the rigid, specific lists of arms that the Coordinating Committee on Multilateral Export Controls employed to interdict the shipment of such items to Soviet bloc nations.[11]

There were of course friendly U.S. bureaucratic enclaves whose residents placed a higher value on perceived military security needs than on soothing irate African leaders, so that decision-making on these matters was a slow process.[12] A case in point was the South African wish to purchase U.S. submarines, which met with such bureaucratic inertia and indecisiveness that the exasperated South African Navy officials ended up purchasing these vessels from the French.[13] The submarine probe not only illustrated the French willingness, especially during the de Gaulle era, to show its disdain for what it perceived as Anglo-American hegemony with NATO as well as for the United Nations[14] but also an apparent American tendency to build linguistic logistical walls. Such walls seemed to exempt naval equipment from an embargo because such equipment was designed for external, seaward defense and presumably could not be employed domestically against the Africans of South Africa or Namibia.[15] The British and French also used the external-internal defense distinction on weaponry.[16] However, the United Nations, however, made no such distinction between internal and external defense,[17] and ironically it was the South African Navy that was reduced as a result of the application of sanctions.[18]

As the South African military establishment became more of a pariah group, particularly after the United Nations Security Council enacted a mandatory embargo in 1977,[19] it turned primarily to France and to Israel to acquire licenses and expertise to manufacture (sometimes by modifying or upgrading existing overseas designs) much of what was needed in the way of naval vessels and aircraft as well as to secure appropriate training to operate this equipment.[20] Paradoxically, this response to the imposition of military sanctions resulted in increased, rather than diminished, employment in the armament industry sector of the economy.[21] In Chapter Seven, I cover the decline of this industry after majority rule became established in South Africa. Gaps in the South African armory were often filled by clandestine techniques that sometimes were uncovered and occasionally resulted in criminal penalties in the United States.[22] Not unexpectedly, various multinational corporations were involved in the technology transfer that enabled South Africa to create its own armaments industry.[23]

The South African Parliament provided their economic and military operatives with a wide range of legislation covering many aspects of sanctions evasion, thus shielding such activities from domestic and foreign journalists, research students, and even their own parliamentarians.[24] Secrecy, moreover, was built into the defense budget in two basic ways. First, there was the Special Defense Account, established in 1974, which modified the 1952 defense acquisitions legislation[25] by combining seven different accounts into one and exempting the new account from scrutiny by the public auditor.[26] In 1952, however, the minister of finance had assured the MPs that there would be parliamentary and auditing oversight for this account.[27] Philip H. Frankel has provided an incisive analysis of the uses of this account.[28] Second, not all defense items were collated in the defense budget, with some scattered throughout other departmental budgets, thus adding another layer of camouflage to military expenditures as well as increasing the defense budget by an estimated twenty per cent[29] or even thirty to thirty-five per cent.[30] Dispersed budgeting also characterized the increasingly expensive research and development costs for top-secret weapons of mass destruction.[31] Moreover, the budget for the police counterinsurgency unit termed *Koevoet* was not part of the regular police budget that could be reviewed and debated in parliament. Rather it was handled through quarterly meetings in Pretoria of a ministerial committee.[32]

In addition to the element of secrecy concerning the foreign purchase and local manufacturing of armaments, the U.S. Defense Intelligence Agency observed that the South African regime was able to sanitize the data that it published in the arms field.[33] South Africa followed a relatively common practice of expropriating arms from its SWAPO foe following successful ground engagements in Angola and even seized arms from on board a foreign ship docked in a South African port before it could deliver its cargo of arms meant for SWAPO. Not only did this booty augment the SADF inventory of infantry weaponry but also it represented an evasion of the international arms boycott.[34] "Ironically," wrote one high-ranking South African Air Force officer, "Angola became probably the biggest arms supplier to South Africa throughout the difficult years of the arms boycotts."[35]

The maxim of enhancing one's own logistical position by depriving one's enemy of access to the weapons of war is hardly a new one, as the American efforts to sever the People's Liberation Armed Force's (commonly termed the Viet Cong) logistical conduit, the so-called Ho Chi Minh Trail, by air strikes in the Vietnam war attest.[36] However, these attacks were unable to close down this supply line.[37] Earlier the French had attempted to sever this supply line, which involved the Viet Minh's use of huge numbers of porters, but met with little success not only because of Viet Minh engineering skills but also because of relatively easy access to a large pool of rather unskilled labor.[38] To succeed in interrupting the flow of weapons to PLAN the SADF needed not only accurate and timely intelligence (often, but hardly always, secured through aerial photography as well as through radio intercepts and spies[39]) but also sufficient and appropriate airpower to destroy critical portions of the weapons transport system, if not the weapons themselves, in a continual fashion.[40]

Such destruction could be successful in those cases where PLAN lacked anti-aircraft weaponry and/or used it with poor effect.[41] As the war continued, PLAN and its allies in Angola acquired the necessary weapons and skills to offset some of this South African advantage. Data are now available which list SAAF aircraft and helicopter loses in the Angolan/Namibian and Rhodesian campaigns from 1974 to 1989, including those that, although hit by enemy fire, were able to return to their base.[42] Indeed, the Cuban regime made a point of sending its best pilots to Cuito Cuanavale in Angola in the latter part of the war.[43] As a former South African soldier who participated in the 1988 Cuito Cuanavale campaign has written, Cuban MIG aircraft activity had a terrifying effect on ground troops.[44] The Cuban strategy involved not only moving their land forces south of their defensive line in Angola (located about 250 or 300 kilometers north of the Namibian border) but also developing an airfield at Cahama, 125 kilometers north of that border, to position its fighter aircraft closer to SADF targets.[45] Not only had they achieved air superiority over the SAAF at Cuito Cuanavale but also they were anxious to take command of Angolan airspace to help force the SADF out of Angola, even though their logistical patrons, the Soviets, were concerned that they might advance too far south.[46] The Cubans, however, feared SADF massive retaliation should their reach extend to the actual invasion of Namibia.[47]

Evading Other Economic Sanctions

Closely associated with the bilateral and multilateral sanctions involving the transfer of weapons and other (often dual-use[48]) military equipment and supplies to the SADF are the ones concerning oil, a vital element in the functioning of any modern military machine. Not unexpectedly, the South African regime had a fairly long lead-time to prepare counter-measures, which are a crucial element in developing a sanctions-busting strategy,[49] and it covered these activities with ample legislation to ensure secrecy concerning its oil operations.[50] Indeed, it was a criminal offense for a South African to advocate sanctions (under the 1962 Sabotage Act, more accurately known as Section 21 of the General Law Amendment Act 76 of 1962[51]), although in practice there seemed to have been no prosecutions for such activities.[52] Even though there is usually a specific admission in the literature regarding sanctions against South Africa that sanctions alone would not suffice to effect a regime change (to non-racial or majority rule),[53] I have not uncovered a clear, logical, detailed, and sequential analysis of just how the oil embargo (by itself) would adversely affect the combat capability or performance of the SADF.

Conventional wisdom would suggest that the embargo would diminish the mobility of SADF air, land, and sea transportation through some sort of rationing arrangement among these three branches. Examining the role of the SADF (and, to a lesser extent, the SAP) in counterinsurgency warfare in Namibia and sometimes in Angola over the 1966–1989 period, one finds little, if any reference, in the literature in English to reduced land mobility which would include SADF tanks, self-propelled artillery, armored personnel carriers or other mine-proofed vehicles, scout cars, trucks, and motorcycles. At least there was no public acknowledgement of fuel shortages, although the existence of any shortages could well have been censored. Still there was fuel rationing and some shortages in the 1980s.[54] Nevertheless, foreign correspondents might well have uncovered these deficiencies, as they were among the first to learn about Operation Savannah, South Africa's incursion into Angola in 1975–1976. This topic has been well covered in the works of Nerys John,[55] Deon Geldenhuys,[56] and Graeme Addison.[57]

The imposition of military sanctions is a clear-cut example of what could be regarded as sectoral, rather than geographically specific, sanctions, that is, those applicable to the military presence and operations in both South Africa and Namibia. These may be necessary but they are not sufficient with respect to the possibility of changing South African policy with respect to its Namibian policy. Members of the five nation Western Contact Group (Canada, France, West Germany, the United Kingdom, and the United States), which assumed the responsibility of achieving independence for Namibia, considered that deficiency. They realized the importance of Namibia-specific sanctions that could be terminated once the country became independent. Thus the Namibian issue could be economically disentangled from the larger, more nettlesome issue of African majority rule and the termination of apartheid in South Africa.[58] In 1985, the proposed U.S. Congressional sanctions seemed to lack specificity with respect to Namibia.[59] Even though the federal government ended the economic sanctions on Namibia following independence in 1990, it took until 1993 for the remaining U.S. state and municipal sanctions on Namibia to be lifted.[60] The Namibian minister of foreign affairs drew attention to this delay in the 1991 foreign affairs budget debate,[61] which underscored the significance of subnational sanctions in federal states, such as three members of the Western Contact Group, namely, Canada, West Germany, and the United States.

Perhaps the best-known example of a Namibia-specific economic sanction concerned the attempt of the United Nations Council for Namibia to deal with the extraction of non-renewable Namibian resources by non–Namibians, that is, for the Council to act as an economic steward for a future nation. Both David de Beer[62] and Alun R. Roberts[63] have analyzed the well-known Council decree no. 1 dealing with these Namibian resources, while Bern Brüggeman has examined the status of that decree following the advent of Namibian independence.[64] This international concern about Namibia's economic patrimony followed logically from the 21 June 1971 advisory opinion of the International Court of Justice that found the South African occupation of the territory to be illegal in light of a prior 27 October 1966 United Nations General Assembly resolution 2145 that terminated South Africa's right to serve as a mandatory power and made the United Nations responsible for the (*de jure*) administration of the territory.[65] That landmark 1966 General Assembly resolution was endorsed by the United Nations Security Council resolution 276 (1970) of 30 January 1970.[66]

In addition to its consular and representational roles,[67] the Council for Namibia assumed the responsibility for safeguarding the resources of the territory for future generations of Namibians by issuing regulations that primarily affected the financial activities of transnational corporations operating in Namibia with the permission of the Pretoria regime. According to 1984 United Nations data, there were 335 foreign corporations in Namibia; the bulk of them were American, British, and South African.[68] Not unexpectedly, most western nations kept their distance from the Council and did not participate in its activities.[69] So far, I have not been able to locate a much needed, full-length academic book in English on the Council, although there is one in German,[70] which regrettably contains no systematic United Nations financial data. This topic needs further research attention.

As noted earlier in Chapter One, the majority of the United Nations General Assembly members had gone on record as being quite critical of these enterprises, although they were more antagonistic to the absence of local control to ensure a more equitable distribution of the wealth those companies created. They were not necessarily hostile to the presence of such companies.[71] As was true in the case of national arms embargoes, the United Nations had no enforcement powers of its own and had to rely on its members and interested journalists, activists, and solidarity groups to monitor the national implementation of such economic measures.[72] Indeed, the United Nations Council for Namibia served as contact point for those non-governmental organizations whose focus and work centered on Namibia.[73]

Walvis Bay as an Economic Hostage[74]

Walvis Bay, located roughly at the midpoint between the northern and southern boundaries of Namibia, was claimed by the British authorities in 1878 and subsequently annexed by the Cape in 1884.[75] The Germans, who began their colonization efforts south of Walvis Bay at Angra Pequena (later known as Luderitz) in 1883, recognized the Cape occupation of Walvis Bay in 1890.[76] During the German colonial era, Walvis Bay remained an extraterritorial enclave of the Cape and then, after the creation of the Union of South Africa in 1910, of the Union itself. When the Union became the Republic of South Africa in 1961, the same relationship continued.[77] Walvis Bay was briefly captured by the Germans at the outset of the First World War, when the newly-formed Union of South Africa became an ally of the United Kingdom in its battle against Germany and its allies.[78] The German regime developed a railway system that emanated from the Swakopmund harbor to their capital of Windhoek as well as to points north and south of Windhoek, yet the line of rail did not extend to the South African border or to the Angolan border. It took the First World War for the South Africans to link their rail system in the Cape with that in German South West Africa; the South Africans utilized this rail link as part of their campaign against the German forces.[79]

Economic activity during the German era depended upon the use of the two ports of Luderitz Bay and Swakopmund as the shallow entry and exit points for imports, exports, and coastal trade, but they were logistically inferior to the better placed and deeper Walvis Bay.[80] Following the First World War, South Africa was awarded the class C mandate for Namibia, and Walvis Bay was administered as if it were an integral part of the mandated territory even though it was never part of German South West Africa.[81] The "as if" phrasing applicable to Walvis Bay was contained in the South West Africa Affairs Act of 1922.[82] A literal reading of clause 119 of the Treaty of Versailles (by which Germany renounced its claim to its colonies) suggests that it was the former German South West Africa that was converted into a mandated territory; there was no mention of Walvis Bay in that treaty clause.[83]

Paul Schamberger has referred to Walvis Bay as Namibia's "front door,"[84] for it has served as the principal seaport for Namibia throughout the mandate era and on into the post World War II era and was thus an integral logistical part of Namibia's seaborne foreign trade as well as the site of the Namibian fishing and canning industries.[85] However, in early 1976 Prime Minister B. J. Vorster made it amply clear that Walvis Bay was South African territory and suggested the possibility of having parliament repeal the 1922 statute that permitted Namibia to administer the enclave.[86] This change was effected on 31 August 1977 by the Walvis Bay Administration Proclamation, which became operational on 1 September 1977. This proclamation essentially turned back the administrative clock fifty-five years and transferred the administration of the bay to the Cape Province of South Africa.[87] Both SWAPO and the United Nations perceived this shift as a serious threat to Namibia's territorial integrity,[88] which occasioned rebukes from the United Nations General Assembly,[89] the United Nations Security Council,[90] and the United Nations Council for Namibia.[91]

From an economic point of view, South African demarche over the bay suggests that it represented a preemptive blow against a future independent Namibia because it would likely mean that the successor government in Windhoek would need to find an alternative harbor on the Atlantic coastline in either Namibia or Angola. That would be a crippling financial blow.[92] As the war in northern Namibia and Angola moved into the 1980s, the members of South African State Security Council realized that South Africa could manipulate or control an independent Namibia by virtue of the economic asymmetry between the two countries.[93] However, they apparently did not fully appreciate the subtleties of economic statecraft at the time of the 1977 transfer even though the Pretoria government provided R 7.2 million in the South West African account as compensation to the territory for the 1977 transfer.[94] Nevertheless, one carefully crafted research study has cautioned that economic factors alone cannot provide an entirely satisfactorily explanation of South African foreign policy regarding the future independence of Namibia.[95]

During the interregnum between the transfer to South Africa and the return of the bay to Namibia after independence (noted in Chapter Seven), Walvis Bay had fallen on hard economic times not only because the white residents were faced with higher South African income taxes than those they had previously paid to the Windhoek authorities[96] but also because there was an exodus of white residents from the bay area due to the sharp decline of the fishing and canning industries.[97]

The fishing industry has been estimated to account for 20 to 25 percent of Namibia's export earnings and perhaps 10 per cent of the gross domestic product.[98] Such a bleak economic scene in Walvis Bay has been attributed to excessive fishing and poor South African environmental stewardship of the fishing grounds,[99] which meant very serious retrenchment in the African contract labor force employed in the canneries.[100] Some of these South African–owned fishing corporations actually transferred their operations to Chile, which suggests the importance the Namibian nationalists attached to the presence and alleged malevolent conduct of transnational firms in Namibia.[101] Indeed, SWAPO criticized the mining and fishing transnational corporations in the 1989 Constituent Assembly election campaign.[102] Conditions in Walvis Bay again underscored the significance of the contract, migrant labor system as a major grievance of SWAPO against the practice of apartheid. The Ovamboland People's Organization (OPO), a precursor of SWAPO, had an established presence in Walvis Bay,[103] and Walvis Bay was also a testing ground for the organizational skills and utility of the strike weapon.[104]

The 1977 annexation of Walvis Bay to the Cape Province, although economically retrogressive from the standpoint of SWAPO and the United Nations, served yet another purpose, that is, it has been described as a "bargaining chip,"[105] a "bargaining pawn," a "hostage," a "bargaining weapon," a "powerful lever,"[106] and even "a stranglehold."[107] It was even suggested that "With Walvis Bay firmly under its control, South Africa ... [was] in a position to exercise a stranglehold on the Namibian economy."[108] To what end? The focus was upon the ground rules of South Africa's negotiations with the members of the Western Contact Group. These five nations were the ones that the Pretoria regime needed to placate because of their protection (three of them were permanent members and wielded veto power in the Security Council) and because of their economic power and economic sanctions. Fear of economic sanctions was a major concern of the Pretoria regime.[109]

Paradoxically, nationals of these five nations had investments in Namibia, particularly in the extraction of minerals, so there has been some concern about just how impartial their diplomats might be.[110] Although they did not recuse themselves because of such investments, later several members of the U.S. Supreme Court did so because of their personal investment portfolios when presented with a case involving claims for reparations from multinational corporations that operated in South Africa. The United Nations had criminalized the policy of apartheid, so that the plaintiffs could apply for damages from those corporations for such alleged misconduct.[111] The South Africa position was essentially a *quid pro quo* with the Contact Group: provided that Walvis Bay was excluded from the agenda of the independence negotiations, South Africa would continue to cooperate with the group in the quest for a mutually acceptable arrangement for independence.[112] This understanding was ambiguously incorporated in a United Nations Security Council resolution,[113] and the diplomatic positions of South Africa, SWAPO, and the United Nations regarding Walvis Bay stayed frozen until Namibia achieved independence in 1990.[114] The subsequent territorial integration of Walvis Bay into an independent Namibia will be covered in Chapter Seven.

No Free War[115]

Considering all the time, effort, and expense the South Africans, in both the public and private sectors, incurred to defend Namibia against bilateral and multilateral attacks from transnational organizations and individual states, one wonders whether the territory was worth all that much to South African and Namibian stakeholders. The response to that question has some bearing on South Africa's strategic posture with respect to that territory.

Was the territory primarily an economic asset or a strategic asset or possibly both and did the economic or strategic value differ over time? These questions are basic to the nature of the colonial enterprise. Arend Lijphart's magisterial analysis of the Dutch and West New Guinea in the post–World War II era of decolonization suggests that, rhetoric notwithstanding, the Dutch held on to New Guinea in spite of the expense. It was an uneconomic venture and consequently other forces, particularly subjective ones, were at work. His crucial finding "disprove[d] the contention that colonialism is solely motivated by objective interests."[116] Albert Memmi, a thoughtful participant-observer of the French colonial presence in Algeria, shrewdly observed that "the colonialist is not unaware that he obliges his home country to maintain an army, and that while the colony is nothing but an advantage for him, it costs the mother country more than he earns for it."[117]

To what extent do these strictures apply to Namibia? Has it been a financial burden on the metropole? Has it been a strategic asset? First, consider German South West Africa (1884–1915). From the metropolitan vantage point, this colony was not cost-effective and needed to be subsidized by Berlin. Namibia was the only German colony without taxes until 1908, the year in which diamonds were discovered.[118] However, the *Deutsche Kolonialgesellschaft für Süd-west Afrika* (German Colonial Society for South West Africa), which became a holding company, did manage to pay significant dividends beginning in 1905.[119] Nevertheless, only one of German's colonies — Togoland — was self-supporting.[120]

Furthermore, in 1923, as part of a South African agreement with the Weimar Republic, the Pretoria regime undertook to pay the pensions of erstwhile German civil servants provided they remained in Namibia and were willing to accept automatic naturalization as South African citizens.[121] It was not until 1936 that a Namibian Commission pointed out that, despite South African loans to balance the Namibian budget, there was no income tax in the territory.[122] That situation lasted until 1942 when Namibia instituted that form of taxation.[123] Namibia was not entirely self-supporting thereafter. Abraham H. du Plessis, a National Party Member of Parliament who represented Windhoek in the South African House of Assembly, observed on 8 April 1969, "We in South-West Africa realize that the Republic of South Africa can do without South-West Africa and that this would not have disastrous economic consequences for South Africa. It can merely cause a little inconvenience. We also realize that South-West Africa cannot forfeit its economic ties with South Africa without entailing for itself tremendous disruption and chaotic conditions."[124] Recognized authorities on Namibia, such as Donald L. Sparks[125] and André du Pisani,[126] have provided complementary analyses of the dependent position of pre-independent Namibia. Yet, this is not to suggest that individual shareholders of multinational firms operating in Namibia fared poorly, although much of their income depended on the fluctuating market value of the individual commodities, which were primarily, but not exclusively, based in the mining sector.[127] Daniel R. Kempton and Roni L. du Preez have explored this topic in terms of the diamond mining operations in Namibia.[128]

As for strategic utility, the South African government invaded the territory at the behest of the imperial British authorities. The thought at the time was that German South West Africa posed a threat to the Royal Navy's dominance of the Southern Atlantic not only because of its short-wave broadcasting facilities (at Windhoek, Luderitz Bay, and Swakopmund) which were valuable communications links for German navy but also because it could offer harbor facilities to German submarines or other naval craft. At the outbreak of that war, the British held Walvis Bay, which was the only really satisfactory harbor in the country. The Germans needed to develop Swakopmund and Luderitz Bay as alternative ports, so the British threat perception was predicated on the Germans' seizure of the enclave of Walvis Bay, a far better harbor for the maintenance, resupply, and refitting of German naval vessels. The Germans did indeed seize Walvis Bay at the beginning of the war.[129]

Once South Africa assumed control (under the nominal auspices of the League of Nations mandate system) of Namibia, what was its strategic utility? Some of the answers are found in Chapter Six, but at this point it would be instructive to turn to the counterfactual aspect of the matter, realizing that this may lapse into *post hoc, ergo propter hoc* thinking. If one agrees with Leo Marquard, the distinguished South African member of the Liberal Party, that "in South Africa no government would be elected that had not promised to maintain white domination,"[130] then focus of the inquiry can readily shift to his assertion that South Africans "have refused to recognise that ... [they] are, in fact, a colonial power."[131] Now the question arises: did the retention of Namibia enhance or detract from South African security? Would early decolonization have saved both blood and treasure? Whose blood? Whose treasure?

The strategic utility of Namibia to South Africa can be seen in the pattern of deployment of military resources during the course of the 1966–1989 war. Two of Namibia's borders, western and northern, feature prominently during that conflict, especially Walvis Bay and the Caprivi Zipfel. That bay held strategic significance for South African air, land, and naval forces[132] (as well as economic importance for both pre- and post-independence Namibia), while the Caprivi was both an early entry point for PLAN units infiltrating Namibia[133] and a military enclave for South African land and air attacks on neighboring states that provided PLAN with rear area bases.[134] Moreover, the Caprivi functioned as an extraterritorial base for UNITA forces[135] and a SADF depot for resupplying UNITA units located in southeastern Angola.[136]

Although it has been conventional wisdom to assert that the defense of white privilege and power in the South African metropole rested on the existence of a *cordon sanitaire* or geographic arc of buffer territories,[137] that contention needs to be revised to take into account the speed and sequence of decolonization in white-ruled Southern Africa as well as the growth of African nationalism within South Africa itself. At one time both the whites and their African nationalist opponents embraced the domino theory of international politics that pervaded much of American strategic thinking, especially regarding Southeast Asia. That is, they assumed that African majority rule along the South African periphery would create the momentum for the triumph of African majority rule throughout all of Southern Africa. This was an untested assumption.[138] Nevertheless, the SADF launched airborne and ground-based attacks on (often purported) ANC communication, logistical, and headquarters sites in neighboring states as part of the destabilization program.[139] Not only did this antagonize these border states and some of their western patrons but also it may have bought South Africa some additional time to inflict greater and periodic damage on the external branches of the ANC.

Extended supply routes and infiltration routes were risky, and Botswana, Zimbabwe, and Mozambique had forbidden the ANC to use their territories as launching sites for raids into South Africa.[140] Perhaps the strategic utility of Namibia has been overrated, but it complements what could be regarded as a kith-and-kin dimension in Namibia, namely the presence of a powerful Afrikaner diaspora in Namibia which could elicit primordial ties with their Afrikaner kinsmen in South Africa.[141] None of the South Africa's other neighbors had such a powerful Afrikaner enclave as Namibia did. Finally, although it may be self-evident, the political situation in Namibia has a direct impact upon that in South Africa and can generate fear and concern among the whites, while giving Africans cause for hope. There is a feedback loop between these white-dominated neighbors.[142]

Turning now to the financial dimension of the Namibian bush war, earlier I drew attention to the propensity of the regime to disaggregate the costs and to spread them among several governmental budgets. Moreover, as the war in Iraq has demonstrated, estimating the cost of a war, particularly for reasons of budget transparency, is not an easy task for researchers as well as for military and legislative planners. There is room for differences of opinion and modes of accounting. Yet financial data on preceding American war costs, with adjustment for inflation, have been published.[143] Amy Belasco fortunately has provided an example how such costs have been calculated.[144]

The common tendency in the literature on the war for Namibian independence has been to report costs on an annual basis, either in South African or U.S. currency, rather than to give an aggregated figure for the entire war. Often the source of the data is omitted, and seldom, if ever, does one learn how the costs were calculated. Indeed, one of the unknown elements in the calculation is the proportion of the annual defense budgets that can be attributed to the Namibian war.[145] Similarly, the same obstacle about the disaggregation of the defense budget occurred with respect to the French-Algerian war.[146]

Turning to aggregated costs, one knowledgeable writer indicated that the entire war cost South Africa R 8 billion, but she did not clearly indicate either the source or the method of accounting adopted.[147] The more frequently used financial data were for annual expenditures, but these estimates vary, depending upon the year, and there are gaps in the years covered, so that one cannot have a consistent record, year by year, of how the costs fluctuated. For the 1984-1985 financial year, Prime Minister P. W. Botha indicated that these defense costs amounted to R450 million.[148] There are differing estimates for 1985, with a low of roughly £ 140 million per annum for South Africa plus £ 30–35 million per annum for South West Africa from Dr. Johan Jones, the secretary of finance in the Multi-Party Conference interim government of South West Africa,[149] to a high of about R 620 per annum (or R 1.7 million per day) in 1985.[150] By 1986, General Jannie Geldenhuys, Chief of the SADF, estimated the annual cost to be R 365 million (or R 1 million per day).[151] That figure, however, doubled to R 2 million per day in 1987, but again nothing was said about how this total was computed.[152]

PART III: THE MILITARY CAMPAIGNS

Chapter Five

The War for the Colonial Spoils[1]

The Call to Arms

Frustration with the decision of the International Court of Justice in July 1966 seemed to be the precipitating factor, which led the Namibian nationalists of SWAPO to resort to arms[2] or to the armed struggle, as SWAPO frequently termed it. Even though he did not use the term of colonial spoils, that notion was implicit in Sam Nujoma's claim in his interview in New York on 28 February 1978 with Cliff Saunders of the South African Broadcasting television service that "We are not fighting even for [African] majority rule. We are fighting to seize power in Namibia, for the benefit of the Namibian people."[3] Mr. Nujoma's statement evoked no official comment from the Western states, as South African Prime Minister B .J. Vorster had hoped there would be.[4] It was commonplace for the Pretoria regime to demonize their SWAPO enemies, and only recently has there been a change in the lexicon, with the South African author David Williams indicating that he preferred the term "insurgent" to alternative nouns because it is a "more neutral word."[5]

The initial encounter between the SWAPO insurgents and the South African Police (SAP) occurred on 26 August 1966 at Ongulumbashe, a remote site near the Angolan border in western Ovamboland. A map of Namibia showing the location of Ongulumbashe is very hard to find notwithstanding the historic significance of the place.[6] Even though there was an SAP account of the incident,[7] it took roughly four decades before a fuller, much more detailed South African narrative was published.[8] That event at Ongulumbashe has been memorialized as Heroes' Day, an official holiday in Namibia.[9] Now there is also a monument marking the site of this encounter in this remote area.[10] On 26 August 1990 (then known as Namibia Day), President Nujoma visited the site to dedicate a monument to those who perished there as well as to accept the salute of those who survived the battle.[11] His remarks there are part of the public record.[12]

That was not the first time that Namibians had resorted to war against their colonizers, so that the Namibians could claim to be following a tradition dating back at least to the Herero-Nama rebellion against the Germans. Indeed, Mr. Nujoma wrote the preface to Horst Drechsler's widely cited text about the response of many Namibians to German African policy in German South West Africa.[13] In this tradition, there was considerable civility in terms of which the Namibians regarded as their enemy, so that the Hereros treated women and children as well as Britons as non-combatants.[14] This stood in sharp contrast, for instance, to the Lakota (Sioux) of Minnesota, who were equally dispossessed of their lands by the whites and who unsuccessfully rebelled against the white settlers in 1862.[15] The U.S. Government hanged a group of thirty-eight Lakota men in Mankato, Minnesota the day after Christmas in 1862 in what the American anthropologist Jack Weatherford claimed was "the largest mass execution in North American history."[16] The 1862 Lakota insurgency in Minnesota is a graphic example of the journalist Adam Hochschild's discerning observation that "In dozens of academic monographs and college courses, South African racial injustice is compared to relations between American whites and blacks. But the closer analogy really is to relations between whites and American Indians."[17]

Sadly enough, however, that early twentieth century Namibian rebellion was characterized by some atrocities,[18] which seem to be a baleful byproduct of guerrilla warfare, as the contemporaneous American military experience in the Philippines suggests.[19] The Namas, who entered the war after the Hereros had taken up arms, proved themselves to be masters of guerrilla warfare, and they produced an exceptionally gifted guerrilla leader, Jakob Marengo.[20] Yet the war against the Germans revealed the extent to which Namibian opposition was fragmented, localized, and uncoordinated. That resistance did not actively involve the Ovambo peoples in the north to any major extent.[21] In addition, the guerrillas had neither international patrons nor completely friendly sanctuaries. All the three borders of Namibia at that time were controlled by colonial powers (Portugal in the north and the United Kingdom in the south and east). Once the Germans drove the Herero eastward into the desert, the Botswana authorities granted asylum to the survivors of that desert trek, and a distinct Herero refugee community flourished thereafter.[22]

The Transit Corridor

With the exception of the Nama campaign, the Namibian insurgency tradition tended to be geographically contained within the borders of the territory even though international colonial border control was rather lax in the early twentieth century.[23] The Germans employed greater firepower, especially artillery, and had correspondingly greater logistical needs in the counterinsurgency campaign, especially when they made use of the railway for transporting men and material.[24] This was a war of maneuver, tracking, stealth, communication, and reconnaissance, with the Germans often at a severe disadvantage. By the 1960s, however, these techniques and characteristics of war in the bush were only partly applicable because of advances in technology as well as in the nature of South African rule in Namibia.

Waging a guerrilla war against the white regime in Namibia would be a daunting task requiring all the skills that the Hereros and Namas had acquired in their campaign against the Germans and a great deal more. It was not sufficient that the United Nations General Assembly denounce the system of colonial rule, depriving it of any international legitimacy,[25] although that type of finding would help the political mobilization process. More to the point, SWAPO needed international legitimacy and recognition, which would be transmuted into more tangible support in terms of military training and supplies and safe havens. In the early 1960s the closest anticolonial port of call was Tanzania, which received its independence (as a United Nations trust territory supervised by the United Kingdom) in late 1961. Indeed, the Tanzanian capital was a well-known Mecca for Southern African exiles.[26]

In order to reach this safe haven, Namibians had a long, arduous journey, often through Botswana and then on through Zambia, but by March, 1961 several SWAPO leaders had reached Dar es Salaam, where they established a party office.[27] The next year, in presenting its petition in Dar es Salaam to the visiting United Nations Committee on South West Africa, SWAPO asked that the mandate for the territory be ended and that the territory be granted independence in 1963. It wanted such a program to be implemented right away and suggested "the use of force if necessary."[28] By 1963, SWAPO had created its military component now known as the People's Liberation Army of Namibia. There are two slightly different chronologies about creation of this armed unit. According to the first one, it was founded as the South West Africa Liberation Army (SWALA) in 1963, then its name was altered to the Namibian People's Army in 1966, and then in 1970 it became the People's Liberation Army of Namibia (PLAN).[29] The second one is that SWALA was created in 1964 and the change of name to PLAN was adopted in 1969.[30]

Sometime between 1962 and October 1963, the Secretary-General of SWAPO, Jacob Kuhangua, negotiated a military pact in Léopoldville, Zaire with the Revolutionary Government of Angola in Exile, the external arm of Holden Roberto's UPA (*União das Populações de Angola*).[31] This pact may have been issued in conjunction with the arrival of an undisclosed number of SWAPO members who journeyed to Kinkuzu, Zaire, in the fall of 1963, mistakenly expecting to receive guerrilla warfare training.[32] Depending upon which source is consulted, there are three different dates cited for that military pact: (1) an undisclosed date in 1962; (2) 17 July 1962; and (3) 26 October 1963.[33] Moreover, none of these three sources published the text of the pact, and Marcum, who made no reference to its military aspects, placed little stock in its utility for the signatories.[34] Talmon provided no commentary on the matter either. This military-diplomatic exercise would suggest that bravura performances might energize insurgents although their enemies may also regard them as diplomatic theatrics.

In June 1964, SWAPO announced that it was "now irrevocably committed to a course of armed revolution."[35] Three months later, the South African mainline press covered this pronouncement.[36] Indeed, SWAPO had considered the option of armed resistance in its first party congress held secretly in Rehoboth, Namibia in 1961,[37] and the following year began to think of war and diplomacy as reinforcing each other, rather than as mutually exclusive pursuits.[38] SWANU (South West Africa National Union), which was the oldest nationalist group, did have a few members who had undergone military training in Egypt and China.[39] Although it claimed that it had arranged for Namibians to be trained in the art of guerrilla warfare for use in future combat, it was unwilling to commit itself to the Liberation Committee of the OAU (Organization of African Unity) to undertake such a war, whereas SWAPO was. Consequently the OAU withdrew its recognition from SWANU in 1965, leaving SWAPO as the sole beneficiary of its legitimacy.[40] Furthermore, in 1967 the authorities in Tanzania advised SWANU that it was no longer welcome in their country.[41] Although SWANU initially lacked sufficient manpower to create its own guerrilla force, by 1975 it felt it could field its own army. However, the OAU would sanction only one army and suggested that SWANU integrate its volunteers into the PLAN. This was the subject of negotiations with the SWAPO leadership, but nothing materialized.[42]

This meant that one insurgent army conducted combat operations, rather than two, as was the case in Zimbabwe, with ZANLA (Zimbabwe African National Liberation Army) and ZIPRA (Zimbabwe People's Revolutionary Army), which served the ZANU (Zimbabwe African National Union) and ZAPU (Zimbabwe African People's Union) organizations, respectively. Notwithstanding the granting of legitimacy, however, the OAU was hardly generous in supplying PLAN with needed arms, much to the annoyance of the SWAPO leadership.[43]

The Pretoria regime dated the insurgency from 27 June 1962 in order to fix criminal liability for the act of armed rebellion.[44] The minister of justice pointed out, in the second reading debate of the 1967 Terrorism Bill, that the June 27th date referred to the date of departure from the territory or from South Africa.[45] The first group to be trained in guerrilla warfare went to Egypt in 1962, and subsequently other recruits were sent to Ghana and to Algeria.[46] Interestingly enough, only one MP (Mrs. Helen Suzman of the Progressive Party) voted against the *ex post facto* clause in the bill,[47] suggesting overwhelming cross-political party support for this legislative legerdemain. The 1962 date is significant because it suggests that either Pretoria had infiltrated its agents into the Namibian traffic flow to and from Dar es Salaam or that the SAP extracted that information from those PLAN members they captured in that engagement or in earlier ones. It was widely believed that the SAP tortured these prisoners, who were tried as a group in the case of *State versus Tuhadeleni and Others*.[48] That belief was confirmed by one of the defendants in the *Tuhadeleni* case,[49] by a leading attorney for the defense,[50] as well as officially nearly three decades later.[51]

This would suggest that by this time the South African security force had developed an intelligence-gathering network. Indeed, Sam Nujoma alleged that Leonard P. Shuuya (with the *nom de guerre* of Castro) was one of the earliest such moles for the South Africans. Shuuya served as the second-in-command of the originally named SWALA. He was subsequently detained in Tanzania, after which he went on to Norway, and he may have returned to Namibia once it became independent.[52] Another Namibian, Keshii P. Nathanael, an activist in the SWAPO Youth League, has contested that interpretation. He was imprisoned with Leonard Shuuya in Keko Prison in Dar es Salaam, Tanzania. Nathanael later went into exile in Sweden, and his account might be flawed or compromised if only because he used another surname (Nanglo) for Shuuya.[53] Another serious setback to the SWAPO security system took place in London in 1966. A member of the South African embassy, working in cooperation with the South African spy, Hans J. Lombard, stole Mr. Nujoma's document-laden briefcase from his London hotel room. This is indicative of SWAPO's fairly lax security procedures at that time.[54]

SWAPO began sending PLAN units into Ovamboland, with the first batch of six guerrillas to arrive in September 1965, followed by a second group in February and March 1966.[55] Eight of the second group were arrested in March, 1966 by the SAP, who learned about the infiltration of PLAN units,[56] and at that point may have turned one of those eight into an informant after imprisonment in Pretoria. President Nujoma asserted that one of the eight guerrillas the South African captured became a police informant,[57] while Sebastian Ballard and Nick Santcross claimed that an unidentified informant tipped off the South Africans, thus setting in motion the Ongulumbashe battle.[58] However, the Ballard-Santcross account claimed that the South Africans had prepared their mole (who was "a high-ranking [guerrilla] soldier ... in the 1950s."[59] Thus these two postwar accounts differ in the dates of the recruitment of a police informer within PLAN, assuming that there was only one such person. A third PLAN group entered Ovamboland (in the north) in July 1966, while a fourth one followed in September 1966.[60]

By the time of the initial engagement in Ongulumbashe, roughly nine hundred Namibians had left their country, some in hopes of completing their education. Of the nine hundred, about two hundred and fifty had received some type of guerrilla training.[61] Such an exodus depended upon a safe passage to Tanzania, which was certainly facilitated by the independence of neighboring Zambia in 1964. The difficult part of the journey lay through Angola or Botswana, which were still under colonial rule. In the case of those who returned to Ongulumbashe, it seems that they traversed southern Angola, but not Botswana, en route to Ovamboland.[62]

Zambia privileged those refugees connected with SWAPO, which was legitimated by the OAU, but would not accept those from SWANU, which resulted in Botswana having to accommodate an increased number of SWANU refugees. Those who transited Botswana became prohibited immigrants once they left Botswana, and those who remained were forbidden to engage in politics.[63]

Botswana's preferred policy, then, was to facilitate the passage of refugees northward, lest they become a financial burden to the treasury or become victimized by those local whites that were sympathetic to the apartheid system. In 1963 that government enacted a prohibition of violence act that precluded the use of Botswana as a springboard for attacks on its neighbors. The refugees were thus relieved to move on to majority-ruled Zambia, signified by the name of the small ferry ("the freedom ferry") that took them across the confluence of the Chobe and Zambezi Rivers in northern Botswana.[64] Notwithstanding these firm policies, some Namibia refugees did manage to traverse Botswana undetected by the authorities, and later on Angola became a more appealing exit corridor for Namibians.[65]

Elusive Internal Bases

Conventional wisdom in insurgency warfare doctrine includes the concept of a base area from which the guerrillas sally forth on their hit and run raids.[66] There apparently is no agreement between the insurgent and the counterinsurgent literature concerning the operational definition of such a zone. Each side has its own definition, which explains much of the confusion and ambiguity found in the literature.[67] Nevertheless, the idea of liberated areas is a significant component of the doctrine of people's liberation parties.[68]

Such a base can provide a larder for arms, communications equipment, food, water, maps, ammunition, and the other paraphernalia of war as well as a site for training. The Ongulumbashe base, which was operational for eleven months (September 1965 to August 1966),[69] apparently was one of five camps the advance party had established to train future guerrillas. The SWAPO guerrillas, who only occupied one camp at a time, provided military training to thirty local Namibians.[70] Yet traditional leaders in Ovamboland reported their presence to the SAP,[71] who began to investigate the matter in March 1966. By August, the SAP were aware of the base camp, and three policemen reconnoitered the elaborate Ongulumbashe site on 23 August 1966. Three days later, a force of thirty-two policemen, ferried in eight helicopters attacked the camp, and the battle was joined. Two SWAPO insurgents were killed, while nine were captured, and an unknown number escaped. There were no casualties among the SAP.[72] More than forty years after the battle, it was disclosed that one of the thirty-two persons was an informer and that several South African Air Force and SADF personnel were also involved.[73] This, then, was the end of PLAN's only long-lasting base within Namibia.[74] Guerrillas also make use of transit camps and staging posts, both of which are located away from the base camp and close to the international border in order to facilitate forays into enemy territory and to process the influx of refugees from that territory.[75] In time, the base (or a cluster of bases) can serve as the headquarters for a zone of liberation, which is administered by the guerrillas. Such a zone enables the guerrillas to have political space in which to develop non-military skills in the art of administration.

A non-territorial alternative was a shadow government, such as the one utilized by the Filipino insurgents that functioned surreptitiously alongside the American military occupation government.[76] Perhaps the guerrillas could also gain experience in the delivery of rudimentary services to the inhabitants of the zone. For example, during the insurgency war against the Portuguese in Guinea-Bissau, the creation of such zones enabled the insurgents to develop a cash-free economy.[77] Performing these functions would build the foundation for subsequent legitimacy and possibly for the claim to be the government-in-waiting. To enable the guerrillas to think in these terms the base would need to be secure against enemy attack, if not surveillance. This, of course, is difficult to accomplish in the age of air power, especially aerial reconnaissance and subsequent helicopter-borne attacks by counterinsurgent forces. Indeed, an aerial photograph of the Ongulumbashe camp has already been published.[78] Using Canberra aircraft, the South African Air Force undertook the task of aerial photography of the area as well as of southern Angola and northern Namibia.[79]

The security branch of the SAP set up a clandestine camp in the Caprivi Zipfel in March 1965 to observe SWAPO activity; Theunis J. Swanepoel, who played a major part in the subsequent attack on the Ongulumbashe base, headed the camp.[80] With the loss of Ongulumbashe, PLAN could not lay claim to semi-liberated or liberated areas within Namibia.[81] There were precedents for such areas during the Viet Minh's campaign in Vietnam,[82] in Fidel Castro's campaign against the Batista regime in Cuba,[83] and the anti–Portuguese war in Guinea-Bissau.[84] Consequently, PLAN needed to revise its logistical planning not only to arrange for external safe havens but also for pre-positioning its arms and ammunition, preferably close to its intended targets.

Until the termination of Portuguese rule in neighboring Angola, there were only two choices for permanent bases in neighboring African majority-ruled states: Botswana or Zambia. The line of supply and troop recruitment and deployment thus ran the geographical gauntlet from Zambia to northern Namibia, and all this needed to be overland transport. Unlike the situation in German-occupied Europe during the Second World War, the Namibian guerrillas could expect no supplies and arms to be dropped from parachute from friendly aircraft or even sent by sea. At one point, the Pan Africanist Congress of

South Africa entertained ideas about seaborne transport for arms and guerrillas, but this came to naught.[85] Similarly, the African National Congress arranged to have the Soviet Union land its guerrillas on the Transkei, but the project was rejected and so never occurred.[86] So far, I have found no corroborative evidence that SWAPO intended to utilize seaborne vessels for its logistical and deployment needs at this early date, although the American Africanist Edwin S. Munger indicated that some "Pan-African strategists in Accra [Ghana] discuss[ed] the advantage of landing a small force ... on the desolate South-West [African] coast."[87] All these unrealized proposals made for a long, vulnerable supply line until supplies could be brought in from the north once Angola became independent.

The lack of an internal base or liberated areas internal base or liberated areas may have disturbed the Organization of African Unity.[88] However, a prominent PLAN official, Rahimisa Kahimise, claimed that there were mobile or "roving" bases inside Namibia.[89] Even though liberated areas or zones are a basic feature of the literature on guerrilla warfare,[90] the absence of these zones seemed to have no discernable impact on the course of the war until the western nations (acting as the Contact Group) began to negotiate with South Africa over the principles and details of the termination of the war and the ensuing transition to internationally recognized independence under the auspices of the United Nations. The U.S. Assistant Secretary of State, Dr. Chester A. Crocker, commented upon SWAPO's lack of liberated areas or permanent bases, which may have suggested that he perceived that SWAPO lacked certain bargaining chips.[91]

Significantly, SWAPO did not directly participate in these negotiations or in the ones that the United States brokered among Angola, Cuba, and South Africa. It seems that the rationale for this exclusion was achieving diplomatic symmetry between SWAPO and the South African–aided group, the National Union for the Total Independence of Angola (UNITA), both of which were non-state actors.[92] In a somewhat similar fashion, the American negotiating team, in drawing up the Treaty of Paris with their Spanish counterparts, excluded the Filipino nationalist diplomats who wanted to secure the independence that their movement had originally proclaimed in 1898.[93] Demilitarization of the country prior to internationally monitored elections is common enough practice, but the challenge in the Namibian case was how to rein in the opposing forces both inside and outside of Namibia. On 15 July 1979, in his meeting with the UN Secretary-General, President Agostinho Neto of Angola suggested a demilitarized zone between his country and Namibia. Later, during the 12–16 November 1979 meeting in Geneva with senior UN Secretariat officials, both SWAPO and the Front Line States (of Angola, Botswana, Mozambique, Nigeria, and Tanzania) indicated their support for such an idea.[94] The South African response to this suggested zone was less enthusiastic and it also emphasized its objection to any PLAN bases within Namibia.[95] Subsequently, the Western Contact Group added its own version to the plan by proposing that a few African nations and the five Contact Group nations send their armed forces, rather than let the UN monitor this zone. Mr. Nujoma of SWAPO objected to this proposal.[96]

Conventionally, in the run-up to internationally supervised elections, the contending armed forces would be confined to their respective bases, thus neutralizing and immobilizing them. Presumably, that would create the necessary political space for the electoral process to unfold in a non-violent fashion. How to determine just where those bases were located and what international agency would undertake to monitor the confinement of those opposing forces to their bases were fundamental issues. What is especially significant in the Namibian case is the geographical and military ambiguity of the noun base and the implications of having a base or bases in terms of status and legitimacy for the protagonists. The South Africans tacitly acknowledged that PLAN did operate on Namibian territory (which would signify a significant level of insurgent military prowess),[97] yet they adamantly refused to permit PLAN bases on Namibian territory (which would be an acknowledgment of their adversary's military success and claim to legitimacy).[98] The UN, in turn, did not deal decisively with the matter of PLAN bases on Namibian territory, treating it in a rather desultory manner, which apparently annoyed the SWAPO leadership. This inattention to detail was to prove embarrassing during the implementation of the UN-supervised transition to independence in early 1989.[99]

Lengthy international negotiations among the key state actors, which excluded SWAPO but included South Africa, Angola, and Cuba, resulted in the agreement to withdraw SADF and Cuban forces from southern Angola as part of a package arrangement known as linkage. Cuban troop withdrawal was the *quid pro quo* for Namibian independence, a formula that met the minimum security needs of both Angola (which depended upon Cuban military manpower and expertise to help its own armed forces [known as FAPLA] in their attempt to keep the SADF at bay in southern Angola) and South Africa (which was anxious about what it perceived as a threatening communist presence bordering on Namibia). Both forces would go home—to Cuba and to South Africa—in phased withdrawals from southern Angola.

Determining the path and timing of the military movements presupposed a functioning civil-military chain of command and identifiable units and base areas as well as a reliable system of international auditing for tracking the affected forces. It also entailed some degree of international cooperation between Namibia's neighbors with respect to PLAN bases. Although Botswana apparently tolerated the traversing of its territory by Zimbabwe guerrillas[100] (and suffered retaliatory raids from the Rhodesians for its purported lack of neutrality[101]), it did not provide any permanent bases for PLAN.[102] Consequently, Botswana would not be directly involved in terms of the monitoring of PLAN troop movements in the prelude to independence. That left Angola, which was the principal sanctuary for PLAN forces once they shifted their headquarters from Zambia.

For the Namibian nationalists a base within their own territory would provide an assembly point which international observers could monitor; this would place PLAN on an equal footing because both opposing forces—PLAN and SADF/SWATF—would be confined to their bases inside Namibia. Such a base would provide a tangible symbol of the legitimacy of SWAPO's armed forces and of their campaign against SADF/SWATF. This would be a graphic negation of the maxim that "they could not expect to gain at the conference table what they had failed to gain on the battlefield."[103] Furthermore, the acquisition of in-country bases would simplify the command and control aspects of the demilitarization exercise involved in the transition period.

The United Nations established 1 April 1989 as the day on which PLAN forces would present themselves to military personnel of the United Nations Transition Assistance Group (UNTAG) and expect to lay down their arms and receive protection en route back to their extraterritorial bases. Similarly, the SADF and SWATF units would be confined to their bases within Namibia. At this time, only a few UNTAG military units were in position in the north to oversee the demilitarization phase of the independence process. Moreover, due in large measure to the frugality of the permanent powers on the United Nations Security Council, the military component of UNTAG was far smaller than the African states wished. Operating through the Non-Aligned Movement (NAM) at the UN, diplomats from a number of NAM states attempted to counter attempts by the five permanent members of the UN Security Council to reduce the cost of UNTAG. These five would jointly be responsible for roughly fifty-seven percent of these costs. The UN Secretary-General did show some flexibility in adjusting the size of the military component to meet future contingencies.[104] Nevertheless, the soldiers in the blue helmets were no real match for the SADF and its SWATF partner.

Earlier SWAPO had agreed to abide by a cease-fire, and there seemed to be no tangible evidence that either side would violate that agreement even though the international peace process resulting in the 1988 New York Accords (which essentially traded Cuban troop withdrawal from Angola for South African troop withdrawal from Namibia, along with Namibian independence) had not included SWAPO as a negotiator or a signatory. By 1 April 1989, the SADF had pulled back from southern Angola and was positioned in its bases in Namibia. For reasons that have yet to be fully explained and documented, between 1 and 28 April 1989 a total of 1,676 armed PLAN soldiers moved from Angola into northern Namibia,[105] where the UNTAG had no infantry deployed.[106]

This precipitated an international incident, for the United Nations Secretary-General granted the South Africans permission to pursue these guerrillas with their own armed forces.[107] Such a move infuriated the African states,[108] and the SADF returned to their bases within two weeks.[109] There was an exceedingly sanguinary battle in early April that cost the lives of 314 PLAN members[110] in what was termed a "turkey shoot."[111] Even though there is compelling evidence to suggest that 18 of the PLAN soldiers were summarily executed following their capture by a special police counterinsurgency unit known as *Koevoet*,[112] that view has been challenged.[113] Why did this infiltration, which reportedly annoyed SWAPO's Angolan hosts,[114] occur? Indeed, SWAPO sent its PLAN units over the border into Namibia without so much as conferring with their Angolan hosts and Cuban allies.[115] Unfortunately Sam Nujoma's memoirs are very opaque, rather rhetorical, and generally unhelpful, thus fuelling some observers' wide-ranging speculations.[116] Mr. Nujoma had indicated SWAPO's willingness to cooperate in an inquiry — presumably an international one, probably under the aegis of the United Nations — into the April 1st events, but this came to naught.[117]

There are three cogent analyses of the tragic April 1st, 1989 events by Lamb,[118] O'Linn,[119] and Thornberry.[120] The first contention is that the Namibian nationalists wanted to acquire something they had not been able to acquire during the course of the war: bases.[121] The Pretoria regime was well aware of this, and it made certain that the United Nations knew that South Africa would not concede to PLAN what it had not secured on the battlefield.[122] To defy or to outmaneuver the South Africans would enable SWAPO to project an image of strength (almost a mirror image of the Afrikaners nationalists' fascination with toughness).[123] A complementary argument is that SWAPO wanted to demonstrate not only that it had a monopoly on the liberation process but also that it could indeed liberate territory within the boundaries of Namibia.[124]

Recent research indicates that President Mugabe of Zimbabwe may have suggested such a stratagem to SWAPO leader Sam Nujoma whose PLAN lacked any liberated zones (comparable to the ones that the Zimbabweans had by 1979). Presumably, such a move would strengthen the political position of SWAPO as well.[125] Norma J. Kriger has furnished ample evidence to support this perspective.[126] Nevertheless, the United Nations Undersecretary-General for Peacekeeping, Mr. Marrack Goulding, warned President Nujoma in Harare on 23 March 1989 that the United Nations peace plan did not permit the creation of SWAPO bases inside Namibia.[127]

The proposition is that SWAPO would present the United Nations with a *fait accompli* and that the United Nations would hold the South Africans at bay for SWAPO.[128] There were two variants of this explanation. The first variant is that SWAPO desired to offset the advantages that it perceived that an undermanned UNTAG military force, a powerful South African administrator-general, and an effective SAP counterinsurgency unit (*Koevoet*) operating inside northern Namibia afforded the South African side.[129] This interpretation complements the first of three contentions briefly listed in Lise Howard's analysis, namely, "that UNTAG could have prevented the incursion [by SWAPO], but ... budgetary and deployment delays precipitated the event."[130] The second variant is that SWAPO wished to dispatch more of its soldiers back into Namibia to improve its electoral strength in the forthcoming Constituent Assembly elections (where it needed a two-thirds majority of the seats to secure its preeminence).[131] Still another explanation for the incursion is that there was a command and control problem within SWAPO and that the civil and military wings were at odds with one another. The incursion was the work of the military hardliners, so it was argued.[132]

A Zimbabwean diplomat, who served at the United Nations during much of this period, presents a thoughtful counter-explanation of the sanguinary events of April 1, 1989. He contends that the confusion surrounding the incursion of PLAN soldiers into Namibia can be traced not only to the exclusion of SWAPO from several decision-making groups and meetings but also to obvious omissions from Western agreements and UN planning documents regarding the presence and location — to say nothing of the lack of definition — of PLAN bases in Namibia and Angola. Moreover, the lengthy debates over the size of the military component of UNTAG and the willingness of two permanent members of the UN Security Council (China and the Soviet Union) to align themselves with the three Western permanent members of the Security Council to trim the proposed budget for the military side of UNTAG are contributing factors, although not as significant as the tardy dispatch of UNTAG to their assigned locations. Faulty UN contingency planning and the UN Special Representative Martii Ahtisaari's ill-advised release of South African security forces to engage the PLAN forces created a dangerous situation, which was resolved by recourse to a multilateral institution, the tripartite (Angola, Cuba, and South Africa with the Soviet Union and United States as observers) joint commission which was not really a UN organization. The upshot of all these acts of omission and commission by some Western and UN institutions and officials would suggest that SWAPO, its leadership, and armed forces were unfairly treated and unjustly vilified.[133]

At this point, which of these explanations seem most likely? Relying on the rule of Occam's razor, I suggest that a *Machtergreifung* explanation is the most satisfactory one in light of the corroborated data. That is, a seizure of power (*Machtergreifung*) independent of Western, although not African, legitimation seems most likely, and how better to demonstrate that quest for power than by heading south over the border, with little anticipated resistance, to establish oneself as master in the chosen land? This act of bravado and overconfidence appeared to be a failed exercise in political theater that delayed the achievement of SWAPO's full political hegemony, something that Mr. Nujoma referred to in his 28 February 1978 interview with Cliff Saunders noted at the beginning of this chapter.

Shifting External Sanctuaries

The loss of the Ongulumbashe base at the outset of the war suggested that PLAN soldiers were vulnerable to detection and attack by SAP units. This underscored the urgency of a secure base from which soldiers, supplies, and armaments could be dispatched for use in hit-and-run attacks on South African targets. At that time the wisest choice was Zambia, which lay astride the northeastern border of the Caprivi Strip portion of Namibia. By 1975 PLAN had managed to build up its force in southwestern Zambia to between 2,000 and 3,000 soldiers.[134] Until 1975, PLAN units operated in the nearby eastern portion of the Caprivi Strip as well in the Okavango River region.[135] The Portuguese were still involved in their counterinsurgency campaign in Angola, which was geographically closer to PLAN's preferred operational area than was Zambia. Moreover, the Portuguese authorities cooperated with the South African ones in order to contain the Namibian guerrillas.[136] SWAPO needed a shorter route to the battlefield, and for a while cooperated with the members of the National Union for the Total Independence of Angola (UNITA) in order to secure a clear passageway for exfiltration from and infiltration to Namibia.[137] It was not until the Portuguese military *coup d'état* of 1974 and the subsequent departure of Portuguese troops from Angola that PLAN could be said to have secure access to neighboring Angola for its rear area bases. In 1976 PLAN moved its military headquarters to Angola,[138] while SWAPO established an office in Luanda that same year.[139]

Once the South Africans launched their attack into Angola in 1975, those rear base areas became the object of SADF concern, with the SADF tending to assume cross-border operation responsibilities. The South African goal was to maximize the space between the Namibian border (or cutline as the Angolan-Namibian border was sometimes termed[140]) and PLAN bases, adding to the distance that PLAN soldiers (with supplies and weapons) had to march to the scene of intended attack[141] and, conversely, to give the South Africans earlier warning of the advance of PLAN infiltrators. In their rear base areas in southern Angola, SWAPO was able to carry on with its political and administrative work, enjoying the protection of FAPLA. In order to deter or to counter the impact of cross-border SADF attacks, PLAN bases in Angola were sited near FAPLA or Cuban military posts, which had the added attraction of being able to rely upon the logistical and communication infrastructures of their allies.[142] Apparently, FAPLA bartered this support and aid to PLAN by requiring PLAN to furnish two brigades to FAPLA that was fighting their joint enemy, UNITA (which, in turn, was supported by the SADF).[143] This diminished PLAN's available mobile forces for cross-border infiltration as well as static forces for the protection of SWAPO refugees in Angola. The SADF raid on Cassinga in Angola on 4 May 1978 demonstrated tragically that this SWAPO/PLAN complex housed both civilian (refugee) and military personnel, which resulted in large collateral damage to the refugee population. That base was neither wholly military nor entirely civilian which created a public relations and diplomatic disaster for the SADF and South Africa,[144] including a rebuke by the United Nations Security Council.[145] Guy Lamb has argued persuasively that this raid fundamentally transgressed the laws of war regarding the treatment of non-combatants.[146]

Military Training and Doctrine

As a League of Nations mandated territory, Namibia was forbidden to have standing armed forces, and thus its Africans were unable to undergo military training. They did, however, have a tradition of guerrilla warfare, which was what they needed to oppose the South Africans in the 1960s. What they lacked was training in the more specialized arts of guerrilla warfare that had developed since their last sustained efforts against the Germans in the early part of the twentieth century. Where and how were they to be trained? The South Africans did recruit Namibians into a non-combatant force (the Native Military Corps) in the Second World War,[147] but they had been anxious about arming Africans for fear of rebellion.[148] Because Namibia was encircled by colonial powers until the mid–1960s, the only place the Namibians could secure the requisite training would be in friendly African, Asian, and Soviet bloc states whose armed forces could serve as instructors. The process began as early as March, 1961, when SWAPO president Sam Nujoma made arrangements with President Gamal Nasser of Egypt to provide military training for its recruits, and in July, 1962 when seven Namibians left for military training in Egypt. By May 1963 SWAPO opened its own training base in Kongwa, Tanzania[149]; this was apparently under the auspices of the Liberation Committee of the Organization of African Unity.[150]

Namibians also received military training in Algeria, China, Cuba, East Germany, Ghana, Nigeria, North Korea, the Soviet Union, and Yugoslavia.[151] Even a very small number of SWANU members received military instruction in China and Egypt.[152] The early Namibian guerrillas then served as instructors for several other Namibians at the Ongulumbashe camp.[153] Initially, the guerrilla recruits were Ovambo migrant workers for the South African mines who fled the Francistown, Botswana labor center before or after their contracts were finished and traveled to Dar es Salaam.[154] In general, these early military recruits had a minimal formal education, and some of them aspired to additional education.[155] This quest for additional education was a postwar problem in Namibia when demobilized veterans with modest educational credentials were unable to transmute political victory into employment and tangible wealth.

The appealing guerrilla model at that early stage was probably the Maoist one. This has been traced to the Yu Chi Chan Club, a Maoist-oriented group in Cape Town to which two prominent Namibians, Kenneth Abrahams and Andreas Shipanga, belonged.[156] Yu Chi Can is the Chinese title of Mao's 1937 work.[157] Although there appeared to be several disparate styles of guerrilla warfare in the beginning,[158] PLAN later seemed to have settled on the Maoist approach and in 1974 sent about eighty of its members to the Soviet Union for advanced training.[159] Guy Lamb has characterized the 1966–1974 operations of PLAN as essentially Maoist style guerrilla warfare.[160] Loren Dobell, however, has questioned the primacy of the Maoist approach of the early Namibian nationalists.[161] Its first commanding officer, Tobias Hanyeko, was killed in combat in 1967; his replacement, Dimo Hamaambo, held this post throughout the remainder of the war.[162] SWAPO, in turn, began to develop a more formal defense organization, with a secretary of defense (Peter Nanyemba, followed by Peter Mueshihange) and a military council; they formed part of SWAPO defense headquarters, which was located in Lubango, Angola.[163]

PLAN developed a force that resembled many standing armies with regard to the division of military labor, with various specialties, such as intelligence, propaganda, reconnaissance, engineering, air defense, sabotage, and artillery.[164] The East Germans evacuated severely wounded PLAN members to East Germany, where the hospital ward where they stayed was named in honor of Jacob Morengo, a renowned Namibian guerrilla who fought the Germans earlier in the century.[165]

PLAN included an elite force, known as Volcano and subsequently Typhoon, which was commanded by the PLAN soldier responsible for the capture of the SADF prisoner of war, Johan van der Mescht. Typhoon specialized in attacks south of Ovamboland in the white farming district of Namibia.[166] In 2010, Rina Jooste made a 52-minute documentary film about Johan van der Mescht's capture, *Captor and Captive: The Story of Danger Ashipala and Johan van der Mescht*, which was shown in Windhoek and by the South African Broadcasting Corporation in 2011.[167] This unit was trained by the East Germans[168] and was held in high regard by Peter Stiff, a South African writer, who was not usually known to comment favorably about SWAPO or PLAN.[169] Indeed, two high-ranking SADF officers gave the East Germans high marks for the quality of the training they gave to PLAN.[170] Other military journalists and SADF, SAAF, and SAP officers, such as Jim Hooper,[171] J. H. Thompson,[172] Richard Lord,[173] Eugene de Kok,[174] and Leopold Scholtz[175] have occasionally indicated their admiration for the training, stamina, and skill of PLAN soldiers. Anthony Clayton, a well known British writer who had been on the faculty of the Royal Military Academy at Sandhurst, agreed with most of these favorable comments, but he took exception to the quality of the training of PLAN members.[176] Conversely, the Cuban military leadership in Angola did not hold PLAN in very high esteem.[177]

With the opening up of Angola after the Portuguese *coup d'état* of 1974 and the attempt of Zambian President Kaunda to arrange a *détente* with South Africa, some fissures opened up within SWAPO and PLAN. A number of SWAPO members were disturbed that their former allies in Angola, UNITA, were now beginning to wage war against FAPLA, so that these Namibians regarded UNITA as a South African cat's paw. To add insult to injury, President Kaunda was clamping down on PLAN, refusing it permission to launch attacks from Zambia; this was seen as placating South African Prime Minister B. J. Vorster. In addition, this dissident group criticized the logistical operations of PLAN as inefficient and claimed that some higher SWAPO leaders were engaged in corrupt practices in Zambia. Such criticism was met with repression, and the dissidents (about half of whom were PLAN members) found themselves in Tanzanian jails. These events formed part of the 1974–1976 crisis within the external wing of SWAPO.[178]

The conduct of the war involved customary guerrilla tactics inside the boundaries of Namibia, on the one hand, and conventional extraterritorial military operations within

Angola once the SADF began to develop a sustained presence in Angola and when PLAN found an allay in FAPLA, the military arm of the MPLA, on the other hand. From the guerrilla perspective, there were hit and run raids from sanctuaries in Zambia and later in Angola across the border to the rural northern reaches of Namibia. These operations focused on the elimination of government personnel and family members regarded as crucial to, or beneficiaries of, separate development structures and policies, such as African traditionalists or notables.[179] There seems to be no published data on the number of those assassinated by PLAN, but it is likely that the numbers are not large perhaps because the South African authorities developed a cadre of bodyguards, known as special constables of the South West Africa Protection Unit for these leaders.[180] Perhaps the best-known instance of assassination of a prominent leader was that of Clements Kapuuo, a Herero leader. There is still a debate about the responsibility for that death.[181] Conversely, SWAPO developed its own bodyguards, trained in East Germany.[182] By way of comparison with Vietnam, the Viet Cong killed some 4,000 village officials in 1960–1961.[183] Such assassinations of collaborators were part of the insurgents' campaign tactics in the Philippine War.[184] Members of the white farming communities located in the Police Zone (separating the northern African reserves or Bantustans from the central and southern white settlement and farming areas) were additional targets.[185]

Other forays involved the establishment of arms, food, and clothing caches within Namibia.[186] Such journeys into Namibia had political as well as military dimensions, and PLAN members surreptitiously engaged in discussions with the locals to politicize them, hoping to create a larger body of SWAPO supporters.[187] This, after all, is the hallmark of guerrilla warfare and in due course creates a larger cadre of Namibians to proffer transiting PLAN members clandestine logistical aid and tactical intelligence.[188] The East Germans furnished Namibians with training in journalism; they published *Namibia Today* on their behalf, provided political education for them, and trained them in military intelligence and counter-intelligence.[189]

Such secret political meetings were standard operating procedures — termed *pungwes* in Shona — for the ZANLA guerrilla units penetrating Zimbabwe.[190] PLAN members thus wore their customary (mustard-colored as well as camouflaged) military uniforms[191] and FAPLA uniforms when in Angolan urban areas,[192] as well as civilian clothes.[193] Wearing military uniforms seemed to lessen the severity of their prison sentences when captured by South African forces.[194] For logistical reasons (especially access to drinking water) these forays into rural northern Namibia predictably took place during the November-to-March rainy season.[195] The rainy season made it difficult for the South Africans to follow the tracks of the infiltrators and for their vehicles to get traction in the wet soil.[196] There was also more cover in the bush areas during the rainy season, which worked to PLAN's advantage.[197] The insurgents concentrated on weakly protected and isolated locales, such as individual farms, or on government structures. Although sabotage of transportation structures, such as highways and bridges, did occur in the central and southern portions of Namibia,[198] this was not a common pattern. However, the SADF acknowledged PLAN's tactical prowess in their internal documents,[199] which later became public knowledge.[200] Moreover, the SADF kept a record of the number of sabotage incidents on an annual basis.[201]

Usually PLAN did not focus its efforts on urban guerrilla warfare,[202] although it was able to transport explosives into urban areas.[203] Following one particularly sanguinary attack on a bank in Oshakati, SWAPO spokesmen insisted that it was not official policy to attack what has been called "soft targets" where substantial civilian deaths could be anticipated, but they declined to state so publicly. Indeed, they remonstrated that they were not responsible for such attacks which, they claimed, had been pseudo operations on the part of their opponents, particularly those in *Koevoet* (the police counterinsurgency unit). Pseudo operations have been used in quite a number of other counterinsurgency campaigns in Africa.[204] The denial was unconvincing, according to one Namibian lawyer recognized for his skill in defending SWAPO members before Namibian courts.[205] Peter Stiff has averred that *Koevoet* was unsuccessful in their attempt to employ this tactic and, with a later single exception, abandoned it.[206] Others are not persuaded that this is so.[207]

Seeking Prisoner Protection

SWAPO's war against the South African regime involved the politics of legitimacy, for it was conceptualized as a war of national liberation (the acronym PLAN included the term liberation). It was important from both a conceptual and pragmatic perspective to legitimize such wars, which involved a change in the relevant portions of public international law.[208] The United Nations General Assembly was the most appropriate forum in which to wage this conceptual battle, if only because of the favored voting position of anti-colonial delegations. Nevertheless, the United Nations Security Council, without referring to SWAPO, acknowledged "the legitimacy of the struggle of the people of Namibia against the illegal presence of the South African authorities in the territory."[209]

The General Assembly, drawing upon the expertise of a committee of jurists, addressed the matter of the legitimacy of national liberation (within the larger context of self-determination). Its member states unanimously passed the Declaration on Principles of International Law on 24 October 1970, which was marked by considerable ambiguity when it came to the matter of the use of armed force.[210] Several days earlier, on 12 October 1970, the General Assembly passed a lengthy resolution spelling out a detailed program to implement its earlier Declaration on the Granting of Independence to Colonial Countries and Peoples. Embedded in that resolution was a declaration that the 1949 Geneva Convention concerning the treatment of prisoners would apply to captured insurgents.[211] It reitered that stand in 1973.[212] Understandably, SWAPO wished to avail itself of that protection for its PLAN soldiers.[213]

South Africa did not acknowledge the legitimacy of SWAPO, which was common practice for states facing armed opponents, as was also the case with Portugal.[214] Indeed, Prime Minister B. J. Vorster publicly demonized SWAPO, stating that it "was conceived and born in communist sin."[215] Consequently, it declined to grant PLAN members prisoner of war (POW) status under the relevant Geneva conventions.[216] Through the International Red Cross,[217] South Africa managed to exchange seven SADF soldiers for three Cuban soldiers captured during Operation Savannah (the code name for its 1975–1976 expedition into Angola).[218] PLAN captured a SADF soldier, Johan van der Mescht, in February 1978,[219] who, along with eight unidentified Western intelligence agents, was exchanged in 1981 for a Soviet spy, Major Aleksei Kozlov.[220]

Gary F. Baines has recently explored this topic in considerable detail, drawing upon

South African archival materials.²²¹ There was one instance, in late December 1983, in which FAPLA captured a SWATF soldier, but it is not known how the Angolan authorities dealt with this case.²²² During the final days of combat, the Cubans captured one wounded South African soldier, Johan Papenfus, who received medical treatment in Cuba.²²³ In several cases, states have pragmatically granted such status without conceding the legitimacy of their opponents: France did so in Algeria and the United States did so in South Vietnam.²²⁴

Despite the rebuff, the United Nations Council for Namibia, which exercised *de jure* (but little, if any, *de facto*) authority in the territory, acceded to the appropriate Geneva conventions,²²⁵ which would add to the stature and legitimacy of SWAPO and PLAN in many international circles. Although Sam Nujoma emphasized the lack of symmetry between SWAPO and South Africa regarding PLAN's willingness (and South Africa's failure) to observe these international norms concerning prisoners, he did not indicate the number of South African prisoners of war involved.²²⁶ Had the numbers of military prisoners and their possible future exchange been the sole considerations in the South African political calculus, the South African regime would have benefited only marginally from such an arrangement because so few SADF soldiers became prisoners of war.²²⁷

Even though the South African regime did not legally regard PLAN members as prisoners of war,²²⁸ in one landmark case tried in the Supreme Court of South West Africa in 1983 involving three such defendants, the defense attorneys drew attention to the Geneva conventions to show that the defendants met the criteria of the conventions to be regarded as such, and, in so doing, distanced PLAN from its South African counterparts (the armed wings of the African National Congress and of the Pan Africanist Congress) which, in their judgment, failed to meet the Geneva criteria. It was thought that this defense strategy was effective in saving the lives of the defendants who were facing a possible death sentence.²²⁹

Toward the end of the conflict, however, there seemed to be few prisoners of war who might benefit from such international norms if, apparently as intimated by an official of the International Committee of the Red Cross, those captured in battle were discreetly executed following their interrogation.²³⁰ Although plausible in the context of a guerrilla war, such an allegation or anecdotal evidence would be very difficult either to confirm or to refute. Furthermore, recent revelations about American disregard of the Geneva conventions with respect to its campaign against Al-Qaida and the Taliban suggests that, even among signatories, there still needs to be third party monitoring and that the chain of command can be broken or circumvented (for example, by the Central Intelligence Agency and its foreign counterparts).²³¹ Such a policy, avers one critic, "…contributes greatly to the institutionalization of torture."²³²

Military Arms and Supplies

In the early stages of the war, military ordinance was in very short supply, with the initial shipment brought by Sam Nujoma and Peter Nanyemba from Algeria to Tanzania by way of Egypt, and from there to Zambia. Thereafter PLAN transported these arms to Katima Mulilo in the Caprivi Zipfel and then on to Ongulumbashe, the first battle site in the war.²³³ The PLAN members were their own arms porters,²³⁴ and they had nothing equivalent to the Ho Chi Minh trail and the system of relays among Vietnamese porters²³⁵ or even the supply system with porters who traversed Mozambique to supply the guerrillas fighting in Rhodesia.²³⁶ Once the Portuguese vacated Angola, PLAN would be able to use the railway and highway systems of Angola, as well as its ports, to facilitate the movement of armaments that they secured from their various Eastern bloc suppliers.²³⁷ Even though it is a commonplace in the literature on guerrilla warfare that the insurgents obtain some of their arms by staging daring raids on enemy arsenals, PLAN used this technique rather infrequently.²³⁸ Indeed, as a visiting PLAN mission to Moscow told their hosts in 1973, in Addis Ababa, Ethiopia, they even displayed their captured South African arms and communications supplies.²³⁹

In the guerrilla phase of warfare, infiltration into Namibia was crucial in carrying the war to the enemy, and this meant the development of a system for bringing in arms from Zambia and/or Angola and then placing them in well-positioned arms caches. PLAN discovered that sometimes weapons malfunctioned after being buried underground for some time,²⁴⁰ and one of the objectives of the South African forces was to locate, utilize, or destroy these caches.²⁴¹ These caches might also include food and clothing, and sometimes anti-personnel mines would protect them.²⁴² Carrying arms and ammunition in backpacks restricted the amount and type of arms and ammunition that PLAN members could take to these caches or on raiding or reconnaissance missions, and they did resort to other means of transport, such as bicycles, donkeys, horses, cattle, and trucks when they were available or could be commandeered or whose owners might be bribed.²⁴³

Because PLAN had no known arms manufacturing facilities, which might be termed cottage industries, they relied on foreign arms and armaments, primarily those of Soviet bloc nations, along with China, and Cuba.²⁴⁴ Although there are some hard data, for example, on East Germany's supply of arms, these data are incomplete²⁴⁵; still the literature on the volume, type, and cost of these exports is disappointingly vague.²⁴⁶ The armaments were appropriate for a light infantry units, although PLAN did acquire heavier weapons and used scout cars as well as armored personnel carriers while in Angola, where it shared some of the FAPLA logistical system.²⁴⁷ At the end of the war, the Namibian Minister of Defense acknowledged that SWAPO (apparently acting as the agent for PLAN) that was making a gift to the newly created Namibian Defense Force (NDF) of weapons and materials left in Zambia and Angola.²⁴⁸ The Minister of Defense declined to put a price tag on the amount of war matériel being transferred to the NDF.²⁴⁹ This would imply not only that PLAN had some means of distinguishing its weaponry from that of FAPLA and of the Zambian Defense Force but also that it regarded the receipt of foreign arms as part of its patrimony. Consequently, it accrued no debt for this arms transfer from its wartime foreign military patrons, and, most interestingly, the SADF also donated military equipment to Namibia.²⁵⁰

International Monitoring by UNTAG

From the perspective of SWAPO, PLAN had been its instrument of military coercion employed to check the combination of the SADF and SWATF, along with the *Koevoet* unit of the SAP, by engaging in both conventional and guerrilla warfare at different times and different places and often with support from their Angolan and Cuban allies. The primary goal was independence under the aegis and hegemony of SWAPO, which had secured a monopoly of international legitimacy, thanks to the patronage of the United Nations General Assembly and the OAU. The SWAPO shadow government received multilateral external funding through various General Assembly organizations, such as the United Nations Council for Namibia, as well as bilateral military and economic assistance from friendly (African and Nordic) governments as well as from solidarity groups within not-so-friendly (usually Western) governments.

From a military perspective, a major source of concern for PLAN was the strength and deployment of countervailing UNTAG military power to balance, if not displace, the South African military presence to enable SWAPO to mobilize the Namibian electorate for the Constituent Assembly elections. The April, 1989 incursion into Namibia from Angola was a substantial setback for PLAN, and it temporarily undercut what respect UNTAG had earned among the Namibian political establishment. Not only were the SWAPO leaders upset with what they regarded as an inadequate funding of UNTAG[251] but also they were visibly angry with Mr. Ahtisaari, the Special Representative of the UN Secretary-General in Namibia, for authorizing the South African security forces to check the April PLAN incursion.[252] These complaints, however, were not simply partisan ones, for subsequent research (involving several individuals personally involved in the operations) has shown that there were other deficiencies in the performance and planning of the UNTAG military unit.[253]

By 24 June 1989, 1,500 SADF members departed from Namibia, and the remaining 1,500 had all left by 21 November 1989.[254] This still did not create the type of environment conducive to free and fair elections for the Constituent Assembly, which would draft the independence constitution. In Chapter Six, I indicate how the SADF, through its opaquely affiliated groups and fronts, engaged in clandestine operations to discredit SWAPO in order to reduce its electoral power in the Constituent Assembly and thereby presumably draft a constitution which accommodated South African economic and minority racial concerns. From the perspective of PLAN, the objective was to neutralize the baleful existence of *Koevoet* whose members frequently terrorized the population of northern Namibia,[255] which probably was intended to reduce the number of pro–SWAPO voters in the Constituent Assembly elections. The South Africans ostensibly demobilized SWATF by 1 June 1989, yet SWATF personnel continued to receive their pay thereafter.[256] Apparently the United Nations Security Council was not impressed by this and specifically instructed South Africa to deactivate SWATF.[257] Despite the United Nations Security Council's two separate admonitions to South Africa to disband *Koevoet*,[258] that task was finally completed a mere week before the Constituent Assembly elections started.[259] Maintaining civil peace was a responsibility assigned to the police observer component of UNTAG (known as CIVPOL), while other elements of UNTAG concerned themselves with electoral registration, election oversight, media monitoring, and fair inter-political party behavior.[260] The Canadian political scientist Douglas G. Anglin has placed these tasks within a much wider framework for analysis,[261] and the United Nations Department of Peacekeeping Operations has issued its own 'Lessons Learned' study of UNTAG, which is rarely mentioned in the literature.[262]

Because the available literature has only slight coverage of PLAN, as an organizational entity,[263] during the run-up phase to the Constituent Assembly elections in early November 1989, it would appear that most of it tacitly disbanded, with individual soldiers returning to their homes and communities. An estimated six hundred former PLAN members remained in Angola, where they guarded the PLAN matériel that was to be transferred to the Namibian Defense Force (NDF). The Angolan government consented to have them there, and in August, 1990 these guards were made members of the NDF. Once the stores had been shipped to Namibia, these NDF members would return to Namibia.[264] As I show in Chapter Seven, some military issues did not disappear with the advent of independence, and the new regime was faced with the inauguration of a new NDF, which (like its counterpart in South Africa[265]) attempted to create an organization which included former PLAN soldiers and their foes from *Koevoet* and SWATF. Notwithstanding the creation of the NDF, the SWAPO government still had to mollify those former PLAN members, who were unemployed, marginalized, and bereft of the economic entitlements they perhaps expected at independence.

Chapter Six

South Africa's Bush War[1]

The Primacy of the Police

Once the First World War had ended, the South African authorities ended the system of military rule in Namibia, and the territory reverted to the civilian pattern common throughout much of southern Africa, especially in the High Commission Territories and Northern and Southern Rhodesia. During the military interregnum, the South African Government deported 1,619 German military personnel and 873 policemen from the territory, and the 1923 London Agreement between South Africa and the Weimar Republic had assured the remaining German-speakers in Namibia that, for the next three decades, they would not be placed in a position where they would be expected to take up arms against Germany.[2]

Territorial security was the province of the police, for the terms of the League of Nations mandate forbade the militarization of the territory. The local administration of the territory had no responsibility for the defense of Namibia; that remained a South African prerogative until 1989.[3] Beginning in 1919, the territory had its own police force even though it fell under the authority of the South African Police (SAP). Two years later, however, there was an administrative change that shifted responsibility for that force to the administrator of the territory. Even though the civil services of both South Africa and Namibia were merged in 1923, the police forces were kept separate. Indeed, the South African Government lacked authority to dispatch members of its own police force to Namibia until legislation (the Police [South-West Africa] Act) combining the two police forces was passed in 1939. That act (Police [South-West Africa] Act) further provided that South Africa would subsidize the territorial police budget in order to expand the size of the Namibian police contingent, which Pretoria regarded as too small for the size of the country.[4] At the time, the territorial police strength was 231 officers and men, which was augmented by 100 more policemen.[5]

The Hertzog Government dispatched heavily armed SAP reinforcements to Windhoek in 1939 to stabilize what British authorities had cautioned South Africa was a volatile political situation in Europe. Justice Minister Smuts feared that the local Germans, impressed by events in Sudetenland, might attempt a *Putsch* on Hitler's birthday in April. Later archival research has shown that he overreacted to events in the territory.[6] During the Second World War, a number of South African policemen volunteered for duty with the Union Defense Force (UDF, as the SADF was called at the time), while others belonged to subversive groups that attempted to undermine the Allied war effort.[7]

During the League of Nations era, the authorities in Namibia turned to their local police officers in order to contain potential or actual violence, which occurred twice, much to the embarrassment of the administration. The first instance, in 1922, concerned the Bondelswarts group of the Nama people in the south of the territory, while the second, in 1924, concerned the mixed race community at Rehoboth. The former had been formidable foes of the Germans early in this century, while the latter sometimes identified with the Germans. In both cases, the South Africans supplemented local police forces with military aircraft from the Union Defense Force (UDF), and each group was coerced into submission.[8] Once the Second World War began, the territory provided both a harbor and airfield — at Walvis Bay and Rooikop (in the Walvis Bay enclave) — for UDF units concerned principally with anti-submarine patrols in the South Atlantic Ocean.[9] To a limited extent it also furnished white and African soldiers for the UDF,[10] including a future Namibian cabinet minister who was tried for treason in Pretoria shortly after the outbreak of the war of independence.[11]

When the Namibian war of independence began at Ongulumbashe on 26 August 1966, the South African response came from the SAP and not from the SADF. Peter Stiff has revealed that several SADF officers, quickly and secretly deputized as SAP members, participated in Operation Blue Wildebeeste, as the attack on Ongulumbashe was termed.[12] Of the forty-seven members participating in that attack, eight were from the SADF, another eight (helicopter pilots) from the South African Air Force (SAAF), thirty from the SAP, and one African informer.[13]

During the 1960s the SADF developed a plan for the defense of the territory as part of Operation Plan Olympus.[14] Although it was not until 1 April 1973 that the SADF took over border security responsibilities from the SAP in Namibia,[15] the SADF and the air force had a small presence in northern Namibia (at Katima Mulilo, Ondangwa, and Rundu) since 1968.[16] In 1968, some SAAF members in Operation *Dikmelk* (Curds and Whey) were dispatched to the Caprivi Zipfel, where they handled electronic warfare, monitoring SWAPO radio transmissions.[17] In addition, in 1967 several SADF members served as SAP members in Ondangua.[18]

There were three reasons why the early years of the war were handled primarily by the Police Force. First, there was a public relations and symbolic element involved in that battle, which the Pretoria regime could portray as one between law and order types and criminal elements,[19] which would tend (in the South African view) to delegitimize the opposition. This would signal that the event was not particularly threatening or significant. There was a Western precedent for this semantic gambit. Even though it was conventional wisdom that "Acknowledging ... unrest as an insurgency confers a politically important element of legitimacy on the opposition," it needs to be emphasized that "such recognition is a de facto admission that something was terribly wrong with the polity — perhaps fatally so."[20] However, the use of such techniques in the counterinsurgency (COIN) repertoire can be dysfunctional in terms of analyzing the nature, strengths, and weaknesses of the insurgents.[21] Following the independence of Namibia, the pejorative terms South African commentators used were often replaced by the more neutral term of insurgent[22] or by a raft of terms that acknowledged the protean character of previously used phrases. As a retired SADF major who served in the elite 1 Reconnaissance Regiment pithily observed in his memoirs, "Depending [upon] who you are and against who[m] you fight either makes you a terrorist, a freedom fighter, a rebel, a dissident, a guer[r]illa or a comrade."[23]

Second, the SADF was not well trained at that time in the intelligence aspect of COIN; it lacked an intelligence network, although the SAP had developed one.[24] One of those police officers, Major General Johannes Dreyer, subsequently created the counter-insurgency unit within the SAP known as *Koevoet*.[25] It was conventional wisdom in COIN doctrine at that time, particularly in British circles, to regard police forces as the principal instruments in the suppression of insurgencies.[26] However, Kevin A. O'Brien observed that the SAP contributed to COIN practices, especially those they learned in Southern Rhodesia, while the SADF handled the theoretical aspects of the doctrine.[27] The South Africans could also point to the terms of the mandate agreement which forbade the militarization of the territory, so that the utilization of the territorial police, rather than the military, could be seen as yet another illustration of Pretoria's adherence to the terms of the mandate agreement.[28]

Third, it was one thing to dispatch the SAP to Namibia, as General Smuts had done in 1939, but it was quite another to send the SADF. The changeover from the outward, Commonwealth oriented Smuts Government to the more regionally oriented Malan Government did not necessarily mean that South Africa had renounced its well-known territorial ambitions; rather, it scaled them back and continued to think in terms of defense cooperation with the United Kingdom, the dominant colonial power in southern and eastern Africa. The essential idea was to move the defense perimeter as far north as allies, capabilities, and the parliament would permit. In this context, it is important to realize, as a veteran South African diplomat observed, "Parliament played no role in foreign policy and the role of the Cabinet tended to be limited to acquiesance or approval."[29] Seaward defense would be an Anglo–South African task that was institutionalized in the Simonstown Agreement, which enabled the South African Navy to enlarge and modernize its fleet while granting the Royal Navy generous facilities at Simonstown, the naval base near Cape Town.[30]

In the 1960s, however, the decolonization perimeter moved southward, and independence wars broke out in adjoining Mozambique and Angola, thus underscoring the need for a line of defense to protect South Africa from such threatening conflict, which would place the white-ruled political system at risk. There was a limited degree of South African–Portuguese defense cooperation in Angola.[31] This cooperation was conducted in a highly secret manner, was tightly controlled by the Portuguese, and was primarily in the logistical and air force support areas.[32] The South African Air Force occasionally furnished support to the Southern Rhodesian forces.[33] From the parliamentary perspective, however, the 1974 South African expedition into Angola demonstrated the extent to which Parliament had been marginalized in the foreign policy process. Executive control over Parliament, particularly in terms of keeping MPs informed about the activities of the SADF in Angola, was ever so obvious,[34] particularly when non–South African journalists were able to reveal the details of military operations.[35] The executive went to Parliament, as it had done *post hoc* 1939 for the SAP in Namibia,[36] to secure greater flexibility in dispatching troops where they were needed. The enabling defense legislation in 1976 meant that the executive, following the advice of the military establishment, could draw or redraw South African defense perimeters, with all that that legally implied for South African servicemen.[37] Considerable SADF conscript combat deaths also proved to be politically unacceptable to the white South African electorate in the latter days of the Namibian war.[38]

Mustering the Military Manpower

Recruiting the manpower for a military establishment raises profound questions concerning the nature of a citizen's duties to the state, especially in time of war. Civic duties and civic exemptions are core matters when a state utilizes an involuntary system of induction into its military forces.[39] In the South African case, there was a strongly nurtured tradition among the Afrikaner population of citizen participation in the armed forces, which acquired an international reputation for their fighting prowess against the British forces in the First (1880) and Second (1899–1902) Anglo-Boer Wars. Yet this Afrikaner civil-military tradition[40] usually seemed to have no place for the conscientious objector, although The Dutch Reformed Church seemed to accept such a position when it came to the 1914 Rebellion and to the Second World War.[41] Even though Africans were sometimes armed in the 1899–1902 Anglo-Boer War, the Afrikaners were leery about arming African auxiliaries.[42] After the close of the second Anglo-Boer War, some Afrikaners did choose a military career, especially in the land forces, and fought on the British side in the First and Second World Wars. The military establishment remained small, however, and much of its leadership gradually shifted into Afrikaner hands after the 1948 general election.[43]

As it began to include more Afrikaners in the upper echelons, the SADF began to assume a more prominent role within the state structure of South Africa. Not only did its budget increase but also it expanded its size by taking in more recruits and by increasing the length of service for the recruits. In addition, it came to rely upon an extensive reserve and mobilization structure, which was anchored in a permanent cadre of officers and non-commissioned officers. This meant that more and more of white South African society were exposed to the rigors of military training and reserve duty. Only very rarely, though, was the SADF used in any type of combat role until the Portuguese withdrawal from Angola. In a few instances it was used as a second line of defense behind the SAP in domestic turbulence involving Africans so that it was not quite as visible as the SAP in terms of institutional support of apartheid.[44] Until 1980, Namibia itself had little in the way of its own armed forces.[45]

When it moved into the combat mode, the SADF confronted two perennial problems that other armies often faced in similar circumstances. The first was how to enlarge the manpower pool in such a way as to minimize the disruption that would cause to employers, a difficulty which plagued the white Rhodesian government as well.[46] The second, complementary challenge was to increase the size of the military forces without engendering citizen hostility to conscription, a problem that earlier faced the Portuguese[47] as well as the Americans in their Vietnam War.[48] To meet the increasing demands for military manpower, the initial response was to lengthen the period of obligation for military service by stretching out the reserve obligation. In this way, the bulk of the military establishment would be non-career personnel who would go through an active tour of duty and a reserve tour of duty.

Nevertheless, based on the American experience, particularly in Vietnam, there are two additional considerations that the current literature on the SADF has yet to address. First, to what extent was there a disconnect between social stratification in the relevant age group of the white male population and military service, particularly combat duty? In the American case, the Vietnam War has been viewed as a blue-collar burden involving the less privileged males.[49] Secondly, to what extent did the sons of the elite, especially the Afrikaner political elite, serve in the SADF, especially in combat roles, during the Namibian War of Independence? Stated differently, was there much evidence of *noblesse oblige* with regard to military and combat service among the more privileged male groups in the apartheid society? Such a question is part of the ongoing dialogue on civic-military responsibility in the United States since the development of an all-volunteer force after the end of the Vietnam War.[50]

Moreover, the SADF made limited use of women volunteers,[51] a policy which the Smuts Government had used in the Second World War.[52] Yet stretching out the limited pool of white men, supplemented by a small number of white women, would still be costly and add to the public payroll. In due course, the regime cautiously began to recruit Africans, thereby reverting to an earlier policy the UDF used in both world wars. The principal difference, however, was that the National Party Government went beyond what the Botha and Smuts Governments had undertaken in the First and Second World Wars, respectively.

As I noted earlier, there were certain political and cultural restraints within Afrikaner political culture against the wholesale arming of Africans, although there had been exceptions to this from time to time. The combat arms units and naval and air components of the UDF were white preserves, but Africans could be a part of support units, undertaking tasks that would not directly pit them against the enemy. Such a policy would tend to minimize subsequent African claims for greater civic rights as a *quid pro quo* for military service. The United States armed forces, at least until the advent of the Korean War, could be said to have elements of such a restrictive civil-military policy.[53] In 1974, the South Africans, drawing upon the principles of apartheid, began to organize ethnically distinct military units in Namibia to shoulder the burdens of war.[54] The SADF dispatched a Colored (mixed-race) unit, the first South African Cape Corps to the Namibian border area in 1975, followed by another one in 1976. In 1978 it sent a company from the 21 Battalion (an African unit) there as well. In its 1988 comparative study of black and white units stationed in Namibia, the SADF reported that it was impressed with the performance, as well as the morale and discipline, of the black soldiers.[55] Such a policy bore a striking resemblance to the Africanization of the Portuguese counterinsurgency forces that had a nominally different attitude to race relations.[56]

One of the most unusual of such military formations was formed from the San (termed Bushmen by many), quite a number of whom were refugees from Angola. This unit was garrisoned in the Caprivi Strip and its Basarwa were highly regarded as trackers.[57] Their recruitment caused concern among several anthropologists,[58] and in 1980 the neighboring Botswana Government enacted legislation forbidding their own nationals from serving in foreign armies without permission of the president.[59] Such legislation may not have been especially effective or stringent because, ironically, beginning in 1987, the Botswana Defense Force (BDF) began to employ some of their San citizens who had served as SADF trackers; the BDF utilized them as trackers for the anti-poaching operations.[60]

Such units functioned as subcontractors for the SADF in some respects, and when they were combined with comparable white units raised in Namibia, they suggested local responsibility for local defense. It also entailed shifting some of the burdens of warfare from white to black soldiers, an argument also heard in the United States at the time it shifted to an all-volunteer force.[61] The development of an indigenous force, the South West Africa Territorial Force (SWATF), raised the nettlesome international legal issue of sovereignty over the territory. Not only had the United Nations General Assembly declared the League of Nations mandate to be at an end and the United Nations to be the sole administrator of the territory[62] but also the International Court had delivered an advisory opinion indicating that South Africa was illegally occupying the territory.[63]

These declarations would tend to undercut the legitimacy of the South African presence in Namibia and serve to cast doubt upon its right to institute conscription in the territory. On 7 October 1980 the South African president published proclamation AG 198, which modified Section 2 of the Defense Act no. 44 of 1957, thereby making Namibian Africans liable for military service. Prior to that time, only Namibian whites were subject to the draft. Subsequently, three affected Namibian Africans (Eric Binga, Alfons Kotjipati, and Edward Amporo) challenged this conscription. The first case (of Eric Binga) went before the territorial Supreme Court in 1983, which upheld the legality of the conscription. The Appeals Court in Bloemfontein then took the Binga case, and in 1988 it too validated the conscription policy. Even though challenges by the other two plaintiffs before the Supreme Court in Windhoek were similarly unsuccessful, not one of the three was ever conscripted.[64]

In practice, however, the authorities were aware of the political proclivities of many Namibians and did not push SWATF recruitment in the northern areas,[65] thereby tacitly acknowledging that these areas were a catchment area for PLAN. This conscription policy had the side effect of alienating younger Namibian males, many of whom chose to leave school early (before reaching the age of sixteen) to avoid registration for SWATF at school.[66] Both SWAPO and the Namibian Council of Churches denounced conscription in Namibia.[67] However, SWAPO benefited from the exodus of these students, who could then be recruited for duty in PLAN.[68]

Indeed, at one point late in the war, a number of SWATF troops were discharged for disciplinary problems, which some observers chose to describe as mutiny.[69] Other observers disagreed.[70] The Southern Rhodesian armed forces also experienced similar difficulties when, in the latter stages of their counterinsurgency war, they attempted to conscript Rhodesian Africans.[71] In the 1954–1962 Algerian war, the French army was able to recruit a considerable number of local Algerians, known as *harkis*, to serve in an auxiliary capacity. After the Algerian Liberation Front emerged as the dominant political force as a result of the negotiated independence, the *harkis* suffered severe retribution at the hands of their erstwhile enemies and received negligible help from the French.[72]

More corrosive of South African legitimacy, however, was the reaction of the white community in South Africa itself. Elements of the Afrikaner community had been outspoken in their denunciation of the First and Second World Wars, regarding them as British undertakings that simply made use of South African manpower to achieve British war aims. There are some parallels with the Quebecquois, who were also alienated by Canadian participation in the world wars.[73] Once they had taken charge of the government and shaped the UDF more to their liking, the Afrikaner government did accept the practice of conscientious objection in the 1957 defense legislation.[74] In general, conscientious objection was associated with the Anglophone churches.[75] As the bush war in Namibia dragged on and military obligations became more onerous, especially to South African university students, hostility toward conscription began to surface and became institutionalized in the End Conscription Campaign (ECC). Using recently declassified archival materials, Merran W. Phillips has provided a detailed analysis of this organization.[76] The ECC, which was created in 1983, appealed more to the English-speaking, rather than to the Afrikaans-speaking, students, and it represented a challenge to the SADF and its manpower policies.[77] It did extend its operations into Namibia, where a branch was established in Katatura, the African township section of Windhoek.[78] Not unexpectedly, the Military Intelligence operators developed and handsomely funded a front organization, Veterans for Victory, to act as a check against the ECC and also to infiltrate the ECC.[79] The ECC was finally banned in 1988.[80]

Strategic Considerations

South African military strategy with respect to Namibia was implicitly linked with the maintenance of the prevailing political system, which meant that the armed forces would be fashioned and utilized in a manner that would maintain the traditional racial hierarchy within the country. These racial attitudes and expectations of white privilege were deeply rooted and not merely the novel creation of the Afrikaner nationalists who fashioned the apartheid system beginning in 1948. Such notions, which were subsumed under what has been termed a social contract between the state and especially the poorer sections of white South African society, were prevalent among the volunteers in the UDF during Prime Minister Smuts' leadership during the Second World War.[81] Indeed, during that war, a very large proportion (estimated at between 50 per cent and 70 per cent) of the ground forces were Afrikaners.[82]

Deon Fourie[83] and Leopold Scholtz,[84] who have been associated with South African universities and the SADF, have provided useful analyses of South African military strategy for Namibia. This strategy included three civil-military principles. The first is that the territory was regarded by the South African leadership as part of the greater South African realm, and that basically meant that internal and external threats to the territory would be treated as though Namibia were part of South Africa for defensive purposes.[85] Indeed, the 1957 Defense Act covered the territory of South West Africa.[86] Both African and white Namibians served in various parts of the UDF during the Second World War,[87] with the returning white veterans receiving far more benefits than their African fellow soldiers.[88] However, I have not been able to ascertain how many whites from the territory served in South African units during this war. Secondly, South African rhetoric underscored the

League of Nations mandate prohibitions about the demilitarization of the territory long after the Pretoria authorities claimed that the mandate was no longer in effect.[89] Thirdly, the defense of the Namibian realm was primarily a police responsibility and the defense force would only be used when the police lacked the manpower or special expertise and weapons inventory to meet the challenge.

With respect to the first two points, Rodney C. Warwick has utilized declassified SADF documents to suggest that South African threat perceptions underlay SADF concerns in the 1960s that the United Nations would be able to muster sufficient military force to invade South Africa. Although the SADF planners' perceptions of such an invasion were not especially realistic in terms of multinational military power projections, they nevertheless prepared contingency plans that entailed the strengthening of the defenses of Walvis Bay, notwithstanding the mandate prohibitions concerning militarization.[90]

In addition to the underlying racial factor in South African strategy for the territory there was also, after 1949, a supplementary political ramification that resembles the pre-independence Algerian case.[91] By virtue of the South West Africa Affairs Amendment Act no. 23 of 1949, the white community in Namibia was represented in both houses of parliament in Cape Town. I have not been able to locate any scholarly studies on the legislative behavior of the Namibian M.P.s and Senators in the bicameral South African Parliament in Cape Town. The Namibian parliamentarians were members of the National Party, and it is probable that their territorial political agendas were not seriously at odds with those of the larger party, which had to accommodate the views prevalent in the four provinces of South Africa. This calls for further research.

The white community had no such representation during the League of Nations mandate period, although its members requested that right at the first congress of the National Party on 22 September 1924.[92] The Pretoria regime did not seriously consider the matter until 1946 when Prime Minister Smuts held discussions with the two white territorial political parties on this and other matters.[93] Paul S. van der Merwe, who served as an M.P. from Namibia and became deputy speaker of the House of Assembly, has examined this topic.[94] Once they secured parliamentary access to the corridors of power in Cape Town, they became legitimated stakeholders in South African domestic politics and could advance or defend their interests with greater ease, not wholly unlike the French residents of Algeria with respect to the French National Assembly.

Namibia was dependent upon South Africa for its defense needs, and its own territorial government had no authority of its own to develop and implement any defense policy, which continued to be a constitutional prerogative of South Africa. Only with the creation of the SWATF in 1977 could Namibia be said to participate in its own defense. It took roughly three years, however, for the SWATF to become operational, that is, from July 1977 until August 1980.[95] Not only did the commanding officer of SWATF simultaneously function as the commanding officer of all SADF units serving in Namibia,[96] South Africa also paid for the SWATF.[97] The overwhelming majority of the soldiers in SWATF were from non-white inhabitants of Namibia,[98] which would be politically significant in terms of the racial mix of combat fatalities in the Namibian theater of operations. By the end of the war, about seventy per cent of the ground troops facing PLAN were from the SWATF,[99] while roughly thirty-five percent of one of component units of

SWATF, namely, the 101 Battalion (from Ovamboland), were former PLAN members whom the South Africans had turned.[100]

The conventional wisdom about the strategy for the defense of Namibia (and of South Africa as well) was initially premised on an extensive buffering perimeter which included white minority governments on the borders of both the territory and the metropole, that is, particularly Angola in the north, Rhodesia in the northeast, and Mozambique in the east.[101] This would afford some spatial protection against land-based attacks (which could include medium-range air support), allowing some lead-time for mobilization. Seaward defense was a matter of coastal and harbor protection and detection, some of which could be handled by aerial and electronic surveillance (through the Silvermine center near Simonstown). As the arms embargo tightened, the navy's blue-water capabilities and missions were drastically reduced.[102] Nevertheless, the navy did participate in counterinsurgency warfare.[103]

Two of the three major the SADF missions were territorial expressions of South Africa's regime structure, that is, protection against internal Black protest, fighting a major conventional war against foreign military foe on South African territory, and the countering of border infiltration.[104] Over time the last two missions segued, and South Africa was faced with an extraterritorial conventional war within Angola that was waged as part of a counterinsurgency war within Namibia. The common thread in these two wars was quite clear, namely, carrying the war into the enemy's territory, thereby (at least temporarily) securing the rear echelon of the metropole. Pieter W. Botha, as Defense Minister, expressed the matter pithily on 2 June 1978 when, in commenting on Operation Reindeer (which entailed the controversial 1978 attack on Cassinga, Angola), he observed that "we do not want war on our soil, and we therefore want to stop the enemy before he comes over our borders."[105]

Military Training and Doctrine

Counterinsurgency doctrine, in the sense of an organized body of knowledge imparted to military personnel that is often revised by combat experience and that receives the imprimatur of the highest echelons of the military establishment, tended to be an informal matter within the South African Defense Force until the 1960s. I have uncovered no evidence that the South African Defense Force intellectuals utilized the German counterinsurgency campaign in Namibia as even a negative lesson, even though there are some comments in the classic British primer on counterinsurgency war.[106]

Although the record seems rather incomplete, there is evidence that several South African police officers did receive some instruction in counterinsurgency from the French in Algeria. The best-known example is Theunis J. ("Rooi Rus") Swanepoel, one of the security police officers who participated in the 1966 attack on the PLAN camp at Ongulumbashe,[107] who was also regarded as one of the principal torturers of the Namibian prisoners in the Tuhadeleni case.[108] The South African military establishment was quite taken with the doctrinal writings of the French general, André Beaufre.[109] His work, however, was in the strategic, rather than in the counterinsurgency, field.[110] Two South African Defense Force officers acted as observers in the Algerian campaign. According to Alom

Peled, Lt. Gen. C. A. Fraser "spent several weeks in Algeria on various occasions observing the French attempts to squash the FLN tactics."[111] The South African journalist, Brian Pottinger, reported that, General Magnus Malan "served briefly on secondment with the French Army in Algeria."[112]

Indeed, it was the South African military attaché in Paris, C.A. ("Pop") Fraser, who introduced the work of Beaufre to the South African strategic community. Fraser, in turn, published a significant tract in the 1960s, *Lessons Learned from Past Revolutionary Wars*, which made a significant impression on SADF officers.[113] South African soldier-diplomat in Luanda, Brigadier Kaas van der Waals, kept abreast of Portuguese military policy in Angola[114] and also took part in the 1966 Operation Blue Wildebeeste against PLAN in Ongulumbashe.[115] General Jannie Geldenhuys also served as Vice-Consul in Luanda before being posted to Windhoek on 1970.[116]

The South African officer corps had access to both British and U.S. military institutions, and it is known that some members of this group attended specialized or command courses in the United States. For example, Colonel Jan D. Breytenbach, who is credited with planning the 1966 attack on the PLAN base at Ongulumbashe, spent nearly a year at an (unspecified) officer's course at Fort Benning, Georgia (a U.S. Army infantry center) in 1963–1964.[117] Another officer, General Magnus Malan, who later became Minister of Defense, attended the U.S. Army Command and General Staff College at Fort Leavenworth, Kansas.[118] Yet another, the Director-General of Civil Affairs for the SADF, Major General Phil Pretorius, attended a specialist course at the Special Warfare School at Fort Bragg, North Carolina.[119] Even though General Georg Meiring, who later became the General Officer Commanding in Namibia from 1983 to 1987, received advanced military training in the United Kingdom,[120] SADF officers were no longer accepted at British officer staff schools after 1961.[121] Interestingly enough, however, Lieutenant General C.A. Fraser did take part in the British counterinsurgency campaign in Malaya.[122]

Members of the elite special forces received training in France in 1970.[123] Moreover, several other SADF members trained with the Rhodesian SAS (Special Air Service) in 1967.[124] In addition, it appears that SADF personnel were able to serve as observers of U.S. Army operations in Vietnam, although this was done in an unobtrusive fashion, perhaps through the back channels of the Central Intelligence Agency.[125] The Israeli Defense Force not only provided instruction in counterinsurgency warfare[126] but also trained South Africans in the development of doctrine for its armored units,[127] in-flight refueling skills,[128] and military planning in the South African Army College.[129] In 1967 the Military Academy added guerrilla warfare to its military history curriculum, and by 1970 the topic became compulsory subject for entry-level cadets.[130] COIN training began in the SAP in 1967, and the SADF introduced such instruction in 1968.[131]

In practical terms, however, Rhodesia served as the training ground in counterinsurgency for the South African Air Force,[132] for both SAP and SADF communications specialists[133] as well as Special Forces members.[134] The SAP sent by far the larger number of members from 1967 to 1975, on the grounds that South Africa was fighting South African insurgents from the African National Congress (ANC) who were tactically allied to the Zimbabwean guerrillas.[135] Even though the performance of some members of the SAP contingent was lackluster,[136] the experience in Rhodesia, particularly with the elite Selous Scouts units that had acquired a reputation for deadly efficiency,[137] provided a basis for the subsequent formation of a comparable SAP organization called *Koevoet* that had an equally chilling reputation.[138] The South African Government helped to fund the Selous Scouts.[139]

Counterinsurgency, as a topic and doctrine, featured in South African military and police instruction, yet the South African military establishment seemed more interested in the practice, rather than the theory, of this type of warfare.[140] SADF officers were keen on the published work of Lt. Col. John J. McCuen of the U.S. Army, *The Art of Counter-Revolutionary War: The Strategy of Counter-insurgency*.[141] Morgan Norval, a former U.S. Marine and military journalist, claimed that McCuen's book "became the bible of the South African counterinsurgency campaign in Namibia."[142] Another favorite author was the British specialist, Sir Robert Thompson,[143] and they were especially interested in the post–World War II guerrilla war in Vietnam.[144]

This was a marked contrast to the earlier South African Afrikaner experience because the higher-ranking Boer officers in the 1899–1902 lacked any formal military training,[145] and yet their style of guerrilla warfare impressed their British foes. An American military historian has observed that even the British had what he termed "historical amnesia" about counterinsurgency doctrine until the time of the post–World War II Malaysian emergency.[146] The military intellectual, it seems, was not held in extremely high esteem in the SADF,[147] and more intellectual effort appears to have been invested in the more encompassing doctrine of total strategy.

This omnibus doctrine, explaining the nature of the threat against South Africa (and Namibia), labeled the "total onslaught," was the intellectual capstone of strategic doctrine. It drew upon Beaufre's work and enjoyed considerable civilian patronage,[148] but it certainly had its critics.[149] This concept could be compared, in some ways, with the antecedent French notion of *la guerre révolutionaire* (revolutionary war), which was equally mesmerized and repelled by Marxist-Leninist-Maoist thought and practice.[150] Both notions suggest the South African and French "penchant for creating self-enclosed universes of ideas, for translating insights into mystiques."[151] Nevertheless, if one accepts the perspective of the late Dr. Bernard B. Fall, an acknowledged expert on Vietnam, that revolutionary war includes both the guerrilla warfare/small war military dimension and a political dimension,[152] then certainly SWAPO and PLAN were waging a revolutionary war. According to Kevin A. O'Brien, in 1985 the South Africans made a lexical shift and moved from COIN to what has been termed counter-revolutionary warfare.[153]

A particularly nettlesome issue in the conduct of warfare, especially in counterinsurgency operations, is the conduct of the soldiers in the field. Counterinsurgency warfare in Namibia has been termed "the dirty war,"[154] perhaps implying that such warfare is "dirtier" than other, more traditional types of battle. Such a label was intimated by Alf A. Haggoy's prescient observation that "counterinsurgent forces" need to "appear to be angels while fighting a dirty war."[155] Although this perception may not be widely shared or accepted by the military, it does direct attention to the significance of the psychological aspects of the well-known policy of winning hearts and minds (WHAM) in such warfare, which rests on the premise that control of, or the tacit support of much of, the population is the focal point of the war. Consequently, torture and atrocities or even mere thoughtless behavior undercut the benign policy of winning hearts and minds, as stressed by Lt. General Constand Viljoen in a 1976 address to members of the Durban Light Infantry stationed at Oshaskati, Namibia.[156] It is advantageous to the counterinsurgent to eliminate, or at least minimize and even punish, such counterproductive behavior. As the investigations of Donald H. Foster and his colleagues have demonstrated, torture became an extremely significant issue in South Africa and Namibia.[157]

In the South African case, the SADF maintained an ethnology unit, employing primarily Afrikaner anthropologists, as part of its civic action program. By 1977, the SADF had sixteen permanent anthropologists in its employ to assist it in its various winning hearts and minds campaigns, and in that year it issued an ethnology booklet for the troops.[158] There, is, however, some doubt whether the use of anthropologists had a continuous and beneficial effect upon troop behavior.[159] The U.S. Army recently turned to anthropologists in the course of its COIN warfare in Afghanistan,[160] but doubt remains about both the wisdom and the ethics of such a practice.[161] J. A. Visser has provided the official view of the SADF's civic action program, especially in the northern reaches of Namibia,[162] while an American naval officer[163] and a noted American expert on the SADF[164] have provided alternative explanations. A later thoughtful analysis, based on archival research and interviews, found that South African WHAM was not an unqualified success.[165] Such programs need not only to be implemented in the early stages of an insurgency but also to be continuous in the delivery of services and must avoid undercutting economic opportunities for local inhabitants.[166] The mere existence of such a program can be construed as evidence of previous socioeconomic neglect and the absence of widespread benefits under the separate development policy of the Pretoria and Windhoek regimes. For example, Robert J. Gordon reported that SADF did undertake civic action among the Bushmen, many of whom served as trackers for the SADF.[167] In this sense, it could be viewed as one of the ironies of counterinsurgency.

Moreover, the African women, particularly in Ovamboland, were able to thwart the intentions of WHAM by providing numerous types of aid and comfort, including intelligence reports, to PLAN guerrillas transiting their areas.[168] No more graphic illustration of the juxtaposition of territory and population loyalty approaches can be found than in the postwar interchange between the two protagonists, Dirk Mudge, leader of the Democratic Turnhalle Alliance (DTA), and his parliamentary opponent. The former asserted that "Swapo never controlled one square inch of this country."[169] This elicited the SWAPO counter-claim that "It is not correct to claim that we never controlled an inch of this country.... We did not use the geographic but a demographic map in our calculation when we were choosing our priorities. We controlled the hearts and minds of our own people."[170]

In the aftermath of the First World War, the British issued a well known Blue Book which reviewed German colonial policy in Namibia and drew attention to unacceptable German civil and military conduct in the territory; the Namibian nationalists and their supporters often cited this document when constructing their case against white minority rule.[171] On two separate occasions, in 1986 and 1988, the president of South Africa granted indemnity to soldiers for acts committed in Namibia, thereby quashing a murder trial and angering the president of the Bar Council of Namibia.[172] The South African minister of justice had invoked these powers in 1984 to terminate litigation to secure the release of Namibian internees in the Mariental detention center.[173] A similar indemnity was extended to South African security forces in the final days of South African rule by the administrator-general of the territory acting apparently within the framework developed by the United Nations for the transition to independence rather than the customary Article 103 ter of the 1957 Defense Act.[174] This proclamation meant that a SADF physician, Dr. Wouter Basson, who was alleged to have murdered two hundred SWAPO detainees by poisonous injections, would not be tried in South Africa on these charges.[175] As Gary F. Baines has suggested, "a culture of impunity" has surrounded South African security legislation and personnel.[176]

Given the close ties that insurgents attempt to develop with the population in order to secure intelligence about the movements and equipment of the enemy, conceal arms caches, rest, and find food, it is common practice for the counterinsurgent forces to blunt or to anticipate such links by arranging to move population groups out of the way, thus depriving their opponents of such succor, shelter, and intelligence. Population resettlement as a technique of counterinsurgency warfare dates back at least to the time of the Spanish repression of the Cuban insurrection in the late nineteenth century.[177] In 1976 the SADF created a one-kilometer wide and sixteen hundred meters long free-fire zone along the Namibian-Angolan border, which resulted in the eviction of the residents living there.[178] The Angolan-Namibian border was also called the cutline, one kilometer south of which was a road known as the Timo Line. The cleared area between the cutline and the Timo Line was termed the Yati Strip, which was closed to all except the military.[179] This, in turn, led to a semblance of fortified villages, which were located away from nearby military encampments.[180] These villages apparently did not replicate the ones in Rhodesia, Vietnam, and in Lusophone Africa presumably because they were unwelcome reminders of the British concentration camps for the Afrikaners in the Second Anglo-Boer War.[181]

Perhaps the most controversial technique in the SADF's counterinsurgency repertoire was the extraterritorial preemptive strike primarily into Angola, which began at the time of the Portuguese evacuation of that country in 1974. There were quite a few of these military operations, each with its own title.[182] According to a high-ranking South African Air Force officer, it appears that the SADF's plans for cross-border operations needed to be cleared with the cabinet.[183] Secondarily, there were occasional retaliatory forays into Zambia, where PLAN operated for a while.[184] In the Angolan case, the SADF took the war to the rear echelon PLAN headquarters, camps, and logistical depots across the Namibian border. The purposes were essentially to disrupt headquarters operations, to capture (and often utilize) weapons as well as enemy operational plans and other intelligence documentation, to force PLAN to extend its supply line, thereby making it more vulnerable to ground and air attack, and to increase both the distance and time PLAN forces would have to travel by truck and foot from their rear to their forward bases before launching cross-border raids into Namibia.

The 4 May 1978 airborne attack on the refugee camp at Cassinga (Kassinga), Angola, codenamed Operation Reindeer, not only accomplished a number of these SADF goals at great cost to PLAN and SWAPO but also this severe setback afforded SWAPO (which termed it a massacre) a public relations bonanza that it was able to utilize to great effect.[185] Indeed, the British Council of Churches and Church Action on Namibia were able to arrange a memorial service in Westminster Abbey in London on 4 May 1988, the tenth anniversary of the attack in honor of those who perished in that SADF action.[186] Cassinga day subsequently became a public holiday in independent Namibia.[187] Perhaps the publicity generated by Cassinga attack could be compared with that connected with the April 26, 1937 (German) Condor Legion bombing of the Basque town of Guernica during the Spanish Civil War, which was the origin of Pablo Picasso's famed painting of that name. The debate over the nature of the attack as well as the nature of the target has not yet been satisfactorily resolved. Edward G. Alexander has written a rather useful South African version on this raid based upon recently declassified files.[188] His study had both a skeptical reception from the South African historian Gary F. Baines[189] as well as tacit approval from a senior American diplomatic historian.[190] Recently, an American scholar, Christian A. Williams, provided yet another interpretation, based on an on-site visit and numerous interviews.[191] The debate over the nature of the attack as well as the nature of the target has not yet been satisfactorily resolved.

With western Zambia off limits to PLAN and with UNITA (National Union for the Total Independence of Angola), an ally of the SADF, effectively blocking PLAN's access to southeastern Angola, the South Africans attempted to funnel PLAN infiltration into the Ovambo region, thereby reducing the geographic spread of their COIN operations within the borders of Namibia.[192] These activities as well as the SADF's cross-border forays into Angola suggested that not only was the SADF waging a counterinsurgency type campaign both within Namibia and Angola but also that in its Angolan operations it was ratcheting up to reach the level of conventional warfare which, from a doctrinal perspective, signifies the final stage of guerrilla warfare.[193] Paul L. Moorcraft asserted that Operation Reindeer marked the SADF's shift into what he called "semi-conventional warfare."[194]

Tank warfare with long-range artillery and air support (countered by increasingly sophisticated radar and anti-aircraft weaponry) in Angola epitomized the conventional warfare aspect of the Namibian bush war. If one adds to this inventory of weapons the frequency of various cross-border operations, the incorporation of former opponents into paramilitary or military units, and the utilization of ethnic preferences and animosities spanning borders, then one shifts from counterinsurgency warfare to what Professors Annette Seegers and André du Pisani have termed frontier warfare.[195] Although neither political scientist has fully developed this taxonomic distinction, indicating the criteria for separating the one type of warfare from the other, nevertheless it has considerable heuristic value.

International Monitoring by UNTAG

Although past studies have suggested the importance of demilitarizing an area whose population will be consulted during an internationally supervised plebiscite,[196] this precept serves as a useful point of departure for exploring the role of the SADF within the larger decolonization framework of the formal trilateral (Angolan, Cuban, and South African) arrangements for the ending of armed hostilities in Namibia and Angola. The United Nations Transition Assistance Group (known as UNTAG) was created by two United Nations Security Council resolutions (435[1978] of 29 September 1978 and 632 [1989] of 16 February 1989)[197] to monitor the shift from Namibia's colonial status to its internationally recognized independent existence during 1989 and 1990. Among its other formally designated tasks, UNTAG helped to consolidate the international legitimacy that the Namibian nationalists and their supporters had worked for over the years.

This international group was a heterogeneous entity, with sub organizations assigned military, voter registration, voter education, electoral oversight, public relations, police oversight, refugee organization and care, and military and civic security responsibilities. Some of these tasks entailed the creation of parallel organizations, alongside the bodies and personnel attached (or seconded from Pretoria) to the *de facto* ruling regime in Windhoek headed by the Administrator-General of South West Africa, who has been termed "South Africa's viceroy of Namibia."[198] The military component of UNTAG dealt with the creation of a climate of physical security and tranquility conducive to fair, transparent, and internationally monitored elections for a Constituent Assembly which would draft a constitution for the nation-to-be.[199] The UN military unit was the principal United Nations group concerned with the phased departure of the SADF from the territory to their metropole as well as with the demobilization of the local military groups, such as SWATF and various South African–sponsored citizen reserve forces. Correspondingly, a special UN task force, UNAVEM (the United Nations Angola Verification Mission), dealt with the return of Angolan-based Cuban units to Cuba over the course of twenty-seven months.[200]

Earlier in Chapter Five, I referred to PLAN's quest for a permanent base within the borders of Namibia and the ensuing firefight beginning on 1 April 1989 between those PLAN members who traversed the international boundary between Angola and Namibia and their opposite numbers in the South West African Police counterinsurgency unit known as *Koevoet*. This proved especially embarrassing to Mr. Martti Ahtisaari, the United Nations Secretary-General's special representative in Namibia, because he authorized the South African authorities to release their armed force, which had been confined to their bases, to staunch the cross-border incursion by fully armed PLAN soldiers.[201] The United Nations military component had not fully deployed in the northern regions of Namibia on that date and thus was both ill equipped and ill positioned to check this southward probe by PLAN forces.

Moreover, the SWAPO leadership failed to prepare a contingency plan to deal with the late arrival and deployment of UNTAG military units.[202] Had SWAPO had such a plan the fatal clash probably might not have occurred or, at worst, have been less sanguinary. According to Peter Stiff, a total of 312 PLAN soldiers, twenty *Koevoet* members, and five SADF soldiers — a total of 337 — lost their lives in this 1–9 April 1989 battle.[203] He claimed that *Koevoet*, rather than the SADF, handled the bulk of the small unit combat operations, while SADF undertook supporting air operations in this final campaign.[204] Stiff tended to present the South African case with skill,[205] and he argued that "nothing in this book was ever subjected to any form of censorship."[206] Nevertheless, a scholarly assessment of the April battle that presents the SWAPO/PLAN view of this battle with as much attention to detail has yet to appear.

If one accepts Leopold Scholtz's contention that this war was "an attempt to win enough time to create the conditions in which Swapo would lose an election,"[207] then one can focus on SADF activities in Namibia following the skirmishes of April, 1989. Such activities were less obtrusive than those of the *Koevoet*, which attracted adverse international attention, particularly the Africa subcommittee of the United States House of

Representatives.[208] As I pointed out in Chapter Five, *Koevoet* behavior also prompted two separate rebukes by the United Nations Security Council. It insisted that the South Africans disband this disruptive and frightening paramilitary police organization as part of the entire demobilization sequence that preceded the elections for the Constituent Assembly. Rather than treat the ensemble of UNTAG-SADF relationships, it is more apposite in this chapter to examine the clandestine work of the military intelligence (MI) branch of the SADF in Namibia during the run up to the 1989 Constituent Assembly election. The overall objective of this branch was to promote anti–SWAPO domestic political parties, especially the Democratic Turnhalle Alliance (DTA), and to denigrate and embarrass SWAPO, thereby thwarting SWAPO's chances of obtaining a two-thirds majority in the Assembly. Such a hegemonic majority was necessary in the Constituent Assembly for SWAPO to fashion the independence constitution without having to compromise with any competing parties.[209]

On 1 April 1989, the very day that fighting broke out between PLAN and *Koevoet* along the Angolan-Namibian border before the UNTAG military units were fully deployed and operational, the United Nations put into effect a 1982 agreement known as the impartiality package that terminated all United Nations financial flows to SWAPO.[210] This agreement, which the Secretary-General did not make public until 23 January 1989, was only published on 16 May 1989, after the April skirmish.[211] The South African regime had consistently and persistently registered its complaint that the United Nations was palpably biased in favor of SWAPO, which had enjoyed its patronage, privileges, and financial support. In effect, the South Africans insisted on a level playing field before they would come to any final agreement about a United Nations–supervised election. However, SWAPO was rather upset about this United Nations policy,[212] that it dubbed "a gentleman's agreement."[213] The impartiality issue has only been marginally covered in the literature.[214]

After Namibia had achieved independence, the South African Foreign Minister Pik Botha openly admitted in mid–1991 that South Africa had funneled a considerable sum of money to SWAPO's opponents in the 1989 Constituent Assembly elections.[215] Peter Stiff indicated that the amount spent was roughly R 100 million.[216] Later, the South African Truth and Reconciliation Commission drew attention to this secret South African funding of SWAPO's opponents in the 1989 Constituent Assembly elections.[217] This revelation led to a full-scale debate in the Namibian National Assembly on the propriety of foreign funding of political parties in the new nation. Not unexpectedly, the Namibian Prime Minister Hage Geingob expressed his deepest displeasure at what he regarded as an egregious South African breach of the impartiality package agreement. In his view, "the United Nations was to stop any support for Swapo, and South Africa [would end support] to any of the internal parties."[218]

Yet the actual text of the 24 September 1982 agreement, which the United Nations Secretary-General sent to the General Assembly in May, 1989, made no explicit reference to South African (public or private) funding,[219] so it is likely that SWAPO assumed that there was to be equivalence between the two major opponents. The language of the Secretary-General's cover letter was sufficiently ambiguous enough to have permitted SWAPO to make such an inference.[220] The logic of the SWAPO position appears to be that it would have secured a two-thirds majority of the seats in the Constituent Assembly had South Africa refrained from funding SWAPO's electoral opponents.[221] Instead, it won

41 of the 72 seats in the Constituent Assembly, which were seven seats short of a majority.[222] Their interpretation of the impartiality clause would seem to legitimize funding for the opposing parties from sources other than the United Nations, on the one hand, and South Africa, on the other hand.[223] Consequently, opposing parties would then have to seek out a wide range of willing, affluent patrons — no easy task, by any means. Only five patron nations were singled out in this debate, namely, Germany, Ghana, Sweden, Switzerland, and the United Kingdom.[224] This condonation and acceptance of foreign financial aid to Namibian political parties went well beyond the 1989 Constituent Assembly elections and seems to be a generally tolerated electoral practice in independent Namibia.[225]

The cluster of South African *sub rosa* activities has been termed Operation 435, while the MI component went by the name of Operation Heyday[226] or Operation Agree.[227] A SADF officer, Nico Basson, served as the military liaison to the DTA,[228] continuing a link begun in 1978 by Theo May, an MI officer who had provided funds for this political party.[229] Major Basson reported to Brigadier Frederik van Wyk, who served in MI as a communications officer, and the Namibia project not only was classified as secret but also was approved by Generals Jannie Geldenhuys and Kat Liebenberg, the chiefs of the SADF. Major Basson created a front organization known as African Communications Project that the SADF funded.[230] Although some accounts list Nico Basson as a SADF major, it is not entirely clear whether he was working on this assignment as an active duty officer. He had been an officer for four years and seemingly functioning as a civilian in Namibia, where his reported remuneration far exceeded that of a serving SADF officer.[231]

From a long-term perspective, one of the most significant effects of this exercise in dissimulation was the publication by this bogus organization of an exposé, *Call Them Spies: A Documentary Account of the Namibian Spy Drama*, edited by Nico Basson and Ben Motinga. It concerned SWAPO's alleged maltreatment of detainees in Angola.[232] Peter Steenkamp has observed that "While the compilation of this book was a covert exercise in South African electoral interference, the documents it contains are authentic. Like all historical documents, they should be treated with due care."[233] Yet it has been cited in no less than thirteen footnotes in American university dissertations dealing with SWAPO.[234]

The detainee topic was brought up in the 1989 Constituent Assembly elections and managed to be a perennial source of dismay to SWAPO, whose leaders wanted closure on the matter as part and parcel of the national goal of reconciliation,[235] and to the critics of SWAPO, who sought greater transparency and possibly an expression of remorse or an apology from the government for its conduct in this matter. Indeed, the detainee issue was ventilated in Namibian parliamentary debates and questions from 1990 to 2006,[236] and the disappointed Namibians have since turned to the International Criminal Court in still another attempt to redress their grievance.[237] Fortunately, this topic has been the subject of careful studies based on extensive interviews.[238]

Above and beyond the SADF MI branch's furtive electoral campaign activities in the months prior to independence, more sinister operations were handled by the murky CCB (Civilian Cooperation Bureau), which was ostensibly part of the military establishment. The Bureau handled more (morally) reprehensible activities that were designed to obfuscate the channels of responsibility and that had an aura of deniability. Their operative succeeded in assassinating Anton Lubowski, a white SWAPO member who was a prominent attorney in Windhoek, and they had drawn up a list of other Namibians to eliminate or neutralize. Other targeted persons included Christo Botha, Christo Lombard, and Gerhard Tötemeyer of the University of Namibia, the editor of *The Namibian* newspaper, Gwen Lister, the lawyers Hartmut Ruppel and Peter Koep, and the activist Michaela Hübschle.[239] Their action in this area was limited to Mr. Lubowski. General Magnus Malan, the Minister of Defense, even publicly claimed that Mr. Lubowski was a secret agent for South Africa, but this accusation persuaded very few South Africans.[240]

Other than the clandestine operations sponsored by the MI branch of the SADF and the opaque activities of the CCB, the SADF had no overt confrontations with the military staff of UNTAG. Relations between the two organizations were tolerable as the roughly 4,500 military officers of UNTAG serving under Lieutenant-General Prem Chand of India monitored the phased withdrawal of SADF units from their bases in Namibia, although the monitors noticed that, as late as October, 1989, slightly less than eight hundred SADF personnel were deployed in managing airfields, providing medical services, and serving as paymasters for SWATF personnel (who were funded until the advent of independence). Mr. Ahtissari was able to diminish the size of this residual SADF component by replacing them by UN employees.[241]

PART IV: THE RESIDUE OF THE CAMPAIGNS

Chapter Seven

The Art of Bending

> ...Learn to bend quickly, white man, before it is too late.
> You'll have to face change and change is always uncomfortable.
> But you will survive and that's what matters in the final analysis.
> — from *The Wild Geese*[1]

Relics of the Namibian War[2]

For the inhabitants of Namibia, the war for independence has ended, at least in a formal sense, and Namibia is an internationally recognized member of the world of states. It has succeeded in its quest not only for legitimacy but also for self-determination, coupled with the maintenance of its territorial integrity. This chapter suggests what has become of several salient issues that were an integral part of the appeal of independence for the African majority of the nation during the 1966–1989 war. These issues are arranged in three major sectoral clusters — diplomatic, economic, and military — that have been used throughout the book. Later, I will suggest answers to the six fundamental questions posed in the preface.

To keep this research manageable and focused, I have omitted two topics that either fall outside the three cluster areas or which seem to be tangential to my purpose. The first topic is the fascinating and continuous inquiry into the nature and quality of the democratic process in postcolonial Namibia, a subject which has attracted a range of observers, Namibian and non–Namibian, and which already has generated a substantial body of literature. Especially noteworthy is the fascinating analysis by a Finnish observer, Lari Kangas,[3] which supplements two studies by Alex Davidson commissioned by the SIDA.[4] There is also a more local perspective on this topic.[5]

Additionally, I have put aside the issue of the Caprivi secession in the northeast even though it does fit within the rubric of territorial integrity, a topic raised in Chapter Two. Both Henning Melber[6] and Bennett Kangumu[7] provide thoughtful analyses of the secession issue. Instead, I have limited the analysis on the subject to the reincorporation of Walvis Bay, which not only has both territorial integrity and economic significance but also international implications.

As a prelude to the sectoral analysis, I would like to focus on a significant constant in the postwar milieu of Namibia, namely, what scholars and observers have termed the politics of memory.[8] Following a protracted war, several subjective questions arose that have fascinated political scientists, sociologists, and psychologists and that help one to place what David Lush has termed "the relics of the Namibian war"[9] into a more specific context. At the very basic level, the question has emerged: who are the Namibians? This is not a banal question but reflects the impact of colonization upon diverse groups who interacted with one another infrequently and may have felt few, if any, bonds with others in the same geographical area.

The search for self-definition can be found in the oft-quoted 1936 query of Ferhat Abbas, an early Algerian nationalist, concerning the nature of Algeria.[10] It continued through the Pretoria trial of thirty-seven African defendants — the Eliazer Tuhadeleni trial — when Toivo Herman Ja Toivo, in a classic speech from the dock on 1 February 1968, drew a sharp distinction between South Africans and Namibians, identifying himself wholly with the latter.[11] Unlike Charles Dickens' character Uriah Heep, the Namibians had not developed an appetite for eating humble pie.[12] Even though this distinguishes colonized from colonizer, it does not provide a long-lasting answer, one that outlasts the colonial era.

There are several ways to answer the question of who is a Namibian, some of which are open to dispute. Bruce Frayne and Wade C. Pendleton have made an empirical attempt to answer that question based upon survey research in Namibia.[13] One approach is to focus on citizenship, which is a legal, constitutional matter and it certainly embraces the customary division between those who hold citizenship by right of birth (*jus sanguinis*) and/or naturalization, on the one hand, and those who reside in the country as citizens of another state, on the other hand. This latter category would apply to South African and German citizens. The South African government dealt with the German residents in the 1920s primarily through a bilateral agreement with the Weimar Republic which attempted to assimilate the Germans into the Namibian body politic while treating them as a privileged minority in terms of language rights, modified pensions, and exemptions from military service under certain circumstances.[14] During the apartheid years, the Germans in Namibia were an integral part of the white community that could organize itself not only to deal with the West German regime but also to engage in unobtrusive contacts with select SWAPO leaders, who were anxious to prevent white flight at independence.[15] These back channel meetings with white business and professional elite, which began as early as 1980, were held in neighboring Zambia and Zimbabwe as well as in France, Germany, Sweden and Switzerland. They apparently led to the post-independence policy of national reconciliation.[16]

Going beyond the topic of citizenship (which would subsume the matter of expatriates living in Namibia and the sometimes controversial matter of dual citizenship with dual passports) one moves to the most enduring aspect, that is, forging trans-ethnic and pan-ethnic identities within one sovereign state. This was an essential part of the nationalist message and a forceful rejection of the centrifugal tendencies of ethnic fragmentation during the colonial regime. Indeed, the intellectual champion of separate development in South Africa, Prime Minister Verwoerd, made it very clear early on that white supremacy could be maintained through the social engineering system termed separate development.[17] This leads into the more contested terrain of political awareness, mobilization, and the hackneyed term struggle. The Portuguese phrase, the struggle continues (*a luta continua*), so widely used in Mozambique, is the mantra, especially for those who have identified with, and continue to identify with, SWAPO. In this formulation, which is enthusiastically accepted by many but rejected by others, SWAPO holds the copyright to independence. Such a construction would derive from the political monopoly granted to SWAPO by the United Nations General Assembly. According to the Namibian jurist, Bryan O'Linn, "SWAPO wanted to retain the tactical advantage of parading as the sole and authentic representative of Namibians whilst portraying the non–SWAPO parties as appendages and stooges of South Africa."[18] SWAPO thus could feel free to define who are the true Namibians and who are the apostates.

Henning Melber recently noted, "The situational application of militant rhetoric as a tool for inclusion and exclusion in terms of the post-colonial national identity is common practice."[19] This is hardly a unique policy, for it is an updated version of a theme found in white South African history and politics, that is, the emphasis upon the *ware Afrikaner* (a true, genuine Afrikaner). In an Orwellian sense,[20] all Afrikaners were equal, but some (*ware Afrikaners*) were more equal than others. Fundamental to this development of the sense of rectitude is the knowledge of how to utilize the politics of memory, including selective recall and convenient forgetfulness, in order to retain control, if not dominance. Johanna Åfreds has undertaken a significant research project involving interviewing Namibian MPs on this subject,[21] while Justine Hunter has provided a well-documented analysis of selective recall in Namibia.[22] Memory management goes beyond the short-lived skills of what have been called spin-doctors and reaches into the more profound subject of historical narrative that, *ab initio*, is usually selective. Indeed, one discerning South African journalist, surveying the demise of the National Party, claimed correctly that "memory ... is a contested terrain."[23] SWAPO has shown itself fully cognizant of the potency of memory,[24] and it has arranged to develop an expensive Valhalla of heroes, known as Heroes' Acre, outside Windhoek[25] as well as to develop its own self-serving version of Namibian history.[26] This commemoration of bygone battles and heroes is hardly a novel policy, for the Germans had done so earlier both in their metropole and in Namibia itself.[27]

Nevertheless, Christian A. Williams' recent research demonstrates that there are several types of narratives that apply to recent Namibian nationalist history, starting with what he has termed "competing narratives"[28] or "competing national histories,"[29] which can then be dichotomized as the "dominant narrative"[30] and the competing "counter-narrative."[31] The challenge, he intimates, is to meld these narratives into what he calls "socially accepted narratives"[32] or "socially accepted national narrative[s]."[33] Given the political paramountcy of the SWAPO establishment and its oft-noted authoritarian approach to the political process (which Henning Melber[34] and Christopher Saunders[35] have attributed to the organizational rigors of decolonization warfare), so far only the dominant narrative is the political coin of the realm.

In the aftermath of the war of independence, an important development in memory politics occurred within a portion of the body politic that had even longer memories than did the veterans of the 1966–1989 war. The Herero element, which had fought the Imperial German *Schutztruppe* (colonial army) and subsequently suffered horribly during and after the German counterinsurgency campaign,[36] took advantage of the American Alien Tort

Claims Act of 1789 to seek damages for this heinous treatment from the German authorities. Jan Grofe has examined the application of that 1789 U.S. statute to non–U.S.-based multinational corporations.[37] Because the Hereros were not a nation state, they could not turn to the International Court of Justice, but in 2001 they sought relief (civil damages) through the U.S. legal system,[38] where the defendants were not the former German Empire, which was defunct, but rather extant multinational corporations based in Germany which were alleged to have acted as agents of the Imperial Government.[39] They also sought an official apology from the current (reunified) German Government,[40] which also has been a major foreign aid donor to Namibia.[41] Reinhart Kössler has written a thoughtful analysis of this matter within the context of current German Namibian relations.[42] Similarly South African groups (Jubilee South Africa and Khulumani Support Group) utilized the 1789 statute in the U.S. judicial system to place a $400 billion claim against a number of multinational corporations that they regarded as important supporters of apartheid.[43]

The Diplomatic Legacy of the Namibian War

Namibia achieved an internationally legitimated independence on 21 March 1990, a day that SWAPO chose because it commemorated the thirtieth anniversary of the 1960 shootings at Sharpeville, South Africa.[44] After independence, Namibia became a recognized member of the world of sovereign states, and this, in turn, entailed the responsibility of establishing formal, diplomatic ties with a range of nation states and international organizations. At this point, Namibia moved beyond legal decolonization and into the challenging period of effective decolonization, as noted in the preface.[45] Previously, the United Nations Council for Namibia had served as a surrogate foreign office for Namibia.[46] Consequently, Namibia not only needed to establish embassies (or lesser status diplomatic posts) but also to recruit and staff these posts with its own foreign service officers. Nevertheless, Namibia did not need to start from scratch because, as noted in Chapter One, it already had a pool of *ersatz* diplomats from the pre-independence era. Nine senior SWAPO chief representatives subsequently served as either high commissioners to Commonwealth nations or as ambassadors.[47] Namibia was qualified to join the Commonwealth owing to the quaint wording of the League mandate agreement that named the United Kingdom as the mandatory power that, in turn, delegated the responsibility to South Africa as its agent.[48] During their years in exile, often in Western states, the SWAPO representatives combined their representational roles with university studies, including both undergraduate and graduate studies.

With the assistance of the Commonwealth Secretariat, prospective Namibian diplomats were able to attend four separate training courses, which began two months after the nation became independent. By September 1990, the Public Service Commission of Namibia provided for the staffing of the Ministry of Foreign Affairs and authorized a total of 210 foreign service positions as well as nine foreign missions.[49] The Commonwealth Secretariat dispatched a Ghanaian diplomat to handle the training program.[50] The nine post-independence foreign missions represented a considerable retrenchment from the number of missions SWAPO maintained prior to independence, namely, twenty-seven.[51]

In addition to performing a range of economic tasks (which will be noted in the next section), Namibian diplomacy provided evidence of gratitude to its patrons and sponsors during the exile period. Mr. Moses M. Garoëb, a SWAPO MP, during the 19 July 1990 foreign affairs debate, observed that "we owe a moral debt ... to the international community which in so many ways contributed to the birth of this new Republic [of Namibia]."[52] The establishment of diplomatic relations with Cuba on 14 September 1990 helped to repay that moral debt.[53] Cuba had undertaken the responsibility of educating some Namibian students before as well as after independence. According to the Deputy Minister of Education and Culture, Cuba hosted 811 Namibian students, 97 of whom were at Cuban universities. Namibia paid N$381,000 for their education.[54] A Hendrik Witbooi School located on the Isle of Pines had been functioning since 1978; it included Namibian children who survived the 1978 SADF attack on Cassinga.[55] The Witbooi School was for secondary school children, while the Hosea Kutako School was for primary school ones.[56] The new Namibian Government also permitted the ANC of South Africa to maintain an office in Windhoek.[57] The ANC had become unbanned in South Africa on 2 February 1990, about six weeks before Namibia became independent.

Initially, the regime established nine embassies, with the intention of adding or doubling that in the near future. Three of the first nine embassies involved access to international organizations (the United Nations [New York], the OAU [Addis Ababa], and the European Economic Community [Brussels]), while three others involved fellow Commonwealth states (Lagos, London, and Lusaka), and the remaining three entailed a balancing of commitments between East (Moscow), West (Washington), and a neutral (Stockholm).[58] The other nine embassies that were to be established later showed roughly the same degree of balance, with two Commonwealth states (India and Zimbabwe), two members of opposing sides in the Cold War (China and Cuba, France and Germany), Algeria, Japan, and South Africa (which presupposed the end of apartheid in the very near future).[59]

For the present, South Africa had what was called the Office of the South African Representative in Windhoek, but this did not entail diplomatic recognition; Namibia permitted this presence for pragmatic reasons involving foreign trade relations and the resolution of the dispute over Walvis Bay.[60] This may well explain why Namibia established a mission in Pretoria in 1992, and in addition it established an embassy in Angola in Luanda in 1992 as well as one in Brazil (which became a patron of the Namibian navy) in 2003. By the year 2004 it had a total of twenty-two diplomatic posts.[61] Further evidence of Namibia's acceptance into the international community was provided by the election of the state to a non-permanent seat in the United Nations Security Council in 1999–2000, on the one hand, and the election of Mr. Theo-Ben Guriab, who served as foreign minister since 1986, as the president of the United Nations General Assembly in that same year, on the other hand.[62]

The Economic Legacy of the Namibian War

Earlier, in Chapter Six, I briefly noted the murky nature of the data dealing with the estimated costs of the Namibian War of Independence. Not only are there different figures but also there are presumably different ways of computing the costs, so that this is one aspect of the war where there is both confusion and a demonstrable absence of transparency. It seems doubtful that researchers will be able to provide an accurate account of this aspect of the war until there is greater access to the South African archives, and assuming that the appropriate documents still exist and have not been destroyed.[63]

On a more prosaic level, the new Namibian state was encumbered with a foreign debt of R 714.1 million, of which R 549.5 million was owed to various South African institutions and R 39.0 million to the Pretoria Government.[64] It seems that South Africa provided subventions to the budget of the South West African territorial administration,[65] while the counter Namibian argument was that the debt was due to South African defense spending in the territory.[66] In 1992 South Africa issued a moratorium on payments of interest as well as principal on the Namibian debt until 30 April 1995, and rescheduled the final payment date, which came due 30 April 2012. There were to be seventeen annual payments of N$78.5 each.[67] The Namibian government, realizing the importance of its international status, chose not to repudiate, but to pay, this debt even though the Namibian people had not been consulted about these pre-independence loans. It negotiated with the South African regime, involving Presidents Nujoma and Mandela as well as their respective finance ministers. On 6 December 1994 the two states agreed that Namibia was not liable for this pre-independence debt. The South African cabinet accepted this cancellation. The Namibian National Assembly ratified a Namibian-South African debt cancellation agreement in 1997, thereby saving Namibia N$1.2 billion (over the course of the subsequent fifteen years).[68]

One of the economic challenges facing the new state was the loss of employment opportunities when the SADF departed from the northern part of Namibia, where the war had begun and had continued even after the SADF conducted operations in neighboring Angola. It was estimated that roughly 25,000 persons in this area became unemployed when the SADF left.[69] Indeed, one SADF information officer indicated that the SADF spent R58 million per annum on its subaltern, ethnic forces in Ovamboland.[70] Ironically enough, several African small businessmen in the north greatly benefited from the generous spending of those soldiers posted to the north.[71]

As pointed out earlier in the section on the economic battlefield in the Introduction, Namibia is a country characterized by economic asymmetry in terms of landholding. This can largely be accounted for by the forceful imposition of colonial rule by the German as well as by the South African regimes that catered to the demands and needs of the white settler communities.[72] Outside of the northern sectors, which were not physically occupied by the German administration and which the South African successor regime designated as reserves for the resident Africans, white farmers usually held the remaining land. The alienation of African land by the white minority governments created a huge imbalance in agricultural land ownership that is illustrated in the skewed proportions in ownership: 94 per cent of the inhabitants owned 48 per cent. of this land, while the remaining 52 per of this land was held by a mere 6 per cent of the population, namely, the white farmers.[73]

Landholding in Namibia involved responses to generally inhospitable geographic conditions involving scant rainfall and cyclical drought, and these, in turn, set limits to the carrying capacity of the land for ranching purposes and for growing crops.[74] Thus,

Namibia was characterized by dual landholding systems, freehold for the white farmers and non-freehold or communal tenure for the African farmers.[75] The large size of many of the farms that the whites own is an economic function of the aridity of the land.[76] From the constitutional perspective, private property is protected in Namibia, although expropriation with proper compensation is not wholly excluded as a result of subsequent land reform legislation passed in 1995 and in 2003. This legislation specifies the conditions under which such expropriation is permissible.[77]

Land reform in post-colonial Namibia has not been a high priority issue for the governing SWAPO party, in part because it draws its political support from the north of the country, where there was little land alienation under both German and South African rule. Indeed, only one-tenth of the Namibian population was dispossessed.[78] Nevertheless, there is certainly a clientele that is anxious for restitution of land,[79] yet that group lacks political muscle, especially compared to the white commercial farmers.[80] Nevertheless, the issue is laden with identity and psychological concerns.[81] There is a general consensus that traditional, ancestral land will not be restored,[82] and there is yet another group whose economic needs are most pressing and who occupy marginal positions within the Namibian economy, namely, the African farm workers.[83] Although the land issue is complex and there are no easy, cost-free solutions, it can be anticipated that to the extent that there is a reduction in rural poverty through legally accepted channels there will also be greater democratic consolidation in Namibia.[84]

A significant feature of the post-colonial era was the negotiated return of the Walvis Bay enclave to the Namibian state, a matter that was both an economic and territorial issue. In 1976, South African legislation designated Walvis Bay as a South African, not a Namibian port,[85] and, as pointed out in Chapter Four, the next year the enclave was incorporated into the Cape Province of the South African metropole. Although SWAPO and the United Nations took very strong exception to this unilateral incorporation, while the Western Contact Group essentially stood aside from the imbroglio, and the matter was relegated to what amounted to a legal and political limbo except for United Nations resolutions endorsing the Namibian claim to the territory.[86]

The government of independent Namibia viewed the return of Walvis Bay as pre-eminently a decolonization issue,[87] one that would constitute the final act of what James Mittelman had termed legal decolonization, as noted in the preface.[88] Indeed, the Namibian minister of foreign affairs described the return of Walvis Bay as "the second independence of our country."[89] The transfer from South Africa to Namibia on 28 February 1994 was a lengthy, complicated procedure involving a period of joint administration as a preliminary step to South African disengagement as well as administrative considerations concerning citizenship, pension rights, residence permits, validity of legal and judicial acts and undertakings, and possible reimbursements concerned with the transfer of title for immovable property to the Namibian regime.[90] The Namibian authorities refused to compensate South Africa for the transfer of the public assets of Walvis Bay, and President Mandela of South Africa absolved Namibia of its debts to South Africa,[91] as I pointed out earlier in this chapter.

There was a military spin-off from the hiatus between the achievement of independence in 1990 and the return of Walvis Bay in 1994, namely, an appreciation of the weakness of the Namibian Defense Force (NDF) with respect to policing its territorial waters effectively to prohibit foreign poaching, which would cut into profits from the fishing industry.[92] This suggested the need for a naval presence which could have both a coastal defense role as well as a fisheries watchdog role.[93] Although the United States military did offer assistance to the NDF concerning small boat handling in Walvis Bay in 1996, the Namibians turned to the Brazilian Ministry of the Navy with which Namibia signed a maritime cooperation agreement in 1994. Brazil undertook the task not only of providing Namibia with a hydrographic survey but also training the NDF naval personnel as well as handling the building of a naval base for the Namibians.[94]

By 1997 the Brazilian navy was conducting the hydrographic survey and was training sixty-five NDF members.[95] Construction of the naval base, apparently an expensive undertaking, was set to begin in 1999, when some of the naval trainees were scheduled to finish their overseas training.[96] A number of naval cadets finished their three year training course in Brazil in 1998, and the government indicated that it would building living quarters for the NDF naval personnel.[97] What is significant about the formation of what is termed the maritime wing of the NDF is that the defense minister stressed that the Walvis Bay base would have a "long-term benefit to the protection of the marine resources of the country."[98] This would suggest a carefully focused environmental and economic role for a rather small branch of the armed forces, bearing some resemblance to the U.S. Coast Guard rather than to larger blue water navies.

Earlier, I had drawn attention to the use of migrant African labor in the fish canning industry in Walvis Bay[99] and to the Namibians' hostility to this type of demeaning employment.[100] Ndeutala Hishongwa has provided a lucid expression of this antipathy in postcolonial Namibia.[101] During the 1970s the Administration engaged in some rather cosmetic improvements in the system, but to little avail, and in June 1989, the consolidated congress of the National Union of Namibian Workers (NUNW) formally denounced the migrant labor system.[102] Freedom of movement and residence were now guaranteed in the Namibian constitution.[103] After independence, with the abolition of the influx control system and passes controlling the flow and direction of African population movement the migrant labor system ended, and the grim buildings housing the laborers in Katatura, the African township outside Windhoek, have been refurbished for community activities.[104]

It seems as though the migrant labor system has been replaced by labor-hire companies located in Walvis Bay, Swakopmund, and Tsumeb that supply laborers to what are called client companies, which include private firms, parastatal organizations, and mining firms. These client companies utilize labor-hire companies not only to deal with fluctuating, short-term needs but also to economize on their administrative costs (by not retaining permanent laborers). The casual workers, who are from northern Namibia, are employed by the labor-hire companies. They are unskilled or semi-skilled workers and not labor union members so the various companies can use them as strikebreakers. Understandably, the NUNW is quite hostile to this new system that treats laborers as commodities.[105]

The Military Legacy of the Namibian War

With the negotiated ending of the Namibian War of Independence, the human and material costs became ever more visible even though neither protagonist had reasonably transparent and inflexible goals and policies during nearly a quarter of a century of warfare. In terms of human costs, there are of course members of the military and paramilitary forces who lost their lives in combat as well as those civilians killed, wounded, and subject to torture and/or lengthy imprisonment.[106] Another hazard of the war, and one with which the American public became even more familiar during the Vietnam and Iraq/Afghanistan campaigns, is the post-traumatic stress disorder (PTSD), which can be very debilitating and expensive to treat.[107] It seems that some French draftees who served in the French-Algerian war suffered similar psychological traumas.[108] Not very much has been published about the presence of PTSD in the Namibian war, and what little has appeared in print more often concerns the SADF[109] rather than their Namibian counterparts[110] or civilians.[111]

Demobilization of Namibians serving in the opposing military and paramilitary units, such as PLAN, SWATF, *Koevoet*, and certain SADF units with non–South African citizens (such as the San) did present an organizational and economic challenge especially because misuse of their military training and skills could prove disruptive and destabilizing to a fragile new nation,[112] as the case of the *Freikorps* (Free Corps) in the Weimar German Republic so graphically illustrated.[113] Lalli Metsola and Henning Melber have examined this issue recently.[114]

Financial compensation (in the form of lump sum payments and/or pensions) and enhanced economic opportunities (often through training and education) are standard rewards allocated to veterans from the public purse. Indeed the South African Government saw to it that white veterans from the Second World War were able to receive agricultural land,[115] and the South West African Administration did not neglect its German-speaking veterans whose military service in the territory ended in 1920.[116] These two Namibian examples suggest the real or perceived power of veterans as mobilizable voters. Even more suggestive is the American experience with World War I veterans, some of whom became militant members of what was termed the Bonus Army whose members sought previously promised benefits from Washington, D.C. This political pressure continued through the Second World War and resulted in those veterans' educational perquisites generally known as the 1944 G. I.[117] Bill of Rights.[118]

The Namibian Government, with a South African pledge of R36 million for this purpose,[119] was able to provide severance pay to a total of nearly 25,000 PLAN, SWATF, and *Koevoet* veterans.[120] Over time, the discourse regarding compensation centered on the emotionally laden question of which group or groups could be regarded as veterans (and hence entitled to emoluments and/or preferred employment in the public sector). Following the terminology of George Orwell, it appeared that all veterans were equal but some were more equal than others. So far, it seems that Namibian legislation privileges the PLAN veterans in that respect.[121]

Beginning in March 1990 the British Army Military Advisory Team provided assistance in the establishment of the fledgling Namibia Defense Force (NDF) until they departed in March 1995.[122] Although the initial NDF intake included both PLAN and SWATF veterans, its budget would permit only a limited number of these veterans.[123] As noted in Chapter Five, SWAPO donated military materiel from its Angolan and Zambian supplies, and this gift helped stretch the NDF budget. Furthermore, the Ministry of Defense preferred 18–25 year old Namibians as soldiers even though the government continued to channel PLAN/SWATF veterans into the NDF.[124] This signified that the

Windhoek regime still had to deal with other unemployed veterans, many of whom had only the most meager educational and vocational credentials and who could not realistically expect highly remunerative civilian employment.[125] This economic challenge was met, in part, by the creation of development brigades (which turned out to be dysfunctional)[126] and by a considerable expansion of the public service, which accommodated roughly 9,000 veterans, if only to secure domestic tranquility.[127]

Despite these public expenditures, the clamor of other veterans did not subside, and political mobilization ensued with veterans' marches that generated further publicity for the plight of the least affluent veterans.[128] As was the case with their opposite numbers in Zimbabwe, these veterans felt strongly about their postwar economic entitlements, all the more so because of the paucity of their educational credentials or vocational preparation.[129] Furthermore, unlike their South African funded opponents in the independence war, PLAN members received no salary during their military service.[130] Consequently, they regarded government largesse as essentially deferred compensation for their time in PLAN.[131] This bore some resemblance to the notion that American veterans considered postwar benefits as a means for redressing the considerable difference between their meager military pay and that earned by civilians who were employed at home during that time.[132]

During the period from 1997 until 2004 the program called the Socio-Economic Integration for Ex-Combatants provided monthly payments to veterans as well as educational stipends for war orphans, and then in 2008 a Ministry of Veterans Affairs was created.[133] Subsequently, the benefits began to include housing for a small number of veterans,[134] along with future subsidies for water, electricity, and transport.[135] By the middle of June 2010 the Ministry of Veterans Affairs was furnishing 80,000 veterans with a monthly stipend of N$ 2,000 monthly; these veterans, however, had very low incomes or were unemployed.[136] This generosity did not go unnoticed, and one Namibian journalist referred to "the culture of entitlement" among the PLAN veterans.[137]

Furthermore, the policy of national reconciliation, designed to ensure domestic racial and political harmony, did not entail a zero-sum approach to the employment opportunities, especially in the public service. Those whites remaining in Namibia generally continued on in their governmental posts, while some highly educated Namibians who spent some, if not most, of the war years in exile acquiring advanced educational credentials, found comfortable and rewarding posts in the higher echelons of the civil service.[138] Somewhat later, there was a brief interlude when foreign contractors attempted to recruit Namibian veterans, but their access to this particular labor market was barred.[139]

One of the troublesome legacies of the war was the presence of landmines, especially in the northern rural areas of the country, a topic that Kristian B. Harpvoken has carefully explored.[140] The Namibian government was able to secure assistance in mine clearance from the American armed forces.[141] When the SADF departed from northern Namibia in 1990, they did not remove all their landmines, and local inhabitants have been killed or injured. Moreover, the task of mine clearance is exceptionally expensive.[142] When the occasion arose in 1997, the Namibian government signed the Ottawa Treaty banning this particularly noxious weapon.[143] At the international level NDF has been quite active and has participated in a number of peace-keeping operations, usually under the auspices of the United Nations but also of the African Union, in Angola, Burundi, Cambodia, Eritrea, Ethiopia, Ivory Coast, Kosovo, and Sudan.[144]

Chapter Eight

Conclusions

The First Question

In the preface, I indicated that I would attempt to answer six different questions concerning the decolonization of Namibia. Taken together, the sequential answers constitute the concluding chapter of this study. The first, most fundamental question was: why was the decolonization of Namibia so protracted? Namibia was certainly an exception to relatively speedy decolonization of other colonies after the end of the Second World War. Neta C. Crawford has provided an exceptionally helpful inventory of explanations to account for that swift decolonization process[1] as well as a list of ideas and concepts that are subsumed under the noun decolonization norm.[2] The companion second query was: how was this decolonization internationalized?

Probably the most obvious and structural answer to the first question was the nature of the metropole, South Africa, and its pervading system of white minority rule.[3] The viability of the system of minority rule in both the center (Pretoria) and periphery (Windhoek) required the South African leadership to play to two separate (white) audiences simultaneously and to balance both sets of expectations and political resources. Robert S. Jaster referred to Prime Minister P. W. Botha as one who was playing at two chessboards.[4] Nevertheless, Namibia was not a crucial issue in South African elections.[5] Implicit in such an answer was a variant of the domino theory of international politics, which reached its zenith in the Vietnam War, that is, the loss of white paramountcy in Namibia would imperil the same system in South Africa.[6] As a corrective, Christopher A. Ford observed that the domino theory was not always uniformly applicable to South African foreign policy.[7] Later this mindset became routinized in the total onslaught formulations of the Pretoria securocrats. Such a formulation implicitly equated the rise of African nationalism (the black peril or *swart gevaar*) with the loss of white privilege and power. The black peril motif featured prominently in the 1929 general election,[8] but this theme was often obscured by highly vocal and robust anti-communism.[9]

The elaborate structures of separate development both in South Africa and Namibia, and the ideological constructs supporting them, were predicated on what seemed to be a zero sum game, consisting of winners and losers. Thus, from the white perspective, to share power was to dilute or to lose power, something the Afrikaners learned the hard way (vis-à-vis the English-speaking whites) ever since their defeat in the Anglo-Boer War of 1899–1902.[10] As one Namibian historian observed, "Afrikaner politicians ... instinctively responded to the white electorate's preference for powerful assertions, in word and deed, of the refusal to dilute white power."[11] Nevertheless, such an attitude was dysfunctional in that it "precluded the sort of meaningful political reforms that could have actually undermined resistance movements," according to an American Rhodes Scholar whose research concerned South African relations with Israel.[12]

This contention leads logically to an ancillary consideration of what could be regarded as a type of white settler diaspora or kith and kin politics. Miles Kahler has undertaken an exceptionally sophisticated analysis of the politics of this type of diaspora.[13] Such kith and kin politics bear a resemblance to what James N. Rosenau has termed linkage politics to explain the melding of international and domestic politics, fields that once were quite disparate. Rosenau's term should not be confused with the notion of linkage used in the latter part of the Namibian War of Independence, where, for reasons of leverage in negotiations, Cuban troop withdrawal from Angola was bundled together with South African military withdrawal from Namibia and Namibian independence.[14] As applied to Namibia, this meant that South African whites, especially Afrikaners, had relatives in Namibia. This bond enhanced their concern about the fate of their kinsmen in Namibia.[15] Similarly, there is a German-speaking diaspora in Namibia.[16] Much the same could be said for the French community in Algeria[17] and the Portuguese one in Angola and Mozambique.[18]

Such a focus on the metropole, however, is a necessary but not sufficient argument because it ignores those instances in which other South African neighbors achieved their independence relatively quickly and with little or no bloodshed. The three former British High Commission Territories (Botswana, Lesotho, and Swaziland) are examples of relatively speedy, pacific decolonization. This is not to deny that they were sometimes perceived as essentially *de facto* clients or vassals of South Africa nor that South Africa did not hesitate to destabilize them in those instances when it felt threatened by their hospitality to exile South African nationalist groups and guerrillas.[19] Nevertheless, these three Southern African states had a different type of metropole (the United Kingdom) which was pro-active in developing policies for gradual, planned decolonization involving recognition of, negotiations with, and searching for consensus with evolving African nationalist groups and leaders.

This is not to imply that British colonial policy in post–World War II Africa was devoid of violence, as Caroline Elkins[20] and Daniel Branch[21] have demonstrated in their revisionist studies of the Mau Mau insurgency. Furthermore, the Kenya Human Rights Commission, representing those who suffered during that insurgency, has undertaken legal action to secure reparations from the British Government.[22] Their legal action was successful.[23] However in the case of the former High Commission Territories, the United Kingdom could serve as their patron and provide them with diplomatic, economic, and military support to keep neighboring South Africa at bay. Namibian African nationalists lacked such a buffer and benefactor.

A second structural approach to answering the question about the length of the decolonization process shifts the focus from the South African metropole to the Security Council of the United Nations, which became the *bête noire* of many African delegations in the United Nations. The gravamen of the complaint is that the Western permanent members — France, the United Kingdom, and the United States — of the Security Council, by means of their (threatening or actual) veto power were able to shield South Africa from very harsh economic and/or military sanctions.[24] This type of argument implied that these three powers (rather than the other two permanent members — China and the Soviet Union) could set or regulate the pace of decolonization. Closely related to this line of reasoning was the constant reiteration of the charge that Western-based multinational corporations were the powerful patrons of South Africa; this was a recurrent theme of General Assembly resolutions.[25] Yet another, complementary explanation involving the UN organization is that the General Assembly essentially wasted too much time in waiting for opinions or decisions by the International Court of Justice. The core complaint was that the status of Namibia was *au fond* a political, not a judicial question.[26] This leads one into the challenging, yet murky field of counterfactuals.[27] In the course of this research I have found only two examples of the use of counterfactuals applied to Namibia, namely, those by Neta C. Crawford[28] and by Leopold Scholtz.[29] It is not altogether clear what a speedier policy, relying upon the growing voting power of the African bloc in the General Assembly, would have accomplished. In this case, African vocal power would be trumped by the economic and military power represented by the Western members of the Security Council. How to win these members to the African point of view was a major challenge facing South Africa's opponents.[30]

The Second Question

The companion second query raised in the preface was: how was this decolonization internationalized? At the outset, one needs to remember that internationalization had been going on for twenty years (1946–1966) before the onset of the independence war and that the United Nations Security Council did not deal with the international status of the territory during these pacific years. Namibia had little, if any, international profile during the League of Nations era, so that African nationalist activity in Namibia was, from a public relations point of view, uneventful. At that time, colonial rule had at least a patina of legitimacy among the major world powers. By the time of the 1950 advisory opinion of the International Court of Justice, the international milieu had shifted away from the uncritical attitude toward the colonial situation to much greater sensitivity to questions of race relations within a colonial context[31] and a more persistent questioning of the legitimacy of the colonial enterprise.

Even though the parliamentary and media management techniques for garnering international attention (and subsequent resources) to the decolonization process had been perfected after the creation of the United Nations,[32] the disposition of the status of Namibia could be said to be characterized by a marked degree of *immobilisme*. Suresh C. Saxena has pointed out that the UN General Assembly paid little attention to the recommendations of its Committee on South West Africa to explore carefully the ramifications of ousting South Africa from Namibia with particular reference to preparing the majority population to assume the responsibilities of independence.[33] It was not until the creation of the UN Institute for Namibia that these matters were systematically investigated.

Honing the art of petitioning the United Nations was the major preoccupation of the Namibian nationalists at this time; it might be thought of as the politics of shame.[34] With the admission of newly independent African states to the United Nations, beginning with Ghana in 1957, there was a cumulative growth of African support for a more assertive declaration of the decolonization norms. David Kay has carefully investigated this process.[35] The change culminated in the passage on 14 December 1960 of United Nations General Assembly resolution 1514 (XV), a resolution that no colonial power opposed; they merely abstained on the vote.[36] Although the center point of the dispute was still located in The Hague with the marathon International Court of Justice case that Ethiopia and Liberia introduced on 4 November 1960,[37] there was a significant development within the territory that changed the nature of the dispute: the institutionalization of African nationalism through the development of a nascent political party system. This went well beyond what Paul R. Mosaka called a "toy telephone" in mid–August 1946 when referring to the ineffectual South African Native Representative Council.[38] It was a real Namibian telephone with extraterritorial connections.

After the Namibian nationalists' expectations were thwarted by the adverse judgment in the 1966 International Court of Justice contentious case, the war began in earnest, followed by the arrest and trial in Pretoria of thirty-seven Namibian nationalists. At that point, the Security Council condemned the 1967 trial,[39] and thereafter the international connections spread to a wider audience, especially with the creation of non-governmental organizations that have often been called solidarity organizations.[40] These groups, along with the Eastern bloc of nations, the Nordic states, and some North and sub–Saharan African nations became patrons of SWAPO and PLAN. Jules Mukumbi wa Nyembo has provided a useful synopsis of African assistance to SWAPO.[41] This external assistance enabled SWAPO to secure arms and military training, furnished them funding for academic scholarships, insured support for Namibian refugees in contiguous nations, and developed a viable nationalist exile organization. Within the context of insurgency, this organization could equally well be characterized as a counter-state.[42] This assistance helped mobilize diplomatic support within the international corridors of power, and to publicize, to shame, and perhaps to undercut the economic advantages that the South African regime had managed to marshal. Once SWAPO secured international legitimation as the sole, authentic representative of the Namibian people by 1976,[43] the United Nations was also able to help with several of these tasks.

This explanation of the internationalization of the decolonization of Namibia needs to be supplemented by the realization that the war era (1966–1989) took place within a larger context, that of the Cold War.[44] The quest for Namibian independence, especially after the Portuguese departure from Angola in 1974, became enmeshed in what is referred to as the realist perspective in post World War II political science. Two examples of the way in which the realist school of international politics has informed academic research on Southern Africa are the works of Ford[45] and of Devraun.[46] That, in turn, led to two competing schools of thought about the situation in Namibia. In the United States, the competing approaches were termed the globalists and the regionalists.[47]

This bifurcation was particularly notable during the Reagan years, when Dr. Chester A. Crocker was the vigorous champion of the globalist approach. He is probably best known for crafting the policy of constructive engagement, one which attempted to secure the independence of Namibia within the context of the Cold War and by means of assessing the security needs of the South African regime and then by balancing threats and payoffs in the more classical style of *Realpolitik*. Joanne E. Davies provides the most recent and well-documented evaluation of this policy.[48] The regionalists, however, took a much less sweeping view of the situation and viewed this independence within the narrower confines of Southern Africa, essentially sidestepping the rhetoric of the Cold War and concentrating more on African goals and perceptions. In brief, the globalists attempted to secure Namibian independence within the harsh milieu of the Cold War, while the regionalists preferred to resolve the issue by not only focusing more closely on the Southern African region but also by keeping the Cold War concerns in the background. Both groups, however, had to cultivate a Congressional constituency for their respective policies.[49]

The Third Question

The third question raised in the preface concerned the issues of similarity, that is, were there any features of the Namibian decolonization process that were found in other decolonization wars? This type of question, *mutatis mutandis*, closely resembles the notion of "analytical reasoning" when comparing different insurgencies.[50] Vincent B. Khapoya has undertaken a pioneering comparative quantitative analysis of the support African states have proffered to terminate white oligarchies in southern Africa, including Namibia,[51] while I have delved into this matter in terms of Namibia.[52] In the Southern African decolonization wars, one of the more obvious characteristics is the nationalists' quest for international attention and succor — something that they shared in common with the Americans who had fought their own war of independence against the British crown. The Americans often refer to their early, eighteenth century anti-colonial credentials. However, there was a marked change in the two centuries separating the American and Southern African decolonization wars, namely, a profound change in the range and speed of international communications, in the composition and nature of both transnational and intergovernmental organizations, and in the lexicon and rhetoric of decolonization.

This is highlighted by the significance of international, regional, national, and solidarity-type organizations, such at the UN, the OAU, legislative and executive bodies, and the various transnational anti-apartheid groups that often included various church denominations. Conversely, the nationalists realized that some of these organizations, including multinational corporations, could be utilized, if not co-opted, by their opponents. This array of protagonists, which was dynamic rather than static, provided a firm empirical basis for the nationalists' repetitive use of one of their favorite terms — struggle. After the Second World War, it seemed nearly conventional wisdom to stress that the lack of foreign support would condemn a guerrilla movement to certain defeat.[53] Researchers from the RAND Corporation have provided two thorough monographs on this topic that utilize a wider database.[54]

In terms of the nationalists' opponents, it seems that the Portuguese,[55] the Southern Rhodesians,[56] and the South Africans were faced with shortages of white manpower for their ground forces, and they met this deficit by recruiting and arming African soldiers Such a policy carried risks, such as possible mutinies[57] and what has been called internal desertion with regard to the French forces,[58] which faced legal obstacles to deploying French conscripts overseas in the early days of the Fourth Republic.[59] White resistance to conscription in South Africa is well covered in the academic literature, sometimes yielding conflicting research strategies and conclusions, such as those by Graeme Callister[60] and Merran W. Phillips.[61] One byproduct of such resistance was emigration,[62] as was also partially true in the case of metropolitan Portugal, where other West European nations offered more attractive economic opportunities.[63] The utilization of reserve forces and frequent military call-ups and deployments in both Southern Rhodesia and South Africa placed a marked strain on their respective economies, especially because of the privileged position of skilled white workers *vis-à-vis* the Africans in the labor force.[64]

From the perspective of the dominant white minority in South Africa, the war in Namibia had occasionally been called South Africa's Vietnam.[65] Professor Baines contends that this comparison with Vietnam "has informed [South African] literary history and cultural memory … as well as the discourse of military personnel and other commentators."[66] However, it seems as though the comparison seems misleading because the United States was an intrusive, rather than a metropolitan, actor in that war. Above all, it was a war between two sovereign (Vietnamese) states, with the United States serving as a patron third party. South Africa, however, was both the metropolitan regime as well as a contiguous state to Namibia, so that it more closely resembled France with its pre–1962 connection.[67] This distinction is significant in terms of threat perception and assumptions as well as in terms of prescriptions for a COIN campaign.

Flawed perceptions lead to flawed policies, and there is the further problem of foreclosed options, opportunity costs, and rigid strategies. These difficulties are currently challenging the American armed forces and their civilian advisers with regard to military operations in Afghanistan and Iraq.[68] Moreover, a distinguished student of French military history who is currently on the faculty of the U.S. Naval Postgraduate School recently cautioned against drawing too many generalizations in the COIN policy field because of changing conditions, environments, and attitudes.[69]

The Fourth Question

Turning to the fourth question, the focus shifts to the uniqueness of the Namibian decolonization. The Namibian experience does not resemble other cases of violent decolonization, especially those in Southern Africa, in one remarkable respect, namely, its international longevity, which can be dated from the inauguration of the mandate in 1920. Moreover, the metropole and the mandate were neighboring territories, a point specifically mentioned in article 22, paragraph six of the League of Nations Covenant; it was the only mandated territory with a mandatory power as a neighbor. Professor I. William Zartman refers to this as "contiguous colonialism."[70] In addition, the Namibian war of independence differed from similar wars in Southern Africa and in Algeria with respect to white emigration. In the case of Angola, estimates suggest that roughly 300,000 Portuguese whites departed,[71] as well as roughly 165,000 from Mozambique.[72]

However, between 25,000 and 35,000 of the returnees from Angola and Mozambique to Portugal were of mixed racial origins, who were subsequently marginalized in Portuguese society.[73] In Algeria the number of departing settlers was roughly one million.[74] The emigration flows were mostly directed to the metropoles of France and Portugal, which were not always welcoming and friendly to these new immigrants whose presence often occasioned economic and political challenges.[75] Some of the Portuguese settlers migrated to South Africa,[76] where there was a community of 700,000 Portuguese.[77] There was also an exodus of whites from Rhodesia not only during the decolonization war but also after the triumph of African majority rule, beginning with roughly 800 per month in 1976, climbing to 46,000 to the period from 1977 to 1979, and to 152,000 for the 1979–1990 years.[78]

Although Thomas,[79] Jowell,[80] and Uys[81] have furnished reasoned arguments and data in the pre-independence literature on Namibia anticipating an appreciable loss of the white inhabitants, it is noteworthy that there was rather a small exodus of whites from Namibia, most of whom were South African civil servants seconded to Namibia and members of the various branches of the South African armed forces posted to Namibia. The total number of these white emigrants was about 50,000.[82] In addition, the SADF relocated the San trackers associated with the SWATF to South Africa.[83] Several of those involved in the 32 Battalion and in *Koevoet* became employed in private South African security companies, including Executive Outcomes.[84]

The Pretoria regime was well aware of its white support base in South Africa and did not wish to antagonize those supporters by accepting a large migration of whites from Namibia. Such a migration might suggest that the regime was forsaking the whites in Namibia. The economic security of the white community was their overriding concern.[85] By way of comparison, roughly 500,000 whites emigrated from South Africa in the period 1994–2007, according to Christi van der Westhuizen.[86] Unfortunately, she provided no source for these data.

Although sixty percent of the 25,000 German-speakers in Namibia were also German citizens,[87] apparently very few of them emigrated to Germany. So far, I have been unable to locate any published hard data on emigration for this language group. Although Esther Schüring refers to the "Namibian Diaspora in Germany," and traces its size from 130 Namibian citizens in 1993 to 409 Namibian citizens in 2003, it is unclear whether these persons hold dual nationality or whether these data include Namibians studying in Germany. Were they emigrating whites, they probably would have acquired German citizenship before emigrating.[88] One informed estimate is that one thousand Germans emigrated after independence.[89]

The Fifth Question

Considering the fifth and sixth questions posed in the preface, there are two complementary queries. The fifth one asks what repertoires did the Namibian nationalists use to secure their goals and, conversely, the sixth one asks how the South African regime attempted to challenge those goals with a competing vision or with what Thomas Henriksen called a counterideology[90] for the future of Namibia? This suggests that the conflict can be interpreted as one of vision versus alternative vision and force versus counterforce. How did these two opponents mesh their diplomatic, economic, and military capabilities in this war, on the one hand, and what were, in the words of Prosser Gifford and William R. Louis, "…the consequences of decolonization…"[91] in terms of these three sectors, primarily for Namibia and secondarily for South Africa, on the other hand?

Fragmented and disconnected Namibian nationalism was the prevailing pattern throughout the German imperial epoch and the pre–World War II League of Nations period, and thereafter these subnational discourses assumed pan-territorial dimensions. It was the Herero people who were the driving force in conceptualizing the sense of African dispossession and its antidote through the aggregation of grievances and aspirations. After 1945, there was an attentive, albeit elite, audience of clergy and other transnational activists in the West to hear and perhaps to respond to this Namibian remonstrance. Although the Liberal Party of South Africa took a brief interest in the cultivation of political consciousness and non-racialism among the Namibian Africans, this amounted to very little[92] and the Africans moved ahead with their own political organization. In due course, the premier nationalist group, SWAPO, began to pursue a course of guerrilla warfare against the South African regime, which assigned the South West African Police the principal responsibility for COIN. Like other guerrillas, PLAN's most significant goal was "…to loosen state control over territory and population" and to corrode their enemy's will to resist.[93]

At the outset, PLAN was poorly armed and had a tortuous overland supply route, but after the Portuguese vacated Angola, the logistics route improved and PLAN was able to secure an array of arms primarily from the Eastern bloc of nations which also supplied FAPLA, facilitating the exchange of weapons. The suppliers of weapons also served as military trainers, and the major emphasis was placed on infiltrating southward into the white farming areas to bring the war right to their doorstep.[94] In some cases they did succeed and were able to sabotage property and infrastructure in a limited way and also to lay landmines and to arrange arms caches within Namibia.

These raids predictably took place in the rainy season, but PLAN was unable to establish liberated zones that were lauded in some of the literature of guerrilla war. Once the PLAN fighters crossed the border back into Angola, their protection came principally from FAPLA. Their South African opponents not only attempted to intercept PLAN units as they crossed the border but also made a determined effort, in terms of conventional war operations, to drive them as far north into Angola as possible, thus making their southward transit to the border an even longer distance.[95] In the course of time, PLAN needed to fight both a guerrilla and a conventional war (which it did with FAPLA and Cuban assistance) in Namibia and Angola, respectively. Although once criticized by "some observers" (who were not identified in the article) as an ineffectual force,[96] their opponents often gave these soldiers high marks for their combat performance.[97] Guerrilla stamina and will power are some of the ingredients of success, which paradoxically can be the absence of loss; a different political calculus can characterize guerrilla, rather than conventional, war.

SWAPO enjoyed considerable success in the diplomatic arena, particularly in the United Nations General Assembly that legitimated their existence and aims. In addition, they engaged in vigorous bilateral diplomacy to secure arms and military training, to fund provisions for Namibian refugees fleeing to African majority-ruled states, to create educational opportunities for talented Namibians, and to cultivate friendly patrons among the attentive and vocal sectors of Western states. In short, they created diplomatic and economic space for their expatriate members. Indeed, they had done so well by the United Nations that their South African opponents complained of the patent partiality of this international organization. Even though the United Nations made an effort in the final days of the war to address this complaint,[98] the South Africans nevertheless advanced this argument from time to time as a dilatory ploy.[99]

The Sixth Question

With regard to the sixth and last question, one finds no counterideology that had a widespread appeal to the Africans of Namibia, that is, one that could trump the nationalists' vision of independence for all the inhabitants of Namibia. South African ideology was, *au fond*, anchored in the white minority's fear and anxiety of African majority rule as well as in a Hobbesian vision of ubiquitous inter-racial conflict. What was paramount was security for the whites.[100] The *swart gevaar* was a familiar concept to the white electorate.[101] This meant that there was a limited freedom of maneuver for the Pretoria regime which not only had to placate two white electorates (in South Africa and Namibia) but also to appeal to policy elites and interest groups in friendly states which could act as a breakwater for South Africa in the United Nations and other international fora. Hence, there were multiple messages or symbols for multiple, sometimes, complementary audiences.

This limited political space was filled to a large extent in symbol manipulation in the United Nations, which was hardly a unique approach to public diplomacy, but it did buy time in the early years, particularly with the western colonial powers. This was the heyday of petitions and the pervasiveness of international law, which appealed to the western members of the Security Council. During these halcyon days there were three International Court of Justice advisory opinions (1950, 1955, and 1956) and the petition process was underway at the General Assembly committee level. Moreover, the Cold War atmosphere enabled the Pretoria regime to cast itself as a valuable ally of the west, complete with strategic minerals (including uranium) and a safe naval redoubt for shipping traversing the Atlantic and Indian Oceans. The accompanying anti-communism resonated with many military and business elites in the west.

One could make a strong case for South Africa's first golden international age that coincided with the League of Nations era in which South Africa was not only able to earn leadership positions in the League but also in which General Jan C. Smuts enjoyed a widespread international reputation. However, after presenting the South African case for the incorporation of Namibia into South Africa, he became thoroughly disillusioned by the United Nations.[102] South Africa's second golden age was cut short in 1960, when Ethiopia and Liberia filed their suit over South Africa's mismanagement of the sacred trust in Namibia. This heralded a direct confrontation with an increasing number of Third World states in the United Nations, which used that organization to delegitimize the entire structure of colonialism and to dedicate themselves to its destruction. Beginning in 1966, when the International Court of Justice decided to reject the plaintiffs' case, thereby undercutting their strategy to turn to the Security Council to enforce the court's judgment against South Africa, the pace quickened. According to A. Ukiomogbe Obozuwa, this was not a realistic expectation because of the probability that the Western permanent members of the UN Security Council would have vetoed such a course of action.[103] The General Assembly terminated South Africa's tenuous link to Namibia by assuming the right to administer the territory until it became independent, and the firefight at Ongulumbashe marked the beginning of the war of independence.

In due course the Pretoria regime became nearly ostracized at the United Nations, particularly in the General Assembly where the anti-colonial bloc was able to utilize its growing numerical strength. The South African diplomacy at the United Nations was characterized by the use of widely accepted symbols, especially self-determination, to explain and justify its separate development policy in Namibia and even to propose yet another plebiscite in the next International Court of Justice advisory opinion (1971). Far more significant was its diplomatic cultivation of the three Western permanent members of the Security Council. This also involved the active, yet low-key participation of the South Africa Foundation members.

Here the issue shifts to the economic and military spheres, where the imposition of sanctions and, in the early stages, possible invasion by the United Nations and/or Afro-Asian military forces[104] were the prevailing concerns. However, it is likely that this perception was not a widespread one within the white South African community.[105] An added threat was the growing geographic enclosure of the nation, both in terms of their opponents' goals of diplomatic and economic isolation and in terms of the shrinking defense perimeter resulting from the decolonization of Angola, Mozambique, and Rhodesia. There was a need for an overarching policy to explain these setbacks and to formulate effective counter-measures. Thus arose the explanatory total onslaught doctrine and the prescriptive total strategy course of action.

With reference to SWAPO and PLAN, the overriding aim of the apartheid regime was "the neutralization of the counter-state"[106] that their opponents were attempting to construct. The SADF developed its COIN doctrines in a syncretistic fashion, borrowing from the French and the Americans. Yet, I have been unable to find few scholarly analyses on the various strategic discourses and counterfactuals that may have driven its policy choices. Although Annette Seegers' *The Military in the Making of South Africa* is a pioneering work, it does not directly address this matter. The scholarly lacuna is probably due to the culture of secrecy surrounding the SADF created by the raft of security legislation that would have precluded research on this topic.

The American example seemed not to extend to the intellectual flaws that characterized much of American counterinsurgency policy in the postwar world.[107] D. Michael Shafer has done a masterful job illuminating the nature of flawed assumptions underlying American COIN policies.[108] It appears as though toleration of dissent is not a widely shared characteristic of the Afrikaner ruling style.[109] Pretoria's diplomatic and military repertoire had an antipodal characteristic summed up in the phrase "talk and thump" style[110] of P. W. Botha that was a well-known technique in statecraft. Equally important was the commonplace bureaucratic difference between the diplomats and warriors in Pretoria.[111] Gillian Gunn has provided a concrete example of this in her assessment of Mozambique.[112] This difference between the diplomats and warriors rests, at least in part, on dissimilar evaluations, and perceptions, of threats against South Africa.[113] The familiar aphorism of "where you stand depends upon where you sit," underscores the ubiquity of bureaucratic wrangling in the formation of foreign policy.[114]

Not unexpectedly, the South African regime interwove military forays and diplomatic gambits,[115] and they varied their policies in accordance with what has been called a three-track policy, namely, the continued military campaign against PLAN and its allies as well as the international track and the domestic, Namibian track.[116] In the military sector, they were able to field an impressive army, even though the professional military leadership was burdened by having to defend "an unacceptable political objective," according to one knowledgeable observer.[117] Both the ground and the air forces were subject to overseas arms embargoes that they were able to counter with domestic arms production, even though, in the final stages of the war in Angola, they were unable to regain effective air superiority over the battlefield. In the case of Walvis Bay, however, they demonstrated their willingness to thump their adversary in the economic battlefield.

In Namibia they unsuccessfully attempted to craft institutions to tame African nationalists and to mollify the resident white community.[118] These fragile institutions (the Multi-Party Conference and the subsequent interim government) were egregiously lacking in legitimacy.[119] Nevertheless, the Namibian institutional building was not a case of tilting at political windmills; rather it was an exercise in social engineering by Pretoria to develop viable institutions in South Africa as part of a cautious attempt to move away from the most odious aspect of apartheid.[120] These shifts were marked by symbol manipulation and by what has been dubbed the "lexicon of obscurity."[121] The subsequent and often violent transition to majority rule ushered in new political actors and policies for South Africa. One of the more noticeable changes was the cancellation of the Namibian debt by the Mandela Government and the vanishing of the securocrats from the corridors of power in Pretoria. No longer would the term "garrison state" apply to South Africa,[122] and Pretoria could now utilize its economic assets for beneficent purposes at home, such as its own negotiated passage to African majority rule.

Appendix: The United Nations and Namibia

Table One
UN General Assembly Resolutions on Namibia: Tabulation for Self-Determination, Trusteeship and Independence, 1946–1960[1]

Resolution Number and Date	Self-Determination	Trusteeship	Independence
65 (I) 14 December 1946	No	Yes	No
141 (II) 1 November 1947	No	Yes	No
227 (III) 26 November 1948	No	Yes	No
337 (IV) 6 December 1949	No	Yes	No
338 (IV) 6 December 1949	No	No	No
449 (V) A/B 13 December 1950	No	Yes (B)	No
570 (VI) A/B 19 January 1952	No	Yes (B)	No
651 (VII) 20 December 1952	No	No	No
749 (VIII) A/B 28 November 1953	No	Yes (B)	No
844 (IX) 11 October 1954	No	No	No
851 (IX) 23 November 1954	No	No	No
852 (IX) 23 November 1954	No	Yes	No
904 (IX) 23 November 1954	No	No	No
934 (X) 3 December 1955	No	No	No
935 (X) 3 December 1955	No	No	No
936 (X) 3 December 1955	No	No	No
937 (X) 3 December 1955	No	No	No
938 (X) 3 December 1955	No	No	No
939 (X) 3 December 1955	No	No	No
940 (X) 3 December 1955	No	Yes	No
941 (X) 3 December 1955	No	No	No
942 (X) 3 December 1955	No	No	No
943 (X) 3 December 1955	No	No	No
1047 (XI) 23 January 1957	No	No	No
1054 (XI) 26 February 1957	No	No	No

Resolution Number and Date	Self-Determination	Trusteeship	Independence
1055 (X) 26 February 1956	No	Yes	No
1056 (XI) 26 February 1957	No	No	No
1057 (X) 26 February 1957	No	No	No
1058 (XI) 26 February 1957	No	No	No
1059 (XI) 26 February 1957	No	Yes	No
1060 (XI) 26 February 1957	No	Yes	No
1061 (XI) 26 February 1957	No	No	No
1138 (XII) 25 October 1957	No	No	No
1139 (XII) 25 October 1957	No	No	No
1140 (XII) 25 October 1957	No	No	No
1141 (XII) 25 October 1957	No	Yes	No
1142 (XII) 25 October 1957	No	No	No
1143 (XII) 25 October 1957	No	No	No
1243 (XIII) 30 October 1958	No	No	No
1244 (XIII) 30 October 1958	No	No	No
1245 (XIII) 30 October 1958	No	No	No
1246 (XIII) 30 October 1958	No	Yes	No
1247 (XIII) 30 October 1958	No	No	No
1333 (XIII) 13 December 1958	No	No	No
1356 (XIV) 17 November 1959	No	No	No
1357 (XIV) 17 November 1959	No	No	No
1358 (XIV) 17 November 1959	No	No	No
1359 (XIV) 17 November 1959	No	Yes	No
1360 (XIV) 17 November 1959	No	Yes	No
1361 (XIV) 17 November 1959	No	No	No
1362 (XIV) 17 November 1959	No	No	No
1563 (XV) 18 December 1960	No	No	No
1564 (XV) 18 December 1960	No	No	No
1565 (XV) 18 December 1960	No	No	No
1566 (XV) 18 December 1960	No	No	No
1567 (XV) 18 December 1960	No	No	No
1568 (XV) 18 December 1960	No	Yes	Yes

Table Two
UN General Assembly Resolutions on Namibia: Tabulation for Self-Determination, Trusteeship and Independence, 1961–1966[2]

Resolution Number and Date	Self-Determination	Trusteeship	Independence
1593 (XV) 16 March 1961	No	No	No
1596 (XV) 7 April 1961	Yes	No	Yes
1702 (XV) 19 December 1961	No	No	Yes
1703 (XV) 19 December 1961	No	No	No
1704 (XV) 19 December 1961	No	No	No
1705 (XV) 19 December 1961	No	No	No
1804 (XVII) 14 December 1962	No	No	No
1805 (XVII) 14 December 1962	No	No	Yes

Resolution Number and Date	Self-Determination	Trusteeship	Independence
1806 (XVII) 14 December 1962	No	No	No
1899 (XVIII) 13 November 1963	Yes	No	Yes
1900 (XVIII) 13 November 1963	No	No	No
1901 (XVIII) 13 November 1963	No	No	No
1979 (XVIII) 16 December 1963	No	No	No
2074 (XX) 17 December 1965	No	No	Yes
2075 (XX) 17 December 1965	No	No	No
2076 (XX) 17 December 1965	No	No	No
2145 (XXI) 27 October 1966	Yes	No	Yes
2235 (XXI) 20 December 1966	No	No	No
2236 (XXI) 20 December 1966	No	No	No

Table Three
UN General Assembly Resolutions on Namibia: Tabulation for Self-Determination, Independence and Legitimacy 1967–1976[3]

Resolution Number and Date	Self-Determination	Independence	Legitimacy
2248 (S-V) 19 May 1967	No	Yes	No
2324 (XXII) 16 December 1967	No	No	No
2325 (XXII) 16 December 1967	No	Yes	No
2372 (XXII) 12 June 1968	No	Yes	Yes
2403 (XXIII) 16 December 1968	Yes	Yes	Yes
2404 (XXIII) 16 December 1968	No	No	No
2498 (XXIV) 31 October 1969	Yes	Yes	Yes
2517 (XXIV) 1 December 1969	Yes	Yes	Yes
2518 (XXIV) 1 December 1969	No	No	No
2678 (XXV) 9 December 1970	Yes	Yes	Yes
2679 (XXV) 9 December 1970	Yes	Yes	No
2680 (XXV) 9 December 1970	No	No	No
2871 (XXVI) 20 December 1971	Yes	Yes	Yes
2872 (XXVI) 20 December 1971	Yes	Yes	No
3030 (XXVII) 18 December 1972	Yes	Yes	No
3031 (XXVII) 18 December 1972	Yes	Yes	Yes
3111 (XXVIII) 12 December 1973	Yes	Yes	Yes
3112 (XXVIII) 12 December 1973	No	No	No
3295 (XXIX) 13 December 1974	Yes	Yes	Yes
3296 (XXIX) 13 December 1974	No	No	Yes
3399 (XXX) 26 November 1975	Yes	Yes	Yes
3400 (XXX) 26 November 1975	No	No	No
31/145 17 December 1976	Yes	Yes	No
31/146 20 December 1976	Yes	Yes	Yes
31/147 20 December 1976	Yes	Yes	No
31/148 20 December 1976	No	No	No
31/149 20 December 1976	No	No	No
31/150 20 December 1976	Yes	Yes	No
31/151 20 December 1976	Yes	Yes	No

Resolution Number and Date	Self-Determination	Independence	Legitimacy
31/152 20 December 1976	No	No	No
31/153 20 December 1976	Yes	Yes	No

Table Four
UN General Assembly Resolutions on Namibia:
Tabulation for Self-Determination, Independence and Legitimacy 1977–1990[4]

Resolution Number and Date	Self-Determination	Independence	Legitimacy
32/9 (Parts A-H) 4 November 1977	Yes (A-D, F)	Yes (A-D, F)	Yes (D)
32/41 7 December 1977	Yes	Yes	No
S-9/2 (Parts I-II) 3 May 1978	Yes (I, II)	Yes (I, II)	Yes (I)
33/182 (Parts A-C) 21 December 1978	Yes (A-C)	Yes (A-C)	Yes (A)
33/206 31 May 1979	Yes	Yes	Yes
34/92 (Parts A-G) 12 December 1979	Yes (A-G)	Yes (A-G)	Yes (G)
34/174 17 December 1979	No	No	No
35/227 (parts A-J) 6 March 1981	Yes (A-H, J)	Yes (A-H, J)	Yes (A)
ES-8/2 14 September 1981	Yes	Yes	No
36/121 (parts A-F) 10 December 1981	Yes (A, C, E)	Yes (A, C, E)	Yes (A)
37/233 (A-E) 20 December 1982	Yes (A-D)	Yes (A-D, F)	Yes (A)
38/36 (parts A-E) 1 December 1983	Yes (A-D)	Yes (A-E)	Yes (A)
39/50 (parts A-E) 12 December 1984	Yes (A-D)	Yes (A-E)	Yes (A)
40/97 (parts A-F) 13 December 1985	Yes (A-D)	Yes (A-F)	Yes (A)
41/39 (parts A-E) 20 November 1986	Yes (A-D)	Yes (A-E)	Yes (A)
41/123 4 December 1986	No	No	No
42/14 (parts A-E) 10 November 1987	Yes (A-D)	Yes (A-E)	Yes (A)
43/26 (parts A-E) 17 November 1988	Yes (A-B, D)	Yes (A-B, D-E)	No
43/134 8 December 1988	No	No	No
44/143 15 December 1989	No	No	No

Resolution Number and Date	Self-Determination	Independence	Legitimacy
44/243 (parts A-B) 11 September 1990	Yes (A)	Yes (B)	No

Table Five
UN Security Council Resolutions on Namibia, 1968–1990: Tabulation for Self-Determination, Independence and Legitimacy[5]

Resolution Number and Date[5]	Self-Determination	Independence	Legitimacy
Res. 245 (1968) 25 January 1968	No	No	No
Res. 246 (1968) 14 March 1968	No	Yes	No
Res. 264 (1969) 20 March 1969	No	Yes	No
Res. 269 (1969) 12 August 1969	No	No	Yes
Res. 276 (1970) 30 January 1970	No	Yes	No
Res. 283 (1970) 29 July 1970	No	Yes	No
Res. 284 (1970) 29 July 1970	No	No	No
Res. 301 (1971) 20 October 1971	Yes	Yes	Yes
Res. 309 (1972) 4 February 1972	Yes	Yes	No
Res. 310 (1972) 4 February 1972	Yes	Yes	No
Res. 319 (1972) 1 August 1972	Yes	Yes	No
Res. 323 (1972) 6 December 1972	Yes	Yes	No
Res. 342 (1973) 11 December 1973	No	No	No
Res. 366 (1974) 17 December 1974	No	No	No
Res. 385 (1976) 30 January 1976	No	No	No
Res. 431 (1978) 27 July 1978	No	No	No
Res. 432 (1978) 27 July 1978	No	No	No
Res. 435 (1978) 29 September 1978	No	No	No
Res. 439 (1978) 13 November 1978	No	No	No
Res. 532 (1983) 31 May 1983	No	Yes	No
Res. 539 (1983) 28 October 1983	No	Yes	No
Res. 566 (1985) 19 June 1985	No	Yes	Yes
Res. 601 (1987) 30 October 1987	No	No	No
Res. 628 (1989) 16 January 1989	No	No	No
Res. 629 (1989) 16 January 1989	No	Yes	No
Res. 632 (1989) 16 February 1989	No	Yes	No
Res. 640 (1989) 29 August 1989	No	Yes	No
Res. 643 (1989) 31 October 1989	Yes	Yes	No
Res. 652 (1990) 17 April 1990	No	No	No

Table Six
United Nations Fund for Namibia, 1972–1990 (Established by UNGA res. 2679 [XXV], operative para. 1, 9 December 1970)

Year	Amount	Source[6]
1972	$50,000	UNGA res. 2872 (XXVI), operative para. 3 20 December 1971
1973	$100,000	UNGA res. 3030 (XXVII), operative para. 2 18 December 1972

Year	Amount	Source
1974	$100,000	UNGA res. 3112 (XXVIII), operative para. 2 12 December 1973*
1975	$200,000	UNGA res. 3296 (XXIX), operative para. 6 13 December 1974
1976	$200,000	UNGA res. 3400 (XXX), operative para. 3 26 November 1975
1977	$300,000	UNGA res. 31/151, operative para. 3 20 December 1976
1978	$500,000	UNGA res. 32/9 B, operative para. 4 4 November 1977
1979	$500,000	UNGA res. 33/182 C, operative para. 5 c 21 December 1978
1980	$500,000	UNGA res. 34/92 E, operative para. 4 12 December 1979
1981	Nothing	UNGA res. 35/227 G 6 March 1981
1982	$1 million	UNGA Res. 36/121 F, operative para. 4 10 December 1981
1983	$1 million	UNGA res. 37/233 E, operative para. 3 20 December 1982
1984	$1 million	UNGA res. 38/36 E, operative para. 5 1 December 1983
1985	$1 million	UNGA res. 39/50 E, operative para. 5 12 December 1984
1986	$1.5 million	UNGA res. 40/97 E, operative para. 7 13 December 1985
1987	$1.5 million	UNGA res. 41/39 E, operative para. 7 20 December 1986
1988	$1.5 million	UNGA res. 42/14 E, operative para. 7 6 November 1987
1989	$1.5 million	UNGA res. 43/26 E, operative para. 7 8 December 1988
1990	$1.5 million	UNGA res. 44/243 B, operative para. 16 11 September 1990

*Operative para. 6 of UNGA res. 3112 (XXVIII) of 12 December 1973 designates the UN Council for Namibia as the trustee for this fund.

Chapter Notes

Abbreviations

AAP — Arms and Armour Press
ACP — African Communications Projects
AD — Andre Deutsch Limited
AJP — Al Jadidah Press
AP — Ashanti Publishing (Pty.) Ltd.
AsP — Ashgate Publishing Limited
AWP — Africa World Press, Inc.
AWS — A.W. Sijthoff
BAB — Basler Afrika Bibliographien
BB — Bantam Books, Inc.
BeP — Beacon Press
BP — Buffalo Publications
BwP — Butterworth Publishers
CbUP — Cambridge University Press
CDB — Covos-Day Books
CFRP — Council on Foreign Relations Press
CH — Croom Helm Ltd.
CKV — Chr. Kaiser Verlag
CnUP — Cornell University Press
col(s). — column(s)
ConP — Contra Press
CoUP — Columbia University Press
CP — Clarendon Press
CS — Content Solutions
DC — Doubleday & Company, Inc.
diss. — dissertation
DPP — David Philip Publishers (Pty.) Ltd.
DUP — Duke University Press
ed. — edition, editor(s)
EIU — The Economist Intelligence Unit
EL — Éditions L'Harmattan
EP — Eyes Publishing
EPC — Ethiope Publishing Company
FaC — Fawcett Columbine
FaF — Faber and Faber
FAP — Frederick A. Praeger, Inc., Publisher
FC — Frank Cass & Co. Ltd.
FHL — Footprint Handbooks Limited
FoP — Fortress Publishers (Pty.) Ltd.
FP — The Foundation Publishers
FrP — The Free Press
FSP — Fokus Suid Publishers
FSV — Franz Steiner Verlag
GalP — Galaxie Press (Pvt.) Ltd.
GaP — Galago Publishing (Pty.) Ltd.
GMP — Gamsberg Macmillan Publishers (Pty.) Ltd.
GP — Greenwood Press
GrP — Grossman Publishers
HBC — History Book Club
HF — Howard Fertig, Inc.
HIP — The Hoover Institution Press
HRE — Hans Robert Engelmann
HSRCP — Human Sciences Research Council Press
HT — Howard Timmins
HUP — Harvard University Press
IBT — I.B. Taurus Publishers
IKOVIK — IKO — Verlag für Interkulturelle Kommunikation
ISS — Institute for Strategic Studies
IUP — Indiana University Press
JaM — Jacanda Media
JBL — J.B. Lippincott Company
JBP — Jonathan Ball Publishers (Pty.) Ltd.
JC — James Currey Ltd.
JHUP — The Johns Hopkins University Press
JM — John Murray
JML — John Meinert Limited
JS — Jeremy Spence
JuC — Juta and Company Limited
KB — Koninklijke Brill NV
KP — Kalinga Publications
KPI — Kegan Paul International Ltd.
LB — Lexington Books
LBC — Little, Brown and Company
LeB — Lemur Books
LGL — Longman Group Limited
LHC — Lawrence Hill and Company, Publishers, Inc.
LPP — Lex Patria Publishers
LRP — Lynne Rienner Publishers
LS — Lyle Stuart
MaC — The Magus Company
MamP — Mambo Press
MaP — Macmillan Press Ltd.
MB — Meridian Books, Inc.
MEN — Macmillan Education Namibia
MES — M. E. Sharpe
MGV — Matthias-Grünewald-Verlag
MITP — MIT Press
ML — The Modern Library
MN — Martinus Nijhoff

MPC — Markham Publishing Company
MPL — The Merlin Press Ltd.
MRP — Monthly Review Press
MTS — Maurice Temple Smith Ltd.
MUP — Manchester University Press
n., nn. — endnote(s), footnote(s)
NAI — Nordic Africa Institute
NALWL — New American Library of World Literature, Inc.
n.d. — no date (of publication)
NeUP — Northeastern University Press
NiP — Nirmal Publications
NIP — Naval Institute Press
NNB — New Namibia Books (Pty.) Ltd.
NP — Ntomeni Publishers
NSP — Nova Science Publishers, Inc.
NSS — Namibia Scientific Society
OAP — Out of Africa Publishers
OB — Owl Books
OcP — Oceana Press
OhUP — Ohio University Press
OP — Osprey Publishing Ltd.
OxUP — Oxford University Press
PA — PublicAffairs
PaB — Panaf Books
PB — Penguin Books, Inc.
PBAL — Penguin Books Australia Ltd.
PBB — Peter Bedrick Books
PBH — Protea Book House
PBSA — Penguin Books (South Africa) (Pty.) Ltd.
PH — Prentice-Hall, Inc.
PHV — Peter Hammer Verlag GmbH
PL — Peter Lang GmbH
PM — Palgrave Macmillan
PnB — Pantheon Books
PP — Pluto Press
PreP — Presidio Press
PrP — Praeger Publishers
PSHY — Pohjois-Suomen Historiallinen Yhdistys
PSI — Praeger Security International
PSP — P. Schlettwein Publishing
PUP — Princeton University Press
PuS — Purnell & Sons (S.A.) (Pty.) Ltd.
QB — Quartet Books
RC — Rex Collings
ReP — Reach Publishers
RH — Random House (Pty.) Ltd.
RLP — Rowman & Littlefield Publishers, Inc.
RP — Ravan Press (Pty.) Ltd.
RSSP — Robert Speller & Sons, Publishers, Inc.
SaP — Sage Press
SAPESB — Southern African Political Economy Series Books
SAWPOB — S. A. Weermag. Openbar Betrekking (South African Defense Force Public Relations Office)
SB — Stackpole Books
SBP — Southern Book Publishers (Pty.) Ltd.
ScP — The Scarecrow Press
SFP — Selous Foundation Press
SkP — Skotaville Publishers
s.l. — without the name of the place of publication (sine loco)
SMP — St. Martin's Press
SoP — Sosiumi Press
SP — Sundeep Prakashan
SUP — Stanford University Press
TAS — Tarus Academic Studies

TC — Thomas Y. Crowell Company
TDSP — Thirty Degrees South Publishers (Pty.) Ltd.
UCLP — University College London Press Limited
UCP — University of California Press
UCTP — University of Cape Town Press
UH — Unwin Hyman Inc.
UIP — University of Ife Press
UKNP — University of KwaZulu-Natal Press
UNCP — University of North Carolina Press
UNDP — University of Notre Dame Press
UNeP — University of Nebraska Press
UNtP — University of Natal Press
UOP — University of Oklahoma Press
UPA — University Press of America
URP — University of Rochester Press
USAP — University of South Africa Press
UTP — University of Toronto Press
vol(s). — volume(s)
WC — Walker & Company
WP — Westview Press
WsUP — Wesleyan University Press
WUP — Witwatersrand University Press
WWN — W. W. Norton & Company
XPC — Xlibris Publishing Company
YUN — Yearbook(s) of the United Nations
YUP — Yale University Press
ZbP — Zebra Press
ZP/B — Zed Press/Books

Preface

1. As of 12 February 2011.
2. Verne Harris, "'They Should Have Destroyed More': The Destruction of Public Records by the South African State in the Final Years of Apartheid, 1990–1994," *Transformation* (Durban) 40 (2000): 29–56, especially 34–35, 37–38, 43–44, and 54.
3. Paulo E. S. L. de F. Correia, "Political Relations between Portugal and South Africa from the End of the Second World War until 1974" (D.Litt. et Phil. diss., University of Johannesburg, 2007), 18.
4. J. Taljaard, "Koevoet Cashing in on Battle Wounds," WM, 13 August 1993, 3.
5. Roger Pfister, *Apartheid South Africa and African States: From Pariah to Middle Power, 1961–1964*, International Library of African Studies, vol. 14 (New York: TAS, 2005), 43–44.
6. Correia, "Political Relations," 16–18.
7. Piero Gleijeses, *Visions of Freedom: Havana, Washington, Pretoria and the Struggle for Southern Africa, 1976–1991* (Chapel Hill: UNCP, 2013), xi and 15.
8. Hans G. Schleicher and Illona Schleicher, *Special Flights: The GDR and the Liberation Movements in Southern Africa* (Harare: SAPESB, 1998), 2.
9. Victor Moukambi, "Relations between South and France with Special Reference to Military Matters, 1960–1990" (D.Phil. diss., Stellenbosch University, 2008), 10 and 293.
10. Vladimir G. Shubin, *The Hot "Cold War": The USSR in Southern Africa* (London: PP; Scottsville: UKNP, 2008), xv.
11. Gary F. Baines, "SADF Soldiers' Stories: Review Article," JNS, 5 (2009): 7–25.
12. Catherine Sasman, "Anti-Colonial History Revisited," NE, 8 December 2009, 4; Ellen N. Namhila, "Filling the Gaps in the Archival Record of the Namibian

Struggle for Independence," IFLAJ, 30, no. 3 [2004]: 224–230, especially 227.

13. Christopher C. Saunders, "History and the Armed Struggle: From Anti-Colonial Propaganda to 'Patriotic History?'" in *Transitions in Namibia: Which Changes for Whom?*, ed. Henning Melber (Uppsala: NAI, 200–7), 21.

14. UNGA res. 1514 (XV) titled *Declaration on the Granting of Independence to Colonial Countries and Peoples*, 14 December 1960.

15. Jean-Claude Fritz, *La Namibie Indépendante: Les Coûts d'une Décolonisation Retardée* (Paris: EL, 1991).

16. Douglas G. Anglin, "Namibian Relations with South Africa: Post-Independence Prospects," in *Prospects for Peace and Development in Southern Africa in the 1990s: Canadian and Comparative Perspectives*, ed. Larry A. Swatuk and Timothy M. Shaw (Lanham, Md.: UPA; Halifax, N.S.: DUCAS, 1991), 107.

17. UNGA, res. 38/36 A of 1 December 1983, operative para. fifteen.

18. Anthony Clayton, *The Wars of French Decolonization* (London: Longman, 1994), 186.

19. Jean Suret-Canale, "From Colonization to Independence in French Tropical Africa: The Economic Background," in *The Transfer of Power in Africa: Decolonization, 1940–1960*, ed. Prosser Gifford and William R. Louis (New Haven: YUP, 1982), 476.

20. Neta C. Crawford, *Argument and Change in World Politics: Ethics, Decolonization, and Humanitarian Intervention*, Cambridge Studies in International Relations no. 81 (New York: CbUP, 2002), 8 n. 7 and 136–137.

21. Rachna Srivastava, *Namibia: A Study in the Process of Decolonization* (Delhi: NiP, 1994), iv-v.

22. Willem Steenkamp, *South Africa's Border War, 1966–1989* (Gibraltar: AP, 1989), 7.

23. Gary F. Baines, "Introduction: Challenging the Boundaries, Breaking the Silences," in *Beyond the Border War: New Perspectives on Southern Africa's Late-Cold War Conflicts*, ed. Gary F. Baines and Peter Vale (Pretoria: USAP, 2008), 5–7.

24. Annette Seegers, *The Military in the Making of Modern South Africa*, International Library of African Studies vol. 1 (London: IBT, 1996), 309–310.

25. Jannie Geldenhuys, *A General's Story: From an Era of War and Peace*, translated by Annemarié Geldenhuys (Johannesburg: JBP, 1995), 91 and 126.

26. Gavin Cawthra, *Brute Force: The Apartheid War Machine* (London: IDAFSA, 1986), 176.

27. "Introduction," in *Namibia: SWAPO Fights for Freedom*, ed. Liberation Support Movement (Oakland, Calif.: LSMIC, 1978), 15 and 18, respectively.

28. Saunders, "History and the Armed Struggle," 15.

29. Clayton, *The Wars of French Decolonization*.

30. Ibid., 182.

31. Anthony Low, "The End of the British Empire in Africa," in *Decolonization and Independence: The Transfers of Power, 1960–1980*, ed. Prosser Gifford and William R. Louis (New Haven: YUP, 1988), 33.

32. William H. Nelson, *The American Tory* (Boston: NeUP, 1992, originally published in 1961), [xv].

33. Rona M. Fields, *The Portuguese Revolution and the Armed Forces Movement* (New York: PrP, 1975), 211, n. 1.

34. Daniel Byman, Peter Chalk, Bruce Hoffman, William Rosenau, and David Brannan, *Trends in Outside Support for Insurgent Movements* (Santa Monica, Calif.: RANDC, National Security Research Division, International Security and Defense Center, 2001), xviii and 83–102.

35. Heribert Adam and Kanya Adam, "The Politics of Memory in Divided Societies," in *After the TRC: Reflections on Truth and Reconciliation in South Africa*, ed. Wilmont James and Linda van de Vijver (Athens: OhUP; Cape Town: DPP, 2000), 32 and 36, respectively for the two quotations.

36. Justine Hunter, "No Man's Land of Time: Reflections on the Politics of Memory and Forgetting in Namibia," in Baines and Vale, ed., *Beyond the Border War*, 302–321.

37. Alexander L. George and Andrew Bennett, *Case Studies and Theory Development in the Social Sciences* (Cambridge: MITP, 2004), 81, 166–167, and 221.

38. George and Bennett, *Case Studies*, 18.

39. Thomas G. Weiss, David Cortright, George A. Lopez, and Larry Minear, "Toward a Framework for Analysis," in *Political Gain and Civilian Pain: Humanitarian Impacts of Economic Sanctions*, ed. Weiss et al. (Lanham, Md.: RLP, 1997), 35–53.

40. Gary F. Baines, "Vietnam Analogies and Metaphors: The Cultural Codification of South Africa's Border War," SJSAAS 13, nos. 1–2 (January-April 2012): 73–90.

41. Thomas H. Henriksen, "Portugal in Africa: Comparative Notes on Counterinsurgency," *Orbis* 21, no. 2 (Summer 1977): 395–412.

42. Kenneth W. Grundy, "The Social Costs of Armed Struggle in Southern Africa," AFS 7, no. 3 (Spring 1981): 445–466.

43. Graeme Callister, "Compliance, Compulsion[,] and Contest: Aspects of Military Conscription in South Africa, 1952–1992" (M.A. thesis, Stellenbosch University, 2007), 2 and 130–141.

44. Elena Torreguitar, *National Liberation Movements in Office: Forging Democracy with African Adjectives in Namibia*. European University Studies, Series XXXI (Political Science), vol. 567 (Frankfurt a.m.: PL, 2009). 413–415 and 466–482.

45. Henri Grimal, *Decolonization: The British, French, Dutch and Belgian Empires, 1919–1963*, translated by Stephan De Vos (Boulder, Colo.: WP, 1978).

46. Kenneth R. Maxwell, "Portugal and Africa: The Last Empire," in Gifford and Louis, ed., *The Transfer of Power in Africa*, 337–385.

47. Tony Smith, "A Comparative Study of French and British Decolonization," CSSH 20, no. 1 (January 1978): 70–102.

48. David B. Abernethy, "Decolonization in Southern Africa: Variations on a Theme" in *Decolonization and Dependency: Problems of Development of African Societies*, ed. Aguibou Y. Yansané, Contributions in Afro-American and African Studies no. 48 (Westport, Conn.: GP, 1980) 196–228.

49. M. Crawford Young, *The African State in Comparative Perspective* (New Haven: YUP, 1994), 275–276.

50. Harry Eckstein, "A Perspective on Comparative Politics, Past and Present" in *Comparative Politics: A Reader*, ed. Harry Eckstein and David E. Apter (New York: FrP, 1963), 3–32, especially 11–12 and 29.

51. Deborah A. Sanders, "Problems and Prospects for the National Liberation Movement: The Dilemma of SWAPO in Namibia," paper presented to the twenty-fifth annual meeting of the ASA, Washington, D.C., 4–7 November 1983, 1–2.

52. James H. Mittelman, "Collective Decolonisation and the U.N. Committee of 24," JMAS, 14, no. 1 (March 1976): 42–44 and 63–64.

53. Ibid., 43.
54. See Chapter One, n. 2 below.
55. R. A. Akindele, "Reflections on the Preoccupation and Conduct of African Diplomacy," JMAS 14, no. 4 (December 1976): 575.
56. Deon J. Geldenhuys, *The Diplomacy of Isolation: South African Foreign Policy Making* (New York: SMP, 1984), 221–231.
57. I. William Zartman, *Ripe for Resolution: Conflict and Intervention in Africa*, updated ed. (New York: OxUP, 1989), 170–254.
58. Vivienne Jabri, *Mediating Conflict: Decision-Making and Western Intervention in Namibia* (Manchester and New York: MUP, 1990).
59. Joanne E. Davies. *Constructive Engagement?: Chester Crocker & American Policy in South Africa, Namibia & Angola* (Oxford: JC.; Auckland Park, South Africa: JaM; Athens: OhUP, 2007).
60. Hans-Joachim Vergau, *Negotiating the Freedom of Namibia: The Diplomatic Achievement of the Western Contact Group*, translated by David R. Ward (Basel: BAB, 2010).
61. Keith Ovenden and Tony Cole, *Apartheid and International Finance: A Program for Change* (Ringwood, Victoria, Australia: PBAL, 1989).
62. Trevor Bell, "The Impact of Sanctions on South Africa," JCAS, 12, no. 1 (1993): 1–28.
63. Kenneth A. Rodman, "Public and Private Sanctions against South Africa," PSQ 109, no. 2 (Summer 1994): 313–334.
64. *How Sanctions Work: Lessons from South Africa*, ed. Neta C. Crawford and Audie J. Klotz (New York: SMP, 1999).
65. Albert Grundlingh, *Fighting Their Own War: South African Blacks and the First World War* (Braamfontein: RP, 1987), 2.
66. Helmoed-Römer Heitman, *South African Armed Forces* (Cape Town: BP, 1990).
67. Helmoed-Römer Heitman, *War in Angola: The Final South African Phase* (Gibraltar: AP, 1990).
68. P. H. R. Snyman, *Beeld van die SWA Gebiedsmag* (Pretoria: SAWOB, 1989), 29–102.
69. Guy Lamb, "Civil Supremacy of the Military in Namibia: An Evolutionary Perspective" (M. Soc. Sci. thesis, University of Cape Town, 1998).
70. Nengovhela J. Livhiwani, "The Role Played by the People's Liberation Army of Namibia (PLAN) during the Namibian Struggle, 1978 to 1989" (M.A. thesis, Rand Afrikaans University, 1999).
71. Ben Connable and Martin C. Libicki, *How Insurgencies End*, prepared for the Marine Corps Intelligence Activity (Santa Monica, Calif.: RANDC, 2010), 69, 132, 158–159, and 165.
72. A. W. Singham and Shirley Hune, *Namibian Independence: A Global Responsibility* (Westport, Conn.: LHC, 1986), 15–37 and 71–82.
73. Suresh C. Saxena, *Namibia and the World: The Birth of a Nation* (Delhi: KP, 1991), 187–214.
74. Ronald Dreyer, *Namibia and Southern Africa: Regional Dynamics of Decolonization, 1945–90* (London: KPI, 1994), 55–59.
75. Christopher C. Saunders, "Namibian Solidarity: British Support for Namibian Independence," JSAS, 35, no. 2 (June 2009): 437–454.
76. George W. Shepherd, Jr., devoted an entire chapter to what he termed "the transnational emergence of Namibia" in his *Anti-Apartheid: Transnational Conflict and Western Policy in the Liberation of South Africa*, Studies in Human Rights no. 3 (Westport, Conn.: GP, 1977), 170–201.
77. Allan D. Cooper, "Preface," in *Allies in Apartheid: Western Capitalism in Occupied Namibia*, ed. Allan D. Cooper (New York: SMP, 1988), x–xi.
78. Roger Fieldhouse, *Anti-Apartheid: A History of the Movement in Britain: A Study in Pressure Group Politics* (London: MPL, 2005), 288.
79. Donald R. Culverson, "The Politics of the Anti-Apartheid Movement in the United States, 1969–1986," PSQ, 111, no. 1 (Spring 1996): 132 and 147.
80. James N. Rosenau, *Turbulence in World Politics: A Theory of Change and Continuity* (Princeton: PUP, 1990), 243–296.
81. Håkan Thörn, *Anti-Apartheid and the Emergence of a Global Society* (London: PM, 2006).
82. Ibid., pp. 18 and 161.
83. Ibid., pp. 4, 10–12, 44, 68–69, 71, and 128.
84. Prosser Gifford and William R. Louis, "Introduction," in Gifford and Louis, ed., *Decolonization*, xxv.
85. Horace Campbell, "The Decolonization Process in Namibia," in *Confrontation and Liberation in Southern Africa: Regional Directions after the Nkomati Accord*, ed. Ibrahim S. R. Msabaha and Timothy M. Shaw (Boulder, Colo.: WP, 1987), 33.
86. Henriksen, "Portugal in Africa," 408–409.
87. Gifford and Louis, "Introduction," in Gifford and Louis, ed., *Decolonization*, xii.

Introduction

1. Peter C. Bennett, "South West Africa/Namibia Issues Related to Political Independence" (M.A. thesis, University of Cape Town, 1983), 8.
2. Keith Gottschalk, "Restructuring the Colonial State: Pretoria's Strategy in Namibia," in *Namibia in Perspective*, ed. Gerhard Tötemeyer, Vezera Kandetu, and Wolfgang Werner (Windhoek: CCN, 1987), 34.
3. http://www.smallwars.quantico.usmc.mil/sw_past.asp, item no. 36.
4. André Wessels, "The South African Navy during the Years of Conflict in Southern Africa, 1966–1989," JCH 31, no. 3 (December 2006): 283 and 295.
5. Raymond Copson, *African Wars and Prospects for Peace* (Armonk, N.Y.: MES, 1994), 12, 20, 54, 57–59, 78, 81–83, 89, 106, 110–111, 136–138, 165, and 168.
6. Ibid., 54 (table 2.2).
7. T. D. P. Dugdale-Pointon, "Namibia 1966–1990," 9 September 2002, http://www.history ofwar.org/articles/wars_namibia.html.
8. Letter to the author from Professor Christopher C. Saunders, Department of Historical Studies, University of Cape Town, dated 2 December 2011.
9. SAP, *Debates,* 16, cols 2782–2783 (14 March 1990, remarks of the minister of foreign affairs during the second reading of the Recognition of the Independence of Namibia Bill).
10. Lauren Dobell, *Swapo's Struggle for Namibia, 1960–1991: War by Other Means*, Basel Namibia Studies Series 3 (Basel: PSP, 1998), 141.
11. Rosemary Preston, "Integrating Fighters after War: Reflections on the Namibian Experience, 1989–1993," JSAS 23, no. 3 (September 1997): 455.
12. UNGA res. 2372 of 12 June 1968, operative para. one.

13. Prime Minister Geingob's reply to Mr. Katjiuongua's question in NPNA, *Debates*, 29, 329–330 (7-22 July 1998).
14. Ingolf Diener, "How to Be a Namibian and a Democrat: On the Question of the Project of Nationhood after Apartheid," in *Contemporary Namibia: The First Landmarks of a Post-Apartheid Society*, ed. Ingold Diener and Olivier Graefe (Windhoek: GMP, 2001), 331.
15. Reinhart Kössler, *In Search of Survival and Dignity: Two Traditional Communities in Southern Namibia under South African Rule* (Windhoek: GMP, 2005), iv.
16. Dobell, *Swapo's Struggle*, 20 and 43.
17. SWAPO of Namibia. Department of Information and Publicity, *To Be Born a Nation: The Liberation Struggle for Namibia* (London: ZP/B, 1981), 255.
18. Dobell, *Swapo's Struggle*, 20 and 23.
19. SWAPO, *To Be Born a Nation*, 255.
20. J. David Singer, "The Level-of-Analysis Problem in International Relations," in *The International System: Theoretical Essays*, ed. Klaus Knorr and Sidney Verba (Princeton: PUP, 1961), 77–92.
21. William R. Louis and Ronald Robinson refer to "A Framework for Studying the Fall of Colonial Empires in the Twentieth Century" in their chapter "The United States and the Liquidation of [the] British Empire in Tropical Africa, 1941-1951," in Gifford and Louis, eds., *The Transfer of Power in Africa: Decolonization, 1940–1960*, 31–55, especially 53–55.
22. Ronald Dreyer, *Namibia and Southern Africa*, especially 2.
23. Mordechai Tamarkin, *The Making of Zimbabwe: Decolonization in Regional and International Politics* (London: FC, 1990), especially 1–8.
24. Joseph S. Nye, Jr., *Soft Power: The Means to Succeed in World Politics* (New York: PA, 2004), 4 (quotation) and 136–137.
25. Sam Nujoma, *Where Others Wavered: The Autobiography of Sam Nujoma* (London PaB, 2001), 123, 192, and 198.
26. Baron F. Barnett, "Southern African Student Exiles: The Function of Politics" (Ph.D. diss., Yale University, 1969), 77.
27. Guy Lamb, "Militarising Politics and Development: The Case of Post-Independence Namibia," in *The Security-Development Nexus: Expressions of Sovereignty and Securitization in Southern Africa*, ed. Lars Buur, Steffen Jensen, and Finn Stepputat (Uppsala: NAI; Cape Town: HSRCP, 2007), 158.
28. Alistair Horne, *The French Army and Politics, 1870–1970* (New York: PBB, 1984), 77–78 (quotation from p. 77).
29. Singer, "The Level-of-Analysis Problem," 92.
30. Yossi Shain, *The Frontier of Loyalty: Political Exiles in the Age of the Nation-State* (Middletown, Conn.: WsUP, 1989), 61.
31. Robert H. Jackson, "The Weight of Ideas in Decolonization: Normative Changes in International Relations," in *Ideas and Foreign Policy: Beliefs, Institutions, and Political Change*, ed. Judith Goldstein and Robert O. Keohane (Ithaca, N.Y.: CnUP, 1993), 111–138, especially 126–133.
32. Letter to the author, dated 3 March 2012.
33. Jackson, "The Weight of Ideas," 137.
34. Crawford, *Argument and Change in World Politics*, 363–380.
35. Michael Hough, "'Legitimacy' and 'Recognition' in Revolutionary Warfare," ISSUPSR, December 1984: 14–19.
36. Timothy J. Lomperis, "Vietnam's Offspring: The Lesson of Legitimacy," CQ, 6, no. 1 (Winter 1986): 18–33.
37. Joanne Wright, "PIRA [Provisional Irish Republican Army] Propaganda: The Construction of Legitimacy," CQ, 10, 3 (Summer 1990): 24–41.
38. Courtney E. Prisk, "The Umbrella of Legitimacy," in *Uncomfortable Wars: Toward a New Paradigm of Low Intensity Conflict*, ed. Max G. Manwaring (Boulder, Colo.: WP, 1991), 69–91.
39. David Burns, "Insurgency as a Struggle for Legitimation: The Case of Southern Africa," SWI 5, no. 1 (Spring 1994): 29–62.
40. Max G. Manwaring, "Toward an Understanding of Insurgency Wars: The Paradigm," in Manwaring, *Uncomfortable Wars*, 25.
41. Peter Novick, *The Resistance versus Vichy: The Purge of Collaborators in Liberated France* (New York: CoUP, 1968), 192 (Appendix A, "The Legitimacy and Legality of Vichy").
42. Samuel P. Huntington, *The Third Wave: Democratization in the Late Twentieth Century* (Norman: UOP, 1991), 46.
43. Shain, *The Frontier of Loyalty*, 165–166.
44. Zartman, *Ripe for Resolution*, 134.
45. Deborah Posel, "The Language of Domination, 1978–1983," in *The Politics of Race, Class, and Nationalism in Twentieth Century South Africa*, ed. Shula Marks and Stanley Trapido (New York: Longman, Inc., 1987), 434.
46. Lawrence S. Finkelstein, "The Politics of Value Allocation in the UN System," in *Politics in the United Nations System*, ed. Lawrence S. Finkelstein (New York: DUP, 1988), 13.
47. Shain, *The Frontier of Loyalty*, 79; Tamarkin, *The Making of Zimbabwe*, 209.
48. Huntington, *The Third Wave*, 89, 97, 128, 151–152, 154, 181, and 184.
49. Finkelstein, "The Politics of Value Allocation," 13.
50. Francis Fukuyama, *The End of History and the Last Man* (New York: Perennial, 1992), 39.
51. Shain, *The Frontier of Loyalty*, 83.
52. Prisk, "The Umbrella of Legitimacy," 70–73 (the indicators are listed on p. 73).
53. Eric A. Nordlinger, *Soldiers in Politics: Military Coups and Governments* (Englewood Cliffs, N.J.: PH, 1977), 93–95.
54. Pierre Englebert, *State Legitimacy and Development in Africa* (Boulder, Colo.: LRP, 2000), 9, 71, 179, and 188–189.
55. Huntington, *The Third Wave*, 20, 46, 48, 86, 100, 146, and 286.
56. M. Crawford Young, "The Colonial State and Post-Colonial Crisis," in Gifford and Louis, eds., *Decolonization*, 30.
57. Inis L. Claude, Jr., "Collective Legitimation as a Political Function of the United Nations," IOr 20, no. 3 (Summer, 1966): 367–379.
58. J. Leo Cefkin, "International Legitimation and Southern Africa: Principles and Practice," paper presented at the sixty-fourth annual meeting of the APSA, Washington, D.C., 2- 7 September 1968, 13–18.
59. André du Pisani, "Namibia: The Quest for Legitimacy," Politeia (Pretoria) 2 no. 1 (1983): 43–51, especially 43–44.
60. Ian Hurd, *After Anarchy: Legitimacy and Power in the United Nations Security Council* (Princeton: PUP, 2007), 2–3.

61. Ibid., 7 and 44.
62. Ibid., 11 (first quotation), 22 (third quotation) 23 (second and fifth quotations), and 83 (fourth quotation).
63. Ibid., 9.
64. M. Stephen Weatherford, "Measuring Political Legitimacy," APSR 86, no. 1 (March 1992): 149–166.
65. Huntington, *The Third Wave*, 50 and 113 (table 3.1).
66. Ibid., 117 and 119.
67. Leonard M. Thompson, *The Political Mythology of Apartheid* (New Haven: YUP, 1985), particularly 25–68.
68. Thomas D. Moodie, *The Rise of Afrikanerdom: Power, Apartheid, and the Afrikaner Civil Religion*, Perspectives on Southern Africa no. 11 (Berkeley: UCP, 1975), especially 295–300.
69. Huntington, *The Third Wave*, 45, 50, and 258–259.
70. Robert L. Bradford, "The Origin and Concession of the League of Nations Class 'C' Mandate for South West Africa and the Fulfillment of the Sacred Trust, 1919–1939" (Ph.D. diss., Yale University, 1965), 159–443.
71. Huntington, *The Third Wave*, 50, 89, 184, and 258–259.
72. *State Legitimacy and Development in Africa*.
73. Ibid., 8.
74. Kalavei J. Holsti, *The State, War, and the State of War*, Cambridge Studies in International Relations no. 51 (Cambridge: CbUP, 1996), 84 and 87–98.
75. Englebert, *State Legitimacy*, 8 (for both quotations).
76. Cedric Thornberry, *A Nation Is Born: The Inside Story of Namibia's Independence* (Windhoek: GMP, 2004), 194.
77. Shain, *The Frontier of Loyalty*, 115.
78. Ibid. 113.
79. Erez Manela, *The Wilsonian Moment: Self-Determination and the International Origins of Anticolonial Nationalism* (New York: OxUP, 2007), 3–17.
80. Jackson, "The Weight of Ideas," 119–126.
81. Manela, *The Wilsonian Moment*, 62.
82. Brad R. Roth, *Governmental Illegitimacy in International Law* (Oxford: CP, 1999), 212–217.
83. Alexander M. Johnston, "Self-Determination in Comparative Perspective: Northern Ireland and South Africa," PSAJPS 17, no. 2 (December 1990): 8.
84. Gifford and Louis, "Introduction," in Gifford and Louis, eds., *Decolonization*, xvii.
85. UNGA res. 1514 (XV) of 14 December 1960, preambular para. two.
86. Anthony G. Gaglione, "Anti-Colonialism and the South West Africa Case: A Study in Majoritarianism at the United Nations" (Ph.D. diss., Rutgers University, 1971), 116–138.
87. UNGA res. 1514 (XV), operative para. six.
88. Hage G. Geingob, "Namibia," in *Conflict and Change in Southern Africa: Papers from a Scandinavian-Canadian Conference*, ed. Douglas G. Anglin, Timothy M. Shaw, and Carl G. Widstrand (Washington, D.C.: UPA, 1978), 121.
89. Frederik J. Nöthling, "Muddy Waters in the New World," in *History of the South African Department of Foreign Affairs, 1927–1993*, ed. Tom F. Wheeler (Johannesburg: SAIIA, 2005), 405–406 and 406, n. 43.
90. Benyamin Neuberger, *National Self-Determination in Postcolonial Africa* (Boulder, Colo.: LRP, 1986), 19–60.
91. Ibid., 41–42 and 55–56.
92. Richard Dale, "Reconfiguring White Ethnic Power in Colonial Africa: The German Community in Namibia, 1923–50," NEP 7, no. 2 (Summer 2001): 75–94; Christo Botha, "Internal Colonisation and an Oppressed Minority?: The Dynamics of Relations between Germans and Afrikaners against the Background of Constructing a Colonial State in Namibia, 1884–1990," JNS, 2 (2007): 7–50.
93. "Schutztruppe Get Pension in South West Africa," WA, 30 March 1958, 17.
94. Neuberger, *National Self-Determination*, 25, 39, and 75.
95. Israel Goldblatt, *History of South West Africa from the Beginning of the Nineteenth Century* (Cape Town: JuC, 1971), 249.
96. *A Survey of Race Relations in South Africa, 1959–1960*, comp. Muriel Horrell (Johannesburg: SAIRR, 1961), 5–8.
97. John H. Wellington, *South West Africa and Its Human Issues* (Oxford: CP, 1967), 399.
98. Wolfgang Werner, "A Brief History of Land Dispossession in Namibia," JSAS 19, no. 1 (March 1993): 135–146.
99. Jeremy Silvester, "Beasts, Boundaries & Buildings: The Survival & Creation of Pastoral Economies in Southern Namibia, 1915–1935," in *Namibia under South African Rule: Mobility & Containment, 1915–46*, ed. Patricia Hayes, Jeremy Silvester, Marion Wallace, and Wolfram Hartmann (Oxford: JC; Windhoek: OAP; and Athens: OhUP, 1998), 106–111.
100. According to the head of the Namibian Archives, the late Brigitte Lau, "The History of Land Dispossession," TN, 8 November 1996, 11 (letter).
101. Ronald Robinson, "Andrew Cohen and the Transfer of Power in Tropical Africa, 1940–1951," in *Decolonisation and After: The British and the French Experience*, Studies in Commonwealth Politics and History no. 7, ed. W.H. Morris-Junes and Dennis Austin (London: FC, 1980), 58.
102. Maxwell, "Portugal and After," 350.
103. Robert J. Gordon, *Mines, Masters and Migrants: Life in a Namibian Mine Compound* (Johannesburg: RP, 1977).
104. Gillian Cronje and Suzanne Cronje, *The Workers of Namibia* (London: IDAFSA, 1979).
105. Wellington, *South West Africa*, 101–103.
106. Herbert W. Dowd, "Non-White Land and Labor Policies in South West Africa from 1918 to 1948" (Ph.D. diss., Tufts University, The Fletcher School of Law and Diplomacy, 1954), 179.
107. Richard Dale, *Botswana's Search for Autonomy in Southern Africa*, Contributions in Political Science no. 358 (Westport, Conn.: GP, 1995), 139–149 and 223–228.
108. Allan D. Cooper, "The Institutionalization of Contract Labour in Namibia," JSAS 25, no. 1 (March, 1999): 121–138.
109. Dowd, "Non-White land and Labor Policies," 185–186.
110. Rauha Voipio, "Contract Work through Ovambo Eyes," in *Namibia: The Last Colony*, ed. Reginald Green, Marja-Liisa Kiljunen, and Kimmo Kiljunen (Harlow, UK: LGL, 1981), 112–131.
111. Martha J. Peterson, *The General Assembly in World Politics*. 2d impression (Boston: UH, 1990), 229.
112. Rosenau, *Turbulence in World Politics*, 36.
113. Quincy Wright, *Mandates under the League of Nations* (New York: GP, 1968, originally published in 1930), 327–328.
114. Lauren Dobell, "SWAPO in Office," in Colin

Leys and John S. Saul, *Namibia's Liberation Struggle: The Two-Edged Sword* (London: JC.; Athens: OhUP, 1995), 174.

115. Isaak I. Dore, *The International Mandate System and Namibia* (Boulder, Colo.: WP, 1985), 33–41 and 54; Gail-Maryse Cockram, *South West African Mandate* (Cape Town: JuC, 1976), 74–84.

116. Cockram, *South West African Mandate*, 81–82, and 98.

117. *Mines and Independence. A Future for Namibia* [No.] 3: Mining (London: CIIR, 1983), 46 and 125–126 (Appendix 2); H. Booysen and G. E. J. Stephan, "Decree No. 1 of the United Nations Council for South West Africa," SAYIL 1 (1975): 63–86.

118. Mahmoud F. El-Said, "The United Nations and Namibia: [The] Implications for Institutional Development of the Organization and the Creation of Norms of International Behavior" (Ph.D. diss., City University of New York, 1986), 181–206 (covering "the United Nations and armed struggle").

119. Tamarkin, *The Making of Zimbabwe*, 5–6.

120. Shain, *The Frontier of Loyalty*, 61.

121. Major General Wally Black, speech to the Associated Scientific and Technical Societies of South Africa, 25 October 1977, as reported in "SA Forces Clash with Terrorists 100 Times a Month," CT, 26 October 1977, 1.

122. Roger Beaumont, "Small Wars: Definitions and Dimensions," AAASPS 541 (September 1995): 20–35.

123. http://smallwars.quantico.usmc.mil/index.asp.

124. Copson, *Africa's Wars*, 3–25.

125. These variations for the Namibian war appear in Copson, *Africa's Wars*, 54 (table 2.2) and 72, n. 48.

126. Walter Laqueur, *Guerrilla: A Historical and Critical Study* (Boston: LBC, 1976), 161 and 202.

127. John W. Turner, *Continent Ablaze: The Insurgency Wars in Africa, 1960 to the Present* (London: AAP, 1998), 35, 37, and 82; Oswin O. Namakalu, *Armed Liberation Struggle: Some Accounts of PLAN's Combat Operations* (Windhoek: GMP, 2004), 5, 22, 24–26, 56, and 152.

128. Thomas H. Henriksen, *Revolution and Counterrevolution: Mozambique's War of Independence, 1964–1974*, Contributions in Intercultural and Comparative Studies no. 6 (Westport, Conn.: GP, 1983), 43–44; Namakalu, *Armed Liberation*, 186–187; and William Minter, *Apartheid's Contras: An Inquiry into the Roots of War in Angola and Mozambique* (Johannesburg: WUP; London: ZB/P, 1994) 4–5, 41, and 194–195.

129. Letter to the author from Professor Saunders dated 2 December 2011.

130. Kenneth W. Grundy, *Soldiers without Politics: Blacks in the South African Armed Forces*, Perspectives on Southern Africa no. 33 (Berkeley: UCP, 1983), 249–272.

131. Heitman, *War in Angola*, 10 (for quotation).

Chapter One

1. This derives from the notion of "the politics of resistance" that the Namibian political scientist André du Pisani used in his "Namibia: The Historical Legacy," in Tötemeyer et al., ed., *Namibia in Perspective*, 23, as well as from the title of Scott Thomas' path-breaking study, *The Diplomacy of Liberation: The Foreign Relations of the African National Congress since 1960*, International Library of African Studies, vol. 2 (London: IBT, 1996).

2. Robert H. Jackson, *Quasi-States: Sovereignty, International Relations, and the Third World* (Cambridge: CbUP, 1990), 21–26; Robert H. Jackson and Carl G. Rosberg, "Why Africa's Weak States Persist: The Empirical and the Juridical in Statehood," WoP 35, no. 1 (October 1982): 1–24.

3. Jackson, *Quasi-States*, 22 and 204, n. 7.

4. Deon J. Geldenhuys, *Isolated States: A Comparative Analysis*, Cambridge Studies in International Relations no. 15 (Cambridge: CbP, 1990), 148, 189, 287, and 563.

5. Christopher Clapham, *Africa and the International System: The Politics of State Survival*, Cambridge Studies in International Relations no. 50 (Cambridge: CbUP, 1996), 224.

6. Geldenhuys, *Isolated States*, 163.

7. Ibid., 162–163.

8. Helmuth Stoecker and Peter Sebald, "Enemies of the Colonial Idea," in *Germans in the Tropics: Essays in German Colonial History*, ed. Arthur J. Knoll and Lewis H. Gann (Westport, Conn: GP, 1987), 59–72.

9. Jeremy Silvester and Jan-Bart Gewald, "Footsteps and Tears: An Introduction to the Construction and Context of the 1918 'Blue Book,'" in Silvester and Gewald, *Words Cannot Be Found: German Colonial Rule in Namibia: An Annotated Reprint of the 1918 Blue Book* (Leiden: KB, 2003), xiii–xxxvii.

10. *South West Africa and the Union of South Africa: The History of a Mandate* (s.l.: Published by authority of the Government of the Union of South Africa and distributed in the United States by the Union of South Africa Government Information Office, New York, circa 1946), 39–40 and 106.

11. Susan Pedersen, "Settler Colonialism at the Bar of the League of Nations," in *Settler Colonialism in the Twentieth Century: Projects, Practices, Legacies*, ed. Caroline Elkins and Susan Pedersen (New York: Routledge, 2005), 117–118.

12. Ibid., 117.

13. William R. Louis, *Great Britain and Germany's Lost Colonies, 1914–1919* (Oxford: CP, 1967), viii–ix and 99–100.

14. Robert C. Eils, "The German Colonial Scandals, 1890–1900" (M.A. thesis, University of Wisconsin-Madison, 1977), ii–iv.

15. Wolfe W. Schmokel, *Dream of Empire: German Colonialism, 1919–1945* (New Haven: YUP, 1964), 83 and 87.

16. King-yuh Chang, "The United Nations and Decolonization, 1960–1968: The Role of the Committee of Twenty-Four" (Ph.D. diss., Columbia University, 1971), 12.

17. Bradford, "The Origin," 160–161 and 448–450.

18. Schmokel, *Dream of Empire*, 84.

19. Wright, *Mandates*, 140.

20. Ibid., 169 and Bradford, "The Origin," 164–166.

21. Bradford, "The Origin," 166, n. 1.

22. Letter to the author from Professor Gerhard K.H. Tötemeyer, dated 26 December 2011.

23. Bryan O'Linn, *Namibia: The Sacred Trust of Civilization: Ideal and Reality* [vol. 1] (Windhoek: GMP, circa 2003), 19 and 191 (quotation from 19).

24. Tilman Dedering, "Petitioning Geneva: Transnational Aspects of Protest and Resistance in South West Africa/Namibia after the First World War," JSAS 35, no. 4 (December 2009): 785–801.

25. ICJPOAD, *South West Africa Cases*, vol. 1, 135 (Memorial of Ethiopia).

26. UNGA res. 1054 (XI) of 26 February 1957, operative para. four (c).

27. Muriel Horrell, *South-West Africa* (Johannesburg: SAIRR, 1967), 19.

28. David Goldsworthy, *Colonial Issues in British Politics: From 'Colonial Government' to 'Wind of Change'* (Oxford: CP, 1971), 68.

29. Solomon I. Slonim, *South West Africa and the United Nations: An International Mandate in Dispute* (Baltimore: JHUP, 1973), 105.

30. Ton J. M. Zuijdwijk, *Petitioning the United Nations: A Study in Human Rights* (New York: SMP, 1982), especially 155–190 and 201–202.

31. Christopher C. Saunders, "Michael Scott and Namibia," AHR 39, no. 2 (December 2007): 25–40.

32. Roger S. Clark, "The International League for Human Rights and South West Africa, 1947–1957: The Human Rights NGO as [a] Catalyst in the International Legal Process," HRQ 3, no. 4 (Fall, 1981): 101–136.

33. ICJRJAOO, *Legal Consequences*, 232, n. 12.

34. ICJRJAOO, *Admissibility*, 32.

35. ICJPOAD, *South West Africa Cases*, vol. 4, 38, n. 3 (counter-memorial of South Africa); Samuel A.P. Mushelenga, "Foreign Policy-Making in Namibia: The Dynamics of the Smallness of a State" (M.A. thesis, University of South Africa, 2008), 41.

36. Ruth First, *South West Africa* (Baltimore: PB, 1963), 195.

37. ICJPOAD, *South West Africa Cases*, vol. 4, 45 (counter-memorial of South Africa).

38. Dobell, *SWAPO's Struggle*, 66.

39. http://209.88.21.36/opencms/opencms/grnnet/MFA/ministry/DeputyMin.html; Mushelenga, "Foreign Policy-Making," 5 (including table 1).

40. Claude, "Collective Legitimation," 376.

41. Rupert Emerson, "Colonialism, Political Development, and the UN," IOr 19, no. 3 (Summer 1965): 493.

42. Alden C. Small, "The United Nations and South West Africa: A Study in Parliamentary Diplomacy" (Ph.D. diss., Tufts University, The Fletcher School of Law and Diplomacy, 1970), 325.

43. Finkelstein, "The Politics of Value Allocation," 18 and 36, n. 50.

44. Robert E. Riggs, "The United Nations and the Rule of Law," in Finkelstein, *Politics in the United Nations System*, 59.

45. Lawrence S. Finkelstein, "Comparative Politics in the UN System," in Finkelstein, *Politics in the United Nations System*, 472.

46. Bradford, "The Origin," 285–295.

47. Lewis H. Gann and Peter J. Duignan, *Burden of Empire: An Appraisal of Western Colonialism in Africa South of the Sahara* (Stanford, Calif.: HIP, 1967), 274.

48. Ibid., 16.

49. Isabel V. Hull, *Absolute Destruction: Military Culture and the Practices of War in Imperial Germany* (Ithaca, N.Y.: CnUP, 2005), 188–190.

50. Casper W. Erichsen, *"The Angel of Death Has Descended Violently among Them": Concentration Camps and Prisoners-of-War in Namibia, 1904–1908*, Research Report 79/2005 (Leiden: ASC, 2005).

51. Published in *Church and Liberation in Namibia*, ed. Peter H. Katjavivi, Per Frostin, and Kaire Mbuende (Winchester, Mass.: PP, 1989), 134–136.

52. Denis Herbstein and John Evenson, *The Devils Are among Us: The War for Namibia* (London: ZP/B, 1989), 57.

53. [Eric Bjornlund], *Nation Building: The U.N. and Namibia* (Washington, D.C.: NDIIA, 1990), 79; Vezera Kandetu, "The Role of the Church in Namibia," in Katjavivi et al., ed., *Church and Liberation in Namibia*, 212–213.

54. G. Michael Scott, *A Time to Speak* (London: FaF, 1967), 219–235, 269–296, and 332–340.

55. Goldsworthy, *Colonial Issues*, 255–278.

56. Philip Steenkamp, "The Churches," in Leys and Saul, *Namibia's Liberation Struggle*, 112, n. 1.

57. NPNA Debates, 15, 238 (11 November 1991) (deputy minister of youth and sport during the debate on financial support to political parties).

58. John Barratt, "The Outlook for Namibian Independence: Some Domestic Constraints," SAIIAIAB 7, no. 1 (1983): 16–17, quotation from 17 (italics in the original).

59. Letter to the author from Professor Tötemeyer, dated 26 December 2011.

60. See the tabulation in Table One of the Appendix.

61. See the tabulation in Table Two of the Appendix.

62. Donald J. Puchala, "The United Nations and Ecosystem Issues: Institutionalizing the Global Interest," in Finkelstein, *Politics in the United Nations System*, 218.

63. Robert E. Jones, "Anti-Colonialism at the United Nations: The Origin and Policy of the United Nations Special Committee on Colonialism, 1960–1967" (Ph.D. diss., University of Notre Dame, 1974), 76.

64. UNGA res. 3383 (XXX), 10 November 1975, 31/33 of 30 November 1976, and 33/23 of 29 November 1978 illustrate this point.

65. UNGA res. 2288 (XXII), 7 December 1967, 2425 (XXIII) of 18 December 1968, 2554 (XXIV) of 12 December 1969, 2703 (XXV) of 14 December 1970, and 2873 (XXVI) of 20 December 1971 are five sequential examples. In these cases, the terms transnational or multinational corporations were not explicitly used in the resolutions, although operative para. four of UNGA res. 31/148 of 20 December 1976 specifically refers to "foreign corporations operating in Namibia."

66. John P. Powelson, "The Balance Sheet on Multinational Corporations in Less Developed Countries," CeD 9, no. 3 (1977): 413–432.

67. UNGA res. 31/146 of 20 December 1976, operative para. 2.

68. See the tabulation in Table Three of the Appendix.

69. See the tabulation in Table Four of the Appendix.

70. Mittelman, "Collective Decolonisation and the UN Committee of 24," 42–46, 53–54, and 64.

71. Gregory L. Wilkins, *African Influence in the United Nations, 1967–1975: The Politics and Techniques of Gaining Compliance to U.N. Principles and Resolutions* (Washington, D.C.: UPA, 1981), 31–32.

72. UNGA res. 3111 (XXVIII) of 12 December 1973, operative para. two of section I.

73. UNGA res. 31/146 of 20 December 1976, operative para. two.

74. UNGA res. 31/152 of 20 December 1976, operative para. one.

75. Ebere Osieke, "Admission to Membership in International Organizations: The Case of Namibia," BYIL 51 (1980): 189–229.

76. For example, UNGA res. 3382 (XXX) of 10 November 1975, operative paras. one and five, UNGA res. 31/34 of 30 November 1976, operative paras. one and three, and UNGA res. 32/14 of 7 November 1977, operative paras. two and three.

77. See Margaret E. Keck and Kathryn Sikkink, *Activists beyond Borders: Advocacy Networks in International Politics* (Ithaca, N.Y.: CnUP, 1998), 16 and 23.

78. This phrase comes from Gaglione, "Anti-Colonialism," 232.

79. See the tabulation in Table Five of the Appendix.

80. Edmund Morris, *Theodore Rex* (New York: The Modern Library, 2001), 185 and 215 (where the rest of the aphorism reads: "you will go far").
81. Tony [i.e., Anthony B.] Emmett, *Popular Resistance and the Roots of Nationalism in Namibia, 1915–1966*, Basel Namibian Studies Series 4 (Basel: PSP, 1999), 286–287 and 289.
82. Ibid., 289.
83. Albert O. Hirschman, *Exit, Voice, and Loyalty: Responses to Declines in Firms, Organizations, and States* (Cambridge: HUP, 1970), 17, 30–33, and 70–71.
84. Emmet, *Popular Resistance*, 139–154.
85. Ibid., 125–138.
86. Ibid., 146–149.
87. Ibid., 111–124.
88. Ibid., 155–167.
89. Hiller B. Zobel, *The Boston Massacre* (New York: WWN, 1970), 3–4.
90. Letter to the author from Professor Tötemeyer, dated 26 December 2011.
91. Michael Crowder, "Tshekedi Khama, Smuts, and South West Africa," JMAS 25, no. 1 (March 1987): 25–42.
92. Dale, *Botswana's Search for Autonomy*, 13–18.
93. Hollis R. Lynch, *Black American Radicals and the Liberation of Africa: The Council on African Affairs, 1937–1955*, Monograph Series No. 5 (Ithaca, N.Y.: CUASRC, 1978), 32–35 and 50–52.
94. William Minter, "An Unfinished Journey," in *No Easy Victories: African Liberation ands American Activists over Half a Century, 1950–2000*, ed. William Minter, Gail Hovey, and Charles Cobb, Jr. (Trenton, N.J.: AWP, 2008), 16–17.
95. UNSC res. 245 (1968) of 25 January 1968, operative para. two.
96. UNIN, *Namibia: A Direct United Nations Responsibility* (Lusaka: UNIN, 1987), 199–229.
97. UNGA res. 2145 (XXI) of 27 October 1966, operative para. four.
98. Newell M. Stultz, *The Apartheid Issue at the Security Council*. The United Nations and Southern Africa Series No. 1 (Braamfontein: SAIIA, 1989), 41–45.
99. Newell M. Stultz, "[The] Evolution of the United Nations Anti-Apartheid Regime," HRQ 13, no. 1 (February 1991): 17–19. John Barratt, "South African Diplomacy at the UN," in *Diplomacy at the UN*, ed. and introduced by Geoffrey R. Berridge and A. Jennings (London and Basingstoke: MaP, 1985), 197–200.
100. John Barratt, "South African Diplomacy at the UN," 197–200.
101. UNGA res. 3411G of 10 December 1975, operative para. six.
102. Stultz, "Evolution," 16–17.
103. Gerhard K. H. Tötemeyer, Vezera Kandetu, and Wolfgang Werner, "Introduction," in Tötemeyer et al., ed., *Namibia in Perspective*, 9.
104. UNGA res. 2145 (XXI) of 27 October 1966, preambular para. one.
105. Gordon S. Wood, *The Americanization of Benjamin Franklin* (New York: PB, 2004), especially 8–13.
106. Cockram, *South West African Mandate*, 285, 382, 428, and 431.
107. Ibid., 279–280 and 380.
108. UNIN, *Namibia: A Direct United Nations Responsibility*, 213.
109. UNGA res. 2248 (S-V), 19 May 1967, Part IV, operative paras one and three.
110. Cockram, South *West African Mandate*, 111–112.
111. Alberto Theodoli, *A Cavallo Di Due Secoli* ([Rome]: La Navicella, [1950]), 159–60. Professor C. John R. Dugard of the University of the Witwatersrand School of Law kindly sent me a copy of the South African Department of Foreign Affairs typescript of their translation of the relevant pages of this book along with the accompanying photocopies of the original text (Professor Dugard's letter to the author dated 4 July 1974).
112. Typescript translation, 1.
113. Ramendra N. Chowdhuri, *International Mandates and Trusteeship Systems: A Comparative Study* (The Hague: MN, 1955), 216–218.
114. Christian M. Rogerson, "A Future 'University of Namibia?': The Rôle of the United Nations Institute for Namibia," *JMAS* 18, no. 4 (December 1980): 675–683.
115. UNGA res. 3296 (XXIX) of 13 December 1974, operative para. five.
116. John J. Grotpeter, *Historical Dictionary of Namibia*, African Historical Dictionaries no. 57 (Metuchen, N.J.: ScP, 1994), 161–162.

Chapter Two

1. André du Pisani utilized the phrase "controlled change" in the title of his article "Namibia: From Incorporation to Controlled Change," JCAS 1, no. 2 (April 1982): 281–305. In a similar vein, the Acting President of the United Nations Council on Namibia, Noel G. Sinclair, indicated in his telegram of 22 February 1985 to the U.S. House of Representatives Subcommittee on Africa that "the regime in Pretoria is endeavouring to control the nature and pace of change in Namibia." USCHRCFA. Subcommittee on Africa, *Namibia: Internal Repression and United States Diplomacy: Hearing, February 21, 1985*, Ninety-Ninth Congress, First Session (hereafter 1985 Wolpe subcommittee hearing) (Washington, D.C.: USGPO, 1985), 167 (Appendix Three).
2. Gary Wasserman, *Politics of Decolonization: Kenya Europeans and the Land Issue, 1960–1965*, African Studies Series no. 17 (Cambridge: CbUP, 1976), 8.
3. Gwendolen M. Carter, *The Politics of Inequality: South Africa since 1948*, rev. ed. (New York: FAP, 1959), title page.
4. SAPHA, *Debates*, 52, col. 3391 (14 March 1945).
5. SAPHA *Debates*, 5, col. 5930 (13 July 1925, speech of General Smuts).
6. Fred E. Bishop, "Apartheid in Theory and Practice, 1948–1959" (senior thesis, Princeton University, 1961), 50.
7. Geisa M. Rocha, *In Search of Namibian Independence: The Limitations of the United Nations* (Boulder, Colo.: WP, 1984), 57; Geldenhuys, *The Diplomacy of Isolation*, 225–226.
8. Robert I. Rotberg, "Political and Economic Realities in a Time of Settlement," in *Namibia: Political; and Economic Prospects*, ed. by Robert I. Rotberg (Lexington, Mass.: LB, 1983), 29.
9. André du Pisani, *SWA/Namibia: The Politics of Continuity and Change* (Johannesburg: JBP, 1985), 63.
10. SAPS, *Debates*, 1956, vol. 3, cols. 3952–3953 (28 May 1956).
11. G. R. Hofmeyr, letter to J. C. Smuts, 30 August 1923, South African State Archives, Pretoria, file PM.LN.

13/4, vol. 5, as quoted in Keith Gottschalk, "Restructuring the Colonial State," 29 and 35.

12. SAPHA, *Debates,* 88, col. 5108 (5 May 1955).

13. Richard Dale, "The Evolution of the South West African Dispute before the United Nations, 1945–1950" (Ph.D. diss., Princeton University, 1962), 95–103.

14. Christopher A. Ford, "South African Foreign Policy since 1965: The Cases of Rhodesia and Namibia" (D.Phil. diss., University of Oxford, 1991), 225.

15. Robert Schrire, *Adapt or Die: The End of White Politics in South Africa* (New York: The FF and the FPA, 1991), 4.

16. Tony Smith, *The French Stake in Algeria, 1945–1962* (Ithaca, N.Y.: CnUP, 1978), 23–26, 28, 42, and 186.

17. Wellington, *South West Africa,* 331–332, 334. 336, 340, 425, and 439.

18. Slonim, *South West Africa,* 4, 6, 33, and 318.

19. Schmokel, *Dream of Empire,* 64–70 and 81.

20. Germany. Reichskolonialamt, *The Treatment of Native and Other Populations in the Colonial Possessions of Germany and England. An Answer to the English Blue Book of August 1918: "Report on the Natives of South-West Africa and Their Treatment by Germany."* Translated from the German (Berlin: HRE, 1919), 27–148.

21. Schmokel, *Dream of Empire,* 83 and 87.

22. Neuberger, *National Self-Determination,* 25, 39, and 75.

23. Richard Dale, "The Ambiguities of Self-Determination for South-West Africa, 1919–1939: A Concept or a Symbol of Decolonization?," PS 5, no. 1 (Spring 1974): 33–39 and 51–54.

24. Schmokel, *Dream of Empire,* 68, n. 91.

25. At J. van Wyk, "South West Africa: Origin of a World Problem," in Wheeler, ed., *History,* 212.

26. Wolfgang Werner, *"No One Will Become Rich": Economy and Society in the Herero Reserves in Namibia, 1915–1946,* Basel Namibia Series Studies 2 (Basel: PSP, 1998), 212–215; Allan D. Cooper, *Ovambo Politics in the Twentieth Century* (Lanham, Md.: UPA, 2001), 209–211 and 231–232, nn. 134–136.

27. Muhammed A. Shukrri, *The Concept of Self-Determination in the United Nations* (Damascus: AJP, 1965), 37 and 43.

28. Ibid., 158–159, n. 147 and 163, n. 158.

29. Ibid., 152.

30. Crawford, *Argument and Change in World Politics,* 325.

31. Peter Walshe, The *Rise of African Nationalism in South Africa: The African National Congress, 1912–1952,* Perspectives on Southern Africa no. 3 (Berkeley: UCP, 1971), 62.

32. "South Africa's Delegation to World Body," *South African Scope* (New York: South African Information Service), December 1974: 4–5.

33. Frederik J. Nöthling, "South Africa and Africa," in Wheeler, ed., *History,* 253.

34. UNGAOR, First Session, Second Part, Fourth Committee, Trusteeship, Part III, SRM of Sub-Committee 2, 47 (Major Hahn's remarks).

35. Lawrence G. Green, *Lords of the Last Frontier: The Story of South West Africa and Its People of All Races,* second, revised ed. (Cape Town: HT, 1962), 168–174.

36. "Items of Interest," WA, 21 December 1946, 3.

37. UNGAOR, First Session, Second Part, Fourth Committee, Trusteeship, Part I, SRM, Annex 13, 231–232.

38. SWALAVP, Fifth Assembly, Second Session, 47 (8 May 1946) and 64 (10 May 1946).

39. UNGA res. 744 (VIII) of 27 November 1953, operative para. one.

40. "Incorporation of S.-W.A.," CT, 28 October 1946, 7.

41. "Native Policy," WA, 5 January 1946, 2 (editorial); "The Future of South West Africa," WA, 9 January 1946, 2 (editorial).

42. "South African Experiment," TE 151, no. 5387 (23 November 1946): 821.

43. John D. Rheinallt Jones, "The Director's Letter: The South West Africa Question," SAIRRRRN 8, no. 5 (May 1946): 38.

44. Brook B. Ballard, Jr., "South West Africa, 1945–50: Union Province or United Nations Trust Territory" (M.A. thesis, University of Chicago, 1955), 98.

45. Bradford, "The Origin and Concession," 449 (Appendix 2).

46. "Lord Hailey's Impressions," WA, 7 September 1946, 8.

47. Dale, "The Evolution," 119–121.

48. Peter Henshaw, "Britain and South Africa at the United Nations: 'South West Africa,' 'Treatment of Indians' and 'Race Conflict,' 1946–1961," SAHJ 31 (November 1994): 84–85.

49. "How S.-W.A. Natives Were Consulted," CT, 6 December 1946, 9.

50. David Johnson, "The South West African Issue in International Law," *Optima* (Johannesburg) 11, no. 3 (September 1961): 121, n. 2 (editor's note).

51. Werner, *"No One Will Become Rich,"* 212; Cooper, *Ovambo Politics,* 211 and 232, n. 136.

52. South Africa, *South West Africa and the Union of South Africa,* 80.

53. UNGAOR, Eleventh Session, Fourth Committee, *Plebiscites Held since 1920 under the Control or Supervision of International Organizations: Memorandum Prepared by the Secretariat,* doc. A/C. 4/351 (20 February 1957), microfiche copy, 2–5 and 50–54.

54. Dale, "The Evolution," 176–183.

55. Ibid., 190 and 192.

56. UNGA res. 65 (I) of 14 December 1946, preambular para. seven.

57. Mansour E. Jahanbani, "The Question of South-West Africa" (M.A. thesis, Columbia University, 1956), 132.

58. UNGA res. 1514 (XV), "Declaration on the Granting of Independence to Colonial Countries and Peoples" of 14 December 1960, operative para. three.

59. Shukrri, *The Concept of Self-Determination,* 143; Michla Pomerance, "Methods of Self-Determination and the Argument of 'Primitiveness,'" CYIL 12 (1974): 38–66, especially 41–46.

60. Emmett, *Popular Resistance,* 250.

61. UNGAOR, Second Session, Second Part, Fourth Committee, Trusteeship, Part I, SRM, annex 3b, 137–138.

62. Harry P. Stumpf, "South West Africa: The Question of Its Incorporation into the Union of South Africa" (M.A. thesis, George Washington University, 1958), 102.

63. Gerhard K. H. Tötemeyer, "Bestuursontwikkelinge in Suidwes-Afrika sedert die Bestaan as Mandaatsgebied tot met die Odendaal-Verslag: 'n Oorsig." Paper prepared for delivery at the course South West Africa: Problems and Alternatives, Summer School, University of Cape Town, Rondebosch, 10–14 February 1975, 10.

64. Emmett, *Popular Resistance,* 250–251; "The Shape of Things" (editorial), TNt 163, no. 20 (16 November 1946): 542.

65. Gerhard K. H. Tötemeyer, "The Legal Framework and Organizational Requirements," in *Elections in Namibia*, ed. Gerhard K. H. Tötemeyer, Arnold Wehmhömer, and Heribert Weiland (Windhoek: GMP, 1996), 22.
66. Roger Hearn, *UN Peacekeeping in Action: The Namibian Experience* (Commack, NY: NSP, 1999), 191–201. ibid., 191 and 194.
67. Ibid., 191 and 194.
68. Bennett Kangumu, *Contesting Caprivi: A History of Colonial Isolation and Regional Nationalism in Namibia*, Basel Namibia Studies Series 10 (Basel: BAB, 2011), 194.
69. James P. Barber and John Barratt, *South Africa's Foreign Policy: The Search for Status and Security, 1945–1988*, Cambridge Studies in International Relations no. 11 (Cambridge: CbUP in association with the SAIIA, 1990), 357–358, n. 33.
70. Unless otherwise indicated, the material in this paragraph comes from Dale, "The Evolution," 121–125.
71. These results are smaller than those recorded for the first referendum, where 208,850 favored incorporation, 33,520 opposed it, and 56,700 were not even consulted (Klaus Dierks, *Chronology of Namibian History from Pre-Historical Times to Independent Namibia* [Windhoek: NSS, 1999], 115).
72. UNGAOR, Second Session, Second Part, Fourth Committee, SRM, 137–138 (Annex 3b).
73. SWALAVP, Fifth Assembly, Third Session, 26–27 (7 May 1947). The original resolution, included in the 1946 South African submission to the United Nations, is published in SWALAVP, Fifth Assembly, Second Session, 44 (7 May 1946) and 50 (8 May 1946).
74. Eric A. Walker, "South Africa and the Empire," in *The Cambridge History of the British Empire. Volume VIII: South Africa, Rhodesia and the High Commission Territories*, ed. Eric A. Walker, second edition (Cambridge: CbUP, 1963), 783–784.
75. Ithiel de Sola Pool with the collaboration of Harold D. Lasswell, Daniel Lerner, et al., *Symbols of Democracy*, Hoover Institute Studies, Series C: Symbols, no. 4 (Stanford: SUP, 1952), 17, 62, and 75 (Appendix).
76. Dr. A. P. Treunicht's motion for the maintenance of the right of self-determination of the whites in SAPHA, *Debates*, 112, cols. 1219–1270 (17 February 1984).
77. Joseph Lelyveld, *Move Your Shadow: South Africa, Black and White* (New York: PB, 1986), 54.
78. See Chapter Two, n. 11 above.
79. Letter to the author from Professor Tötemeyer, dated 26 December 2011.
80. Theodor Hanf, Heribert Weiland, and Gerda Vierdag in collaboration with Lawrence Schlemmer, Rainer Hampel, and Burkhard Krupp, *South Africa, The Prospects of Peaceful Change: An Empirical Enquiry into the Possibility of Democratic Conflict Regulation* (London: RC; Cape Town: DPP; Bloomington: IUP, 1981), 47.
81. South Africa. Commission of Enquiry into South West Africa Affairs, *Report*. R.P. no. 12/1964 ([Pretoria]: [Government Printer], 1964), 55 (paras. 184 and 190) and 515 (paras. 1554–1555).
82. SAPHA, *Debates*, 23, col. 4998 (9 May 1968).
83. Sam C. Nolutshungu, "South Africa and the Transfers of Power in Africa," in Gifford and Louis, ed., *Decolonization*, 481.
84. UNGA res. 2145 (XXI) of 27 October 1966, operative paras. four and five.
85. UNSC res. 264 (1969) of 20 March 1969, operative para. one.
86. UNSC res. 276 (1970) of 30 January 1970, preambular para. three, which reiterated UNSC res. 264 (1969) of March 1969.
87. UNSC res. 284 (1970) of 29 July 1970, operative para. one, which referred to UNSC res. 276 (1970) of 30 January 1970.
88. ICJPOAD, *Legal Consequences*, vol. II, 22–23, 165–169, 471, 475, 492–496, 509–516, 524–525, and 601–602.
89. Letter to the author from Professor Tötemeyer, dated 4 August 2004.
90. ICJRJAOO, *Legal Consequences*, 20–21 and 57–58.
91. Speech of Mr. Colin Legum of the Progressive Party to the SAI IA, Cape Town, 1 February 1972, as quoted in *The South West Africa/Namibia Dispute: Documents and Scholarly Writings on the Controversy between South Africa and the United Nations*, Perspectives on Southern Africa no. 9, ed. John Dugard (Berkeley: UCP, 1973), 539.
92. Ibid., 538–539.
93. Ibid., 540–541.
94. Grotpeter, *Historical Dictionary*, 186–187 and 604 and USCHRCFA. Subcommittee on Africa, *Critical Developments in Namibia: Hearings, February 21 and April 4, 1974*. Ninety-Third Congress. Second Session (hereafter Diggs subcommittee hearings) (Washington, D.C.: USGPO, 1974), 26 (reply to the question of Congressman Edward H. Biester, Jr.).
95. UN doc. S/10832 incorporating doc. S/10832/Corr. 1, 15 November 1972, Annex II, pars. seven, twelve through twenty-one-, and twenty-three.
96. S[uresh] C. Saxena, *Namibia: Challenge to the United Nations* (Dehli: SP, 1978), 218–221.
97. Stanley Uys, "SA Given an Ultimatum on SWA: Waldheim's 'Diplomatic' Warning: End Deadlock or Face Trouble," ST, 12 March 1972, 3).
98. S. Keith Panter-Brick, "La Francophonie with Special Reference to Educational Links and Language Problems," in *Decolonisation and After: The British and French Experience*, Studies in Commonwealth Politics and History no. 7, ed. W. H. Morris-Jones and Georges Fischer (London: FC, 1980), 337.
99. Saul H. Dubow, *Racial Segregation and the Origins of Apartheid in South Africa, 1919–36* (Houndmills, Basingstoke, Hampshire, England: MaP, 1989), 3, 11–12, 26, 45, 52, 66, 70, 80, 86, 99, 101, 106–107, 109, 122, 132, 171–172, and 178–180.
100. André du Pisani, "State and Society under South African Rule," in *State, Society[,] and Democracy: A Reader in Namibian Politics*, ed. Christiaan Keulder (Windhoek: GMP, 2000), 69.
101. Joshua B. Forrest, *Namibia's Post-Apartheid Regional Institutions: The Founding Year* (Rochester: URP, 1998), 35–39.
102. du Pisani, "State and Society," 69 and 71.
103. David Soggot, *Namibia: The Violent Heritage* (New York: SMP, 1986), 186.
104. Ibid., 195–197.
105. Ibid., 201–202; Marion Wallace with John Kinahan, *A History of Namibia from the Beginning to 1990* (New York: CoUP, 2011), 286.
106. Wallace with Kinahan, *A History*, 287.
107. Soggot, *Namibia*, 203.
108. The author's interview with Mr. Dirk F. Mudge in Windhoek on 25 May 1976. I am grateful to Mrs. Johanna C. F. Schoeman of Windhoek for arranging this interview.

109. Gerhard K.H. Tötemeyer, "The Interim Government and Its Rule: The Legitimacy Crisis," in Tötemeyer et al., ed., *Namibia in Perspective*, 54–68.
110. Luther H. Evans, "Are 'C' Mandates Veiled Annexations?" SWPSSQ 7, no. 4 (March 1927): 381–400.
111. Zedekia Ngavirue, *Political Parties and Interest Groups in South West Africa (Namibia): A Study of a Plural Society (1972)*, Basel Namibia Studies Series 1 (Basel: PSP, 1997), 172.
112. O'Linn, *Namibia*, [vol. 1], 7–8.
113. Ibid.
114. SAPHA, *Debates*, 8, cols. 1323–1324 (11 March 1927).
115. du Pisani, *SWA/Namibia*, 205, n. 21.
116. Wallace with Kinahan, *A History*, 269.
117. John Dugard, "South West Africa and the 'Terrorist Trial,'" AJIL 64, no. 1 (January 1970): 21–22.
118. Ibid., 19.
119. George Bizos, *Odyssey to Freedom* (Houghton: RH, 2007), 331.
120. In the case of *State v. [Fillimon] Nangola* (1976), as recounted in O'Linn, *Namibia*, [vol. 1], 202.
121. Sagay, *The Legal Aspects of the Namibian Dispute*, 127–131.
122. Dale, *Botswana's Search*, 24–25; Kangumu, *Contesting Caprivi*, 76–78.
123. ICJPOAD, *South West Africa Cases*, vol. 1, 193–194 (memorial of Ethiopia), vol. 4, 106–118 (counter-memorial of South Africa), vol. 6, 409–414 (rejoinder of South Africa), and Dierks, *Chronology of Namibian History*, 110 and 159.
124. Lynn Berat, *Walvis Bay: Decolonization and International Law* (New Haven: YUP, 1990), 47–67.
125. ICJPOAD, *South West Africa Cases*, vol. 4, 106–107 and 110–111 (counter-memorial of South Africa).
126. See Wellington, *South West Africa*, 331–332 and 338–339 and Frederik J. Nöthling, "The South West Africa Dispute, 1948–1966," in Wheeler, ed., *History*, 328–330.
127. SAPHA, *Debates*, vol. 101, col. 5564 (11 May 1959, speech of the minister of external affairs during the external affairs budget debate).
128. The partition suggestion appears in UNGAOR, Sixth Session, Plenary Meetings (First Phase), Annexes, Agenda Item 38: Question of South West Africa, Appendix III, 15, para. ten of UN doc. A/1901/Add. 2, 15 November 1951.
129. Wellington, *South West Africa*, 332.
130. UN doc. A/1901/Add. 2, 15 November 1951, 13, para. three [b]).
131. UNGA res. 1243 (XIII) of 30 October 1958, operative para. one.
132. ICJPOAD, *Legal Consequences*, vol. 1, 91, para. sixty-two (written statement of the United Nations Secretary-General).
133. See Chapter Two, n, 82 above.
134. Peter Stiff, *Warfare by Other Means: South Africa in the 1980s and 1990s* (Alberton: GaP, 2001), 129.
135. Richard Dale, "African Nationalism and Subnationalism in Namibia: The Conflict over Self-Determination, 1945–1971," CRSN 15, nos. 1–2 (1988): 25–32.
136. Kössler, *In Search of Survival*, 95 and 98.
137. J. H. de Beer, "The Independence of the TBVC States: The Africa Branch from 1976," in Wheeler, ed., *History*, 583–595.
138. Jan H. P. Serfontein, *Namibia?* (Randburg: FSP, 1976), 299–301 and 418–420 (Annexure J). The newspaper article was by Caroline Clark, "Partition Scheme for SWA: Independent White, Black States Urged," ST, 13 October 1974, 1–2.
139. Dreyer, *Namibia and Southern Africa*, 84–86.
140. Barratt, "The Outlook," 19–20; "South West Africa: Exit the Ovambos?," FM, 4 October 1974, 37–38.
141. Dreyer, *Namibia and Southern Africa*, 85–86.
142. Julian Burgess et al., *The Great White Hoax: South Africa's International Propaganda Machine* (London: AB, 1977).
143. Pienaar, *South Africa and International Relations*, 6–12.
144. Bradford, "The Origin and Concession," 174, 175–176, 203–206, 212–215, 419–420, 427–428, 437, and 440–441.
145. SAPHA, *Debates*, vol. 55, col. 2412 (26 February 1946, speech of Eric H. Louw, who became minister of external affairs in 1955).
146. Pienaar, *South Africa and International Relations*, 10.
147. Pedersen, "Settler Colonialism at the Bar of the League of Nations," 114.
148. Pienaar, *South Africa and International Relations*, 64–66 and 80.
149. Rayford W. Logan, *The Operation of the Mandate[s] System in Africa, 1919–1927, with an Introduction on the Problem of the Mandates in the Post-War World* (Washington, D.C.: FP, 1942), 16, 16 n. 29, 17, and 50.
150. Itsejuwa Sagay, *The Legal Aspects of the Namibian Dispute* (Ile Ife, Nigeria: UIP, 1975), 9, 39, 41–42, 44–45, 56–57, 105, 111, and 138.
151. Schrire, *Adapt or Die*, 4.
152. Andries M. Fokkens, "The Role and Application of the Union Defence Force in the Suppression of Internal Unrest" (M.Mil. thesis, Stellenbosch University, 2006), 56–73.
153. Ibid., 73–82; Patrick Pearson, "The Rehoboth Rebellion," WPSAS, 2, ed. Philip Bonner (Johannesburg: RP, 1981), 31–51.
154. Dale, "Reconfiguring White Ethnic Power," 83–85.
155. van Wyk, "South West Africa," 212–219.
156. Deon J. Geldenhuys, *The Diplomacy of Isolation: South African Foreign Policy Making* (New York: SMP, 1984), 3, 7, and 16–17; Wheeler, ed., *History*, Annexure A, 676; Grotpeter, *Historical Dictionary*, 606.
157. Kurt M. Campbell, *Soviet Policy towards South Africa* (New York: SMP, 1986), 56, 62, and 66.
158. Christopher Saunders, "From Apartheid to Democracy in Namibia and South Africa: Some Comparisons," in Henning Melber and Christopher Saunders, *Transition in Southern Africa: Comparative Aspects: Two Lectures*, Discussion Paper no. 10 (Uppsala: NAI, 2001), 10 and 15.
159. Per Strand, *SWAPO and Nation Building in Namibia: Transfer of Power in the Post-Communist Era*, Discussion Paper no. 8 (Windhoek: UNNISER, 1991), 32–44.
160. Christof Maletsky, "Communist Party Back to the Drawing Boards," TN, 14 January 2010, 5; Christof Maletsky, "Ten Parties Forfeit Election Deposits," TN, 8 December 2009, 2, respectively.
161. André van Deventer and Philip Nel, "The State and 'Die Volk' versus Communism, 1922–1941," PSAJPS, 17, no. 2 (December 1990): 64–81; Wessel Visser, "The Production of Literature on the 'Red Peril' and 'Total On-

slaught' in Twentieth-Century South Africa," *Historia* (Pretoria) 49, no. 2 (November 2004): 105-128.

162. W. A. Dorning, "A Concise History of the South African Defence Force (1912-1987)," MOPJSADF 17, no. 2 (1987): 17.

163. Dermot M. Moore, "The South African Air Force in Korea: An Assessment," MHJ 6, no. 3 (June 1984): 88-94.

164. James P. Barber, *South Africa's Foreign Policy, 1945-1970* (London: OxUP, 1973), 9-10, 82, and 82, n. 1.

165. Roger S. Boulter, "F C Erasmus and the Politics of South African Defence, 1948-1959" (Ph.D. diss., Rhodes University, 1997), 183-185 and 191.

166. Geoffrey R. Berridge, *South Africa, the Colonial Powers[,] and 'African Defence'; The Rise and Fall of the White Entente, 1948-60* (New York: SMP, 1992).

167. Frederik J. Nöthling, "The Search for Defence Co-Operation," in Wheeler, ed., *History*, 365-388.

168. Sam[uel] C. Nolutshungu, *South Africa in Africa: A Study in Ideology and Foreign Policy* (Manchester: MUP, 1975), 46-48 and 62-63.

169. Susan Riveles, "Human Rights as a Political Catalyst in South African Policy toward Namibia" (Ph.D. diss., Howard University, 1991), 103.

170. William J. Foltz, "United States Policy toward Southern Africa: Economic and Strategic Constraints," PSQ 92, no. 1 (Spring 1977): 47-64.

171. Martha S. van Wyk, "The 1963 United States Arms Embargo against South Africa: Institution and Implementation" (M.A. thesis, University of Pretoria, 1998), 84.

172. James Sanders, *Apartheid's Friends: The Rise and Fall of South Africa's Secret Service* (London: JM, 2006), 15, 31, 44, 54, and 314.

173. Campbell, *Soviet Policy,* 127-139.

174. Peter Vanneman, *Soviet Strategy in Southern Africa: Gorbachev's Pragmatic Approach* (Stanford, Calif.: HIP, 1990), 19-20, 41-42, and 46-47.

175. 1985 Wolpe subcommittee hearing, 98-99.

176. Keck and Sikkink, *Activists beyond Borders*, 1-38.

177. Kevin Danaher, *In Whose Interest?: A Guide to U.S.-South Africa Relations* (Washington, D.C.: IPS, 1984), 185.

178. This account draws on Louis B. Gerber, *Friends and Influence: The Diplomacy of Private Enterprise* (Cape Town: PuS, 1973), [vi], 18, 20, 42, 58, 86-88, 99, 104-105, 140, 153, and 156). For an opposing viewpoint, see Ruth First, Jonathan Steele, and Christabel Gurney, *The South African Connection: Western Investment in Apartheid* (London: MTS, 1972), 221-233.

179. Sanders, *Apartheid's Friends*, 114 and 418, n. 48; Danaher, *In Whose Interest?*, 146 and 163.

Chapter Three

1. This term was used in the statement of Assistant Secretary of State for African Affairs, Chester A. Crocker, before the USHRCFA. Subcommittees on International Economic Policy and Trade and on Africa, *The Anti-Apartheid Act of 1985: Hearings and Markup ... on H.R. 1460, April 17, 18, 30, May 2, 1985*. Ninety-Ninth Congress, First Session (Washington: USGPO, 1986), 48 (17 April 1985).

2. Crawford and Klotz, ed., *How Sanctions Work: Lessons from South Africa,* ed. Neta C. Crawford and Audie J. Klotz (New York: SMP, 1999).

3. Neta C. Crawford and Audie J. Klotz, "How Sanctions Work: A Framework for Analysis," in Crawford and Klotz, ed., *How Sanctions Work,* 27 (table 2.1) and 31 (table 2.2); Audie Klotz, "Making Sanctions Work: Comparative Lessons," in Crawford and Klotz, ed., *How Sanctions Work,* 266 (table 14.1).

4. Thomas, *The Diplomacy of Liberation,* 19.

5. Lasswell, *Politics: Who Gets What, When, How* (New York: MB, 1958).

6. Alistair Horne, *A Savage War of Peace: Algeria, 1954-1962,* revised ed. (New York: PB, 1987), 237-238, 261, 416-417.

7. Laqueur, *Guerrilla,* 188 and 425, n. 75.

8. *Constitution of the South West People's Organisation (SWAPO) of Namibia Adopted by the Meeting of the Central Committee, July 28th–August 1st, 1976, Lusaka, Zambia* (Lusaka: SWAPO Department for Publicity and Information, n.d.), as reprinted in USCSCJ. Subcommittee on Security and Terrorism, *The Role of the Soviet Union, Cuba, and East Germany in Fomenting Terrorism in Southern Africa: Hearings, March 22, 24, 25, 29, and 31, 1982* (hereafter Denton subcommittee hearings, with the volume number). Volumes 1 and 2. Ninety-Seventh Congress, Second Session (Washington, D.C.: USGPO, 1982), vol. 1, 623.

9. Ibid., 636.

10. Zartman, *Ripe for Resolution,* 179 (for both quotations).

11. Jeffrey Record, *The Wrong War: Why We Lost in Vietnam* (Annapolis, Md.: NIP, 1998), 65.

12. Charles Maechling, Jr., "Insurgency and Counterinsurgency: The Role of Strategic Theory," PJUSAWC 14, no. 3 (Autumn 1984): 32.

13. Ibid.

14. Record, *The Wrong War,* 65-66.

15. Cawthra, *Brutal Force: The Apartheid War Machine.*

16. UNGA res. 3111 (XXVIII) of 12 December 1973, part I, operative para. two and UNGA res. 31/146 of 20 December 1976, operative para. two.

17. UNGA res. 31/152 of 20 December 1976, operative pars. one through three.

18. Rocha, *In Search of Namibian Independence,* 117.

19. Erik Suy, "The Status of Observers in International Organizations," RdC, 160 (1978, part 2), 101.

20. UNGA res. 3280 (XXIX), 10 December 1974, operative para. six.

21. Klaas van Walraven, *Dreams of Power: The Role of the Organization of African Unity in the Politics of Africa, 1963-1993,* ASC Research Series 13/1999 (Aldershot, Hants, England: AsP, 1999), 243-244.

22. Shubin, *The Hot "Cold War,"* 205.

23. van Walraven, *Dreams of Power,* 212-213, 215, 241, and 366.

24. Ansprenger, *Die Befreiungspolitik der Organisation für Afrikanische Einheit, 1963 bis 1975,* Studien zum Konflikt im Südlichen Afrika. Entwicklung und Frieden. Wissenschaftliche Reihe 8 (München: CKV; Mainz: MGV, 1975), 217-221.

25. Hage G. Geingob, "State Formation in Namibia: Promoting Democracy and Good Governance" (Ph.D. diss., University of Leeds, 2004), 52-53.

26. UNGA res. 3295 (XXIX), of 13 December 1974, part III, operative para. two.

27. Berat, "Namibia: The Road to Independence and the Problem of Succession of States," in *Governments-in-Exile in Contemporary World Politics,* ed. Yossi Shain (New York: Routledge, 1991), 32.

28. Peter H. Katjavivi, *A History of Resistance in*

Namibia (London: JC.; Addis Ababa: OAU Inter-African Cultural Fund; and Paris: UNESCO Press, 1988), 52–53.

29. ICJRJAOO, *Legal Consequences*, 58.

30. UNSC res, 276 (1970) of 30 January 1970, operative para. two.

31. Dobell, *SWAPO's Struggle*, 62.

32. Khalil Makkawi, "The Fourth Committee of the United Nations General Assembly" (Ph.D. diss., Columbia University, 1968), 109–110.

33. Ibid., 67 and 69.

34. Ibid., 92 and 317.

35. Ibid., 102.

36. See "Information Newsletter: Meeting on South West Africa/Namibia in Geneva, 7–14 January 1981," [2]-[3], supplement to the SAD, 6 February 1981.

37. This was an enclosure in a letter of 4 November 1982 to the author from Mr. J.J. Grobler, Consul (Information), South African Consulate, Chicago.

38. SAPHA *Debates*, 83, cols. 172–176 (23 February 1979), reply of the minister of foreign affairs to Mr. J. D. duP. Basson's question.

39. Margaret P. Karns, "Ad Hoc Multilateral Diplomacy: The United States, The Contact Group, and Namibia," IOr, 41, no. 1 (Winter 1987): 107.

40. Jan C. Heunis, *United Nations versus South Africa: A Legal Assessment of United Nations and United Nations Related Activities in Respect of South Africa* (Cape Town and Johannesburg: LPP, 1986), 7.

41. Nina Drolsum, "The Norwegian Council for Southern Africa (NOCOSA): A Study in Solidarity and Activism," in *Norway and National Liberation in Southern Africa*, ed. Torre L. Eriksen (Uppsala: NAI, 2000), 228.

42. Mark Israel, *South African Political Exile in the United Kingdom* (New York: SMP, 1999), 182.

43. Gretchen Bauer, *Labor and Democracy in Namibia, 1971–1996* (Athens: OhUP, 1998), 9.

44. See Bradford, "The Origin," 285–295.

45. Nils O. Oermann, *Mission, Church and State Relations in South West Africa under German Rule (1884–1915)*, Missionsgeschichtliches Archiv, Bd. 5 (Stuttgart: FSV, 1999), 242.

46. Hull, *Absolute Destruction*, 188.

47. Iina Soiri and Pekka Peltola, *Finland and National Liberation in Southern Africa* (Uppsala: NAI, 2000), 55–66 and 189–197.

48. Casimir S. B. Knight, "The British Churches and the Namibian Struggle" (M.A. thesis, Queen's University, 1991), 29 and 50–51.

49. Letter to the author from Professor Tötemeyer, dated 26 December 2011.

50. Gerhard K.H. Tötemeyer, *Church and State in Namibia: The Politics of Reconciliation* (Freiburg i. B.: ABI, 2010), 93.

51. Knight, "The British Churches," 27–28.

52. Per Frostin, "The Theological Debate on Liberation," in Katjavivi et al., ed., *Church and Liberation in Namibia*, 51–92.

53. Testimony of Martin A. Sovik, Assistant Director of the Office of Governmental Affairs of the Lutheran Council in the United States in 1985 Wolpe subcommittee hearing, 99–100 and 116. Siegfried Groth provides limited data on this in his *Namibia; The Wall of Silence*.

54. Siegfried Groth, *Namibia; The Wall of Silence: The Dark Days of the Liberation Struggle*, Introductions by Heinz H. Held and Carl Mau, translated from the German by High Beyer (Wuppertal: PHV, 1995), 38–45.

55. David Lan, *Guns & Rain: Guerrillas & Spirit Mediums in Zimbabwe*, Perspectives on Southern Africa no. 38 (London: JC; Berkeley: UCP, 1985).

56. Edward C. May, *Report on the Wingspread Conference on Namibia Convened by [the] Lutheran Council in the U.S.A. and the Johnson Foundation, May 1976* (Racine, Wisconsin: JF, 1976), 22.

57. 1985 Wolpe subcommittee hearing, 88–118.

58. *SWA/Namibia Today*, ed. Marlien de Beer (Windhoek: DGASLS, 1988), 76–77.

59. Prepared statement of Martin A. Sovik, Assistant Director of the Office of Governmental Affairs of the Lutheran Council in the United States, in 1985 Wolpe subcommittee hearing, 92.

60. Knight, "The British Churches," 85.

61. Philip Steenkamp, "The Churches," 94–114.

62. Knight, "The British Churches," 44.

63. Ibid., 89–90.

64. Andreas Shipanga, *In Search of Freedom: The Andreas Shipanga Story. As Told to Sue Armstrong* (Gibraltar: AP, 1989), 140.

65. Knight, "The British Churches," 89.

66. Groth, *Namibia: The Wall of Silence*; Lauren Dobell, "Namibia's Wall of Silence," SAR 11, no. 4 (July 1996): 30–33.

67. Stiff, *Warfare by Other Means*, 382–383; Steenkamp, "The Churches," 113, n. 29.

68. Knight, "The British Churches," 69 and 26, respectively.

69. *South West Africa: Travesty of Trust: The Expert Papers and Findings of the International Conference on South West Africa, Oxford 23–26 March 1966...*, ed. Ronald Segal and Ruth First (London: AD, 1967), 8.

70. Knight, "The British Churches," 54 and 71–72; Herbstein and Evenson, *The Devils Are among Us*, 57.

71. Knight, "The British Churches," 60 and 108.

72. Al Cook, "The International Defence and Aid Fund for Southern Africa or IDAF," in *The Road to Democracy in South Africa* (Pretoria: USAP, 2008), vol. 3, International Solidarity, Part 1, 141–253.

73. Letter to the author from Mr. Moore Crossey, Curator of the African Collection, Yale University Library, dated November 7, 2001.

74. Letter to the author from Dr. Peter Limb, Africana Bibliographer, Michigan State University, dated November 7, 2001.

75. Denis Herbstein, *White Lies: Canon Collins and the Secret War against Apartheid* (Cape Town: HSRCP; Oxford: JC, 2004), 133–152.

76. Statement of Douglas P. Wachholz, Attorney, Lawyers Committee for Civil Rights under Law, in Diggs subcommittee hearings, 3.

77. Knight, "The British Churches," 30–32.

78. Tristan A. Borer, *Challenging the State: Churches as Political Actors in South Africa, 1980–1994* (Notre Dame, Indiana: UNDP, 1998), 55.

79. Ibid., 54–56, 105–106, 119, and 125.

80. Ibid., 2–7, 21–22, 43, 52–53, 61–62, 68–69, 80, 82, 126, 137–139, and 156–157.

81. Ibid., 55, 60, 63–64, 80–81, and 196–197.

82. Ibid., 59, 81, 138, and 153.

83. Janet Cherry, "'Just War' and 'Just Means': Was the TRC Wrong about the ANC?," *Transformation*, no. 42 (2000): 9–28.

84. NPNA, *Debates*, vol. 16, 38 (19 November 1991) for both quotations.

85. Borer, *Challenging the State*, 53–54.

86. Knight, "The British Churches," 35–36 and 38.

87. Ibid., 109.
88. Annemarie Heywood, *The Cassinga Event: An Investigation of the Records*, second revised ed. (Windhoek: NAN, 1996).
89. Dobell, *SWAPO's Struggle for Namibia, 1960–1991*, 70, n. 10.
90. Leo Barnard, "Die Gebeure by Cassinga, 4 Mei 1978: 'n Gevallestudie van die Probleme van 'n Militêre Historikus," *Historia* 41, no. 1 (May 1996): 88–99.
91. Gary F. Baines, *The Battle for Cassinga: Conflicting Narratives and Contested Meanings*, BAB Working Paper no. 2, 2007 (Basel: BAB, 2007), 1–12.
92. This phrase is from Heribert Adam and Kanya Adam, "The Politics of Memory in Divided Societies," 32.
93. Tor Sellström, *Sweden and National Liberation in Southern Africa: Volume I: Formation of a Popular Opinion (1950–1970)* (Uppsala: NAI, 1999), 19 n. 4; *Liberation in Southern Africa: Regional and Swedish Voices: Interviews from Angola, Mozambique, Namibia, South Africa, Zimbabwe, the Frontline States [,] and Sweden*, ed. Tor Sellström (Uppsala: NAI, 1999), 7, n. 1.
94. Tor Sellström, *Sweden and National Liberation in Southern Africa. Volume II: Solidarity and Assistance, 1970–1994* (Uppsala: NAI, 2002), 867; Soiri and Peltola, *Finland and National Liberation*, 11–16.
95. Sellström, *Sweden and National Liberation*, vol. 1, 293 and 293 n. 1. The date of the foreign exchange rate was 7 February 2014.
96. Eva H. Østbye, "The Namibian Liberation Struggle: Direct Norwegian Support to SWAPO," in Eriksen, *Norway and National Liberation*, 89. The date of the foreign exchange rate was 7 February 2014.
97. Soiri and Peltola, *Finland and National Liberation*, 177 (appendix 1). The date of the foreign exchange rate was 7 February 2014.
98. Hiifikepunye Pohamba, former chief SWAPO representative to Tanzania, interviewed by Tor Sellström in Windhoek, 15 March 1995; Aaron Mushimba, former SWAPO representative to Angola and to Zambia, interviewed by Tor Sellström in Windhoek, 16 March 1995 in Sellström, *Liberation in Southern Africa*, 95–96 and 85, respectively; Dr. Nickey Iyambo, a member of the Namibian Cabinet, interviewed by Iina Soiri in Windhoek, 20 August 1996, in Soiri and Peltola, *Finland and National Liberation*, 211–212; and Østbye, "The Namibian Liberation Struggle," 128.
99. Sellström, *Sweden and National Liberation*, vol. 2, 363 n. 4.
100. Janice Love, *The U.S. Anti-Apartheid Movement: Local Activism in Global Politics* (New York: PrP, 1985), 29–50; Earl H. Fry, *The Expanding Role of State and Local Governments in U.S. Foreign Affairs* (New York: CFRP, 1998), 5, 82, 94–95, and 98.
101. Linda Freeman, *The Ambiguous Champion: Canada and South Africa in the Trudeau and Mulroney Years* (Toronto: UTP, 1997), 137–139.
102. Eva H. Østbyte, "Pioneering Local Activism: The Namibian Association of Norway," in Eriksen, *Norway and National Liberation*, 353–372.
103. Østbye, "The Namibian Liberation Struggle," 121–123.

Chapter Four

1. The phrase comes from Signe Landgren, *Embargo Disimplemented: South Africa's Military Industry* (New York: OxUP, 1989), 21.
2. Philip H. Frankel, *Pretoria's Praetorians: Civil-Military Relations in South Africa* (Cambridge: CbUP, 1984), 40.
3. Fieldhouse, *Anti-Apartheid*, 42. The source of this claim is contained in files CAB 21/4634, PREM 11/4486, and PREM 11/5114 in the British PRO (ibid., 65, n. 49).
4. Geldenhuys, *Isolated States*, 472–474 and 503; and Moukambi, "Relations between South Africa and France," 19–20, 29–30, 75, 101, and 104.
5. Moukambi, "Relations between South Africa and France," 93–96, 100, 105–107, 109, 114–115, 117–118 and 121–122; Michael Brzoska, "Arming South Africa in the Shadow of the UN Arms Embargo," DA, 7, no. 1 [March 1991]: 24–25, 28, and 31; Richard Leonard, *South Africa at War: White Power and the Crisis in Southern Africa* (Westport, Conn.: LHC, 1983), 133–134 and 137 (table 5–1); Sasha Polakow-Suransky, *The Unspoken Alliance: Israel's Secret Relationship with Apartheid South Africa* (New York: PnB, 2010), 96, 98, 132, and 231.
6. van Wyk, "The 1963 United States Arms Embargo," 18, 84, 98, 101–102, and 132.
7. Ibid., 34.
8. UNSC res. 181 (1963) of 7 August 1963, operative para. four.
9. UNSC res. 418 (1977) of 4 November 1977, operative paras. one through five.
10. Les [Lourens E. S.] de Villiers, *In Sight of Surrender: The U.S. Sanctions Campaign against South Africa, 1946–1993* (Westport, Conn.: PrP, 1995), 20–21.
11. Brzoska, "Arming South Africa," 32–33, and 34, n. 7; Landgren, *Embargo Disimplemented*, 7–8.
12. van Wyk, "The 1963 United States Arms Embargo," 16–18, 20–21, 23–25, and 29–31.
13. Ibid., 17–18, 49–56, 61, 63–64, and 66–67.
14. Moukambi, "Relations between South Africa and France," 69, 86, 89–91, and 102.
15. van Wyk, "The 1963 United States Arms Embargo," 21 and 34.
16. Landgren, *Embargo Disimplemented*, 196 and 210.
17. Leonard, *South Africa at War*, 133.
18. Brzoska, "Arming South Africa," 23.
19. UNSC res. 418 (1977) of 4 November 1977, operative paras. one through five.
20. Landgren, *Embargo Disimplemented*, 37, 63–65, 70–71, 113–117, 220, 231–232, and 261–265 (appendix 4); Moukambi, "Relations between South Africa and France," 93–94, 101, 105, 107–115, and 117–118; Polakow-Suransky, *The Unspoken Alliance*, 96, 132, 151–152, 182, 215, and 224.
21. Neta C. Crawford, "The Humanitarian Consequence of Sanctioning South Africa: A Preliminary Analysis," in Weiss et al., ed., *Political Gain and Civilian Pain*, 77.
22. Martha S. van Wyk, "The 1977 United States Arms Embargo against South Africa: Institution and Implementation to 1997" (D.Phil. diss., University of Pretoria, 2004), 227–233, 289–295, and 350–352.
23. Brzoska, "Arming South Africa," 29 and 36, n. 42; Landgren, *Embargo Disimplemented*, 233–234.
24. Kathy Satchwell, "The Power to Defend: An Analysis of Various Aspects of the Defence Act," in *Society at War: The Militarisation of South Africa*, ed. Jacklyn Cock and Laurie Nathan (New York: SMP, 1989), 46–49; Kate Philip, "The Private Sector and the Security Establishment," in Cock and Nathan, ed., *Society at War*, 206;

Graeme Simpson, "The Politics and Economics of the Armaments Industry in South Africa," in Cock and Nathan, ed., *Society at War*, 225.

25. Speech of the minister of finance moving the second reading of the Defense Special Equipment Account Bill in SAPHA, *Debates*, 77 (21 February 1952), col. 1540.

26. Speech of the deputy minister of finance moving the second reading of the Defense Special Account Bill in SAPHA, *Debates*, 47 (14 February 1974), cols. 912–913.

27. SAPHA, Debates, 77 (21 February 1952), cols. 1547-1548.

28. Frankel, *Pretoria's Praetorians*, 74–75.

29. Cawthra, *Brutal Force*, 82.

30. Landgren, *Embargo Disimplemented*, 25.

31. Helen E. Purkitt and Stephen F. Burgess, *South Africa's Weapons of Mass Destruction* (Bloomington: IUP, 2005), 73.

32. Peter Stiff, *The Covert War: Koevoet Operations [in] Namibia, 1979–1989* (Alberton: GaP, 2004), 488.

33. Brzoska, "Arming South Africa," 34, n. 11.

34. Landgren, *Embargo Disimplemented*, 42, 124, 134, n. 27, and 231.

35. Dick [Richard S.] Lord, *From Fledgling to Eagle: The South African Air Force during the Border War* (Johannesburg: TDSP, 2008), 479.

36. Record, *The Wrong War*, 75, 101, and 117.

37. Ibid., 57.

38. George K. Tanham, *Communist Revolutionary Warfare: The Vietminh in Indochina* (New York: FAP, 1961), 69–72 and 106–108.

39. Letter to the author from Professor Baines, dated 3 March 2012.

40. Dick [Richard S.] Lord, *Vlamgat: The Story of the Mirage FI in the South African Air Force* (Weltevreden Park, South Africa: CDB, 2000), 59; Lord, *From Fledgling to Eagle*, 138, 185, 238, and 298.

41. Lord, *From Fledgling to Eagle*, 74, 141, 149, 159, 221–222, 233, 246, 257, 304, 318, 394, 435, 479, and 487.

42. Lord, *Vlamgat*, 259–268 (Appendix 7).

43. Edward George, *The Cuban Intervention in Angola, 1965–1991: From Che Guevara to Cuito Cuanavale* (New York: FC, 2005), 211 and 215.

44. Clive Holt, *At Thy Call We Did Not Falter* (Cape Town: ZbP, 2005), 85, 87, 90, 94, and 105.

45. Piero Gleijesis, *Visions of Freedom: Havana, Washington, Pretoria, and the Struggle for Southern Africa, 1976–1991* (Chapel Hill, N.C.: UNCP, 2013), 6, 364, 428, and 430.

46. Ibid., 366, 405, 413, 425, and 428.

47. Ibid., 454.

48. Gay McDougall, "Implementation of the [Comprehensive] Anti-Apartheid Act of 1986," in *Sanctioning Apartheid*, ed. Robert E. Edgar (Trenton, N.J.: AWP, 1990), 42–43, n. 4.

49. Merle Lipton, *Sanctions and South Africa: The Dynamics of Economic Isolation*, Special Report no. 1119 (London: EIU, 1988), 77.

50. Jaap Woldendorp, "The Oil Embargo against South Africa: Effects and Loopholes," in Edgar, ed., *Sanctioning Apartheid*, 169–172.

51. John Dugard, *Human Rights and the South African Legal Order* (Princeton: PUP, 1978), 176, n. 144.

52. Borer, *Challenging the State*, 60 and 229, n. 64; Lipton, *Sanctions*, 120.

53. Crawford, "The Humanitarian Consequence," 60.

54. Letter to the author from Professor Baines, dated 3 March 2012.

55. Nerys John, "South African Intervention in the Angolan Civil War, 1975–1976: Motivations and Implications" (M.A. thesis, University of Cape Town, 2002).

56. Geldenhuys, *The Diplomacy of Isolation*, 186.

57. Graeme N. Addison, "Censorship of the Press in South Africa during the Angolan War: A Case Study of News Manipulation and Suppression" (M.A. thesis, Rhodes University, 1980).

58. Marianne A. Spiegel, "The Namibia Negotiations and the Problem of Neutrality," in *International Mediation in Theory and Practice*, ed. Saadia Touval and I. William Zartman, SAIS Papers in International Affairs no. 6 (Boulder, Colo.: WP with the Foreign Policy Institute, SAIS, 1985), 115.

59. Marc A. Levy, "Mediation of Prisoners' Dilemma Conflicts and the Importance of the Cooperation Threshold: The Case of Namibia," JCR 29, no. 4 (December 1985): 602.

60. "End SA Sanctions Says Mandela, But Free Namibia Still Has Them," WeA, 25–26 September 1993, 5.

61. NPNA, *Debates*, 14, 90 (14 June 1991).

62. David de Beer, "The Netherlands and Namibia: The Political Campaign to End Dutch Involvement in the Namibian Trade," in Cooper, ed., *Allies in Apartheid*, 125–130.

63. Alun R. Roberts, "British Economic Involvement in South African–Occupied Namibia, 1845–1986," in Cooper, ed., *Allies in Apartheid*, 164–171.

64. Bern Brüggeman, "The United Nations Council for Namibia with Especial Emphasis on Its Decree No. 1" (LL.M. thesis, University of Cape Town, 1992), 119–162.

65. ICJRJAOO, *Legal Consequences*, 58.

66. UNSC res. 276 (1970) of 30 January 1970, preambular para. two.

67. S[uresh] C. Saxena, "[The] Role of the U. N. Council for Namibia," AQ 17, no. 3 (January 1978): 10–11 and 14–16.

68. UNIN, *Namibia: Perspectives for National Reconstruction and Development* (Lusaka: UNIN, 1986), 41 and 55, n. 52.

69. Karin Arts, "The Legal Status and Functioning of the United Nations Council for Namibia," LJIL. 2, no. 2 (November 1989): 206.

70. Andreas Junius, *Der United Nations Council for Namibia*, Europöische Hochschulschriften. Reihe II, Rechtswissenschaft, Bd. 817 (Frankfurt a.M.: PL, 1989).

71. Mittleman, "Collective Decolonization," 44, 55, and 60–61.

72. Brzoska, "Arming South Africa," 21 and 28.

73. Saxena, *Namibia and the World*, 235–237.

74. The phrase is modified from Graham Hopwood, *Walvis Bay: South Africa's Hostage* (London: CIIR; Amsterdam: AEI; London: CAN, 1990).

75. Goldblatt, *History*, 62–63 and 87.

76. Berat, *Walvis Bay*, 13 and 43–46.

77. Ibid., 13.

78. Gerald L'Ange, *Urgent Imperial Service: South African Forces in German South West Africa, 1914–1915* (Rivonia: AP, 1991), 7.

79. Ibid., 280–281.

80. Richard Moorsom, *Walvis Bay: Namibia's Port* (London: IDAFSA in cooperation with the UNCN, 1984), 11 and 25; Green, *Lords of the Last Frontier*, 218–219.

81. Berat, *Walvis Bay*, 13.

82. Ronald Dreyer, "Dispute over Walvis Bay: Origins

and Implications for Namibian Independence," AA 83, no. 333 (February 1984): 503.

83. Anton du Plessis. *The Strategic Significance of Walvis Bay and the Penguin Islands*, ad hoc publication no. 28 (Pretoria: ISSUP, 1991), 27, n. 4.

84. Paul Schamberger, "The Front Door to SWA," TS, 29 May 1975 (second city late ed.), 28.

85. Moorsom, *Walvis Bay*, 10–11 and 58.

86. SAPHA, *Debates*, 61, col. 5278 (23 April 1976).

87. Daan S. Prinsloo, *Walvis Bay and the Penguin Islands: Background and Status*, Study Report no. 8 (Pretoria: FAA, 1977), 17.

88. Moorsom, *Walvis Bay*, 11 and 18–21.

89. UNGA res. 32/9 (D), 4 November 1977, preambular para. nine and operative paras. six through eight; UNGA res. S9/2, 3 May 1978, preambular para. six, part I, operative para. eleven, and part II, para. thirty-seven; and UNGA res. 35/227 (A) of 16 March 1981, preambular para. sixteen and operative paras. three and seventeen.

90. UNSC res. 432, 27 July 1978, preambular para. three and operative paras. one through four.

91. Berat, *Walvis Bay*, 95.

92. Moorsom, *Walvis Bay*, 60–61; "Coastal Bavaria," *Namibia: A Survey* (supplement to the FM, 22 July 1983), 31.

93. Andreas G. Velthuizen, "Applying Military Force for Political Ends: South Africa in South-Western Africa, 1987–1988" (M.A. thesis, University of South Africa, 1994), 124.

94. Donald L. Sparks, "Namibia's Coastal and Marine Development Potential," AA 83, no. 333 (October 1984): 493.

95. Ford, "South African Foreign Policy," 180–204.

96. Moorsom, *Walvis Bay*, 47.

97. Ibid., 45.

98. Sparks, "Namibia's Coastal and Marine Development," 485.

99. Moorsom, *Walvis Bay*, 11 and 29–32.

100. Ibid., 33–36.

101. Richard Moorsom, *Exploiting the Sea*, A Future for Namibia, vol. 5 (London: CIIR, 1984), 53–55 and 57–58.

102. Brian Harlech-Jones, *A New Thing?: The Namibian Independence Process, 1989–1990* (Windhoek: University of Namibia, EIN, 1997), 170.

103. Emmett, *Popular Resistance*, 263.

104. Moorsom, *Walvis Bay*, 42–43.

105. David M. Stone, "Namibia 1979: Another Angola?" (M.A. thesis, [U.S.] Naval Postgraduate School, 1979), 24.

106. The next four terms are from Moorsom, *Walvis Bay*, 19 (second and third terms), 69 (fourth term), and 70 (fifth term).

107. Hopwood, *Walvis Bay*, 7 (sixth term).

108. David Dorward, *Namibia: International Dimensions to Its Decolonisation*, Occasional Paper no. 3 (East Melbourne: The Australian Institute of International Affairs [Victorian Branch] and Geelong, Victoria: Deakin University, School of Social Sciences, 1989), 11.

109. Gleijeses, *Visions*, 150–155, 157–158, 177–178, 215–216, 289–293, 295–296, and 388–389 (these are merely illustrative of the many more other pages referring to sanctions).

110. Jabri, *Mediating Conflict*, 49–54 and 57, n. 40.

111. Patrick Bond, "Can Reparations for Apartheid Profits Be Won in U.S. Courts?" AI 38, no. 2 (September 2008): 14.

112. Berat, *Walvis Bay*, 94–96; Moorsom, *Walvis Bay*, 20 and 68.

113. UNSC res. 432, 27 July 1978, preambular para. three and operative paras. one through four.

114. du Plessis, *The Strategic Significance*, 18–19.

115. The term stems from the assertion that "there is no free lunch, and there are no free wars" (Joseph E. Stiglitz and Linda J. Bilmes, *The Three Trillion Dollar War: The Truth of the Cost of the Iraq Conflict* [New York: WWN, 2008], 55).

116. Arend Lijphart, *The Trauma of Decolonization: The Dutch and West New Guinea*, Yale Studies in Political Science, no. 17 (New Haven: YUP, 1966), 286–289 (quotation from p. 289).

117. Albert Memmi, *The Colonizer and the Colonized*, expanded ed., introduction by Jean-Paul Sartre, afterword by Susan G. Miller (Boston: BeP, 1967), 64.

118. Gilbert I. Schrank, "German South West Africa: Social and Economic Aspects of Its History, 1884–1915" (Ph.D. diss., New York University, 1974), 231.

119. Lewis H. Gann and Peter J. Duignan, *The Rulers of German Africa, 1884–1914* (Stanford: SUP, 1977), 260 (table E.11).

120. Mary E. Townsend, *The Rise and Fall of Germany's Colonial Empire, 1884–1918* (New York: HF, 1966, first published in 1930), 264.

121. Dale, "Reconfiguring White Ethnic Power in Namibia," 81.

122. South Africa. South West Africa Commission. *Report.* U.G.26 (Pretoria: GP, 1936), 69, para. 348 (a).

123. Goldblatt, *History of South West Africa*, 266 (table C).

124. SAPHA, *Debates*, 26, col. 3556; Grotpeter, *Historical Dictionary*, 113–114.

125. Donald L. Sparks, "Namibia's Economy at Independence," paper prepared for delivery at the twenty-third annual meeting of the ASA, Philadelphia, 15–18 October 1980.

126. André du Pisani, "Namibia: The Political Economy of Transition," SAI 15, no. 3 (January 1985): 150–156.

127. Letter to the author from Professor Saunders, dated 2 December 2011.

128. Daniel R. Kempton and Roni L. du Preez, "Namibian-De Beers State-Firm Relations: Cooperation and Conflict," JSAS 23, no. 4 (December 1997): 585–613.

129. L'Ange, *Urgent Imperial Service*, 7, 9, 17, 40, 89, and 260; Louis, *Great Britain and Germany's Lost Colonies*, 156.

130. Leo Marquard, *South Africa's Colonial Policy: Presidential Address Delivered at the Annual Meeting of the Council of the South African Institute of Race Relations in Hiddingh Hall, Cape Town, on January 16, 1957* (Johannesburg: SAIRR, 1957), 16.

131. Ibid., 9.

132. Moorsom, *Walvis Bay*, 63–66 and 84.

133. Paul R. Moorcraft, *African Nemesis: War and Revolution in Southern Africa (1945–2010)* (London: Brassey's [UK], 1990), 104.

134. Kangumu, *Contesting Caprivi*, 134 and 154.

135. Ibid., 160.

136. Gleijeses, *Visions*, 446.

137. Moorcraft, *African Nemesis*, 63–64.

138. Kenneth W. Grundy, *Guerrilla Struggle in Africa: An Analysis and Preview* (New York: GrP, 1971), 69 and 148.

139. Robert S. Jaster, *The Defence of White Power: South African Foreign Policy under Pressure* (London: MaP, 1988), 119–124.

140. Gleijeses, *Visions*, 335; Joseph Hanlon, *Beggar Your Neighbours: Apartheid Power in Southern Africa* (London: CIIR and JC; Bloomington: IUP, 1986), 144 and 324, n. 29.

141. Gleijeses, *Visions*, 156.

142. Kenneth W. Grundy, *The Militarization of South African Politics* (Bloomington: IUP, 1986), 26; Gleijeses, *Visions*, 458–459, 489, and 519.

143. Ron Scherer, "How U.S. Is Deferring War Costs," CSM, 16 January 2007, 1 and 10–11; Mark Trumbull, "How Able Are Americans to Bear the Costs of War?," CSM, 20 (March 2008), 11.

144. Amy Belasco, *The Cost of Iraq, Afghanistan, and Other Global Wars on Terror Operations since 9/11*, CRS Report RL 33110 (Washington, D.C.: CRS, 2010).

145. Crawford, *Argument and Change*, 364.

146. Horne, *A Savage War of Peace*, 538.

147. Susan Brown, "Diplomacy by Other Means: SWAPO's Liberation War," in Leys and Saul, *Namibia's Liberation Struggle*, 37.

148. "R1[,]143-m for Namibia from SA," TS, 12 July 1984, 6.

149. "What War on Swapo Costs," *Sowetan* (Johannesburg), 27 June 1985, 19.

150. "R 600[,]000: That's the Price of a Dead Guerrilla," STr, 22 September 1985, 23.

151. Interview with Gen. J. J. Geldenhuys, *Défense et Armements* [place of publication not given], no. 47 [January, 1986], 51, as reported in Landgren, *Embargo Disimplemented*, 57 and 59, n. 44.

152. David Simon and Richard Moorsom, "Namibia's Political Economy: A Contemporary Perspective," in Tötemeyer et al., ed., *Namibia in Perspective*, 84.

Chapter Five

1. The phrase "the colonial spoils" is from Tamarkin, *The Making of Zimbabwe*, 130, 157, and 265.

2. Katjavivi, *A History of Resistance*, 59.

3. As reported in Willem Steenkamp, *Borderstrike!: South Africa into Angola* (Durban: BwP, 1983), 9.

4. "West Mum on SWAPO Statement," TS, 1 March 1978, stop press ed., 5.

5. *On the Border: The White South African Military Experience, 1965–1990* (Cape Town: Tafelberg, 2008), 12.

6. Two sources do show the location, namely, Helmoed-Römer Heitman, *Modern African Wars, 3: South-West Africa*, Men-at-Arms Series no. 242 (London: OP, 1991), 6; Paul J. Els, *Ongulumbashe: Where the Bushwar [sic] Began* (Wandsbeck, South Africa: ReP, 2007), 65, 129, 184, and 239.

7. "Die S.A. Polisiester vir Voortreflike Diens," SARP (Pretoria), 7, no. 10 (August 1971): 26–27.

8. Els, *Ongulumbashe*.

9. NPNA, *Debates* vol. 7, 10 (19 November 1990) (speech of the deputy minister of home affairs during the second reading debate on the Public Holidays Bill).

10. Nujoma, *Where Others Wavered*, 165 (photograph); Els, *Ongulumbashe*, 222 (photograph).

11. David Lush, *Last Steps to Uhuru: An Eye-Witness Account of Namibia's Transition to Independence* (Windhoek: NNB, 1993), 299.

12. Sam Nujoma, "24th Anniversary of the Launching of the Armed Liberation Struggle in Namibia, August 26, 1990, Ongulumbashe," in *Ten Years of Freedom, Peace & Prosperity: Speeches of the President, March 1990—March 20, 1995*, ed. Amy Schoeman ([Windhoek]: Ministry of Information and Broadcasting, The Directorate [of] Print Media and Regional Offices, circa 2000), 34–37.

13. Horst Drechsler, *"Let Us Die Fighting"*: The Struggle of the Herero and Nama against German Imperialism (1884–1915) (London: ZP/B, 1980), vii–xi.

14. Ibid., 143–144.

15. Duane Schultz, *Over the Earth I Come: The Great Sioux Uprising of 1862* (New York: SMP, 1992).

16. Jack Weatherford, *Native Roots: How Indians Enriched America* (New York: FaC, 1991), 165.

17. Adam Hochschild, *The Mirror at Midnight: A South African Journey* (New York: PB, 1990), 238.

18. Arnold V. Wallenkampf, "The Herero Rebellion in South West Africa, 1904–1906: A Study in German Colonialism" (Ph.D. diss., University of California, Los Angeles, 1969), 345–349.

19. Richard E. Welch, Jr., "American Atrocities in the Philippines: The Indictment and the Response," PHR 43, no. 2 (May 1974): 233–253.

20. The most current study is John Masson's *Jakob Marengo: An Early Resistance Hero of Namibia* (Windhoek: OAP, 2001).

21. Martii Eirola, *The Ovambogefahr: The Ovamboland Reservation in the Making: Political Responses of the Kingdom of Ondonga to the German Colonial Power, 1884–1910*, Studia Historica Septentrionalia no. 22 (Rovaniemi, Finland: PSHY, 1992), 163–185.

22. Frank R. Vivelo, "The Entry of the Herero into Botswana," BNR 8 (1976): 39–46; Boammaruri B. Kebonanang, "The History of the Herero in Mahalapye, Central District: 1922–1984," BNR, 21 (1989): 43–60.

23. John M. Bridgman, *The Revolt of the Hereros*, Perspectives on Southern Africa no. 30 (Berkeley: UCP, 1981), 141.

24. Ibid., 66–68, 140, and 169.

25. UNGA res. 1514 (XV) of 14 December 1960.

26. Harvey Glickman, "Dar es Salaam: Where Exiles Plan—and Wait." AR, vol. 8, no. 7 (July, 1973): 3–6.

27. Steenkamp, *South Africa's Border War*, 20.

28. UN, *Report of the Committee on South West Africa Concerning the Implementation of General Assembly Resolutions 1568 (XV) and 1596 (XV)*, UNGAOR, Sixteenth Session, Supplement no. 12A (A/4926) (New York: UN, 1962), 18.

29. Dierks, *Chronology*, 128, 131, and 135.

30. Namakalu, *Armed Liberation Struggle*, 1.

31. John A. Marcum, *The Angolan Revolution, Volume I: The Anatomy of an Explosion (1950–1962)* (Cambridge, Mass.: MITP, 1969), 310–311 and 310, n. 74; Stefan Talmon, *Recognition of Governments in International Law: With Particular Reference to Governments in Exile* (New York: OxUP, 1998), 339 (Appendix III).

32. John A. Marcum, *The Angolan Revolution, Volume II: Exile Politics and Guerrilla Warfare (1962–1976)* (Cambridge: MITP, 1978), 116–117.

33. Marcum, *The Angolan Revolution, Volume 1*, 310; "Angolan, South West Freedom Movements to Collaborate," *Contact* (Cape Town), 5, no. 16 (9 August 1962): 1; Talmon, *Recognition of Governments in International Law*, 339 (Appendix III), respectively.

34. Marcum, *The Angolan Revolution*, Volume 1, 310–311.

35. "What Prize [sic] Unity?," *South West Africa Today*

(Dar es Salaam: SWAPO Information Service), no volume or number (June, 1964), [1].
36. The phrasing also appears in "Violence New Tactic of South West Africa Party," TS. 23 September 1964, 24.
37. Joe Putz, Heidi von Egidy, and Perri Caplan, *Political Who's Who of Namibia*. (Windhoek: MaC, 1987), 120.
38. Dierks, *Chronology*, 127.
39. Johan A. Müller, *"The Inevitable Pipeline into Exile": Botswana's Role in the Namibian Liberation Struggle* (Basel: BAB, 2012), 121 and 142.
40. Tor Sellström's interview with Charles Kauraisa (former chairman of the External Council of SWANU), Windhoek, 20 March 1985, in Sellström, *Liberation in Southern Africa: Regional and Swedish Voices*, 74; Sellström, *Sweden and National Liberation in Southern Africa*, vol. 1, 272, n. 1.
41. "Tanzania Bans S.W.A. Rebels," TS, city late ed., 30 September 1967, 9.
42. Elena Torreguitar's interview with Zedekia Ngavirue (a founding member of SWANU) in Windhoek, 28 April 1994 in Torreguitar, *National Liberation Movements*, 166, n. 67 and 488.
43. Shubin, *The Hot "Cold War,"* 205.
44. Clause 9 (1) of the Terrorism Act, No. 83 of 1967 (South Africa: *Government Gazette Extraordinary*, no. 1771, 21 June 1967, 86).
45. SAPHA *Debates*, 21, col. 7031 (1 June 1967).
46. Susan Brown, "Diplomacy by Other Means: SWAPO's Liberation War," in Leys and Saul, *Namibia's Liberation Struggle*, 20.
47. SAPHA *Debates*, 21, col. 7121 (2 June 1967).
48. Richard A. Falk, "The Observer's Report: The State versus Elisar Tuhadeleni and Others," in *Erosion of the Rule of Law in South Africa* (Geneva: IComJ, 1968), 53.
49. John Ya-Otto with Ole Gjerstad and Michael Mercer, *Battlefront Namibia: An Autobiography* (Westport, Conn.: LHC, 1981), 87–104.
50. Joel Carlson, *No Neutral Ground* (New York: TC, 1973), 169, 171, 173, 177, 183–184, 187, 206, and 208–209.
51. TRCSA, *Report*, vol. 2, 200.
52. Nujoma, *Where Others Wavered*, 163, 170–172, and 180.
53. Keshii P. Nathanael, *A Journey to Exile: The Story of a Namibian Freedom Fighter* (Aberystwyth, Wales: SoP, 2002), 167–169, 173–174, and back cover.
54. Nujoma, *Where Others Wavered*, 145; Gordon Winter, *BOSS: South Africa's Secret Police* (Harmondsworth, Middlesex, England: PB, 1981), 316 and 318.
55. Michael Morris, *Armed Conflict in Southern Africa: A Survey of Regional Terrorisms from Their Beginnings to the Present, with a Comprehensive Examination of the Portuguese Position* (Cape Town: JS, 1974), 3.
56. "First Terrorists Were Caught Six Months Ago," TS, 30 September 1966, city late ed., 4.
57. Nujoma, *Where Others Wavered*, 171–172.
58. Sebastian Ballard and Nick Santcross, *Namibia Handbook* (Bath, England: FHL, 1997), 170.
59. Ibid., 70 for both quotations.
60. Helmoed-Römer Heitman, *South African War Machine* (Novato, Calif.: PreP, 1985), 138.
61. SAPHA, *Debates*, 17, col. 2738 (22 September 1966, statement of the deputy minister of police).
62. Ibid., col. 1522 (26 August 1966, statement of the minister of justice).
63. Müller, *"The Inevitable Pipeline into Exile,"* 62, 66, 72, 75, and 114–115.
64. Dale, *Botswana's Search for Autonomy*, 27, 32–33, 41–42, and 55.
65. Müller, *"The Inevitable Pipeline into Exile,"* 86 and 121.
66. Ko-wang Mei, "The Theory and Practice of Modern Guerrilla Warfare" (Ph.D. diss., Michigan State University, 1965), 114–120.
67. Paresh Pandya, *Mao Tse-tung and Chimurenga: An Investigation into Zanu's Strategies* (Braamfontein: SkP, 1988), 55–58.
68. Lucien W. Pye, *Guerrilla Communism in Malaya: Its Social and Political Meaning* (Princeton: PUP, 1956), 30–32.
69. Hidipo L. Hamutenya and Gottfried H. Geingob, "African Nationalism in Namibia," in *Southern Africa in Perspective: Essays in Regional Politics*, ed. Christian P. Potholm and Richard Dale (New York: FrP, 1972), 91.
70. Morris, *Armed Conflict*, 3.
71. Steenkamp, *South Africa's Border War*, 21.
72. Morris, *Armed Conflict*, 3–4; Chris Vermaak, "South West Africa: The Case for 'Namibia,'" in Reg Shay and Chris Vermaak, *The Silent War* (Salisbury: GalP, 1971), 171–177.
73. Els, *Ongulumbashe*, 127 and 253–254.
74. South African Defense Force. Military Information Bureau, "The War in SWA [South West Africa]/N[amibia]," ISSUPB 4/87 (24 September 1987): 2.
75. Pandya, *Mao Tse-tung and Chimurenga*, 47–49.
76. Brian M. Linn, *The U.S. Army and Counterinsurgency in the Philippine War, 1899–1902* (Chapel Hill: UNCP, 1989), 37–38, 40–43, 51, 135–136, and 166.
77. Gérard Chaliand, *Armed Struggle in Africa: With the Guerrillas in "Portuguese" Guinea*, translated by David Rattray and Robert Leonhardt (New York and London: MRP, 1969), 17.
78. Els, *Ongulumbashe*, 139.
79. Ibid., 29 and 59.
80. TRCSA, *Report*, vol. 2, 14 and 24.
81. Willem Steenkamp, "Politics of Power: The Border War," in *Southern Africa within the African Revolutionary Context: An Overview*, ed. Al. J. Venter (Gibraltar: AP, 1989), 219–220.
82. Robert Taber, *The War of the Flea: A Study of Guerrilla Warfare Theory and Practise* (New York: LS, 1965), 76–78.
83. Ibid., 40–44.
84. Basil Davidson, *The Liberation of Guiné: Aspects of an African Revolution* (Harmondsworth, Middlesex, England: PB, 1969), 17, 43 n., 45 n., 73, 80–81, 88, 102–103, 107, 117–118, 120, 124 n., 125–126, and 135–136.
85. Sellström, *Sweden and National Liberation in Southern Africa*, vol. 2, 500, n. 2.
86. Vladimir Shubin, "Unsung Heroes: The Soviet Military and the Liberation of Southern Africa," in *Cold War in Southern Africa: White Power, Black Liberation*, Cold War History Series no. 24, ed. Sue Onslow (New York: Routledge, 2009), 158–159.
87. Edwin S. Munger, "South-West Africa: Evolution or Revolution? [ESM-6-61]," *American Universities Field Staff Reports Service*, Central & Southern African series, 10, no. 6 (July 1961): 1.
88. Tor Sellström's interview with Ben Amathila (former SWAPO representative to Austria, West Germany, and Scandinavia, later Minister of Broadcasting and Information), Stockholm, 19 May 1995, in Sellström, *Liberation in Southern Africa: Regional and Swedish Voices*, 65.

89. Peter H. Katjavivi's interview with Kahimise, place and date not given, as paraphrased and quoted in Peter H. Katjavivi, "The Rise of Nationalism in Namibia and Its International Dimensions" (D.Phil. diss., University of Oxford, 1986), 280 n. 2 and 285 (quotation).
90. Laquer, *Guerrilla*, 133, 135, 189, 231, 284, 312, 334, 394, and 404.
91. Chester A. Crocker, *High Noon in Southern Africa: Making Peace in a Rough Neighborhood* (New York: WWN, 1992), 130 and 130 n.
92. Ibid., 193 and 220.
93. Paul A. Kramer, "Introduction: Decolonizing the History of the Philippine-American War," in Leon Wolff, *Little Brown Brother: How the United States Purchased and Pacified the Philippine Islands at the Century's Turn*, Francis Parkman Prize ed. (New York: HBC, 2006), and xiii.
94. *Supplementary Report of the Secretary-General concerning the Implementation of Security Council Resolutions 435 (1978) and 439 (1978) concerning the Question of Namibia*, UN doc. S/13634 of 23 November 1979, paras. three, four, seven, eight, and ten.
95. "Letter dated 5 December 1979, from the South African Foreign Minister to the UN Secretary-General, concerning the Proposed Demilitarized Zone," SARc 20 (August 1980): 14.
96. TH, 30 May 1981, as cited in Cleophas J. Tsokodayi, *Namibia's Independence Struggle: The Role of the United Nations* ([Bloomington, Ind.]: XPC, 2011), 74, n. 153.
97. Tsokodayi, *Namibia's Independence*, 56, n. 110 and Gleijeses, *Visions*, 205–206, 497, and 607, n. 59.
98. Gleijeses, *Visions*, 497.
99. Tsokodayi, *Namibia's Independence*, 59, 134, 136, 145, and 159–160; Gleijeses, *Visions*, 205–206 and 497.
100. Tamarakin, *The Making of Zimbabwe*, 221.
101. Dale, *Botswana's Search for Autonomy*, 28, 43, and 54.
102. Ibid., 55; Heitman, *South African War Machine*, 157, 160, and 165.
103. Thornberry, *A Nation Is Born*, 98.
104. Cleophas Tsokodayi, who was the deputy permanent representative of Zimbabwe at the UN at this time, provides an observer-participant view of the NAM lobbying over this issue in his *Namibia's Independence*, 23, 117, 123, 116–139, and 144.
105. These were South African estimates published in Peter Stiff, *Nine Days of War* (Alberton, South Africa: LeB, 1989), 231.
106. Moorcraft, *African Nemesis*, 246.
107. UNDPI, *The Blue Helmets: A Review of United Nations Peace-keeping*, second ed. (New York: UN, 1990), 362.
108. Steenkamp, *South Africa's Border War*, 182.
109. Richard Dale, "The UN and African Decolonization: UNTAG in Namibia," TAF 8, no. 3 (Fall 1991): 41.
110. Stiff, *Nine Days*, 231.
111. Lush, *Last Steps*, 158.
112. Alun R. Roberts, "Namibia: What They Didn't Tell Us," AR 34, no. 4 (July-August 1989): 62.
113. Stiff, *Nine Days*, 259.
114. "Treacherous Crossing: Namibian Independence Debacle," SAR 5, no. 1 (July 1989): 16.
115. Gleijeses, *Visions*, 498 an 607, n. 65.
116. Nujoma, *Where Others Wavered*, 396–400.
117. Ibid., 405–406.
118. Lamb, "Civil Supremacy," 135–144.
119. O'Linn, *Namibia*, [vol. 1], 315–335.
120. Thornberry, *A Nation Is Born*, 87–140.
121. Crocker, *High Noon*, 130 and 484.
122. SAPHA, *Debates*, 79, cols. 1858–1862 (6 March 1979, speech of the prime minister).
123. Steenkamp, *South Africa's Border War*, 182.
124. Letter to the author from Professor Tötemeyer, dated 26 December 2011.
125. Christopher C. Saunders, "Liberation and Democracy: A Critical Reading of Sam Nujoma's Autobiography," in *Re-examining Liberation in Namibia: Political Culture since Independence*, ed. Henning Melber (Uppsala: NAI, 2003), 93.
126. Norma J. Kriger, *Guerrilla Veterans in Post-War Zimbabwe: Symbolic and Violent Politics, 1980–1987*, African Studies Series no. 103 (Cambridge: CbUP, 2003), 46–47, 51, 116, and 195.
127. Thornberry, *A Nation Is Born*, 137.
128. Morgan Norval, *Death in the Desert: The Namibian Tragedy* (Washington, D.C.: SFP, 1989), 258–259.
129. Hearn, *UN Peacekeeping*, 105.
130. Lise Howard, "UN Peace Implementation in Namibia: The Causes of Success," IP, 9, no. 1 (Spring, 2002): 108–109.
131. Matthew S. Shugart, "Guerrillas and Elections: An Institutionalist Perspective on the Costs of Conflict and Competition," ISQ 36, no. 2 (June 1992): 142; "Treacherous Crossing," 16; Harlech-Jones, *A New Thing?*, 98.
132. Lynda Schuster, "Guerrillas at Odds: Namibia Pact in Jeopardy," CSM, 6 April 1989, 1–2 and Lush, *Last Steps to Uhuru*, 159–160.
133. This synthesis is based on Tsokodayi, *Namibia's Independence Struggle*, 100–102, 116, 130–137, 145–152, 154–161, and 215.
134. John S. Saul and Colin Leys, "SWAPO: The Politics of Exile," in Leys and Saul, *Namibia's Liberation Struggle*, 48.
135. Lionel Cliffe with Ray Bush et al., *The Transition to Independence in Namibia* (Boulder, Colo.: LRP, 1994), 27.
136. Robert Rinehart, "National Security," in *South Africa: A Country Study*, Foreign Area Studies, The American University, DA Pam 550–93, second edition, ed. Harold D. Nelson (Washington, D.C.: Headquarters, Department of the Army, 1981), 304–305; Marcum, *The Angolan Revolution, Volume II*, 266; Willem S. van der Waals, *Portugal's War in Angola, 1961–1974* (Rivonia: AP, 1993), 208–209 and 211–12.
137. Brown, "Diplomacy by Other Means," 24–26.
138. Ibid., 24.
139. William Minter, *Apartheid's Contras: An Inquiry into the Roots of War in Angola and Mozambique* (London: ZP/B.; Johannesburg: WUP, 1994), 30.
140. Steenkamp, *Borderstrike!*, 4 and 259, n. 1.
141. Brown, "Diplomacy by Other Means," 32.
142. Edward G. M. Alexander, "The Cassinga Raid" (M.A. thesis, University of South Africa, 2003), 30 and 38; Turner, *Continent Ablaze*, 83.
143. Turner, *Continent Ablaze*, 35 and 43.
144. Alexander, "The Cassinga Raid," 159–181.
145. UNSC res. 428 (1978) of 6 May 1978, preambular paragraphs six, seven, and eight and operative paragraph one.
146. Guy Lamb, "Putting Belligerents in Context: The Cases of Namibia and Angola," in *Civilians in War*, ed. Simon Chesterman (Boulder, Colo: LRP, 2001), 27.

147. Robert F. Gordon, "The Impact of the Second World War on Namibia," JSAS 19, no. 1 (March 1993): 152–162.
148. Grundy, *Soldiers without Politics*, 44–45, 66, and 99–100.
149. Nujoma, *Where Others Wavered*, 115, 154, and 158–159.
150. Brown, "Diplomacy by Other Means," 20.
151. Nujoma, *Where Others Wavered*, 115, 154–155, and 159; Schleicher and Schleicher, *Special Flights*, 186 and 214–215.
152. "Müller, *"The Inevitable Pipeline into Exile,"* 142–143.
153. South Africa. Supreme Court. Transvaal Division. *State versus Eliaser Tuhadeleni and 36 Others* (hereafter 1968 Tuhadeleni judgment) (s.l.: n.p., judgment of 26 January 1968, mimeographed copy), 34–35.
154. Emmett, *Popular Resistance*, 331–332; Brown, "Diplomacy by Other Means," 20–21.
155. Somadoda Fikeni, "Exile and Return: The Politics of Namibia's 'Returnees'" (M.A. thesis, Queen's University, 1992), 44–45, 63, and 82.
156. Kenneth Abraham, interviewed by Somadoda Fikeni, Windhoek, 5 July 1991, as reported in ibid., 45 and 45 n. 1.
157. Mao Tse-Tung, *On Guerrilla Warfare*, translated with an introduction by Samuel B. Griffith (New York: FAP, 1961), 37.
158. Emmett, *Popular Resistance*, 336.
159. Brown, "Diplomacy by Other Means," 24.
160. Lamb, "Civil Supremacy," 71.
161. Dobell, *Swapo's Struggle*, 29 and 29, n. 12.
162. Grotpeter, *Historical Dictionary*, 405.
163. Brown, "Diplomacy by Other Means," 31.
164. Heitman, *Modern African Wars*, 24 and 33.
165. Schleicher and Schleicher, *Special Flights*, 168, 178, 182–183, 186, and 192–197.
166. Namakulu, *Armed Liberation Struggle*, 173.
167. Letter (with enclosures) to the author from Mr. Werner W. Hillebrecht, Head of the National Archives of Namibia, dated 13 December 2011; letter from Professor Saunders, dated 2 December 2011.
168. Anthony Clayton, *Frontiersmen: Warfare in Africa since 1950* (London: UCLP, 1999), 127–128.
169. Stiff, *Covert War*, 87, 192, and 259.
170. Schleicher and Schleicher, *Special Flights*, 214–215 and 243, nn. 154–155.
171. Jim Hooper, *Beneath the Visiting Moon: Images of Combat in Southern Africa* (Lexington, Mass.: LB, 1990), 161–162.
172. J. H. Thompson, *An Unpopular War: From Afkak to Bosbefok: Voices of South African National Servicemen* (Cape Town: ZbP, 2006), 113–114 and 175.
173. Lord, *From Fledgling to Eagle*, 16, 87, 186, 192–193, 223, and 362.
174. Eugene de Kok, as told to Jeremy Gordon, *A Long Night's Damage: Working for the Apartheid State* (Saxonwold, South Africa: ConP, 1998), 79–80.
175. Leopold Scholtz, "The Namibian Border War: An Appraisal of the South African Strategy," SM, 34, no. 1 (2006): 36 and 43.
176. Clayton, *Frontiersmen*, 142.
177. Shubin, *The Hot "Cold War,"* 226; Gleijeses, *Visions*, 209.
178. Colin Leys and John S. Saul, "Liberation with Democracy?: The Swapo Crisis of 1976," JSAS 20, no. 1 (March 1994): 123–147.

179. Brown, "Diplomacy by Other Means," 22 and 25; Turner, *Continent Ablaze*, 37 and 78.
180. Heitman, *Modern African Wars*, 7, 9, and 22.
181. Jan-Bart Gewald, "Who Killed Clements Kapuuo?," JSAS, 30, no. 3 (September 2004): 559–576.
182. Schleicher and Schleicher, *Special Flights*, 213–214 and 228.
183. Bernard B. Fall, *Last Reflections on a War* (Garden City, N.Y.: DC, 1967), 219.
184. Linn, *The U.S. Army*, 133–135.
185. *State versus Ruben Hengula, Michael Shikongo, and Lazarus Guieb*, as discussed in O'Linn, *Namibia*, [vol. 1], 201–202.
186. Johannes "Mistake" Gaomab, "With the People's Liberation Army of Namibia in Angola," in *Histories of Namibia: Living through the Liberation Struggle: Life Histories*, ed. and comp. Colin Leys and Susan Brown (London: MPL, 2005), 64–65; Piet[er] Nortje, *32 Battalion: The Inside Story of South Africa's Elite Fighting Unit* (Cape Town: ZbP, 2003), 167–168 and 194.
187. Namakulu, *Armed Liberation Struggle*, 157; Peter Stiff, *The Covert War: Koevoet Operations [in] Namibia, 1979–1989* (Alberton: GaP, 2004), 88.
188. Namakulu, *Armed Liberation Struggle*, 62 and 186.
189. Schleicher and Schleicher, *Special Flights*, 167, 182, 184, 213–219, and 230.
190. Pandya, *Mao Tse-tung and Chimurenga*, 145–150.
191. Nortje, *32 Battalion*, 83.
192. Heitman, *South African War Machine*, 147.
193. Ibid., 158; Namakulu, *Armed Liberation Struggle*, 61.
194. Christa van der Schiff, "Considerations of International Humanitarian Law in [the] Sentencing of Members of SWAPO — *S v Sagartius* 1983 1 SA 833 (SWA)," SAYIL 9 (1983): 112–116.
195. Brown, "Diplomacy by Other Means," 32.
196. Wilhelm S. Barnard, "The Border War: After 19 Years," in *Kompas op Suidwes-Afrika/Namibië*, ed. Wilhelm S. Barnard. Society for Geography Special Publication no. 5 (Demmesig, South Africa: SG, 1985), 196.
197. Heitman, *Modern African Wars*, 5.
198. *State versus Johannes A. Pandeni, Pewtrus N. Iilonga, and Willem Bow*, as discussed in O'Linn, *Namibia*, [vol. 1], 210–212.
199. "Minutes of the Security Conference Held at Windhoek 17–18 May," doc. no. SWA/T1/552/1 (marked secret), June 1984, p. E, as translated from the Afrikaans and quoted in Katjavivi, *A History*, 87 and 139, n. 8.
200. Dennis Herbstein, "Secret Pretoria Fear for Namibia Troops," TO, 9 September 1984, 6.
201. G[eorg] L. Meiring, "Current SWAPO Activity in South West Africa," ISSUPSR (June, 1985): 16 (table 1).
202. The exceptions involving urban sabotage are *State versus Paulus Andreas* and *Stephanus Nghifikwa*, *State versus Afunda Nghiyolwa*, and *State versus Leonard Sheehama*, respectively, as discussed in O'Linn, *Namibia*, [vol. 1], 249–262.
203. *State versus Johnny Heita and Seven Others*, as discussed in ibid., 245–249.
204. Lawrence E. Cline, *Pseudo Operations and Counterinsurgency: Lessons from Other Countries* (Carlisle, Penn.: USAWCSSI, 2005), especially 4–31.
205. O'Linn, *Namibia*, [vol.1], 253–262 (*State versus Leonard Sheehama*) and 302–303.
206. Stiff, *The Covert War*, 62 and 207.
207. Ann-Charlotte Andersen, "Koevoet: A Brief His-

tory" (B.A. [Hons.] thesis, University of Cape Town, 1997), 31, 52, and 69.

208. See the analysis of "the legitimacy of armed struggle" in El-Said, "The United Nations and Namibia," 183–190.

209. UNSC res. 269 (1969) of 12 August 1969, operative para. four.

210. Heather A. Wilson, *International Law and the Use of Force by National Liberation Movements* (Oxford: CP, 1988), 97–100 and 103. The relevant phrasing was contained in UNGA res. 2625 (XXV) of 24 October 1970, Annex, Preamble, Section titled "The Principles of Equal Rights and Self-Determination of Peoples," unnumbered para. five.

211. UNGA res. 2621 (XXV) of 12 October 1970, operative para. three, subparagraph six (a).

212. UNGA res. 3103 (XXVIII) of 12 December 1973, operative para. four.

213. The SWAPO position is set forth in IDAFSA. Research, Information, and Publication Department, "Prisoners of War in Namibia: The Capture and Treatment of Combatants of the People's Liberation Army of Namibia (PLAN) and Other Prisoners-of-War." RI/COM II/002E. No. 010. International Conference in Solidarity with the Frontline States, Lisbon, 25–27 March 1983, 1–10.

214. Wilson, *International Law*, 124 and 126.

215. SAPHA, *Debates*, vol. 60, col. 361 (30 January 1976 during the debate on the motion of no confidence).

216. Wilson, *International Law*, 160 and 172.

217. "POW Interlude in Angola," POMSADF 29, no. 10 (October 1978): 10.

218. John, "South African Intervention in the Angolan Civil War," 19, 32 n. 192, 70, 70 n. 51, 72, 72 n. 64, 93, and 93 n. 237.

219. Nujoma, *Where Others Wavered*, 316–319, with a photograph on p. 317.

220. Sanders, *Apartheid's Friends*, 163, 195, 429, n. 36, and 435, n. 49.

221. Baines, "The Saga of South African POWs in Angola, 1975–82," SM, 40, 2 (2012): 102–141.

222. Lord, *From Fledgling to Eagle*, 306.

223. Heitman, *War in Angola*, 298; Nortje, *32 Battalion*, 249.

224. Wilson, *International Law*, 124–125 and 152–153.

225. Ibid., 172.

226. Nujoma, *Where Others Wavered*, 398.

227. Stiff, *The Covert War*, 333.

228. See the extended analysis of the South African position in H. Booysen, "Terrorists, Prisoners of War, and South Africa," SAYIL 1 (1975): 14–45 and H. Booysen, "Prisoner of War Status for South African Citizens or Persons Owing Allegiance to the State," ISSUPSRSA 10, no. 1 (May 1988): 91–105.

229. *The State versus Sagarius, Jason, and Malamo*, as discussed in O'Linn, *Namibia*, [vol. 1], 216–221 and 281, n. 33; "Namibia: Prisoner-of-War Status," FPRSA 41 (July-August 1982): 1 and 4; "Prisoners-of-War," FPRSA 42 (September-October 1982): 10.

230. According to Nicolas de Rougement, representative of the International Committee of the Red Cross, in a conversation with Cedric Thornberry of the United Nations on 28 March 1989 in Windhoek (as reported in Thornberry, *A Nation is Born*, 76).

231. Jane Mayer, *The Dark Side: The Inside Story of How the War on Terror Turned into a War on American Ideals* (New York: Doubleday, 2008), 123.

232. Jessica Wolfendale, "Preventing Torture in Counter-Insurgency Operations," in *Ethics Education for Irregular Warfare*, ed. Don Carrick, James Connelly, and Paul Robinson (Farnham, Surrey, England: AsP, 2009), 68.

233. Dierks, *Chronology*, 132.

234. Namakula, *Armed Liberation Struggle*, 157–158.

235. Tanham, *Communist Revolutionary Warfare*, 69–72.

236. Henrik Ellert, *The Rhodesian Front War: Counter-Insurgency and Guerrilla War in Rhodesia, 1962–1980* (Gweru, Zimbabwe: MamP, 1989), 22.

237. Barnard, "The Border War," 199.

238. Namakalu, *Armed Liberation Struggle*, 26, 64, 73, 92, 95, and 97.

239. Shubin, *The Hot "Cold War,"* 209.

240. Namakalu, *Armed Liberation Struggle*, 45 and 158.

241. Nortje, *32 Battalion*, 167 and 193.

242. Ibid., 138–139, 157 168, and 194.

243. Namakalu, *Armed Liberation Struggle*, 5, 68–69, 86, 111, and 139; Stiff, *The Covert War*, 111–112 and 456; Brown, "Diplomacy by Other Means," 29; Gaomab, "With the People's Liberation Army in Angola," 65.

244. Nortje, *32 Battalion*, 8 provides an inventory of PLAN's weaponry.

245. Schleicher and Schleicher, *Special Flights*, 186 and 212–214.

246. See also Gareth M. Winrow, *The Foreign Policy of the GDR in Africa,* Soviet and East European Studies no. 78 (Cambridge: CbUP, 1990), 145–148; Denton subcommittee hearings, vol. 1, 7 (testimony of Assistant Secretary of State for African Affairs Dr. Chester A. Crocker on 22 March 1982).

247. Heitman, *South African War Machine*, 141, 146, and 156.

248. NPNA, *Debates*, 13, 80 and 84 (10 June 1991, statement of the minister of defense in the defense budget debate).

249. NPNA, *Debates*, 1, 340 (30 May 1990, question 6, answer of the minister of defense to Mr. Gende's question).

250. NPNA, *Debates*, 9, 82–83 (15 March 1991, statement of the minister of defense).

251. Saxena, *Namibia and the World*, 207.

252. Nujoma, *Where Others Wavered*, 396–397.

253. *The Namibian Peace Process: Implications and Lessons for the Future*, ed. Heribert Weiland and Matthew Braham, Freiburger Beiträger zu Entwicklung und Politik, 12 (Freiburg i. B.: ABI, 1994), 73–81 and 92–113.

254. UNDPI, *The Blue Helmets*, 371; Thornberry, *A Nation Is Born*, 156.

255. USCHRCFA. Subcommittee on Africa, *Namibian Independence: Review of the Process and the Process and Progress: Hearing, July 20, 1989*. One Hundred First Congress, First Session (Washington, D.C.: USGPO, 1990), 36 and 67 (hereafter 1989 Wolpe subcommittee hearing) (statements of Ms. Gay McDougall, and of Professor Christopher Eadley, Harvard University Law School, respectively).

256. Hearn, *UN Peacekeeping*, 116.

257. UNSC res. 643 of 31 October 1989 operative para. six.

258. UNSC res. 640 of 29 August 1989, operative para. two and UNSC res. 643 of 31 October 1989, operative para. six.

259. Hearn, *UN Peacekeeping*, 139.

260. Ibid., 121–205.

261. Anglin, *International Monitoring as a Mechanism*

for Conflict Resolution in Southern Africa, Working Paper no. 17, Southern African Perspectives (Bellville: UWCC-SAS, 1992), 1–42.

262. Tsokodayi, *Namibia's Independence Struggle*, 205.

263. UNDPI, *The Blue Helmets*, 360, 366–367, and 373.

264. NPNA, *Debates*, 6, 334–335 (30 October–15 November 1990, question 44, answer of the minister of defense to Mr. Gende's question).

265. Philip H. Frankel, *Soldiers in a Storm: The Armed Forces in South Africa's Democratic Transition* (Boulder, Colo.: WP, 2000), 47–100.

Chapter Six

1. The term "bush war" in the context of Namibia appears in Stefan Sonderling, *Bushwar* [,] *Bosoorlog* [,] *Buschkrieg* (Windhoek: EP, 1980).

2. Du Pisani, *SWA/Namibia*, 47–48 and 52.

3. T.A.P. du Plessis provides a synopsis of defense arrangements in Namibia from 1920 until 1960 in his "Die Ontwikkeling van die SWA Weermag," MOPJSADF 13, no. 1 (1983): 28–31.

4. SAPS, *Debates*, 1939, cols. 380–388 (1 May 1939, speech of the minister of justice).

5. "Police Strength in S.-W. Africa," TF, 20 May 1939, 11.

6. Henry J. Martin and Neil D. Orpen, *South Africa at War: Military and Industrial Organization and Operations in Connection with the Conduct of the War, 1939–1945*, South African Forces, World War II, vol. 7 (Cape Town: PuS, 1979), 19–20; Robert Citino, *Germany and the Union of South Africa in the Nazi Period* (Westport, Conn.: GP, 1991), 196–197.

7. Martin and Orpen, *South Africa at War*, 62–63, 82, 221, and 360.

8. For the Bondelswarts and Rehoboth cases, see the analyses in Emmett, *Popular Resistance*, 111–124 and 155–167, respectively.

9. Martin and Orpen, *South Africa at War*, 28–30, 44, 46, 114, 168, 229, 259, 264, 275, 315, 268, 275, and 335.

10. Ibid., 58, 70, 119, 126, 223–224, and 360; Gordon, "The Impact," 152–161.

11. "Statement by Toivo Herman Ja Toivo Delivered in Open Court on February 1, 1968," in *Erosion of the Rule of Law in South Africa* (Geneva: IComJ, 1968), 59 (Appendix 1).

12. Peter Stiff, *The Silent War: South African Recce Operations, 1969–1994* (Alberton, South Africa: GaP, 1999), 36–37.

13. Els, *Ongulumbashe*, 127 and 253–254.

14. Rodney C. Warwick, "The South African Military under Verwoerd: SADF Popularisation among the White Community, 1960–66." Paper presented to the biennial conference of the South African Historical Society, Cape Town, 29 June 2005, 4, n. 16.

15. Magnus A. de M. Malan, *My Life with the SA Defence Force* (Pretoria: PBH, 2004), 108.

16. Heitman, *Modern African Wars*, 14.

17. Els, *Ongulumbashe*, 50–51.

18. Ibid., 166–167.

19. Moorcraft, *African Nemesis*, 106; "Paramilitary Shock Troops," *Resister* 37 (May 1985), as reproduced in *War and Resistance: Southern African Reports: The Struggle for Southern Africa as Documented by Resister Magazine*, ed. Gavin Cawthra, Gerald Kraak, and Gerald O'Sullivan (London and Basingstoke: MaP, 1994), 116; Els, *Ongulumbashe*, 153.

20. Connable and Libicki, *How Insurgencies End*, 211 (for both quotations).

21. See D. Michael Shafer, "The Unlearned Lessons of Counterinsurgency," PSQ 103, no. 1 (Spring 1988): 74.

22. David Williams, *On the Border: The White South African Military Experience, 1965–1990* (Cape Town: Tafelberg, 2008), 12.

23. Jack Greeff, *A Greater Share of Honour* (Ellisras, South Africa: NP, 2001), i–ii (biography) and 101 (quotation).

24. Moorcraft, *African Nemesis*, 106.

25. Jim Hooper, *Koevoet!* (Johannesburg: SBP, 1988), 108–109.

26. Douglas S. Blaufarb, *The Counterinsurgency Era: U.S. Doctrine and Performance, 1950 to the Present* (New York: FrP, 1977), 194; Nathan Leites and Charles Wolf, *Rebellion and Authority: An Analytic Essay on Insurgent Conflicts* (Chicago: MPC, 1970), 74.

27. Kevin A. O'Brien, *The South African Intelligence Services: From Apartheid to Democracy, 1948–2005* (New York: Routledge, 2011), 42.

28. Morris, *Terrorism*, 176–178.

29. Donald Sole, "South African Foreign Policy Assumptions and Objectives from Hertzog to De Klerk," SAJIA 2, no. 1 (Summer 1994): 104.

30. Berridge's archival-based *South Africa, The Colonial Powers and "African Defence"* provides a detailed analysis of South African defense policy in the 1948–1960 transitional period.

31. Consult van der Waals, *Portugal's War in Angola*, 133–134, 140, 151, 200, 208–209, and 211–212 as well as Marcum, *The Angolan Revolution*, vol. 2, 266.

32. Correia, "Political Relations between Portugal and South Africa," 8, 101–107, 110, 137–139, 141–142, 144–151, 155–157, 170–171, 180 n. 150, 208, 214, 216, 223, and 253; Lord, *From Fledgling to Eagle*, 48–51, 53–54, 58, and 501.

33. Details are provided in Purkitt and Burgess, *South Africa's Weapons*, 90–91 and 264, n. 16 and in Lord, *From Fledgling to Eagle*, 54, 59–63, 93–102, 116–117, 126–130, 135, 137, and 501–502.

34. Geldenhuys, *The Diplomacy of Isolation*, 44–69 and 75–84.

35. For a pioneering theoretical and empirical analysis of this challenging subject, see Graeme A. Addison, "Censorship of the Press in South Africa during the Angolan War: A Case Study of News Manipulation and Suppression" (Rhodes University, unpublished M.A. thesis, 1980).

36. SAPS, *Debates*, 1939, col. 388 (1 May 1939, speech of the minister of justice on the second reading of the Police [South-West Africa] Bill).

37. Kenneth W. Grundy, *Defense Legislation and Communal Politics: The Evolution of a White South African Nation as Reflected in the Controversy over the Assignment of Armed Forces Abroad, 1912–1976*, Papers in International Studies, Africa Series no. 33 (Athens: OUCISAP, 1978), 40–51.

38. George, *The Cuban Intervention in Angola*, 225, 231, and 245; Michael Clough and Jeffrey Herbst, *South Africa's Changing Regional; Strategy: Beyond Destabilization*, Critical Issues 1989, no. 4 (New York: CFR, 1989), 22.

39. Eliot A. Cohen, *Citizens and Soldiers: The Dilemmas of Military Service* (Ithaca, N.Y.: CnUP, 1985), 117–151 and 206–211.

40. Frankel, *Pretoria's Praetorians*, 19–28.
41. [Laurie Nathan], *Out of Step: War Resistance in South Africa* (London: CIIR, 1989), 78.
42. André Wessels, "Afrikaners at War," in *The Boer War: Direction, Experience and Image*, ed. John Gooch (London: FC, 2000), 103–104.
43. Rinehart, "National Security," 304; Boulter, "F[rans] C[hristiaan] Erasmus and the Politics of South African Defence," 46–71.
44. Frankel, *Pretoria's Praetorians*, 101–103.
45. du Plessis, "Die Ontwikkeling van die SWA Weermag," 28–32.
46. Tamarkin, *The Making of Zimbabwe*, 122.
47. John P. Cann, *Counterinsurgency in Africa: The Portuguese Way of War, 1961–1974*, Contributions in Military Studies no. 167 (Westport, Conn.: GP, 1997), 87–93.
48. Robert B. Smith, "Disaffection, Delegitimation, and Consequences: Aggregate Trends for World War II, Korea and Vietnam," in *Public Opinion and the Military Establishment*, ed. Charles C. Moskos, Jr. (Beverly Hills, Calif.: SaP, 1971), 221–251.
49. Christian G. Appy, *Working-Class War: American Combat Soldiers and Vietnam* (Chapel Hill: UNCP, 1993), 11–43.
50. Kathy Roth-Douquet and Frank Schaeffer, *AWOL: The Unexcused Absence of America's Upper Classes from Military Service and How It Hurts Our Country* (New York: Collins, 2007), 36, 45, 120, 206, 208, 220, and 246.
51. Jacklyn Cock, "Manpower and Militarisation: Women and the SADF," in *Society at War: The Militarisation of South Africa*, ed. Jacklyn Cock and Laurie Nathan (New York: SMP, 1989), 51–66.
52. Martin and Orpen, *South Africa at War*, 64, 287, and 346.
53. Martin Binkin and Mark J. Eitelberg with Alvin J. Schexnider and Marvin M. Smith, *Blacks and the Military* (Washington, D.C.: BI, 1982), 9–38.
54. Grundy, *Soldiers without Politics*, 254.
55. Alom Peled, *A Question of Loyalty: Military Manpower Policy in Multiethnic States* (Ithaca, N.Y.: CnUP, 1998), 62–63 and 74–75.
56. Cann, *Counterinsurgency*, 93–106.
57. Ian Uys, *Bushmen Soldiers: Their Alpha and Omega* (Germiston: FoP, 1993).
58. Richard Lee, "The Gods Must Be Crazy, But the State Has a Plan: Government Policies towards the San in Namibia and Botswana," in *Namibia, 1884–1984: Readings on Namibia's History and Society*, ed. Brian Wood (London: NSC in cooperation with the UNIN, Lusaka, 1988), 539–550, especially 540–543 and 545–546; Robert J. Gordon, *The Bushman Myth: The Making of a Namibian Underclass* (Boulder, Colo.: WP, 1992), 185–192 and 260–261.
59. Dale, *Botswana's Search for Autonomy*, 51–52 and 186, nn. 61–63.
60. Dan Henk, "The Botswana Defense Force and the War against Poachers in Southern Africa," *SWI* 16, no. 2 (June 2005): 177 and 190, nn. 46 and 47.
61. Binkin et al., *Blacks and the Military*, 78–83.
62. UNGA res. 2145 (XXI) of 27 October 1966, operative paras. four and five.
63. ICJRJAOO, *Legal Consequences*, 58.
64. Riveles, "Human Rights," 159, 161–170, 179–180, and 186. See also Gerhard Erasmus, "Mandates, Military Service and Multiple Choice," *SAYIL* 11 (1985–1986): 115–137.
65. Tony Weaver, "The South African Defence Force in Namibia," in Cock and Nathan, ed., *Society at War*, 96.

66. Tessa Cleaver and Marion Wallace, *Namibia: Women in War* (London: ZP/B, 1990), 65.
67. Cawthra, *Brutal Force*, 202 and 204.
68. Kenneth Abrahams, "A Doctor in the Struggle at Home and in Exile," in Leys and Brown, ed. and comp., *Histories*, 155.
69. Mark Verbaan's two articles, "Mutiny as Troops Say No to Angola," *WM*, 20–26 November 1987, 1–2; and "Troops Charged for Refusing to Obey," *WM*, 27 November–3 December 1987, 1–2.
70. "No Mutiny, But We Did Discharge Troops," *TS*, international airmail weekly ed., 24 November 1987, 1.
71. Tamarakin, *The Making of Zimbabwe*, 226–227.
72. Martin Evans, "The *Harkis*: The Experience and Memory of France's Muslim Auxiliaries," in *The Algerian War and the French Army, 1954–62: Experiences, Images, Testimonies*, ed. Martin S. Alexander, Martin Evans, and John F.V. Keiger (Basingstoke, Hampshire, England: PM, 2002), 117–133.
73. Frankel, *Pretoria's Praetorians*, 199, n. 23.
74. *A Survey of Race Relations in South Africa, 1974*, comp. Muriel Horrell, Dudley Horner, and Jane Hudson (Johannesburg: SAIRR, 1975), 58.
75. *War and Conscience in South Africa: The Churches and Conscientious Objection* (London: CIIR and PC, 1982), especially 41–66 (titled "The Politics of Conscientious Objection").
76. Merran W. Phillips, "The End Conscription Campaign, 1983–1988: A Study of White Extra-Parliamentary Opposition to Apartheid" (M.A. thesis, University of South Africa, 2002).
77. Laurie Nathan, "'Marching to a Different Beat': The History of the End Conscription Campaign," in Cock and Nathan, ed., *Society at War*, 309–321.
78. Riveles, "Human Rights," 174.
79. Stiff, *Warfare by Other Means*, 284–287.
80. Nathan, "'Marching,'" 308.
81. Neil Roos, *Ordinary Springboks: White Servicemen and Social Justice in South Africa, 1939–1961* (Aldershot, England: AsP, 2005), 195–198.
82. Ibid., 30; Albert M. Grundlingh, "The King's Afrikaners?: Enlistment and Ethnic Identity in the Union of South Africa's Defence Force during the Second World War, 1939–45," *JAH* 40, no. 3 (1999): 354 and 354, n. 10.
83. Deon F. S. Fourie, "The Strategic Significance of South West Africa." Paper prepared for delivery at the course South West Africa: Problems and Alternatives, Summer School, University of Cape Town, Rondebosch, 10–14 February 1975.
84. Scholtz, "The Namibian Border War," 19–48.
85. Sally E. Crocker, "South West Africa: A Test Case for the International Trusteeship System of the United Nations" (senior thesis, Radcliffe College, 1954), 67–68.
86. O'Brien, *The South African Intelligence Services*, 22–23.
87. Gordon, "The Impact," 153–154 and 161–162; G[eoffrey] Tylden, *The Armed Forces of South Africa with an Appendix on the Commandos*, Frank Connock Publication no. 2 (Johannesburg: CJAM, 1954), 28 and 182–183.
88. Brigitte Lau, "The History of Land Dispossession," (letter), *TN*, 8 November 1996, 11.
89. ICJPOAD, *South West Africa Cases*, vol. 4, 47–62 (counter-memorial of South Africa).
90. Rodney C. Warwick, "White South Africa and Defence, 1960–1968: Militarization, Threat Perception, and Counter Strategies" (Ph.D. diss., University of Cape Town, 2009), 170–186.

91. Miles Kahler, *Decolonization in Britain and France: The Domestic Consequences of International Relations* (Princeton: PUP, 1984), 323.
92. du Pisani, *SWA/Namibia*, 71.
93. SAPHA, *Debates*, vol. 66, cols. 1278–1281, 16 February 1949 (speech of prime minister Daniel F. Malan during the second reading of the South West Africa Affairs Amendment bill).
94. Paul S. van der Merwe, "Die Ontwikkeling van Selfbestuur in Suidwes-Afrika, 1919–1960" (M.A. thesis, University of South Africa, 1963), 53–57.
95. Dierks, *Chronology*, 155 and 165.
96. Moorcraft, *African Nemesis*, 216.
97. Grotpeter, *Historical Dictionary*, 492.
98. Geldenhuys, *A General's Story*, 98.
99. Heitman, *Modern African Wars*, 17.
100. Ibid., 18.
101. Moorcroft, *African Nemesis*, 63.
102. Rinehart, "National Security," 334–336.
103. Helmoed-Römer Heitman, "Equipment of the Border War," JCH 31 no. 3 (December 2006): 107–108.
104. Rinehart, "National Security," 308–309.
105. *P.W. Botha: A Political Backgrounder* (London: South African Embassy, September, 1978), 57 as quoted in Robert S. Jaster, "War and Diplomacy," in Robert S. Jaster, Moeletsi Mbeki, Morley Nkosi, and Michael Clough, *Changing Fortunes: War, Diplomacy, and Economics in Southern Africa* ([New York]: FF and FPA, 1992), 24 and 181, n. 2.
106. Charles E. Callwell, *Small Wars: Their Principles and Practice*, third edition. (Lincoln: UNeP, 1996, originally published in 1906), xiv, 61, 93, 130, 145, 255, 362, 369, 416, and 441.
107. Stephen Ellis, "The Historical Significance of South Africa's Third Force," JSAS 24, no. 2 (June 1998): 269.
108. Carlson, *No Neutral Ground*, 187.
109. Seegers, *The Military*, 140–141.
110. Scholtz, "The Namibian Border War," 24, n. 17.
111. Peled, *A Question of Loyalty*, 40.
112. Brian Pottinger, *The Imperial Presidency: P.W. Botha: The First 10 Years* (Bergvlei: SBP, 1988), 370.
113. Seegers, *The Military*, 133; Geldenhuys, *A General's Story*, 82, 85, and 302, respectively.
114. van der Waals, *Portugal's War in Angola*, rear outside cover.
115. Alexander, "The Cassinga Raid," 26, n. 46.
116. Geldenhuys, *A General's Story*, 37–40.
117. Paul Els, *We Fear Naught But God: The Story of the South African Special Forces, "The Recces"* (Weltevreden Park, South Africa: CDB, 2000), 199.
118. Malan, *My Life*, 42–43.
119. P. Coetzee, "'n Loopbaan vol Hoogtepunte," POMSADF 28, no. 3 (March 1978): 6.
120. Hilton Hamann, *Days of the Generals* (Cape Town: ZbP, 2001), xvi–xvii.
121. Peled, *A Question of Loyalty*, 42.
122. Ellis, "The Historical Significance of South Africa's Third Force," 270.
123. Els, *We Fear Naught*, 11.
124. Alexander, "The Cassinga Raid," 99.
125. Discussion with Professors Leo Barnard and André Wessels of the Department of History, University of the Free State, Bloemfontein, 13 September 2004 and with retired SADF Major General Chris Thirion, former Deputy Chief of Staff Intelligence, Pretoria, 29 September 2004.

126. *Tel Aviv New Outlook*, March-April 1983, 31–35, as cited in James Adams, *The Unnatural Alliance* (London: QB, 1984), 89–90 and 208; Moorcraft, *African Nemesis*, 105 and 109, n. 10.
127. Evert Jordaan, "The Role of South African Armour in South West Africa/Namibia and Angola, 1975–1989," JCH 31, no. 3 (December 2006), 169–170, 183, and 185–186.
128. Leo Barnard, "The South African Air Force's Transport Aircraft: Acquisition and Utilisation during the Border War," JCH 31, no. 3 (December 2006): 248–249.
129. G[eorge] P. H. Kruys, "Doctrine Development in the South African Armed Forces up to the 1980s," in *Selected Military Issues with Specific Reference to the Republic of South Africa*, ed. M[icheal] Hough and L[ouis] du Plessis, ad hoc Publication no. 38 (Pretoria: UPISS, 2001), 16.
130. Deon Visser, "Marrying Sparta and Athens: The South African Military Academy and Task-Orientated Junior Officer Development in Peace and War, 1950–2001," JCH, 27, no. 3 (December 2002): 194.
131. Christi van der Westhuizen, *White Power and the Rise and the Fall of the National Party* (Cape Town: ZbP, 2007), 104.
132. Leo Barnard, "Die Suid-Afrikaanse Lugmag (SALM) se Optrede in die Teaters Angola en Rhodesië (circa 1966–1974) as Aanloop tot die Grensoorlog," JCH, 31, no. 3 (December 2006): 80–90.
133. Ellert, *The Rhodesian Front War*, 83.
134. Els, *We Fear Naught*, 19 and 43.
135. M[ichael] Evans, *Fighting against Chimurenga: An Analysis of Counter-Insurgency in Rhodesia, 1972–79*, Local Series no. 37 (Salisbury: HAZ, 1981), 3 and 9.
136. Bruce Hoffman, Jennifer Taw, and David Arnold, *Lessons for Contemporary Counterinsurgencies: The Rhodesian Experience*, R-3998-A (Santa Monica, Calif.: RANDC, 1991), 60.
137. Jakkie Cilliers, *Counter-Insurgency in Rhodesia* (London: CH, 1985), 118–134.
138. Frederik J. Burger, "Teeninsurgensie in Namibië: Die Rol van die Polisie" (M.A. thesis, University of South Africa, 1992), 298 and 307–311; Gavin Cawthra, *Policing South Africa: The SAP & the Transition from Apartheid* (London: ZP/B, 1993), 92–93.
139. Ellert, *The Rhodesian Front War*, 90.
140. Seegers, *The Military*, 137 and 141.
141. London: FaF, 1966.
142. Morgan Norval, *Death in the Desert: The Namibian Tragedy* (Washington, D.C.: SFP, 1989), 70.
143. Alexander, "The Cassinga Raid," 14.
144. Turner, *Continent Ablaze*, 70.
145. Wessels, "Afrikaners at War," 78–79.
146. Thomas R. Mokaitis, *British Counterinsurgency, 1919–60* (New York: SMP, 1990), 188–189.
147. Annette Seegers, "If Only ... The Ongoing Search for Method in Counter-Insurgency" (review article), JCAS, 8–9, nos. 1–2 (1989–1990): 210–211; Evert Jordaan, "The Role of South African Armour," 184.
148. Steven K. Metz, "Pretoria's 'Total Strategy' and Low-Intensity Warfare in Southern Africa," CSt, 6, no. 4 (1987): 437–469 and 460, n. 1.
149. Neta C. Crawford, *The Domestic Sources and Consequences of Aggressive Foreign Policies: The Folly of South Africa's "Total Strategy,"* Working Paper no. 41, Southern African Perspectives (Bellville: UWCCSAS, 1995).

150. Donn A. Starry, "La Guerre Révolutionaire," MR, 47, no. 2 (February 1967): 61–70.
151. George A. Kelley, *Lost Soldiers: The French Army and Empire in Crisis, 1947–1962* (Cambridge: MITP, 1965), 107–125, quotation from 109.
152. Fall, *Last Reflections on a War*, 210–211, 220, and 223.
153. Kevin A. O'Brien, *The South African Intelligence Services*, 93 and 135.
154. "Dirty War in Namibia," SAR, 1, no. 1 (June 1985): 12–13.
155. Alf A. Haggoy, *Insurgency and Counterinsurgency in Algeria* (Bloomington: IUP, 1972), 265.
156. As reported in Rick Andrew's autobiography of his SADF service in Namibia (*Buried in the Sky* [Rosebank, Johannesburg: PBSA, 2001], 79–81).
157. Donald H. Foster, with Dennis Davis and Dianne Sandler, *Detention & Torture in South Africa: Psychological, Legal & Historical Studies* (Claremont: DPP, 1987), 10, 25–26, 51, 54, 83, and 89.
158. Robert J. Gordon, "Anthropology in the Service of Apartheid," SAR, 4, no. 3 (December 1988): 22–25.
159. Robert J. Gordon, "Anthropology on High: The South West Africa Case at the World Court" (unpublished manuscript dated 6 March 2000), 19–20.
160. Scott Peterson, "US Army's Afghan Strategy: Better Anthropology," CSM, 7 September 2007, 1 and 4.
161. Lindy Heinecken and Donna Winslow, "The Human Terrain: The Need for Cultural Intelligence," in *South Africa and Contemporary Counterinsurgency: Roots, Practices, Prospects*, edited by Deane-Peter Baker and Evert Jordaan (Claremont: UCTP, 2010), 197–208, especially 204; H. R. McMaster, "Preserving Soldiers' Moral Character in Counter-Insurgency Operations," in Carrick, Connelly, and Robinson, *Ethics Education for Irregular Warfare*, 23.
162. J. A. Visser, *The South African Defence Force's Contribution to the Development of South West Africa* ([Pretoria]: SADF Military Information Bureau, circa 1983).
163. Michael S. McCrary, "Guerrilla Warfare in Namibia and Associated Implications for External Military Involvement" (M.A. thesis, [U.S.] Naval Postgraduate School, 1979), 154–156.
164. Kenneth W. Grundy, *The Militarization of South African Politics* (Bloomington: IUP, 1986), 60–62.
165. Lieneke E. de Visser, "Winning Hearts and Minds in the Namibian Border War," SM 39, no. 1 (2011): 85–100.
166. Edward B. Glick, *Peaceful Conflict: The Non-Military Use of the Military* (Harrisburg, Penn.: SB, 1967), 175–176, 178, and 181–183; Cleaver and Wallace, *Namibia*, 12.
167. Gordon, *The Bushman Myth*, 190–191 and 261, n. 9.
168. Heike Becker, *Namibian Women's Movement, 1980 to 1992: From Anti-Colonial Resistance to Reconstruction*, Wissenschaftliche Reihe/ISSA, Bd. 23 (Frankfurt a. M.: IKOVIK, 1995), 167 and 200, n. 26.
169. NPNA, *Debates*, vol. 15, 246 (11 November 1991 during the debate concerning financial support to political parties).
170. NPNA, *Debates*, 16, 72 (20 November 1991, remarks of the deputy minister of home affairs 1991 during the debate concerning financial support to political parties).
171. Dale, "Reconfiguring Ethnic Power," 77–79.
172. "SADF Murder," FPRSA 67 (November-December 1986): 10; "Shifidi Lilling: Appeal Heard," FPRSA, *Focus* 79 (November-December 1988): 3; David Smuts, "The Interim Government and Human Rights," in Tötemeyer et al., ed., *Namibia in Perspective*, 221–222.
173. Weaver, "The South African Defence Force," 94–95.
174. Michelle Sieff, "Reconciling Order and Justice?: Dealing with the Past in Post-Conflict States" (Ph.D. diss., Columbia University, 2002), 57–59.
175. Marléne Burger and Chandré Gould, *Secrets and Lies: Wouter Basson and South Africa's Chemical and Biological Warfare Programme* (Cape Town: ZbP, 2002), 190–191.
176. Gary F. Baines, "Perpetuating a Culture of Impunity: War Crimes, Indemnity[,] and Amnesia in Namibia and South Africa" (unpublished draft manuscript, dated 1 May 2012).
177. Jonathan Hyslop, "The Invention of the Concentration Camp: Cuba, Southern Africa[,] and the Philippines, 1896–1907," SAHJ 63, no. 2 (June 2011): 251–276.
178. Francis Toase, "The South African Army: The Campaign in South West Africa/Namibia since 1966," in *Armed Forces and Modern Counter-Insurgency*, ed. Ian F.W. Beckett and John Pimlott (London: CH, 1985), 210.
179. Nortje, *32 Battalion*, 301–302; Lord, *From Fledgling to Eagle*, 482 and 490.
180. König, *Namibia*, 12–13.
181. Scholtz, "The Namibian Border War," 41.
182. These are annotated and listed in Turner, *Continent Ablaze*, 263–264, Appendix 2 ("South African Cross-Border Operations Undertaken from Northern Namibia, 1978–1987").
183. R[ichard] S. Lord, "SAAF Fighter Involvement in the Border War, 1965–1988," JCH, 31, no. 3 (December 2006): 259 and 261.
184. Stiff, *The Silent War*, 222–233.
185. O'Linn, *Namibia* [vol. 1], 133–135.
186. Knight, "The British Churches," 109.
187. See the second reading debate of the Public Holidays Bill in NNA, *Debates*, vol. 7, 10 and 12–18 (19 November 1990).
188. Alexander, "The Cassinga Raid."
189. Baines, *The Battle for Cassinga: Conflicted Narratives and Contested Meanings*.
190. Gleijeses, *Visions*, 537, n. 92.
191. Christian A. Williams, "Exile History: An Ethnography of the SWAPO Camps and the Namibian Nation" (Ph.D. diss., University of Michigan, 2009), 29–72.
192. Scholtz, "The Namibian Border War," 39 and 43–44.
193. Edward E. Rice, *Wars of the Third Kind: Conflict in Underdeveloped Countries* (Berkeley: UCP, 1988), 79–89.
194. Moorcraft, *African Nemesis*, 219.
195. Seegers, *The Military*, 239, 265, and 309–310; André du Pisani, *Beyond the Barracks: Reflections on the Role of the SADF in the Region*, Occasional Paper (Braamfontein: SAIIA, 1988), 4–7 and 20, n. 2.
196. Harold S. Johnson, *Self-Determination within the Community of Nations* (Leyden: AWS, 1967), 135–140.
197. *The Blue Helmets: A Review of United Nations Peace-keeping*, second edition ([New York]: UNDPI, 1990), 445 (appendix II).
198. Thornberry, *A Nation Is Born*, 193.
199. Hearn, *UN Peacekeeping*, 87–120.
200. *The Blue Helmets*, 335–340.
201. Hearn, *UN Peacekeeping*, 94–100.

202. Saunders, "Liberation and Democracy," 93.
203. Stiff, *The Covert War*, 465.
204. Ibid., 336–466.
205. Piero Gleijeses indicated that Stiff had excellent access to both the SADF and intelligence communities (*Visions*, 288 and 499).
206. Stiff, *The Covert War*, [8].
207. Scholtz, "The Namibian Border War," 33.
208. 1989 Wolpe subcommittee hearing, 2, 11–12, 22, and 94–95.
209. Sanders, *Apartheid's Friends*, 250.
210. [Bjornlund], *Nation Building*, v, 18–19, and 115–116 (Appendix IX).
211. Tsokodayi, *Namibia's Independence Struggle*, 81, n. 189.
212. Theo-Ben Gurirab, "The Genesis of the Namibian Constitution: The International and Regional Setting," in *Constitutional Democracy in Namibia: A Critical Analysis after Two Decades*, ed. Anton Bösl, Nico Horn and André du Pisani (Windhoek: MEN, 2010), 114.
213. Tsokodayi, *Namibia's Independence Struggle*, 81–82, n. 190.
214. "Some Observations regarding the Settlement Plan for Namibia," ISSUPB 2/89 (March 1989): 3; Zartman, *Ripe for Resolution*, 205; Vergau, *Negotiating the Freedom of Namibia*, 14, 48, 52, 61, 72, 77, 83, 88–90, 92, 99, and 104.
215. Gwen Lister, "DTA Bust by Pik," TN, 26 July 1991, 1–2.
216. Stiff, *Warfare by Other Means*, 380.
217. Christof Maletsky, "SA govt[.] Bankrolled DTA's Campaign," TN, 4 November 1998 (http://www.namibian.com.na/Netstories/November98/DTAfunds.html).
218. NPNA, *Debates*, 15, 230–231 (11 November 1991), quotation from p. 231.
219. "Letter dated 16 May 1989 from the Secretary-General to the President of the Security Council." UN doc. S/20635, 16 May 1989, annex titled "Namibia: Informal Check List," paragraph eleven. Bjorlund (*Nation Building*, 18) indicated that the 1982 document was sent to the General Assembly; the same UN doc. S/20635 also bore the General Assembly document designation A/44/280.
220. He wrote that "in separate discussions with the Western Contact Group, the Government of South Africa also confirmed its agreement to those understandings which relate to its responsibilities under the plan" (UN doc. S/20635).
221. NPNA, *Debates*, 16, 70 (20 November 1991, remarks of the deputy minister of home affairs, who did not explicitly mention this, but strongly implied it).
222. Lionel Cliffe with Ray Bush et al., *The Transition to Independence in Namibia* (Boulder, Colo.: LRP, 1994), 183 (Table 8.1).
223. NPNA, *Debates*, 15, 336 (18 November 1991, remarks of the minister of information and broadcasting).
224. NPNA, *Debates*, 15, 269 (12 November 1991) and 310 (13 November 1991).
225. Debie LeBeau and Edith Dima, *Multiparty Democracy and Elections in Namibia*. EISA Research Report no. 13 (Johannesburg: EISA, 2005), 94–95.
226. Terry Bell with Dumisa B. Ntsebeza, *Unfinished Business: South Africa, Apartheid, and Truth* (London: Verso, 2003), 266–267.
227. James Sanders refers to it as Operation Agree (*Apartheid's Friends*, 250), as did Nico Basson himself (Pat Deveraux, "Paid R1-m To Smear Swapo: Nico Basson," TS, 31 July 1991 [international airmail weekly ed.], 4).
228. Sanders, *Apartheid's Friends*, 251.
229. O'Linn, *Namibia*, [vol. 1], 124–125. Bell, however, dates the DTA-MI link to 1977 (*Unfinished Business*, 268).
230. Charles Leonard, "Agent Paid R 1-m to 'Sell' Army Role," TS, 27 March 1991 (international airmail weekly ed.), 4.
231. Ibid.
232. *Call Them Spies: A Documentary Account of the Namibian Spy Drama*, ed. Nico Basson and Ben Motinga (Windhoek and Johannesburg: ACP, 1989).
233. Steenkamp, "The Churches," 113, n. 29.
234. Torreguitar, *National Liberation Movements*, 242–243, 246–247, 257–258, 260, 268, 272–274, and 278; Williams, "Exile History," 159, 165, 168–169, 182, 184, 187, and 192.
235. Geingob, "State Formation in Namibia," 197–205.
236. John S. Saul and Colin Leys, "Lubango and After: 'Forgotten History' as Politics in Contemporary Namibia," JSAS, 29, no. 2 (June 2003): 335–353; Brigitte Weidlich, "Swapo Rejects Motion on Lubango Victims," TN, 26 October 2006, 1.
237. Stephanie Harries, "Namibia Turns to World for Answers," CSM, 24 January 2008, 7.
238. Torreguitar, *National Liberation Movements*, 229–283; Williams, "Exile History," 119–156.
239. Gerhard K. H. Tötemeyer, *Church and State in Namibia: The Politics of Reconciliation*, Freiburger Beiträge zu Entwicklung und Politik no. 38 (Freiburg i. Br: ABI, 2010), 141.
240. Stiff, *Warfare by Other Means*, 375–412.
241. UNDPI, *The Blue Helmets*, 370–371 and 445 (appendix II).

Chapter Seven

1. Julius Limbani's remark in Daniel Carney's novel, *The Wild Geese* (New York: Bantam Books, Inc., 1977), 226.
2. The phrase is from Lush, *Last Steps to Uhuru*, 285.
3. Lari Kangas, "Namibian Democracy: Consolidated?" (M.A. thesis, Stellenbosch University, 2006).
4. Alex Davidson, *Democracy and Development in Namibia: The State of Democracy and Civil Rights, 1989–1991*, Uppsala Studies in Democracy no. 2 (Uppsala: UUDG, 1991); and *Government and Opposition in Namibia: Four Years after Independence*, Uppsala Studies in Democracy no. 8 (Uppsala: UUDG, 1994).
5. *Building Democracy: Perceptions and Performance of Government and Opposition in Namibia: Summary of [the] Proceedings of a Conference presented by the Namibia Institute for Democracy in Windhoek on 30 November 1996* (Windhoek: NID and KAS, 1996).
6. Henning Melber, "One Namibia, One Nation?: The Caprivi as Contested Territory," JCAS, 27, no. 4 (October 2009): 463–481.
7. Bennett Kangumu, *Contesting Caprivi*, 237–262 and 270–271.
8. Heribert Adam and Kanya Adam, "The Politics of Memory in Divided Societies," 32.
9. See Chapter Seven, n. 2 above.
10. Quoted in Horne, *A Savage War of Peace*, 40.
11. See Chapter Six, n. 10 above.

12. Charles Dickens, *David Copperfield*, with an introduction and notes by Jeremy Tambling (London: PB, 1996 [first published in 1850]), 531.
13. Bruce Frayne and Wade C. Pendleton, *Mobile Namibia: Migration Trends and Attitudes*, Migration Policy Series no. 27 (Cape Town: IDASA [and Kingston, Ontario]: Queen's University, 2002), 37–40 (including table 3.4).
14. See Introduction, nn. 93 and 94 above.
15. Vergau, *Negotiating the Freedom of Namibia*, xii, 2, and 100–103.
16. NMFA, *Namibia's Foreign Policy and Diplomacy Management* ([Windhoek]: NMFA, 2004), 46.
17. SAPHAD, *Debates*, vol. 5, col. 242 (25 January 1963 [the prime minister's speech during the debate on the motion of no confidence]).
18. Bryan O'Linn, *Namibia: The Sacred Trust of Civilization*, [vol. 1], 154.
19. Henning Melber, "'Namibia, Land of the Brave': Selective Memories on War and Violence within Nation Building," in *Rethinking Resistance: Revolt and Violence in African History*, ed. Jon Abbink, Mirjam de Bruijn, and Klaas van Walraven (Leiden: KB, 2003), 322.
20. George Orwell, *Animal Farm: A Fairy Story*, with an introduction by C.M. Woodhouse (New York: NALWL, 1946), 123.
21. Johanna Åfreds, *History and Nation-Building: The Political Uses of History in Post-Colonial Namibia*, MFS-Reports 2000: 2 (Uppsala: UUDEH, 2000).
22. Justine Hunter, "Dealing with the Past in Namibia: Getting the Right Balance between Justice and Sustainable Peace?," in *The Long Aftermath of War: Reconciliation and Transition in Namibia*, Freiburger Beiträge zu Entwicklung und Politik, 27, ed. André du Pisani, Reinhart Kössler, and William A. Lindeke (Freiburg i. Br.: ABI, 2010), 403–433.
23. van der Westhuizen, *White Power & the Rise and Fall of the National Party*, 287.
24. Reinhart Kössler, "Public Memory, Reconciliation[,] and the Aftermath of War: A Preliminary Framework with Special Reference to Namibia," in *Re-examining Liberation in Namibia: Political Culture since Independence*, ed. Henning Melber (Uppsala: NAI, 2003), 99–112.
25. Melber, "'Namibia, Land of the Brave,'" 319–320 (photograph on p. 319); Brigitte Weidlich, "Windhoek's Heroes' Acre Running up Unheroic Costs," TN, 19 October 2006, 3.
26. Letter to the author from Professor Saunders, dated 2 December 2011.
27. Consult Joachim Zeller, "Symbolic Politics: Notes on the German Colonial Culture of Remembrance," in *Genocide in German South-West Africa: The Colonial War of 1904–1908 and Its Aftermath*, ed. Jürgen Zimmerer and Joachim Zeller, translated and introduced by Edward J. Neather (Monmouth, Wales: MPL, 2003), 231–251; Andreas Vogt, *National Monuments in Namibia: An Inventory of Proclaimed National Monuments in the Republic of Namibia* (Windhoek: GMP, 2004), 85–132.
28. Williams, "Exile History," 273.
29. Ibid., 24.
30. Ibid., 8–9 and 64.
31. Ibid., iii, 11, 22, 64, and 221.
32. Ibid., 264 and 270.
33. Ibid., 252.
34. Henning Melber, "'Presidential Indispensability' in Namibia: Moving out of Office But Staying in Power," in *Legacies of Power: Leadership Change and Former Presidents in African Politics*, ed. Roger Southall and Henning Melber (Pretoria: HSRCP, 2006), especially 100–101 and 111.

35. Saunders, "History and the Armed Struggle," 24.
36. Jan-Bart Gewald, "Herero Genocide in the Twentieth Century: Politics and Memory," in Abbink et al., ed., *Rethinking Resistance*, 279–304.
37. Jan Grofe, "Shadows of the Past: Chances and Problems for the Herero in Claiming Reparations from Multinationals for Past Human Rights Violations" (L.L.M. thesis, University of the Western Cape, 2002), 69–81.
38. Jeremy Sarkin, *Colonial Genocide and Reparation Claims in the 21st Century: The Socio-Legal Claims under International Law by the Herero against Germany for Genocide in Namibia, 1904–1908* (Westport, Conn.: PSI 2009), 148–154, 189, and 191.
39. Ibid., 154–155 and 191–192.
40. Ibid., 131–137 and 191.
41. Esther Schüring, "'History Obliges': The Real Motivations behind German Aid Flows in the Case of Namibia" (M.A.L.D. thesis, Tufts University, Fletcher School of Law and Diplomacy, 2004), 23–26 and 89.
42. Reinhart Kössler, "Genocide and Reparations: Dilemmas and Exigencies in Namibian-German Relations," in du Pisani, Kössler, and Lindeke, ed., *The Long Aftermath of War: Reconciliation and Transition in Namibia*, 215–241.
43. Bell with Ntsebeza, *Unfinished Business*, 349–350; Bond, "Can Reparations for Apartheid Profits Be Won in U.S. Courts?," 13–14, 16, and 22; Julian Simcock, "Will a U.S. Court Case Set Right South Africa's Apartheid Past?," CSM, 20 June 2011, 33.
44. Christopher C. Saunders, "Transition in Namibia, 1989–1990 and the South African Case," in *Peace, Politics[,] and Violence in the New South Africa*, ed, Norman Etherton (London: HZP, 1992), 214.
45. See the Preface, nn. 28–29 above.
46. Brüggermann, "The United Nations Council for Namibia," 92–103.
47. Mushelenga, "Foreign Policy-Making in Namibia," 68–69.
48. Donald L. Sparks and December Green, *Namibia: The Nation after Independence* (Boulder: WP, 1992), 68–69.
49. NPNA, *Debates*, 14, 81–82, and 85 (17 June 1991 [speech of the minister of foreign affairs in the foreign affairs budget debate]).
50. Mushelenga, "Foreign Policy-Making in Namibia," 105.
51. NPNA, *Debates*, 3, 203 (19 July 1990 [speech of the minister of foreign affairs in the foreign affairs budget debate]).
52. Ibid., 228.
53. Mushelenga, "Foreign Policy-Making in Namibia," 97.
54. NPNA, *Debates*, 29, 292 (12 March–1 April 1993 [reply to Mr. Pretorius' question]).
55. *Changing the History of Africa: Angola and Namibia*, ed. David Deutschmann (Melbourne: OcP, 1989), xvii.
56. Williams, "Exile History," 147, n. 412.
57. Mushelenga, "Foreign Policy-Making in Namibia," 102.
58. Ibid., 150; NPNA, *Debates*, 3, 231–232 (19 July 1990 [speech of the minister of foreign affairs in the foreign affairs budget debate]).
59. NPNA, *Debates*, 3, 232 (19 July 1990 [speech of the minister of foreign affairs in the foreign affairs budget debate]).
60. Ibid., 206–207 (19 July 1990 [speech of the minister of foreign affairs in the foreign affairs budget debate]).

61. NMFA, *Namibia's Foreign Policy*, 46.
62. NPNA *Debates*, 32, 99 (10 March 1999, speech of Mr. Moses K. Katjiuongua of the Democratic Coalition of Namibia [an opposition party] during the debate on a motion concerning the foreign and defense policies of Namibia); Grotpeter, *Historical Dictionary*, 186–187; Mushelenga, "Foreign Policy-Making in Namibia," 165–166.
63. Letter to the author from Dr. Henning Melber, Research Director of the Nordic Africa Institute, Uppsala, dated 13 April 2003.
64. *Namibia Country Profile, 1990–91: Annual Survey of Political and Economic Background* (London: EIU, 1990), 47.
65. André du Pisani, "Namibia: Impressions of Independence," in *The Dynamics of Change in Southern Africa*, ed. Paul B. Rich (New York: SMP, 1994), p. 216, n. 1.
66. Graham Evans, "Across the Orange River: Namibia and Colonial Legacies," in *From Pariah to Participant: South Africa's Evolving Foreign Relations, 1990–1994*, ed. Greg Mills (Braamfontein: SAIIR, 1994), 153, n. 3.
67. *Namibia, Swaziland Country Profile, 1993–94* (London: EIU, 1994), 64.
68. NPNA, *Debates*, 17, 117 (10 April 1997) and 243–244 (14 April 1997) (speech of the minister of finance).
69. "Namibia: Beauty v[s.] Beast," TE 318, no. 7694 (16 February 1991): 34–35.
70. Chris Louw, "Stryd Begin vir die Hart van 'n Nuwe Namibia," SA 20 (April 1989): 10.
71. Chris Tapscott, "War, Peace & Social Classes," in Leys and Saul, *Namibia's Liberation Struggle*, 159.
72. Justine Hunter, "Who Should Own the Land?: An Introduction," in *Who Should Own the Land?: Analysis and Views on Land Reform and the Land Question in Namibia and Southern Africa*, ed. Justine Hunter (Windhoek: KAS and NID, 2004), 1.
73. Ibid.
74. Wolfgang Werner, "Agriculture and Land," in *Namibia: A Decade of Independence, 1990–2000*, ed. Henning Melber, NEPRU Publication no 7 (Windhoek: NEPRU, 2000), 29 and 34.
75. Ibid., 29.
76. Kangas, "Namibian Democracy," 40 and 91.
77. Ibid., 40.
78. Hunter, "Who Should Own the Land?," 3.
79. Donna Pankhurst, *A Resolvable Conflict?: The Politics of Land Reform in Namibia*, Peace Research Report no. 36 (Bradford, West Yorkshire, England: UBDPS, 1996), 102–111.
80. Hunter, "Who Should Own the Land?," 3.
81. Ibid., 4.
82. Werner, "Agriculture and Land," 41–42.
83. Wolfgang Werner, "Promoting Development among Farm Workers: Some Options for Namibia," in Hunter, ed., *Who Should Own the Land?*, 24.
84. Kangas, "Namibian Democracy," 118–121.
85. Berat, *Walvis Bay*, 91, n. 6.
86. UNGA res. 32/9 D of 4 November 1977, preambular para. eight and operative paras. six and seven as well as UNSC res. 432 (1978) of 27 July 1978, preambular paras one and two and operative paras. one and two.
87. NPNA *Debates*, 36, 93–95 (3 February 1994, speech of the minister of foreign affairs during the second reading debate of the Walvis Bay and the Off-Shore Islands bill).
88. Preface, n. 28.
89. NPNA *Debates*, 35, 205 (25 November 1993, speech of the minister of foreign affairs during the first reading debate of the Walvis Bay and the Off-Shore Islands bill).
90. David Simon, "Strategic Territory and Territorial Strategy: The Geopolitics of Walvis Bay's Reintegration into Namibia," PG 15, no. 2 (April 1996): 195, 205–207, 209–210, and 213.
91. Ibid., 209–210.
92. *Walvis Bay: A Report of a Fact-Finding Mission, October 1990*. NEPRU Working Papers no. 13 (Windhoek: NEPRU, 1992), 21 and NPNA, *Debates*, 13, 99–100 (11 June 1991, speech of the deputy minister of state security during the defense budget debate).
93. Graham Evans, "Walvis Bay: South Africa, Namibia[,] and the Question of Sovereignty," IA 66, no. 3 (July 1990): 560.
94. NPNA, *Debates, 7*, 365 and 367–368 (2 April 1996, speech of the minister of defense during the defense budget debate).
95. NPNA, *Debates*, 17, 8 and 13 (8 April 1997, speech of the minister of defense during the defense budget debate).
96. NPNA, *Debates*, 25, 328–329 (16 April 1998, speech of the minister of defense during the defense budget debate).
97. NPNA, *Debates*, 34, 78 and 80 (29 April 1999, speech of the minister of defense during the defense budget debate).
98. NPNA, *Debates*, 25, 328 (reference to the maritime wing) and 329 (quotation) (16 April 1998, speech of the minister of defense during the defense budget debate).
99. See Chapter Four, n. 237 above.
100. See Introduction, n. 111 above.
101. Ndeutala Hishongwa, *The Contract Labour System and Its Effect on Family and Social Life in Namibia: A Historical Perspective* (Windhoek: GMP, 1992), especially 87–112.
102. Gretchen Bauer, *Labor and Democracy in Namibia, 1971–1996* (Athens: OhUP; London: JC, 1998), 39, 92 and 128.
103. Kangas, "Namibian Democracy," 41.
104. Letter to the author from Dr. Botha, dated 28 October 2009.
105. *Playing the Globalisation Game: The Implications of Economic Liberalisation for Namibia*, ed. Herbert Jauch ([Windhoek]: LRRI, 2001), 89–95.
106. See Introduction, nn. 6–7 above.
107. Brad Knickerbocker, "The Cost of War: Wounded Troops Overwhelm Care," CSM, 22 October 2007, 1 and 11; Gordon Lubold, "Demand on V[eterans] A[ffairs] Grows," CSM, 30 August 2009, 21.
108. Bernard W. Sigg, "The Children of the Occupation and Colonial Ideology," in Alexander et al., ed., *The Algerian War*, 220–221.
109. Gary F. Baines, "South Africa's Vietnam: Literary History and Cultural Memory of the Border Wars," in *Telling Wounds: Narrative, Trauma & Memory: Working through the SA Armed Conflicts of the 20th Century: Proceedings of the Conference Held at the University of Cape Town, 3–5 July 2002*, ed. Chris N. van der Merwe and Rolf W. Wolfswinkel (Midrand, Bellville: CS, 2004), 167; TRCSA, vol. 4, 236–241.
110. Gwinyayi A. Dzinesa, "Postconflict Disarmament, Demobilization, and Reintegration of Former Combatants in Southern Africa," ISP, 8, no. 1 (February 2007): 86; Debie LeBeau, *An Investigation into the Lives of Namibian Ex-Fighters Fifteen Years after Independence*

(Windhoek: PEACEC, 2005), 30, 32–34, and 149–152; Selma Shipanga, "Ex-Combatants Suffer from Post-War Trauma," TN, 31 July 2012 (no pagination given in e-version).

111. Ellen N. Namhila, *The Price of Freedom* (Windhoek: NNB, 1997), 43; Chris Tapscott and Ben Mulongeni, *An Evaluation of the Welfare and Future Prospects of Repatriated Namibians in Northern Namibia*, Research Report [no.] 3 (Windhoek: UNNISER, 1990), 19–20.

112. Nat J. Colletta, Markus Kostner, Ingo Wiederhofer, with the assistance of Emilio Mondo, Taimi Sitari, and Tadesse A. Woldu, *Case Studies in War-to-Peace Transition: The Demobilization and Reintegration of Ex-Combatants in Ethiopia, Namibia, and Uganda*, Africa Technical Department Series, WB Discussion Paper no. 331 (Washington, D.C.: WB, 1996), 144.

113. Robert G.L. Waite, *Vanguard of Nazism: The Free Corps Movement in Postwar Germany, 1918–1923* (Cambridge: HUP, 1952).

114. Lalli Metsola and Henning Melber, "Namibia's Pariah Heroes: SWAPO Ex-Combatants between Liberation Gospel and Security Interests," in Buur et al., ed., *The Security-Development Nexus*, 85–105.

115. Brigitte Lau, "The History of Land Dispossession," TN, 8 November 1996, 11 (letter); NPNA, *Debates*, 30, 209 (10 November 1998, remarks of Mrs. Kaura).

116. Ordinance no. 31 of 1958 in *Union Legislation Affecting South West Africa and Proclamations, Ordinances[,] and Principal Government Notices Issued in South West Africa during 1958*. Published by Order of the Honourable Administrator of South West Africa (Windhoek: JML, 1959), 451, 453, and 455; Introduction, n. 78 above.

117. G.I. (which stands for Government Issue) is the American slang term for a member of the armed forces, customarily the army.

118. Paul Dickson and Thomas B. Allen, *The Bonus Army: An American Epic* (New York: WC, 2004).

119. NPNA, *Debates*, 6, 3–4 and 33–67 (30 October and 1 November 1990, respectively on Mr. Moses Katjiuongua's motion).

120. Colletta et al., *Case Studies in War-to-Peace Transition*, 145 and 146 (table 4.1).

121. Brigitte Weidlich, "New Bill Defines Struggle Credentials," TN, 24 October 2007 (http://www.namibian.com.na/2007/October/national/07C45E54E4.html).

122. Laurie Nathan, *Marching to a Different Drum: A Description and Assessment of the Formation of the Namibian Police and Defence Force*, Southern African Perspectives: A Working Paper Series no. 4 (Bellville: UWCCSAS, 1991), 5; NPNA, *Debates*, 7, 365 (2 April 1996, remarks of the minister of defense).

123. Colletta et al., *Case Studies in War-to-Peace Transition*, 149.

124. NPNA, *Debates*, 34, 79 (29 April 1999, speech of the minister of finance during the defense budget debate).

125. Preston, "Integrating Fighters," 457.

126. Colletta et al., *Case Studies in War-to-Peace Transition*, 155–167.

127. Geingob, "State Formation in Namibia," 173 and 176–177; Henning Melber, "Public Sector and Fiscal Policy," in Melber, ed., *Namibia: A Decade of Independence*, 100, 103, and 105; Klaus Schade, "Poverty," in ibid., 121.

128. Reinhart Kössler and Henning Melber, "Political Culture and Civil Society: On the State of the Namibian State," in *Contemporary Namibia: The First Landmarks of a Post-Apartheid Society*, ed. Ingolf Diener and Olivier Graefe (Windhoek: GMP, 2001), 151; Chris Tapscott, "Class Formation and Civil Society in Namibia," in Diener and Graefe, ed., *Contemporary Namibia*, 318–319.

129. Norma Kriger, *Guerrilla Veterans in Post-War Zimbabwe: Symbolic and Violent Politics, 1980–1987*, African Studies Series no. 3 (Cambridge: CbUP, 2003), 22 and 140.

130. NPNA, *Debates*, 14, 32 (29 November 1996, remarks of the prime minister).

131. Preston, "Integrating Fighters," 458.

132. Dickson and Allen, *The Bonus Army*, 18–19 and 29.

133. Catherine Sasman, "DPA Says Vet[eran]s Benefits [Are] Divisive," TN, 7 December 2011 (no pagination given in e-version).

134. "Gov[ernmen]t Will Not Cave in to Demands for N$200[,]000 Cash Payments for Veterans," TN, 13 February 2012 (no pagination given in e-version).

135. "More Cash Coming for Registered Veterans," TN, 7 March 2012 (no pagination given in e-version).

136. Luqman Cloete, "80[,]000 Veterans Benefit from N$2[,]000 Monthly Subsidy," TN, 21 June 2010 (no pagination given in e-version).

137. Gwen Lister, the editor of *The Namibian*, in "Political Perspective," TN, 29 April 2011 (no pagination given in e-version).

138. See Fikeni, "Exile and Return: The Politics of Namibia's 'Returnees,'" 134–138 as well as Chris Tapscott, "Namibia: A Class Act?," SAR, 7, no. 2 (November 1991): 3–6.

139. Stephanie Hanes, "Security Firms Look to Africa for Recruits," CSM, 8 January 2008, 6.

140. Kristian B. Harpvoken, "Landmines in Southern Africa: Regional Initiatives for Clearance and Control," CSP, 18, no. 1 (April 1997): 83–108.

141. NPNA, *Debates*, 29, 88 (14 July 1998, statement of the minister of foreign affairs during the debate on the ratification of the convention on anti-personnel mines).

142. Alex Vines, "Still Killing: Land-mines in Southern Africa," in *From Defence to Development: Redirecting Military Resources in South Africa*, [ed.] Jacklyn Cock and Penny Mckenzie (Cape Town: DPP; Ottawa: IDRC, 1998), 152–153 and 155; Mushelenga, "Foreign Policy-Making in Namibia," 141 (table 12); LeBeau, *An Investigation*, xiv, xxi, 41, 43, 83, 86, 89, 92–93, 96, 150, 180, 182, and 187.

143. Mushelenga, "Foreign Policy-Making in Namibia," i–ii, 72, and 141–145.

144. Ibid., 99–100, 130, 219, and 220 (table 14).

Chapter Eight

1. Neta C. Crawford, "Decolonization as an International Norm: The Evolution of Practices, Arguments, and Beliefs," in *Emerging Norms of Justified Intervention: A Collection of Essays from a Project of the American Academy of Arts and Sciences*, ed. Laura W. Reed and Carl Kaysen (Cambridge, Mass.: AAAS, 1993), 46–48.

2. Ibid., 50 and 52.

3. Thomas Ohlson, "The End of the Cold War and Conflict Resolution in Southern Africa," in *Sub-Saharan Africa: A Sub-Continent in Transition*, ed. Rukhsana A. Siddiqui (Aldershot: Avebury, AsP, 1993), 250.

4. Robert S. Jaster, *South Africa in Namibia: The Botha Strategy* (Lanham, Md.: UPA, 1985), 101–107.

5. Ford, "South African Foreign Policy," 205.

6. See Chapter Two, nn. 6–9 above.

7. Ford, "South African Foreign Policy," 156–157.
8. Henriëtte J. Lubbe, "The Myth of 'Black Peril': *Die Burger* and the 1929 Election," SAHJ, 37 (November 1997): 107–132.
9. Jaster, *South Africa in Namibia*, 26–27.
10. Newell M. Stultz, *Afrikaner Politics in South Africa, 1934–1948*, Perspectives on Southern Africa no. 13 (Berkeley: University of California Press, 1974), 12 and 14.
11. Christo B. Botha, "South Africa's Total Strategy in the Era of Cold War, Liberation Struggles[,] and the Uneven Transition to Democracy," JNS, 4 (2008): 100.
12. Polakow-Suransky, *The Unspoken Alliance*, 130.
13. Kahler, *Decolonization in Britain and France*, 316–353.
14. James N. Rosenau, "Introduction: Political Science in a Shrinking World," in *Linkage Politics: Essays on the Convergence of National and International Systems*, ed. James N. Rosenau (New York: FrP, 1969), 1–17.
15. Ford, "South African Foreign Policy," 225.
16. Vergau, *Negotiating the Freedom of Namibia*, 1, n. 1.
17. Benjamin Stora, "The 'Southern' World of the *Pieds Noirs*: References to and Representations of Europeans in Colonial Algeria," in Elkins and Pedersen, ed., *Settler Colonialism*, 225–241.
18. Stephen C. Lubkemann, "Unsettling the Metropole: Race and Settler Reincorporation in Postcolonial Portugal," in Elkins and Pedersen, ed., *Settler Colonialism*, 257–270.
19. Hanlon, *Beggar Your Neighbours*, 91–129 and 219–233.
20. Caroline Elkins, *Imperial Reckoning: The Untold Story of Britain's Gulag in Kenya* (New York: OB, 2005).
21. Daniel Branch, *Defeating Mau Mau, Creating Kenya: Counterinsurgency, Civil War, and Decolonization*, African Studies Series no. [111] (New York: CbUP, 2009).
22. Mukoma Wa Ngugi, "To Save Africa: A Missing Step," CSM, 13 November 2007, 9.
23. Alan Cowell, "Britain to Compensate Kenyan Victims of Colonial-Era Torture," NYT, 7 June 2013, A8.
24. Theophilus Igboeli, "The Internal Politics of the United Nations: A Case Study of Namibia's Independence, 1967–1972" (Ph.D. diss., Howard University, 1972), 19–22, 59, 70, 110, 122, 147, 149, and 153–155.
25. Ibid., 115–116, 132, 139, 150, and 170–171; Chapter One, n. 58 above.
26. Saxena, *Namibia: Challenge to the United Nations*, 283–285.
27. David Sullivan and Stephen Majeski, "A Methodology for the Study of Historical Counterfactuals," ISQ, 42, no. 1 (March 1998): 79–108.
28. Neta C. Crawford, *Argument and Change in World Politics*, 363–385.
29. Leopold Scholtz, "The Standard of Research on the Battle of Cuito Cuanavale, 1987–1988," SM 39, no. 1 (2011): 115–137, particularly 127–128.
30. Saxena, *Namibia: Challenge to the United Nations*, 288–290.
31. Audie J. Klotz, *Norms in International Relations: The Struggle against Apartheid* (Ithaca, N.Y.: CnUP, 1995), 40–48.
32. Mohamed Alwan, *Algeria before the United Nations* (New York: RSSP, 1959), especially 14–32, 40–45, and 71–76.
33. Saxena, *Namibia: Challenge to the United Nations*, 126–137.
34. Keck and Sikkink, *Activists beyond Borders*, 16 and 23.
35. David A. Kay, "The Impact of African States on the United Nations," IOr, 23, no. 1 (Winter, 1969): 20–47.
36. Crawford, "Decolonization as an International Norm," 44.
37. ICJRJAOO, *Preliminary Objections*, 321.
38. Colin M. Tatz, *Shadow and Substance in South Africa: A Study in Land and Franchise Policies Affecting Africans, 1910–1960* (Pietermaritzburg: UNtP, 1962), 116 and 122, nn. 89 and 92.
39. UNSC res. 245 (1968) of 25 January 1968, operative para. two; UNSC res. 246 (1968) of 14 March 1968, operative paras. one and two.
40. Drolsum, "The Norwegian Council," 228.
41. Jules Mukumbi wa Nyembo, "The Assistance Given to SWAPO by Certain African Countries and Organisations, 1960–1985" (B.A. [Hons.] thesis, University of Cape Town, 2002), 8–82.
42. Thomas A. Marks, "Counterinsurgency in the Age of Globalism," JCS, 27, no. 1 (Summer 2007): 22–23.
43. See Chapter One, nn. 72–73 above.
44. Christopher C. Saunders and Sue Onslow, "The Cold War and Southern Africa, 1976–1990," in *The Cambridge History of the Cold War, vol. III: Endings*, ed. Melvyn P. Leffler and Odd A. Westad (New York: CbUP, 2010), 222–243.
45. Ford, "South African Foreign Policy," 5–12 and 147–180.
46. L. Joan D. Devraun, "South African Foreign Relations with Angola, 1975–1988: A Structural Perspective" (M.A. thesis, University of Cape Town, 1997), 20–32, 90–92, 125–126, 162–164, and 174.
47. Howard E. Wolpe, "The Dangers of Globalism," and Peter Duignan, "Africa from a Globalist Perspective," in *African Crisis Areas and U.S. Foreign Policy*, ed. Gerald J. Bender, James S. Coleman, and Richard L. Sklar (Berkeley: UCP, 1985), 284–290 and 291–307, respectively.
48. Joanne E. Davies, *Constructive Engagement?*.
49. Anne F. Holloway, "Congressional Initiatives on South Africa," in Bender et al., ed., *African Crisis Areas*, 89–94.
50. Austin Long, *On "Other War": Lessons from Five Decades of RAND Counterinsurgency Research*, Prepared for the Office of the Secretary of Defense (Santa Monica: RANDC, 2006), 13.
51. Vincent B. Khapoya, *The Politics of Decision: A Comparative Study of African Policy toward the Liberation Movements*, Monograph Series in World Affairs, 12, no. 3 (Denver: UDSSFGSIS, [1975]), 5, 11, 14–15, 26, 55, and 64.
52. Richard Dale, "A Comparative Reconsideration of the Namibian Bush War, 1966–89," SWI, 18, no. 2 (June 2007): 196–215.
53. Paresh Pandya, "Foreign Support to ZANU and ZANLA during the Rhodesian War," ISSUPSR, November 1987, 3.
54. See the Preface, nn. 21 and 36 above.
55. Douglas L. Wheeler, "African Elements in Portugal's Armies in Africa (1961–1974)," AFS, 2, no. 2 (February 1976): 233–250.
56. Peter McLaughlin, "Victims as Defenders: African Troops in the Rhodesian Defence System[,]1890–1980," SWI 2, no. 2 (August 1991): 240–275, especially 265–271.
57. See Chapter Six, nn. 69–70 above.
58. Bernard B. Fall, *Hell in a Very Small Place: The*

Siege of Dien Bien Phu (Philadelphia: JBL, 1967), 209 and 453.
59. Ibid., viii-ix.
60. See the Preface, n. 25 above.
61. See Chapter Six, n. 76 above.
62. Laurence Nathan, "Force of Arms, Force of Conscience: A Study of the Militarisation, the Military, and the Anti-Apartheid War Resistance Movement in South Africa, 1970–1988" (M.Phil. thesis, University of Bradford, 1990), [108]-[110] and [225]-[226].
63. Cann, *Counterinsurgency in Africa*, 89–91 and 192; Fields, *The Portuguese Revolution*, 49.
64. Peter Godwin and Ian Hancock, *"Rhodesians Never Die": The Impact of War and Political Change on White Rhodesia, c. 1970–1980* (Harare: BaoB, 1995), 135–136; Cawthra, *Brutal Force*, 83–85.
65. Gary F. Baines, "South Africa's Vietnam? Literary History and Cultural Memory of the Border War," SAHJ 49 (November 2003): 172–192.
66. Letter to the author from Professor Baines, dated 3 March 2012.
67. François Jaques, "The Decolonization of French-Speaking Territories in Africa as Reflected in the South African Press: A Case Study of Algeria and the Belgian Congo," JES, 36, no. 1 (March 2006): 36–41; Al J. Venter, "The South African–Algerian Connection: Why Algeria?," in *Challenge: Southern Africa within the African Revolutionary Context: An Overview*, ed. Al J. Venter (Gibraltar: AP, 1989), 31–62.
68. See Jeffrey H. Michaels and Michael Ford, " Bandwagonistas: Rhetorical Re-description, Strategic Choice[,] and the Politics of Counter-insurgency," SWI, 22, no. 2 (May 2011): 352–384.
69. Douglas Porch, "The Dangerous Myths and Dubious Promise of COIN," SWI, 22, no. 2 (May 2011): 239–257.
70. Zartman, *Ripe for Resolution*, 171.
71. Gillian Gunn, "The Angolan Economy: A Status Report," in *Angola, Mozambique[,] and the West*, The Washington Papers no. 130, ed. Helen Kitchen (New York: PrP; published with the Center for Strategic and International Studies, Washington, D.C., 1987), 57.
72. Lubkemann, "Unsettling the Metropole," 259.
73. Ibid., 266–267.
74. Martin S. Alexander, Martin Evans, and John F. V. Keiger, "The 'War without a Name,' the French Army, and the Algerians," in Alexander et al., ed., *The Algerian War*, 27.
75. Lubkemann, "Unsettling the Metropole," 257–270; Benjamin Stora, "The 'Southern' World of the *Pieds Noirs*," 225–241.
76. Lubkemann, "Unsettling the Metropole," 258–259.
77. Gillian Gunn, "Post-Nkomati Mozambique," in Kitchen, ed., *Angola, Mozambique[,] and the West*, 86.
78. Godwin and Hancock, *"Rhodesians Never Die,"* 149, 286, and 315, respectively.
79. Wolfgang H. Thomas, "The Economy in Transition to Independence," in Rotberg, ed., *Namibia: Political and Economic Prospects*, 73, 75, 79–82, and 84–85.
80. Kate Jowell, "Economic Priorities for an Independent Namibia," in Rotberg, ed., *Namibia*, 94.
81. Stanley Uys, "SWAPO and the Postindependence Era," in Rothberg, ed., *Namibia*, 105–106 and 110.
82. Letter to the author from Dr. Botha, dated 18 September 2009.
83. Uys, *Bushman Soldiers*, 249–270.
84. Nortje, *32 Battalion*, 283; Sisingi Kamongo and Leon Bezuidenhout, *Shadows in the Sand: A Koevoet Tracker's Story of an Insurgency War* (Pinetown, South Africa: TDSP, 2011), 222.
85. Secret cable titled "Pik and the Prospects of a SWAPO Victory," sent 23 October 1981 from the U.S. Consulate in Cape Town to the Secretary of State, Washington, D.C. in the Ronald Reagan Presidential Library, White House staff and office files, Herman J. Cohen files, 1987–1988, African Affairs Directorate, National Security Council, boxes 91875 and 91876, as cited in Davies, *Constructive Engagement*, 136–137 and 144, n. 8.
86. van der Westhuizen, *White Power*, 287.
87. Vergau, *Negotiating the Freedom of Namibia*, 1–2, n. 1.
88. Schüring, "'History Obliges,'" 75.
89. Letter to the author from Professor Tötemeyer, dated 26 December 2011.
90. Henriksen, "Portugal in Africa," 408–409.
91. Gifford and Louis, "Introduction," in Gifford and Louis, ed., *Decolonization*, xii.
92. Israel Goldblatt, *Building Bridges: Namibian Nationalists: Clemens Kapuuo, Hosea Kutako, Brendan Simbwaye, Samuel Witbooi*, ed. Dag Henrichsen, Naomi Jacobson, and Karen Marshall, Lives, Legacies, Legends series no. 7 (Basel: BAB, 2010), xix, 5, 11, 68, 89–90, 92–93, 108, and 132.
93. Azeem Ibrahim, "Conceptualisation of Guerrilla Warfare," SWI, 15, no. 3 (Winter 2004): 113.
94. Brown, "Diplomacy by Other Means," 24 and 32.
95. Ibid., 32.
96. [Patrick Bulger], "Swapo Is Likely to Have the Edge in Namibian Poll," TS, international airmail weekly ed., 29 August 1983, 15.
97. See Chapter Five, nn. 169–175 above.
98. Hearn, *UN Peacekeeping*, 232–233. The details of the arrangements are published in SADFA, *Namibian Independence and Cuban Troop Withdrawal* (Pretoria: GPr, 1989), 5–6.
99. Zartman, *Ripe for Resolution*, 205–206.
100. Jaster, *In Defence of White Power*, xiv.
101. See Chapter Eight, n. 8 above.
102. van Wyk, "South West Africa: Origin of a World Problem," 216–218.
103. A. Ukiomogbe Obozuwa, *The Namibian Question: Legal and Political Aspects*, Ethiope Law Series no. 2 (Benin City, Nigeria: EPC, 1973), 204.
104. Warwick, "White South Africa and Defence," 159, 168–169, 172, 182, 198–199, 223, and 226.
105. Letter to the author from Professor Baines, dated 3 March 2012.
106. Marks, "Counterinsurgency in the Age of Globalism," 22.
107. Michaels and Ford, "Bandwagonistas," 359–361.
108. D. Michael Shafer, *Deadly Paradigms: The Failure of U.S. Counterinsurgency Policy* (Princeton: PUP, 1988).
109. Jaster, *The Defence of White Power*, 6.
110. Pottinger, *The Imperial Presidency*, 203 and 215.
111. Ford, "South African Foreign Policy," 215.
112. Gillian Gunn, "Mozambique after Machel," in Kitchen, ed., *Angola, Mozambique[,] and the West*, 134.
113. Letter to the author from Professor Baines, dated 3 March 2012.
114. Graham T. Allison, *Essence of Decision: Explaining the Cuban Missile Crisis* (Boston: LBC, 1971), 176 and 316, n. 71 (where he attributes the maxim to Don K. Price).
115. Amy Biehl, "Chester Crocker and the Negotia-

tions for Namibian Independence: The Role of the Individual in Recent American Foreign Policy" (senior thesis, Stanford University, 1989), 97, n. 19.
  116. Thomas Ohlson, *Power Politics and Peace Policies: Intra-State Conflict Resolution in Southern Africa*. Report no. 50 (Uppsala: UUPCR, 1998), 92.
  117. Kevin A. O'Brien, "Special Forces for Counter-Revolutionary Warfare: The South African Case," SWI, 12, 2 (Summer 2001): 105 (quotation).
  118. Laurent C.W. Kaela, *The Question of Namibia* (New York: SMP, 1996), 84–90 and 107–110.
  119. Gottschalk, "Restructuring the Colonial State," 31; Gerhard Tötemeyer, "The Interim Government and Its Rule: The Legitimacy Crisis," in Tötemeyer et al., ed., *Namibia in Perspective*, 54–68.
  120. Ford, "South African Foreign Policy," 227, 229–231, 234, 239, 243, and 251.
  121. Pottinger, *The Imperial Presidency*, 168 and 140 (quotation).
  122. Moorcraft, *African Nemesis*, 395–419.

Appendix

  1. The listing for the years 1946–1960, inclusive, is based on ICJPOAD, *Legal Consequences,* Vol. I, Annex A, 112–116 (Written Statement of the Secretary-General). The tabulation includes both the preambular and operative paragraphs of General Assembly resolutions.
  2. The listing for the years 1961–1966, inclusive, is based on ICJPOAD, *Legal Consequences*, vol. 1, Annex a, 112–116 (Written Statement of the Secretary-General), although resolution 1593 (XV) of 16 March 1961 has been added to that list. The tabulation includes both the preambular and operative paragraphs of those General Assembly resolutions that deal expressly with Namibia rather than with the more inclusive subject of Southern Africa.
  3. The listing for the years 1967–1969, inclusive, is based on ICJPOAD, *Legal Consequences*, vol. 1, Annex A, 112–116 (Written Statement of the Secretary-General), although resolution S-V 2248 of 19 May 1967 has been added to that list. The listing for 1970–1976, inclusive, is drawn from the appropriate YUN. The tabulation includes both the preambular and operative paragraphs of those General Assembly resolutions that deal expressly with Namibia rather than with the more inclusive subject of Southern Africa.
  4. The listing for 1977–1990, inclusive, is drawn from the appropriate YUN. The tabulation includes both the preambular and operative paragraphs of those General Assembly resolutions that deal expressly with Namibia rather than with the more inclusive subject of Southern Africa. The trend was to move to omnibus resolutions on Namibia, with each sub-resolution or part designated by sequential letters of the alphabet. Thus, UNGA res. 35/227 of 6 March 1981 contains ten sub-resolutions, namely, A through J.
  5. The listing for 1968–1990, inclusive, is drawn from the appropriate YUN.
  6. The sources are the same as those used for tables three and four.

Bibliography

This bibliography is divided into sections: Documents. Books. Monographs and Pamphlets. Articles in Journals and Yearbooks. Conference and Other Papers. Theses and Dissertations.

Documents

Basson, Nico, and Ben Motinga, editors. *Call Them Spies: A Documentary Account of the Namibian Spy Drama.* Windhoek and Johannesburg: African Communications Projects, 1989.

Cline, Lawrence E. *Pseudo Operations and Counterinsurgency: Lessons from Other Countries.* Carlisle, Penn.: U.S. Army War College, Strategic Studies Institute, 2005.

Colletta, Nat J., Markus Kostner, Ingo Wiederhofer, with the assistance of Emilio Mondo, Taimi Sitari, and Tadesse A. Woldu. *Case Studies in War-to-Peace Transition: The Demobilization and Reintegration of Ex-Combatants in Ethiopia, Namibia, and Uganda.* World Bank Discussion Paper no. 331. Africa Technical Department Series. Washington, D.C.: The World Bank, 1996.

de Beer, Marlien. *SWA/Namibia Today.* Windhoek: Department of Governmental Affairs, Section Liaison Services, 1988.

Dugard, John, editor. *The South West Africa/Namibia Dispute: Documents and Scholarly Writings on the Controversy between South Africa and the United Nations.* Perspectives on Southern Africa no. 9. Berkeley: University of California Press, 1973.

Germany. Reichskolonialamt. *The Treatment of Native and Other Populations in the Colonial Possessions of Germany and England. An Answer to the English Blue Book of August 1918: "Report on the Natives of South-West Africa and Their Treatment by Germany."* Translated from the German. Berlin: Hans Robert Engelmann, 1919.

Great Britain. Union of South Africa. *Report on the Natives of South-West Africa and Their Treatment by Germany. Prepared in the Administrator's Office, Windhuk, South-West Africa, January, 1918.* Cmd. 9146. London: HMSO, 1918. Reprinted as Jeremy Silvester and Jan-Bart Gewald, *Words Cannot Be Found: German Colonial Rule in Namibia: An Annotated Reprint of the 1918 Blue Book.* Leiden: Koninklijke Brill NV, 2003.

Heywood, Annemarie. *The Cassinga Event: An Investigation of the Records.* Second revised edition. Windhoek: National Archives of Namibia, 1996.

International Court of Justice. Pleadings, Oral Arguments, Documents. *Legal Consequences for States of the Continued Presence of South Africa in Namibia (South West Africa) Notwithstanding Security Council Resolution 276 (1970). Volume I: Request for Advisory Opinion, Written Statements.* [The Hague]: International Court of Justice, 1971.

———. Pleadings, Oral Arguments, Documents. *Legal Consequences for States of the Continued Presence of South Africa in Namibia (South West Africa) Notwithstanding Security Council Resolution 26 (1970). Volume II: Oral Statements and Correspondence.* [The Hague]: International Court of Justice, 1972.

———. Pleadings, Oral Arguments, Documents. *South West Africa Cases (Ethiopia v. South Africa; Liberia v. South Africa)* [The Hague]: International Court of Justice, n.d., vols. 1, 4, and 6.

———. Reports of Judgments, Advisory Opinions and Orders. *Admissibility of Hearings of Petitioners by the Committee on South West Africa: Advisory Opinion of June 1st, 1956.* [The Hague]: International Court of Justice, n.d.

———. Reports of Judgments, Advisory Opinions and Orders. *Legal Consequences for States of the Continued Presence of South Africa in Namibia (South West Africa) Notwithstanding Security Council Resolution 276 (1970): Advisory Opinion of 21 June 1971.* [The Hague]: International Court of Justice, 1972.

"Letter Dated 5 December 1979, from the South African Foreign Minister to the UN Secretary- General, concerning the Proposed Demilitarized Zone." *Southern Africa Record* 20 (August 1980): 14.

Namibia. Ministry of Foreign Affairs. *Namibia's Foreign Policy and Diplomacy Management.* [Windhoek]: Ministry of Foreign Affairs, 2004.

Namibia. Parliament. National Assembly. *Debates*, 1 (1990), 3 (1990) 6 (1990), 7 (1990), 9 (1991), 13 (1991), 14 (1991), 15 (1991), 16 (1991), 29 (1993), 35 (1993), 36 (1994), 7 (1996), 14 (1996) 17 (1997), 25 (1998) 29 (1998), 30 (1998), 32 (1999), and 34 (1999).

[Republic of] South Africa. Commission of Enquiry into South West Africa Affairs. *Report.* R.P. no. 12/1964. [Pretoria]: [Government Printer], 1964.

[Republic of] South Africa. Department of Foreign Affairs. *Namibian Independence and Cuban Troop Withdrawal.* Pretoria: Government Printer, 1989.

[Republic of] South Africa. Department of Foreign Affairs, compiler. *South West Africa: Basic Documents, 30 January 1976 to 2 May 1979.* s.l.: Issued by the Department of Foreign Affairs, circa 1979.

[Republic of] South Africa. *Government Gazette Extraordinary*, no. 1771, 21 June 1967.

[Republic of] South Africa. Parliament. *Debates*, 16 (1990).

[Republic of] South Africa. Parliament. House of Assembly. *Debates*, 5 (1963), 17 (1966), 21 (1967), 23 (1968), 26 (1969), 47 (1974), 60 (1976), 61 (1976), 79 (1979), 83 (1979), and 112 (1984).

[Republic of] South Africa. Supreme Court. Transvaal Division. *State versus Eliaser Tuhadeleni and 36 Others*. S.l.: n.p., judgment of 26 January 1968. Mimeographed copy.

Rinehart, Robert. "National Security." In *South Africa: A Country Study*. Foreign Area Studies, The American University. DA Pam 550-93. Second edition, edited by Harold D. Nelson, 293-373. Washington, D.C.: Headquarters, Department of the Army, 1981.

Schoeman, Amy, editor. *Ten Years of Freedom, Peace & Prosperity: Speeches of the President, March 1990–March 20, 1995*. [Windhoek]: Ministry of Information and Broadcasting, The Directorate [of] Print Media and Regional Offices, circa 2000.

South West Africa. *Votes and Proceedings of the Legislative Assembly. Second Session—Fifth Assembly. 25th to 27th March and 26th April to 10th May, 1946*.

_____. *Votes and Proceedings of the Legislative Assembly. Third Session—Fifth Assembly. 3rd to 5th February and 1st to 14th May, 1947*.

S[outh] W[est] A[frica] P[eople's] O[rganization] of Namibia. Department of Information and Publicity. *To Be Born a Nation: The Liberation Struggle for Namibia*. London: Zed Press, 1981.

Truth and Reconciliation Commission of South Africa. *Report*. 7 vols. s.l.: Truth and Reconciliation Commission, 1998 (vols. 1–5), 2002 (vol.7), and 2003 (vol. 6).

Union Legislation Affecting South West Africa and Proclamations, Ordinances[,] and Principal Government Notices Issued in South West Africa during 1958. Published by Order of the Honourable Administrator of South West Africa. Windhoek: John Meinert, 1959.

[Union of] South Africa. Parliament. House of Assembly. *Debates*, 5 (1925), 8 (1927), 34 (1939), 37 (1940), 52 (1945), 55 (1946), 66 (1949), 77 (1952), 88 (1955), and 101 (1959).

[Union of] South Africa. Parliament. Senate. *Debates*, 1939 and 1956, vol. 3.

[Union of] South Africa. *South West Africa and the Union of South Africa: The History of a Mandate*. s.l.: Published by authority of the Government of the Union of South Africa and distributed in the United States by the Union of South Africa Government Information Office, New York, circa 1946.

[Union of] South Africa. South West Africa Commission. *Report*. U.G.26. Pretoria: The Government Printer, 1936.

United Nations. *Official Records of the Second Part of the First Session of the General Assembly. Fourth Committee. Trusteeship. Part I. Summary Record of Meetings. 1 November–12 December 1946*. Lake Success, N.Y.: United Nations, n.d.

_____. *Official Records of the Second Part of the First Session of the General Assembly. Fourth Committee. Trusteeship. Part III. Summary Records of Meetings of Sub-Committee 2. 16 November–5 December 1946*. Lake Success, N.Y.: United Nations, n.d.

_____. *Official Records of the Second Session of the General Assembly. Fourth Committee. Trusteeship. Part I. Summary Records of Meetings. 16 September–6 November 1947*. Lake Success, N.Y.: United Nations, 1947.

_____. *Official Records of the Sixth Session of the General Assembly. Plenary Meetings (First Phase). Annexes. Agenda Item 38: Question of South West Africa. Report of the Ad Hoc Committee on South West Africa to the General Assembly. Second Addendum, Appendix III*. United Nations doc. A/1901/Add. 2 (15 November 1951). Paris: United Nations, 1951–1952.

_____. *Report of the Committee on South West Africa concerning the Implementation of General Assembly Resolutions 1568 (XV) and 1596 (XV)*. General Assembly Official Records, Sixteenth Session, Supplement no. 12A (A/4926). New York: United Nations, 1962.

_____. *Supplementary Report of the Secretary-General concerning the Implementation of Security Council Resolutions 435 (1978) and 439 (1978) concerning the Question of Namibia*. United Nations doc. S/13634 (23 November 1979).

United Nations. Department of Public Information. *The Blue Helmets: A Review of United Nations Peace-keeping*. Second ed. s.l.: United Nations, 1990.

United Nations. Department/Office of Public Information. *Yearbook of the United Nations*, vols. 24 (1970) through 44 (1990). Place of publication and publisher varies.

United Nations. General Assembly. Eleventh Session. Fourth Committee. *Plebiscites Held since 1920 under the Control or Supervision of International Organizations: Memorandum Prepared by the Secretariat*. Doc. A/C. 4/351 (20 February 1957).

United Nations. Institute for Namibia. *Namibia: A Direct United Nations Responsibility*. Lusaka: United Nations Institute for Namibia, 1987.

_____. *Namibia: Perspectives for National Reconstruction and Development*. Lusaka: United Nations Institute for Namibia, 1986.

United States Congress. House of Representatives. Committee on Foreign Affairs. Subcommittee on Africa. *Critical Developments in Namibia: Hearings, February 21 and April 4, 1974*. Ninety-Third Congress, Second Session. Washington, D.C.: U.S. Government Printing Office, 1974.

_____. *Namibia: Internal Repression and United States Diplomacy: Hearing, February 21, 1985*. Ninety-Ninth Congress, First Session. Washington, D.C.: U.S. Government Printing Office, 1985.

_____. *Namibian Independence: Review of the Process and Progress: Hearing, July 20, 1989*. One Hundred First Congress, First Session. Washington, D.C.: U.S. Government Printing Office, 1990.

United States Congress. House of Representatives. Committee on Foreign Affairs. Subcommittees on International Economic Policy and Trade and on Africa. *The Anti-Apartheid Act of 1985: Hearings and Markup ... on H.R. 1460, April 17, 18, 30, May 2, 1985*. Ninety-Ninth Congress, First Session. Washington, D.C.: U.S. Government Printing Office, 1986.

United States Congress. Senate. Committee on the Judiciary. Subcommittee on Security and Terrorism. *The Role of the Soviet Union, Cuba, and East Germany in Fomenting Terrorism in Southern Africa: Hearings, March 22, 24, 25, 29, and 31, 1982*. Volumes 1 and 2. Ninety-Seventh Congress, Second Session. Washington, D.C.: U.S. Government Printing Office, 1982.

Visser, J.A. *The South African Defence Force's Contribution to the Development of South West Africa*. [Pretoria]: SADF Military Information Bureau, circa 1983.

Books, Monographs and Pamphlets

Adams, James. *The Unnatural Alliance*. London: Quartet Books, 1984.

Åfreds, Johanna. *History and Nation-Building: The Political Uses of History in Post-Colonial Namibia*. MFS-Reports 2000: 2. Uppsala: Uppsala University Department of Economic History, 2000.

Allison, Graham T. *Essence of Decision: Explaining the Cuban Missile Crisis*. Boston: Little, Brown, 1971.

Alwan, Mohamed. *Algeria before the United Nations*. New York: Robert Speller & Sons, 1959.

Andrew, Rick. *Buried in the Sky*. Rosebank, Johannesburg: Penguin Books (South Africa), 2001.

Anglin, Douglas G. *International Monitoring as a Mechanism for Conflict Resolution in Southern Africa*. Working Paper no. 17. Southern African Perspectives. Bellville: University of the Western Cape, Centre for Southern African Studies, 1992.

Ansprenger, Franz. *Die Befreiungspolitik der Organisation für Afrikanische Einheit, 1963 bis 1975*. Studien zum Konflikt im Südlichen Afrika. Entwicklung und Frieden. Wissenschaftliche Reihe 8. München: Chr. Kaiser Verlag; Mainz: Matthias-Grünewald-Verlag, 1975.

Appy, Christian G. *Working-Class War: American Combat Soldiers and Vietnam*. Chapel Hill: University of North Carolina Press, 1993.

Baines, Gary F. *The Battle for Cassinga: Conflicting Narratives and Contested Meanings*. BAB Working Paper no. 2: 2007, Basel: Basler Afrika Bibliographien, 2007.

Ballard, Sebastian, and Nick Santcross. *Namibia Handbook*. Bath, England: Footprint Handbooks, 1997.

Barber, James P. *South Africa's Foreign Policy, 1945–1970*. London: Oxford University Press, 1973.

_____, and John Barratt, *South Africa's Foreign Policy: The Search for Status and Security, 1945–1988*. Cambridge Studies in International Relations no. 11. Cambridge: Cambridge University Press in association with the South African Institute of International Affairs, 1990.

Bauer, Gretchen. *Labor and Democracy in Namibia, 1971–1996*. Athens: Ohio University Press, 1998.

Becker, Heike. *Namibian Women's Movement, 1980 to 1992: From Anti-Colonial Resistance to Reconstruction*. Wissenschaftliche Reihe/ISSA, Bd. 23. Frankfurt a. M.: IKO-Verlag für Interkulturelle Kommunikation, 1995.

Belasco, Amy. *The Cost of Iraq, Afghanistan, and Other Global Wars on Terror Operations since 9/11*. CRS Report RL 33110. Washington, D.C.: Congressional Research Service, 2010.

Bell, Terry, with Dumisa B. Ntsebeza. *Unfinished Business: South Africa, Apartheid, and Truth*. London: Verso, 2003.

Berat, Lynn. *Walvis Bay: Decolonization and International Law*. New Haven: Yale University Press, 1990.

Berridge, Geoffrey R. *South Africa, the Colonial Powers and "African Defence": The Rise and Fall of the White Entente, 1948–60*. New York: St. Martin's, 1992.

Binkin, Martin, and Mark J. Eitelberg with Alvin J. Schexnider and Marvin M. Smith. *Blacks and the Military*. Washington, D.C.: The Brookings Institution, 1982.

Bizos, George. *Odyssey to Freedom*. Houghton: Random House, 2007.

[Bjornlund, Eric]. *Nation Building: The U.N. and Namibia*. Washington, D.C.: National Democratic Institute for International Affairs, 1990.

Blaufarb, Douglas S. *The Counterinsurgency Era: U.S. Doctrine and Performance, 1950 to the Present*. New York: The Free Press, 1977.

Borer, Tristan A. *Challenging the State: Churches as Political Actors in South Africa, 1980–1994*. Notre Dame, Ind.: University of Notre Dame Press, 1998.

Branch, Daniel. *Defeating Mau Mau, Creating Kenya: Counterinsurgency, Civil War, and Decolonization*. African Studies Series no. 111. New York: Cambridge University Press, 2009.

Bridgman, John M. *The Revolt of the Hereros*. Perspectives on Southern Africa no. 30. Berkeley: University of California Press, 1981.

Building Democracy: Perceptions and Performance of Government and Opposition in Namibia: Summary of [the] Proceedings of a Conference presented by the Namibia Institute for Democracy in Windhoek on 30 November 1996. Windhoek: Namibia Institute for Democracy and Konrad-Adenauer-Stiftung, 1996.

Burger, Marléne, and Chandré Gould. *Secrets and Lies: Wouter Basson and South Africa's Chemical and Biological Warfare Programme*. Cape Town: Zebra Press, 2002.

Burgess, Julian, et al. *The Great White Hoax: South Africa's International Propaganda Machine*. London: The Africa Bureau, 1977.

Byman, Daniel, Peter Chalk, Bruce Hoffman, William Rosenau, and David Brannan. *Trends in Outside Support for Insurgent Movements*. Santa Monica, Calif.: RAND Corporation, National Security Research Division, International Security and Defense Center, 2001.

Callwell, Charles E. *Small Wars: Their Principles and Practice*. Third edition. Introduction to the Bison Books edition by Douglas Porch. Lincoln: University of Nebraska Press, 1996 (originally published in 1906).

Campbell, Kurt M. *Soviet Policy towards South Africa*. New York: St. Martin's, 1986.

Cann, John P. *Counterinsurgency in Africa: The Portuguese Way of War, 1961–1974*. Contributions in Military Studies no. 167. Westport, Conn.: Greenwood, 1997.

Carlson, Joel. *No Neutral Ground*. New York: Thomas Y. Crowell Company, 1973.

Carney, Daniel. *The Wild Geese*. New York: Bantam, 1977.

Carter, Gwendolen M. *The Politics of Inequality: South Africa since 1948*. Rev. ed. New York: Frederick A. Praeger, 1959.

Cawthra, Gavin. *Brutal Force: The Apartheid War Machine*. London: International Defence and Aid Fund for Southern Africa, 1986.

_____. *Policing South Africa: The SAP & the Transition from Apartheid*. London: Zed Books, 1993.

Chaliand, Gérard. *Armed Struggle in Africa: With the Guerrillas in "Portuguese" Guinea*. Introduction by Basil Davidson. Translated by David Rattray and Robert Leonhardt. New York and London: Monthly Review Press, 1969.

Chowdhuri, Ramendra N. *International Mandates and Trusteeship Systems: A Comparative Study*. The Hague: Martinus Nijhoff, 1955.

Cilliers, Jakkie [Jacobus K.]. *Counter-Insurgency in Rhodesia*. London: Croom Helm, 1985.

Citino, Robert. *Germany and the Union of South Africa in the Nazi Period*. Westport, Conn.: Greenwood, 1991.

Clapham, Christopher. *Africa and the International System: The Politics of State Survival*. Cambridge Studies in International Relations no. 50. Cambridge: Cambridge University Press, 1996.

Clayton, Anthony. *Frontiersmen: Warfare in Africa since 1950*. London: UCL Press, 1999.

_____. *The Wars of French Decolonization*. New York: Longman Publishing, 1994.

Cleaver, Tessa, and Marion Wallace. *Namibia: Women in War*. London: Zed Books, 1990.

Cliffe, Lionel, with Ray Bush, et al. *The Transition to Independence in Namibia*. Boulder, Colo.: Lynne Rienner Publishers, 1994.

Clough, Michael, and Jeffrey Herbst. *South Africa's Changing Regional Strategy: Beyond Destabilization*. Critical Issues 1989, no. 4. New York: Council on Foreign Relations, 1989.

Cockram, Gail-Maryse. *South West African Mandate*. Cape Town: Juta and Company, 1976.

Cohen, Eliot A. *Citizens and Soldiers: The Dilemmas of Military Service*. Ithaca, N.Y.: Cornell University Press, 1985.

Connable, Ben, and Martin C. Libicki. *How Insurgencies End*. Prepared for the Marine Corps Intelligence Activity. Santa Monica, Calif.: RAND Corporation, 2010.

Cooper, Allan D. *Ovambo Politics in the Twentieth Century*. Lanham, Md.: University Press of America, 2001.

Copson, Raymond. *African Wars and Prospects for Peace*. Armonk, N.Y.: M.E. Sharpe, 1994.

Crawford, Neta C. *Argument and Change in World Politics: Ethics, Decolonization, and Humanitarian Intervention*. Cambridge Studies in International Relations no. 81. New York: Cambridge University Press, 2002.

_____. *The Domestic Sources and Consequences of Aggressive Foreign Policies: The Folly of South Africa's "Total Strategy."* Working Paper no. 41. Southern African Perspectives. Bellville: University of the Western Cape, Centre for Southern African Studies, 1995.

_____, and Audie J. Klotz, editors. *How Sanctions Work: Lessons from South Africa*. New York: St. Martin's, 1999.

Crocker, Chester A. *High Noon in Southern Africa: Making Peace in a Rough Neighborhood*. New York: W.W. Norton, 1992.

Cronje, Gillian, and Suzanne Cronje. *The Workers of Namibia*. London: International Defence and Aid Fund for Southern Africa, 1979.

Dale, Richard. *Botswana's Search for Autonomy in Southern Africa*. Contributions in Political Science no. 358. Westport, Conn.: Greenwood, 1995.

Danaher, Kevin. *In Whose Interest?: A Guide to U.S.–South African Relations*. Washington, D.C.: Institute for Policy Studies, 1984.

Davidson, Alex. *Democracy and Development in Namibia: The State of Democracy and Development in Namibia: The State of Democracy and Civil Rights, 1989-1991*. Uppsala Studies in Democracy no. 2. Uppsala: Uppsala University, Department of Government, 1991.

_____. *Government and Opposition in Namibia: Four Years after Independence*. Uppsala Studies in Democracy no. 8. Uppsala: Uppsala University, Department of Government, 1994.

Davidson, Basil. *The Liberation of Guiné: Aspects of an African Revolution*. With a foreword by Amilcar Cabral. Harmondsworth, Middlesex, England: Penguin Books, 1969.

Davies, Joanne E. *Constructive Engagement?: Chester Crocker & American Policy in South Africa, Namibia & Angola*. Oxford: James Currey; Auckland Park, South Africa: Jacana Media; Athens: Ohio University Press, 2007.

De Kok, Eugene, as told to Jeremy Gordin. *A Long Night's Damage: Working for the Apartheid State*. Saxonwold, South Africa: Contra Press, 1998.

Deutschmann, David, editor. *Changing the History of Africa: Angola and Namibia*. Melbourne: Oceana Press, 1989.

de Villiers, Les [Lourens E. S.]. *In Sight of Surrender: The U.S. Sanctions Campaign against South Africa, 1946–1993*. Westport, Conn.: Praeger, 1995.

Dickens, Charles. *David Copperfield*. With an introduction and notes by Jeremy Tambling. London: Penguin Books, 1996 (first published in 1850).

Dickson, Paul, and Thomas B. Allen. *The Bonus Army: An American Epic*. New York: Walker & Company, 2004.

Dierks, Klaus. *Chronology of Namibian History from Pre-Historical Times to Independent Namibia*. Windhoek: Namibia Scientific Society, 1999.

Dobell, Lauren. *Swapo's Struggle for Namibia, 1960-1991: War by Other Means*. Basel Namibia Studies Series 3. Basel: P. Schlettwein Publishing, 1998.

Dore, Isaak I. *The International Mandate System and Namibia*. Boulder, Colo.: Westview, 1985.

Dorward, David. *Namibia: International Dimensions to Its Decolonisation*. Occasional Paper no. 3. East Melbourne: The Australian Institute of International Affairs [Victorian Branch]; Geelong, Victoria: Deakin University, School of Social Sciences, 1989.

Drechler, Horst. *"Let Us Die Fighting": The Struggle of the Herero and Nama against German Imperialism (1884–1915)*. London: Zed Press, 1980.

Dreyer, Ronald. *Namibia and Southern Africa: Regional Dynamics of Decolonization, 1945-90*. London: Kegan Paul, 1994.

Dubow, Saul H. *Racial Segregation and the Origins of Apartheid in South Africa, 1919-36*. Houndmills, Basingstoke, Hampshire, England: Macmillan, 1989.

Dugard, John. *Human Rights and the South African Legal Order*. Princeton: Princeton University Press, 1978.

du Pisani, André. *Beyond the Barracks: Reflections on the Role of the SADF in the Region*. Occasional Paper. Braamfontein: South African Institute of International Affairs, 1988.

_____. *SWA/Namibia: The Politics of Continuity and Change*. Johannesburg: Jonathan Ball Publishers, 1985.

du Plessis, Anton. *The Strategic Significance of Walvis Bay and the Penguin Islands*. Ad hoc publication no. 28. Pretoria: Institute of Strategic Studies, University of Pretoria, 1991.

Eirola, Martii. *The Ovambogefahr: The Ovamboland Reservation in the Making: Political Responses of the Kingdom of Ondonga to the German Colonial Power, 1884-1910*. Studia Historica Septentrionalia no. 22. Rovaniemi, Finland: Pohjois-Suomen Historiallinen Yhdistys, 1992.

Elkins, Caroline. *Imperial Reckoning: The Untold Story of Britain's Gulag in Kenya*. New York: Owl Books, 2005.

Ellert, Henrik. *The Rhodesian Front War: Counter-Insurgency and Guerrilla War in Rhodesia, 1962-1980*. Gweru, Zimbabwe: Mambo Press, 1989.

Els, Paul. *Ongulumbashe: Where the Bushwar Began*. Wandsbeck, South Africa: Reach Publishers, 2007.

_____. *We Fear Naught But God: The Story of the South African Special Forces, "The Recces."* Weltevreden Park, South Africa: Covos-Day Books, 2000.

Emmett, Tony [Anthony B.]. *Popular Resistance and the Roots of Nationalism in Namibia, 1915-1966*. Basel Namibia Studies Series 4. Basel: P. Schlettwein Publishing, 1999.

Englebert, Pierre. *State Legitimacy and Development in Africa*. Boulder, Colo.: Lynne Rienner Publishers, 2000.

Erichsen, Casper W. *"The Angel of Death Has Descended Violently among Them": Concentration Camps and Prisoners-of-War in Namibia, 1904–08*. Research Report 79/2005. Leiden: African Studies Centre, 2005.

Evans, M[ichael]. *Fighting against Chimurenga: An Analysis of Counter-Insurgency in Rhodesia, 1972–79*. Local Series no. 37. Salisbury: The Historical Association of Zimbabwe, 1981.

Fall, Bernard B. *Hell in a Very Small Place: The Siege of Dien Bien Phu*. Philadelphia: J. B. Lippincott, 1967.

———. *Last Reflections on a War*. Garden City, N.Y.: Doubleday, 1967.

Fieldhouse, Roger. *Anti-Apartheid: A History of the Movement in Britain: A Study in Pressure Group Politics*. London: The Merlin Press, 2005.

Fields, Rona M. *The Portuguese Revolution and the Armed Forces Movement*. New York: Praeger, 1975.

First, Ruth. *South West Africa*. Baltimore: Penguin, 1963.

———, Jonathan Steele, and Christable Gurney. *The South African Connection: Western Investment in Apartheid*. London: Maurice Temple Smith, 1972.

Forrest, Joshua B. *Namibia's Post-Apartheid Regional Institutions: The Founding Year*. Rochester: University of Rochester Press, 1998.

Foster, Donald H., with Dennis Davis and Dianne Sandler. *Detention & Torture in South Africa: Psychological, Legal & Historical* Studies. Claremont: David Philip Publisher, 1987.

Frankel, Philip H. *Pretoria's Praetorians: Civil-Military Relations in South Africa*. Cambridge: Cambridge University Press, 1984.

———. *Soldiers in a Storm: The Armed Forces in South Africa's Democratic Transition*. Boulder, Colo.: Westview, 2000.

Freeman, Linda. *The Ambiguous Champion: Canada and South Africa in the Trudeau and Mulroney Years*. Toronto: University of Toronto Press, 1997.

Fritz, Jean Claude. *La Namibie Indépendante: Les Coûts d'une Décolonisation Retardée*. Paris: Éditions L'Harmattan, 1991.

Fry, Earl H. *The Expanding Role of State and Local Governments in U.S. Foreign Affairs*. New York: Council on Foreign Relations Press, 1998.

Galula, David. *Counterinsurgency Warfare: Theory and Practice*. New York: Frederick A. Praeger, 1964.

Gann, Lewis H., and Peter J. Duignan. *Burden of Empire: An Appraisal of Western Colonialism in Africa South of the Sahara*. Stanford, Calif.: Hoover Institution Press, 1967.

Geldenhuys, Deon J. *The Diplomacy of Isolation: South African Foreign Policy Making*. New York: St. Martin's, 1984.

———. *Isolated States: A Comparative Analysis*. Cambridge: Cambridge University Press, 1990.

Geldenhuys, Jannie. *A General's Story: From an Era of War and Peace*. Translated by Annemarié Geldenhuys. Johannesburg: Jonathan Ball Publishers, 1995.

George, Edward. *The Cuban Intervention in Angola, 1965–1991: From Che Guevara to Cuito Cuanavale*. New York: Frank Cass, 2005.

Gerber, Louis B. *Friends and Influence: The Diplomacy of Private Enterprise*. Cape Town: Purnell & Sons, 1973.

Gleijeses, Piero. *Visions of Freedom: Havana, Washington, Pretoria and the Struggle for Southern Africa, 1976–1991*. Chapel Hill: University of North Carolina Press, 2013.

Glick, Edward B. *Peaceful Conflict: The Non-Military Use of the Military*. Harrisburg, Penn.: Stackpole Books, 1967.

Godwin, Peter, and Ian Hancock. *"Rhodesians Never Die": The Impact of War and Political Change on White Rhodesia, c. 1970–1980*. Harare: Baobab Books, 1995.

Goldblatt, Israel. *Building Bridges: Namibian Nationalists: Clemens Kapuuo, Hosea Kutako, Brendan Simbwaye, Samuel Witbooi*. Edited by Dag Henrichsen, Naomi Jacobson, and Karen Marshall. Lives, Legacies, Legends series no. 7. Basel: Basel Afrika Bibliographien, 2010.

———. *History of South West Africa from the Beginning of the Nineteenth Century*. Cape Town: Juta & Company, 1971.

Goldsworthy, David. *Colonial Issues in British Politics: From "Colonial Development" to "Wind of Change."* Oxford: Clarendon Press, 1971.

Gordon, Robert J. *The Bushman Myth: The Making of a Namibian Underclass*. Boulder, Colo.: Westview, 1992.

———. *Mines, Masters and Migrants: Life in a Namibian Mine Compound*. Johannesburg: Ravan Press, 1977.

Greeff, Jack. *A Greater Share of Honour*. Ellisras, South Africa: Ntomeni Publications, 2001.

Green, Lawrence G. *Lords of the Last Frontier: The Story of South West Africa and Its People of All Races*. Second, revised edition. Cape Town: Howard Timmins, 1962.

Grimal, Henri. *Decolonization: The British, French, Dutch and Belgian Empires, 1919–1963*. Translated by Stephan De Vos. Boulder, Colo.: Westview, 1978.

Groth, Siegfried. *Namibia: The Wall of Silence: The Dark Days of the Liberation Struggle*. Introductions by Heinz H. Held and Carl Mau. Translated from the German by Hugh Beyer. Wuppertal: Peter Hammer Verlag, 1995.

Grotpeter, John J. *Historical Dictionary of Namibia*. African Historical Dictionaries no. 57. Metuchen, N.J.: Scarecrow, 1994.

Grundlingh, Albert. *Fighting Their Own War: South African Blacks and the First World War*. Braamfontein: Ravan Press, 1987.

Grundy, Kenneth W. *Defense Legislation and Communal Politics: The Evolution of a White South African Nation as Reflected in the Controversy over the Assignment of Armed Forces Abroad, 1912–1976*. Papers in International Studies, Africa Series no. 33. Athens: Ohio University Center for International Studies, Africa Program, 1978.

———. *Guerrilla Struggle in Africa: An Analysis and Preview*. New York: Grossman Publishers, 1971

———. *The Militarization of South African Politics*. Bloomington: Indiana University Press, 1986.

———. *Soldiers without Politics: Blacks in the South African Armed Forces*. Perspectives on Southern Africa no. 33. Berkeley: University of California Press, 1983.

Hamann, Hilton. *Days of the Generals*. Cape Town: Zebra Press, 2001.

Hanf, Theodor, Heribert Weiland, and Gerda Vierdag in collaboration with Lawrence Schlemmer, Rainer Hampel, and Burkhard Krupp. *South Africa, the Prospects of Peaceful Change: An Empirical Enquiry into the Possibility of Democratic Conflict Regulation*. London: Rex Collings; Cape Town: David Philip; Bloomington: Indiana University Press, 1981.

Hanlon, Joseph. *Beggar Your Neighbours: Apartheid Power in Southern Africa*. London: The Catholic Institute for International Relations, and James Curry; Bloomington: Indiana University Press, 1986.

Harlech-Jones, Brian. *A New Thing?: The Namibian Independence Process, 1989–1990*. Windhoek: University of Namibia, Ecumenical Institute for Namibia, 1997.

Hearn, Roger. *UN Peacekeeping in Action: The Namibian*

Experience. Commack, N.Y.: Nova Science Publishers, 1999.

Heggoy, Alf A. *Insurgency and Counterinsurgency in Algeria*. Bloomington: Indiana University Press, 1972.

Heitman, Helmoed-Römer. *Modern African Wars. 3. South-West Africa*. Men-at-Arms Series no. 242. London: Osprey, 1991.

———. *South African Armed Forces*. Cape Town: Buffalo Publications, 1990.

———. *South African War Machine*. Novato, Calif.: Presidio Press, 1985.

———. *War in Angola: The Final South African Phase*. Gibraltar: Ashanti Publishing, 1990.

Henriksen, Thomas H. *Revolution and Counterrevolution: Mozambique's War of Independence, 1964–1974*. Contributions in Intercultural and Comparative Studies no. 6. Westport, Conn.: Greenwood, 1983.

Herbstein, Denis, *White Lies: Canon Collins and the Secret War against Apartheid*. Cape Town: HSRC Press; Oxford: James Currey Publishers, 2004.

———, and John Evenson. *The Devils Are Among Us: The War for Namibia*. London: Zed Books, 1989.

Heunis, Jan C. *United Nations versus South Africa: A Legal Assessment of United Nations and United Nations Related Activities in Respect of South Africa*. Johannesburg and Cape Town: Lex Patria Publishers, 1986.

Hirschman, Albert O. *Exit, Voice, and Loyalty: Responses to Decline in Firms, Organizations, and States*. Cambridge: Harvard University Press, 1970.

Hishongwa, Ndeutala. *The Contract Labour System and Its Effect on Family and Social Life in Namibia: A Historical Perspective*. Windhoek: Gamsberg Macmillan, 1992.

Hochschild, Adam. *The Mirror at Midnight: A South African Journey*. New York: Penguin Books, 1990.

Hoffman, Bruce, Jennifer Taw, and David Arnold. *Lessons for Contemporary Counterinsurgencies: The Rhodesian Experience*. R-3998-A. Santa Monica, Calif.: RAND [Corporation], 1991.

Holsti, Kalevi J. *The State, War, and the State of War*. Cambridge Studies in International Relations no. 51. Cambridge: Cambridge University Press, 1996

Holt, Clive. *At Thy Call We Did Not Falter*. Cape Town: Zebra Press, 2005.

Hooper, Jim. *Beneath the Visiting Moon: Images of Combat in Southern Africa*. Lexington, Mass.: D.C. Heath and Company, 1990.

———. *Koevoet!* Johannesburg: Southern Book Publishers, 1988.

Hopwood, Graham. *Walvis Bay: South Africa's Hostage*. London: Catholic Institute for International Relations; Amsterdam: African-European Institute; London: Church Action on Namibia, 1990.

Horne, Alistair. *The French Army and Politics, 1870–1970*. New York: Peter Bedrick Book, 1984.

———. *A Savage War of Peace: Algeria, 1954–1962*. Revised edition. New York: Viking Penguin, 1987.

Horrell, Muriel. *South-West Africa*. Johannesburg: South African Institute of Race Relations, 1967.

———, compiler. *A Survey of Race Relations in South Africa, 1959–1960*. Johannesburg: South African Institute of Race Relations, 1961.

———, Dudley Horner, and Jane Hudson, compilers. *A Survey of Race Relations in South Africa, 1974*. Johannesburg: South African Institute of Race Relations, 1975.

Hull, Isabel V. *Absolute Destruction: Military Culture and the Practices of War in Imperial Germany*. Ithaca, N.Y.: Cornell University Press, 2005.

Huntington, Samuel P. *The Third Wave: Democratization in the Late Twentieth Century*. Norman: University of Oklahoma Press, 1991.

Hurd, Ian. *After Anarchy: Legitimacy and Power in the United Nations Security Council*. Princeton: Princeton University Press, 2007.

Israel, Mark. *South African Political Exile in the United Kingdom*. New York: St. Martin's, 1999.

Jabri, Vivienne. *Mediating Conflict: Decision-Making and Intervention in Namibia*. Manchester and New York: Manchester University Press, 1990.

Jackson, Robert H. *Quasi-States: Sovereignty, International Relations, and the Third World*. Cambridge: Cambridge University Press, 1990.

Jaster, Robert S. *The Defence of White Power: South African Foreign Policy under Pressure*. London: Macmillan, 1988.

———. *South Africa in Namibia: The Botha Strategy*. Lanham, Md.: University Press of America, 1985.

Jauch, Herbert, editor. *Playing the Globalisation Game: The Implications of Economic Liberalisation for Namibia*. Windhoek: Labor Resource and Research Institute, 2001.

Johnson, Harold S. *Self-Determination within the Community of Nations*. Leyden: A.W. Sijthoff, 1967.

Junius, Andreas. *Der United Nations Council for Namibia*, Europöische Hochshulschriften. Reihe II. Rechtswissenschaft, Bd. 817. Frankfurt a. M.: Peter Lang, 1989.

Kahler, Miles. *Decolonization in Britain and France: The Domestic Consequences of International Relations*. Princeton: Princeton University Press, 1984.

Kangumu, Bennett. *Contesting Caprivi: A History of Colonial Isolation and Regional Nationalism in Namibia*. Basel Namibia Studies Series 10. Basel: Basel Afrika Bibliographien, 2011.

Katjavivi, Peter H. *A History of Resistance in Namibia*. London: James Currey; Addis Ababa: Organization of African Unity Inter-African Cultural Fund; and Paris: UNESCO Press, 1988.

———, Per Frostin, and Kaire Mbuende, editors. *Church and Liberation in Namibia*. London and Winchester, Mass., Pluto Press, 1989.

Keck, Margaret E., and Kathryn Sikkink. *Activists beyond Borders: Advocacy Networks in International Politics*. Ithaca: Cornell University Press, 1998.

Kelley, George A. *Lost Soldiers: The French Army and Empire in Crisis, 1947–1962*. Cambridge, Mass.: The M.I.T. Press, 1965.

Khapoya, Vincent B. *The Politics of Decision: A Comparative Study of African Policy toward the Liberation Movements*. Monograph Series in World Affairs, 12, no. 3. Denver: University of Denver, The Social Science Foundation and Graduate School of International Studies, [1975].

Klotz, Audie J. *Norms in International Relations: The Struggle against Apartheid*. Ithaca, N.Y.: Cornell University Press, 1995.

Kössler, Reinhart. *In Search of Survival and Dignity: Two Traditional Communities in Southern Namibia under South African Rule*. Windhoek: Gamsberg Macmillan, 2005.

Kriger, Norma J. *Guerrilla Veterans in Post-War Zimbabwe: Symbolic and Violent Politics, 1980–1987*. African Studies Series no. 103. Cambridge: Cambridge University Press, 2003.

Lan, David. *Guns & Rain: Guerrillas & Spirit Mediums in Zimbabwe*. London: James Currey; Berkeley: University of California Press, 1985.

Landgren, Signe. *Embargo Disimplemented: South Africa's Military Industry*. New York: Oxford University Press, 1989.

L'Ange, Gerald. *Urgent Imperial Service: South African Forces in German South West Africa, 1914–1915*. Rivonia: Ashanti Publishing, 1991.

Laqueur, Walter. *Guerrilla: A Historical and Critical Study*. Boston: Little, Brown, 1976.

Lasswell, Harold D. *Politics: Who Gets What, When, How*. New York: Meridian Books, 1958.

LeBeau, Debie. *An Investigation into the Lives of Namibian Ex-Fighters Fifteen Years after Independence*. Windhoek: People's Education, Assistance, and Counseling for Empowerment Center, 2005.

———, and Edith Dima, *Multiparty Democracy and Elections in Namibia*. EISA Research Report no. 13. Johannesburg: Electoral Institute of Southern Africa, 2005.

Leites, Nathan, and Charles Wolf. *Rebellion and Authority: An Analytic Essay on Insurgent Conflicts*. Chicago: Markham, 1970.

Lelyveld, Joseph. *Move Your Shadow: South Africa, Black and White*. New York: Penguin Books, 1986.

Leonard, Richard. *South Africa at War: White Power and the Crisis in Southern Africa*. Westport, Conn.: Lawrence Hill and Company, 1983.

Lijphart, Arend. *The Trauma of Decolonization: The Dutch and West New Guinea*. Yale Studies in Political Science, no. 17. New Haven: Yale University Press, 1966.

Linn, Brian M. *The U.S. Army and Counterinsurgency in the Philippine War, 1899–1902*. Chapel Hill: University of North Carolina Press, 1989.

Lipton, Merle. *Sanctions and South Africa: The Dynamics of Economic Isolation*. Special Report no. 1119. London: The Economist Intelligence Unit, 1988.

Logan, Rayford W. *The Operation of the Mandate[s] System in Africa, 1919–1927, with an Introduction on the Problem of the Mandates in the Post-War World*. Washington, D.C.: The Foundation Publishers, 1942.

Long, Austin. *On "Other War": Lessons from Five Decades of RAND Counterinsurgency Research*. Prepared for the Office of the Secretary of Defense. Santa Monica: RAND Corporation, 2006.

Lord, Dick [Richard S.]. *From Fledgling to Eagle: The South African Air Force during the Border War*. Johannesburg: Twenty Degrees South Publishers, 2008.

———. *Vlamgat: The Story of the Mirage F1 in the South African Air Force*. Weltevreden Park, South Africa: Covos-Day Books, 2000.

Louis, William R. *Great Britain and Germany's Lost Colonies, 1914–1919*. Oxford: Clarendon Press, 1967.

Love, Janice. *The U.S. Anti-Apartheid Movement: Local Activism in Global Politics*. New York: Praeger, 1985.

Lush, David. *Last Steps to Uhuru: An Eye-Witness Account of Namibia's Transition to Independence*. Windhoek: New Namibia Books, 1993.

Lynch, Hollis R. *Black American Radicals and the Liberation of Africa: The Council on African Affairs, 1937–1955*. Monograph Series No. 5. Ithaca, N.Y.: Cornell University, Africana Studies and Research Center, 1978.

Malan, Magnus A. de M. *My Life with the SA Defence Force*. Pretoria: Protea Book House, 2004.

Manela, Erez. *The Wilsonian Moment: Self-Determination and the International Origins of Anticolonial Nationalism*. New York: Oxford University Press, 2007.

Mao Tse-Tung. *On Guerrilla Warfare*. Translated with an Introduction by Samuel B. Griffith. New York: Frederick A. Praeger, 1961.

Marcum, John A. *The Angolan Revolution, Volume I: The Anatomy of an Explosion (1950–1962)*. Cambridge, Mass.: The M.I.T. Press, 1969.

———. *The Angolan Revolution, Volume II: Exile Politics and Guerrilla Warfare (1962–1976)*. Cambridge, Mass.: The MIT Press, 1978.

Marquard, Leo. *South Africa's Colonial Policy: Presidential Address Delivered at the Annual Meeting of the Council of the South African Institute of Race Relations in Hiddingh Hall, Cape Town, on January 16, 1957*. Johannesburg: South African Institute of Race Relations, 1957.

Martin, Henry J., and Neil D. Orpen. *South Africa at War: Military and Industrial Organization and Operations in Connection with the Conduct of the War, 1939–1945*. South African Forces, World War II, volume 7. Cape Town: Purnell & Sons, 1979.

Masson, John. *Jakob Marengo: An Early Resistance Hero of Namibia*. Windhoek: Out of Africa Books, 2001.

May, Edward C. *Report on the Wingspread Conference on Namibia Convened by [the] Lutheran Council in the U.S.A. and the Johnson Foundation, May 1976*. Racine, Wisconsin: The Johnson Foundation, 1976.

Mayer, Jane. *The Dark Side: The Inside Story of How the War on Terror Turned into a War on American Ideals*. New York: Doubleday, 2008.

McCuen, John J. *The Art of Counter-Revolutionary War: The Strategy of Counter-insurgency*. London: Faber and Faber, 1966.

Memmi, Albert. *The Colonizer and the Colonized*. Expanded edition. Introduction by Jean-Paul Sartre. Afterword by Susan G. Miller. Boston: Beacon Press, 1967.

Miller, Stuart C. *"Benevolent Assimilation": The American Conquest of the Philippines, 1899–1903*. New Haven: Yale University Press, 1982.

Mines and Independence. A Future for Namibia [no.] 3: Mining. London: The Catholic Institute for International Relations, 1983.

Minter, William. *Apartheid's Contras: An Inquiry into the Roots of War in Angola and Mozambique*. London: Zed Books; Johannesburg: Witwatersrand University Press, 1994.

Mockaitis, Thomas R. *British Counterinsurgency, 1919–60*. New York: St. Martin's, 1990.

Moodie, Thomas D. *The Rise of Afrikanerdom: Power, Apartheid, and the Afrikaner Civil Religion*. Perspectives on Southern Africa no. 11. Berkeley: University of California Press, 1975.

Moorcraft, Paul R. *African Nemesis: War and Revolution in Southern Africa (1945–2010)*. London: Brassey's, 1990.

Moorsom, Richard. *Exploiting the Sea*. A Future for Namibia, vol. 5. London: Catholic Institute for International Relations, 1984.

———. *Walvis Bay: Namibia's Port*. London: International Defense and Aid Fund for Southern Africa in Cooperation with the United Nations Council for Namibia, 1984.

Morris, Edmund. *Theodore Rex*. New York: The Modern Library, 2001.

Morris, Michael. *Armed Conflict in Southern Africa: A Survey of Regional Terrorisms from Their Beginnings to the Present, with a Comprehensive Examination of the Portuguese Position*. Cape Town: Jeremy Spence, 1974.

———. *Terrorism: The First Full Account in Detail of Ter-*

rorism and Insurgency in Southern Africa. Cape Town: Howard Timmins, 1971.

Müller, Johan A. *"The Inevitable Pipeline into Exile": Botswana's Role in the Namibian Liberation Struggle*. Basel: Basel Afrika Bibliographien, 2012.

Namakalu, Oswin O. *Armed Liberation Struggle: Some Accounts of PLAN's Combat Operations*. Windhoek: Gamsberg Macmillan, 2004.

Namhila, Ellen N. *The Price of Freedom*. Windhoek: New Namibia Books, 1997.

Namibia Country Profile, 1990–91: Annual Survey of Political and Economic Background. London: The Economist Intelligence Unit, 1990.

Namibia, Swaziland Country Profile, 1993/94. London: The Economist Intelligence Unit, 1994.

Nathan, Laurie. *Marching to a Different Drum: A Description and Assessment of the Formation of the Namibian Police and Defence Force*. Southern African Perspectives: A Working Paper Series no. 4. Bellville: University of the Western Cape, Centre for Southern African Studies, 1991.

[Nathan, Laurie]. *Out of Step: War Resistance in South Africa*. London: Catholic Institute for International Relations, 1989.

Nathanael, Keshii P. *A Journey to Exile: The Story of a Namibian Freedom Fighter*. Aberystwyth. Wales: Sosiumi Press, 2002.

Nelson, William H. *The American Tory*. Boston: Northeastern University Press, 1992 (originally published in 1961).

Neuberger, Benyamin. *National Self-Determination in Postcolonial Africa*. Boulder, Colo.: Lynne Rienner Publisher, 1986.

Ngavirue, Zedekia. *Political Parties and Interest Groups in South West Africa (Namibia): A Study of a Plural Society (1972)*. Basel Namibia Studies Series 1. Basel: P. Schlettwein Publishing, 1997.

Nolutshungu, Sam[uel C.] *South Africa in Africa: A Study in Ideology and Foreign Policy*. Manchester: Manchester University Press, 1975.

Nordlinger, Eric A. *Soldiers in Politics: Military Coups and Governments*. Englewood Cliffs, N.J.: Prentice-Hall, 1977.

Nortje, Piet[er]. *32 Battalion: The Inside Story of South Africa's Elite Fighting Unit*. Cape Town: Zebra Press, 2003.

Norval, Morgan. *Death in the Desert: The Namibian Tragedy*. Washington, D.C.: Selous Foundation Press, 1989.

Novick, Peter. *The Resistance versus Vichy: The Purge of Collaborators in Liberated France*. New York: Columbia University Press, 1968.

Nujoma, Sam. *Where Others Wavered: The Autobiography of Sam Nujoma*. London: Panaf Books, 2001.

Nye, Jr., Joseph S. *Soft Power: The Means to Succeed in World Politics*. New York: PublicAffairs, 2004.

Obozuwa, A. Ukiomogbe. *The Namibian Question: Legal and Political Aspects*. Ethiope Law Series no. 2. Benin City, Nigeria: Ethiope Publishing Company, 1973.

O'Brien, Kevin A. *The South African Intelligence Services: From Apartheid to Democracy*. New York: Routledge, 2011.

Oermann, Nils O. *Mission, Church and State Relations in South West Africa under German Rule (1884–1915)*. Missiongeschichtliches Archiv, Bd. 5. Stuttgart: Franz Steiner Verlag, 1999.

Ohlson, Thomas. *Power Politics and Peace Policies: Intra-State Conflict Resolution in Southern Africa*. Report no. 50. Uppsala: University of Uppsala, Department of Peace and Conflict Research, 1998.

O'Linn, Bryan. *Namibia: The Sacred Trust of Civilization: Ideal and Reality*. [vol. 1] Windhoek: Gamsberg Macmillan, circa 2003.

Orwell, George. *Animal Farm: A Fairy Story*. With an introduction by C.M. Woodhouse. New York: New American Library of World Literature, 1946.

Ovenden, Keith, and Tony Cole. *Apartheid and International Finance: A Program for Change*. Ringwood, Victoria, Australia: Penguin Books Australia, 1989.

Pandya, Paresh. *Mao Tse-tung and Chimurenga: An Investigation into Zanu's Strategies*. Braamfontein: Skotaville Publishers, 1988.

Pankhurst, Donna. *A Resolvable Conflict?: The Politics of Land Reform in Namibia*. Peace Research Report no. 36. Bradford, West Yorkshire, England: University of Bradford, Department of Peace Studies, 1996.

Peled, Alom. *A Question of Loyalty: Military Manpower Policy in Multiethnic States*. Ithaca, N.Y.: Cornell University Press, 1998.

Peterson, Martha J. *The General Assembly in World Politics*. 2nd impression. Boston: Unwin Hyman, 1990.

Pfister, Roger. *Apartheid South Africa and African States: From Pariah to Middle Power, 1961–1964*. International Library of African Studies, vol. 14. New York: Tarus Academic Studies, 2005.

Pienaar, Sara. *South Africa and International Relations between the Two World Wars: The League of Nations Dimension*. Johannesburg: Witwatersrand University Press, 1987.

Polakow-Suransky, Sasha. *The Unspoken Alliance: Israel's Secret Relationship with Apartheid South Africa*. New York: Pantheon Books, 2010.

Pool, Ithiel de Sola, with the collaboration of Harold D. Lasswell, Daniel Lerner et al. *Symbols of Democracy*. Hoover Institute Studies, Series C: Symbols, no. 4. Stanford: Stanford University Press, 1952.

Pottinger, Brian. *The Imperial Presidency: P.W. Botha: The First 10 Years*. Bergvlei: Southern Book Publishers, 1988.

Prinsloo, Daan S. *Walvis Bay and the Penguin Islands: Background and Status*. Study Report no. 8. Pretoria: Foreign Affairs Association, 1977.

Purkitt, Helen E., and Stephen F. Burgess. *South Africa's Weapons of Mass Destruction*. Bloomington: Indiana University Press, 2005.

Pye, Lucien W. *Guerrilla Communism in Malaya: Its Social and Political Meaning*. Princeton: Princeton University Press, 1956.

Record, Jeffrey. *The Wrong War: Why We Lost in Vietnam*. Annapolis, Md.: Naval Institute Press, 1998.

Rice, Edward E. *Wars of the Third Kind: Conflict in Underdeveloped Countries*. Berkeley: University of California Press, 1988.

Rocha, Geisa M. *In Search of Namibian Independence: The Limitations of the United Nations*. Boulder, Colo.: Westview, 1984.

Roos, Neil. *Ordinary Springboks: White Servicemen and Social Justice in South Africa, 1939–1961*. Aldershot, England: Ashgate, 2005.

Rosenau, James N. *Turbulence in World Politics: A Theory of Change and Continuity*. Princeton: Princeton University Press, 1990.

Roth, Brad R. *Governmental Illegitimacy in International Law*. Oxford: Clarendon Press, 1999.

Roth-Douquet, Kathy, and Frank Schaeffer. *AWOL: The*

Unexcused Absence of America's Upper Classes from Military Service and How It Hurts Our Country. New York: Collins, 2007.

Sagay, Itsejuwa. *The Legal Aspects of the Namibian Dispute*. Ile Ife, Nigeria: University of Ife Press, 1975.

Sanders, James. *Apartheid's Friends: The Rise and Fall of South Africa's Secret Service*. London: John Murray, 2006.

Sarkin, Jeremy. *Colonial Genocide and Reparation Claims in the 21st Century: The Socio-Legal Claims under International Law by the Herero against Germany for Genocide in Namibia, 1904–1908*. Westport, Conn.: Praeger Security International, 2009.

Saxena, Suresh C. *Namibia and the World: The Story of the Birth of a Nation*. Delhi: Kalinga Publications, 1991.

———. *Namibia: Challenge to the United Nations*. Dehli: Sundeep Prakashan, 1978.

Schleicher, Hans G., and Illona Schleicher. *Special Flights: The GDR and the Liberation Movements in Southern Africa*. Harare: SAPES Books, 1998.

Schmokel, Wolfe W. *Dream of Empire: German Colonialism, 1919–1945*. New Haven: Yale University Press, 1964.

Schrire, Robert. *Adapt or Die: The End of White Politics in South Africa*. [New York]: Ford Foundation and Foreign Policy Association, 1991.

Schultz, Duane. *Over the Earth I Come: The Great Sioux Uprising of 1862*. New York: St. Martin's, 1992.

Scott, G. Michael. *A Time to Speak*. London: Faber and Faber, 1967.

Seegers, Annette. *The Military in the Making of Modern South Africa*. International Library of African Studies vol. 1. London: I.B. Taurus, 1996.

Segal, Ronald, and Ruth First, editors. *South West Africa: Travesty of Trust: The Expert Papers and Findings of the International Conference on South West Africa, Oxford 23–26 March 1966....* London: Andre Deutsch, 1967.

Sellström, Tor, editor. *Liberation in Southern Africa: Regional and Swedish Voices*. Uppsala: Nordic Africa Institute, 1999.

———. *Sweden and National Liberation in South Africa. Volume I: Formation of a Popular Opinion (1950–1970)*. Uppsala: Nordic Africa Institute, 1999.

———. *Sweden and National Liberation in South Africa. Volume II: Solidarity and Assistance, 1970–1994*. Uppsala: Nordic Africa Institute, 2002.

Serfontein, Jan H. P. *Namibia?* Randburg: Fokus Suid Publishers, 1976.

Shafer, D. Michael. *Deadly Paradigms: The Failure of U.S. Counterinsurgency Policy* Princeton: Princeton University Press, 1988.

Shain, Yossi. *The Frontier of Loyalty: Political Exiles in the Age of the Nation-State*. Middletown, Conn.: Wesleyan University Press, 1989.

Shepherd, Jr., George W. *Anti-Apartheid: Transnational Conflict and Western Policy in the Liberation of South Africa*. Studies in Human Rights no. 3. Westport, Conn.: Greenwood, 1977.

Shipanga, Andreas. *In Search of Freedom: The Andreas Shipanga Story. As Told to Sue Armstrong*. Gibraltar: Ashanti Publishing, 1989.

Shubin, Vladimir G. *The Hot "Cold War": The USSR in Southern Africa*. London: Pluto Press; Scottsville: University of KwaZulu-Natal Press, 2008.

Shukrri, Muhammed A. *The Concept of Self-Determination in the United Nations*. Damascus: Al Jadidah Press, 1965.

Singham, A. W., and Shirley Hune. *Namibian Independence: A Global Responsibility*. Westport, Conn.: Lawrence Hill and Company, 1986.

Slonim, Solomon I. *South West Africa and the United Nations: An International Mandate in Dispute*. Baltimore: The Johns Hopkins University Press, 1973.

Smith, Tony. *The French Stake in Algeria, 1945–1962*. Ithaca, N.Y.: Cornell University Press, 1978.

Snyman, P. H. R. *Beeld van die SWA Gebiedsmag*. Pretoria: S.A. Weermag, Openbare Betrekkinge, 1989.

Soggot, David. *Namibia: The Violent Heritage*. New York: St. Martin's, 1986.

Soiri, Iina, and Pekka Peltola. *Finland and National Liberation in Southern Africa*. Uppsala: Nordic Africa Institute, 1999.

Sonderling, Stefan. *Bushwar[,] Bosoorlog[,] Buschkrieg*. Windhoek: Eyes Publishing, 1980.

South West Africa People's Organization of Namibia. Department of Information and Publicity. *To Be Born a Nation: The Liberation Struggle for Namibia*. London: Zed Press, 1981.

Sparks, Donald L., and December Green. *Namibia: The Nation after Independence*. Boulder, Colo.: Westview, 1992.

Srivastava, Rachna. *Namibia: A Study in the Process of Decolonization*. Delhi: Nirmal Publications, 1994.

Steenkamp, Willem. *Borderstrike!: South Africa into Angola*. Durban: Butterworths Publishers, 1983.

———. *South Africa's Border War, 1966–1989*. Gibraltar: Ashanti Publishing, 1989.

Stiff, Peter. *The Covert War: Koevoet Operations [in] Namibia, 1979–1989*. Alberton: Galago Publishing, 2004.

———. *Nine Days of War*. Alberton: Lemur Books, 1989.

———. *The Silent War: South African Recce Operations, 1969–1994*. Alberton: Galago Publishing, 1999.

———. *Warfare by Other Means: South Africa in the 1980s and 1990s*. Alberton: Galago Publishing, 2001.

Stiglitz, Joseph E., and Linda J. Bilmes. *The Three Trillion Dollar War: The Truth of the Cost of the Iraq Conflict*. New York: W.W. Norton, 2008.

Strand, Per. *SWAPO and Nation Building in Namibia: Transfer of Power in the Post-Communist Era*. Discussion Paper no. 8. Windhoek: University of Namibia, Namibian Institute for Social and Economic Research, 1991.

Stultz, Newell M. *Afrikaner Politics in South Africa, 1934–1948*. Perspectives on Southern Africa no.13. Berkeley: University of California Press, 1974.

———. *The Apartheid Issue at the Security Council*. The United Nations and Southern Africa Series no. 1. Braamfontein: The South African Institute of International Affairs, 1989.

Taber, Robert. *The War of the Flea: A Study of Guerrilla Theory and Practise*. New York: Lyle Stuart, 1965.

Talmon, Stefan. *Recognition of Governments in International Law: With Particular Reference to Governments in Exile*. New York: Oxford University Press, 1998.

Tamarkin, Mordechai. *The Making of Zimbabwe: Decolonization in Regional and International Politics*. London: Frank Cass & Co., 1990.

Tanham, George K. *Communist Revolutionary Warfare: The Vietminh in Indochina*. New York: Frederick A. Praeger, 1961.

Tapscott, Chris, and Ben Mulongeni, *An Evaluation of the Welfare and Future Prospects of Repatriated Namibians in Northern Namibia*. Research Report [no.] 3. Windhoek: University of Namibia, Namibian Institute for Social and Economic Research, 1990.

Theodoli Alberto. *A Cavallo Di Due Secoli*. [Rome]: La Navicella, [1950].

Thomas, Scott. *The Diplomacy of Liberation: The Foreign Relations of the African National Congress since 1960*. International Library of African Studies, vol. 2. London: I.B. Taurus, 1996.

Thompson, J.H. *An Unpopular War: From Afkak to Bosbefok: Voices of South African National Servicemen*. Cape Town: Zebra Press, 2006.

Thompson, Leonard M. *The Political Mythology of Apartheid*. New Haven: Yale University Press, 1985.

Thörn, Håkan *Anti-Apartheid and the Emergence of a Global Society*. London: Palgrave Macmillan, 2006.

Thornberry, Cedric. *A Nation Is Born: The Inside Story of Namibia's Independence*. Windhoek: Gamsberg Macmillan, 2004.

Torreguitar, Elena. *National Liberation Movements in Office: Forging Democracy with African Adjectives in Namibia*. European University Studies, Series XXXI (Political Science), vol. 567. Frankfurt a. M.: Peter Lang, 2009.

Tötemeyer, Gerhard K. H. *Church and State in Namibia: The Politics of Reconciliation*. Freiburg i. B.: Arnold Bergstraesser Institut, 2010.

Townsend, Mary E. *The Rise and Fall of Germany's Colonial Empire, 1884–1918*. With an introduction by Carleton J. H. Hayes. New York: Howard Fertig, 1966, first published in 1930.

Tsokodayi, Cleophas J. *Namibia's Independence Struggle: The Role of the United Nations*. [Bloomington, Ind.]: Xlibris, 2011.

Turner, John W. *Continent Ablaze: The Insurgency Wars in Africa, 1960 to the Present*. London: Arms and Armour Press, 1998.

Tylden, G[eoffrey]. *The Armed Forces of South Africa with an Appendix on the Commandos*. Frank Connock Publication no. 2. Johannesburg: City of Johannesburg Africana Museum, 1954.

Uys, Ian. *Bushmen Soldiers: Their Alpha and Omega*. Germiston: Fortress Publishers, 1993.

van der Waals, Willem S. *Portugal's War in Angola, 1961–1974*. Rivonia: Ashanti Publishing, 1993.

van der Westhuizen, Christi. *White Power and the Rise and the Fall of the National Party*. Cape Town: Zebra Press, 2007.

Vanneman, Peter. *Soviet Strategy in Southern Africa: Gorbachev's Pragmatic Approach*. Stanford, Calif.: Hoover Institution Press, 1990.

van Walraven, Klaas. *Dreams of Power: The Role of the Organization of African Unity in the Politics of Africa, 1963–1993*. African Studies Centre Research Series 13/1999. Aldershot, Hants, England: Ashgate, 1999.

Vergau, Hans-Joachim. *Negotiating the Freedom of Namibia: The Diplomatic Achievement of the Western Contact Group*. Translated by David R. Ward. Basel: Basel Afrika Bibliographien, 2010.

Vogt, Andreas. *National Monuments in Namibia: An Inventory of Proclaimed National Monuments in the Republic of Namibia*. Windhoek: Gamsberg Macmillan, 2004.

Waite, Robert G. L. *Vanguard of Nazism: The Free Corps Movement in Postwar Germany, 1918–1923*. Cambridge: Harvard University Press, 1952.

Wallace, Marion, with John Kinahan. *A History of Namibia from the Beginning to 1990*. New York: Columbia University Press, 2011.

Walshe, Peter. *The Rise of African Nationalism in South Africa: The African National Congress, 1912–1952*. Perspectives on Southern Africa no. 3. Berkeley: University of California Press, 1971.

Walvis Bay: A Report of a Fact-Finding Mission, October 1990. NEPRU Working Papers no. 13. Windhoek: Namibian Economic Policy Research Unit, 1992.

War and Conscience in South Africa: The Churches and Conscientious Objection. London: Catholic Institute for International Relations and Pax Christi, 1982.

Wasserman, Gary. *Politics of Decolonization: Kenya Europeans and the Land Issue, 1960–1965*. African Studies Series no. 17. Cambridge: Cambridge University Press, 1976.

Weatherford, Jack. *Native Roots: How Indians Enriched America*. New York: Fawcett Columbine, 1991.

Weiland, Heribert, and Matthew Braham, editors. *The Namibian Peace Process: Implications and Lessons for the Future*. Freiburger Beiträger zu Entwicklung und Politik 12. Freiburg i. B: Arnold Bergstraesser Institut, 1994.

Wellington, John H. *South West Africa and Its Human Issues*. Oxford: The Clarendon Press, 1967.

Werner, Wolfgang. *"No One Will Become Rich": Economy and Society in the Herero Reserves in Namibia, 1915–1946*. Basel Namibia Studies Series 2. Basel: P. Schlettwein Publishing, 1998.

Wilkins, Gregory L. *African Influence in the United Nations, 1967–1975: The Politics and Techniques of Gaining Compliance to U.N. Principles and Resolutions*. Washington, D.C.: University Press of America, 1981.

Williams, David. *On the Border: The White South African Military Experience, 1965–1990*. Cape Town: Tafelberg, 2008.

Wilson, Heather A. *International Law and the Use of Force by National Liberation Movements*. Oxford: Clarendon Press, 1988.

Winrow, Gareth M. *The Foreign Policy of the GDR in Africa*. Soviet and East European Studies no. 78. Cambridge: Cambridge University Press, 1990.

Winter, Gordon. *BOSS: South Africa's Secret Police*. Harmondsworth, Middlesex, England: Penguin, 1981.

Wood, Gordon S. *The Americanization of Benjamin Franklin*. New York: Penguin, 2004.

Wright, Quincy. *Mandates under the League of Nations*. New York: Greenwood, 1968, originally published in 1930.

Ya-Otto, John. With Ole Gjerstad and Michael Mercer. *Battlefront Namibia: An Autobiography*. Westport, Conn.: Lawrence Hill & Company, 1981.

Young, M. Crawford. *The African Colonial State in Comparative Perspective*. New Haven: Yale University Press, 1994.

Zartman, I. William. *Ripe for Resolution: Conflict and Intervention in Africa*. New York: Oxford University Press, 1985.

Zobel, Hiller B. *The Boston Massacre*. New York: W. W. Norton, 1970.

Zuijdwijk, Ton J.M. *Petitioning the United Nations: A Study in Human Rights*. New York: St. Martin's, 1982.

Chapters in Books

Abernethy, David B. "Decolonization in Southern Africa: Variations on a Theme." In *Decolonization and Dependency: Problems of Development of African Societies*, edited by Aguibou Y. Yansané, 196–228. Contributions in Afro-American and African Studies no. 48. Westport, Conn.: Greenwood, 1980.

Abrahams, Kenneth. "A Doctor in the Struggle at Home and in Exile." In *Histories of Namibia: Living through the Liberation Struggle: Life Histories*, compiled and edited by Colin Leys and Susan Brown, 139–157. London: The Merlin Press, 2005.

Adam, Heribert, and Kanya Adam. "The Politics of Memory in Divided Societies." In *After the TRC: Reflections on Truth and Reconciliation in South Africa*, edited by Wilmot James and Linda van de Vijver, 32–47. Athens: Ohio University Press; Cape Town: David Philip Publishers, 2000.

Alexander, Martin S., Martin Evans, and John F. V. Keiger. "The 'War without a Name': The French Army and the Algerians: Recovering Experiences, Images, and Testimonies." In *The Algerian War and the French Army, 1954–62: Experiences, Images, Testimonies*, edited by Martin S. Alexander, Martin Evans, and John F. V. Keiger, 1–39. Basingstoke, Hampshire, England: Palgrave Macmillan, 2002.

Anglin, Douglas G. "Namibian Relations with South Africa: Post-Independence Prospects." In *Prospects for Peace and Development in Southern Africa in the 1990s: Canadian and Comparative Perspectives*, edited by Larry A. Swatuk and Timothy M. Shaw, 93–113. Lanham, Md.: University Press of America; Halifax, N.S.: Dalhousie University Centre for African Studies, 1991.

Baines, Gary F. "Introduction: Challenging the Boundaries, Breaking the Silences." In *Beyond the Border War: New Perspectives on Southern Africa's Late-Cold War Conflicts*, edited by Gary F. Baines and Peter Vale, 1–21. Pretoria: University of South Africa Press, 2008.

———. "South Africa's Vietnam: Literary History and Cultural Memory of the Border Wars." In *Telling Wounds: Narrative, Trauma & Memory: Working through the SA Armed Conflicts of the 20th Century: Proceedings of the Conference Held at the University of Cape Town, 3–5 July 2002*, edited by Chris N. van der Merwe and Rolf W. Wolfswinkel, 59–170. [Midrand, Bellville]: Content Solutions, 2004.

Barnard, Wilhelm S. "The Border War: After 19 Years." In *Kompas op Suidwes-Afrika/Namibië*. Special Publication no. 5, edited by Wilhelm S. Barnard, 188–207. Demmesig, South Africa: Society for Geography, 1985.

Barratt, John. "South African Diplomacy at the UN," in *Diplomacy at the UN*, edited and introduced by Geoffrey R. Berridge and A. Jennings, 191–203. London and Basingstoke: Macmillan Press Ltd., 1985.

Berat, Lynn. "Namibia: The Road to Independence and the Problem of Succession of States." In *Governments-in-Exile in Contemporary World Politics*, edited by Yossi Shain, 18–41. New York: Routledge, 1991.

Brown, Susan. "Diplomacy by Other Means: SWAPO's Liberation War." In *Namibia's Liberation Struggle: The Two-Edged Sword*, by Colin Leys and John S. Saul with contributions from Susan Brown et al., 19–39. London: James Currey; Athens: Ohio University Press, 1995.

Campbell, Horace. "The Decolonization Process in Namibia." In *Confrontation and Liberation in Southern Africa: Regional Directions after the Nkomati Accord*, edited by Ibrahim S. R. Masbaha and Timothy M. Shaw, 33–49. Boulder, Colo.: Westview, 1987.

Cock, Jacklyn. "Manpower and Militarisation: Women and the SADF." In *Society at War: The Militarisation of South Africa*, edited by Jacklyn Cock and Laurie Nathan, 51–66. New York: St. Martin's, 1989.

Cook, Al. "The International Defence and Aid Fund or Southern Africa or IDAF." In *The Road to Democracy in South Africa*, vol. 3, International Solidarity, Part 1, 141–253. Pretoria: UNISA Press, 2008.

Cooper, Allan D. "Preface." In *Allies in Apartheid: Western Capitalism in Occupied Namibia*, edited by Allan D. Cooper, x-xi. New York: St. Martin's, 1988.

Crawford, Neta C. "Decolonization as an International Norm: The Evolution of Practices, Arguments, and Beliefs." In *Emerging Norms of Justified Intervention: A Collection of Essays from a Project of the American Academy of Arts and Sciences*, edited by Laura W. Reed and Carl Kaysen, 37–61. Cambridge, Mass.: American Academy of Arts and Sciences, 1983.

———, and Audie J. Klotz. "How Sanctions Work: A Framework for Analysis." In *How Sanctions Work*, edited by Neta C. Crawford and Audie J. Klotz, 25–42. New York: St. Martin's, 1999.

de Beer, David. "The Netherlands and Namibia: The Political Campaign to End Dutch Involvement in the Namibian Trade." In *Allies in Apartheid: Western Capitalism in Occupied Namibia*, edited by Allan D. Cooper, 124–135. New York: St. Martin's, 1988.

de Beer, J. H. "The Independence of the TBVC States: The Africa Branch from 1976." In *History of the South African Department of Foreign Affairs, 1927–1993*, edited by Tom F. Wheeler, 583–595. Johannesburg: The South African Institute of International Affairs, 2005.

Diener, Ingolf. "How to Be a Namibian and a Democrat: On the Question of the Project of Nationhood after Apartheid." In *Contemporary Namibia: The First Landmarks of a Post-Apartheid Society*, edited by Ingold Diener and Olivier Graefe, 327–353. Windhoek: Gamsberg Macmillan, 2001.

Dobell, Lauren. "SWAPO in Office." In *Namibia's Liberation Struggle: The Two-Edged Sword*, by Colin Leys and John S. Saul with contributions from Susan Brown et al., 171–195. London: James Currey; Athens: Ohio University Press, 1995.

Drolsum, Nina. "The Norwegian Council for Southern Africa (NOCOSA): A Study in Solidarity and Activism." In *Norway and National Liberation in Southern Africa*, edited by Torre L. Eriksen, 211–265. Uppsala: Nordic Africa Institute, 2000.

Duignan, Peter. "Africa from a Globalist Perspective." In *African Crisis Areas and U.S. Foreign Policy*, edited by Gerald J. Bender, James S. Coleman, and Richard L. Sklar, 291–307. Berkeley: University of California Press, 1985.

du Pisani, André. "Namibia: The Historical Legacy." In *Namibia in Perspective*, edited by Gerhard H. K. Tötemeyer, Vezera Kandetu, and Wolfgang Werner, 13–26. Windhoek: Council of Churches in Namibia, 1987.

———. "Namibia: Impressions of Independence." In *The Dynamics of Change in Southern Africa*, edited by Paul B. Rich, 199–21. New York: St. Martin's, 1994.

———. "State and Society under South African Rule." In *State, Society[,] and Democracy: A Reader in Namibian Politics*, edited by Christiaan Keulder, 49–76. Windhoek: Gamsberg Macmillan, 2000.

Eckstein, Harry. "A Perspective on Comparative Politics, Past and Present." In *Comparative Politics: A Reader*, edited by Harry Eckstein and David E. Apter. 3–32. New York: The Free Press, 1963.

Evans, Graham. "Across the Orange River: Namibia and Colonial Legacies." In *From Pariah to Participant: South Africa's Evolving Foreign Relations, 1990–1994*, edited by Greg Mills, 138–157. Braamfontein: South African Institute of International Relations, 1994.

Evans, Martin. "The *Harkis*: The Experience and Memory of France's Muslim Auxiliaries." In *The Algerian War and the French Army, 1954–62: Experiences, Images, Testimonies*, edited by Martin S. Alexander, Martin Evans, and John F. V. Keiger, 117–133. Basingstoke, Hampshire, England: Palgrave Macmillan, 2002.

Falk, Richard A. "The Observer's Report: The State v. Eliaser Tuhadeleni and Others." In *Erosion of the Rule of Law in South Africa*, 40–54. Geneva: International Commission of Jurists, 1968.

Finkelstein, Lawrence S. "Comparative Politics in the UN System." In *Politics in the United Nations System*, edited by Lawrence S. Finkelstein, 446–483. Durham, N.C.: Duke University Press, 1988.

———. "The Politics of Value Allocation in the UN System." In *Politics in the United Nations System*, edited by Lawrence S. Finkelstein, 1–40. Durham, N.C.: Duke University Press, 1988.

Frostin, Per. "The Theological Debate on Liberation." In *Church and Liberation in Namibia*, edited by Peter H. Katjavivi, Per Frostin, and Kaire Mbuende, 51–92. London: Pluto Press, 1989.

Gaomab, Johannes "Mistake." "With the People's Liberation Army in Angola." In *Histories of Namibia: Living through the Liberation Struggle: Life Histories*, edited and compiled by Colin Leys and Susan Brown, 63–75. London: The Merlin Press, 2005.

Gewald, Jan-Bart. "Herero Genocide in the Twentieth Century: Politics and Memory." In *Rethinking Resistance: Revolt and Violence*, edited by Jon Abbink, Mirjam de Bruijn, and Klaas van Walraven, 279–304. Leiden: Koninklijke Brill, 2003.

Gifford, Prosser, and William R. Louis. "Introduction." In *Decolonization and African Independence: The Transfers of Power, 1960–1980*, edited by Prosser Gifford and William R. Louis, ix-xxix. New Haven: Yale University Press, 1988.

Gottschalk, Keith. "Restructuring the Colonial State: Pretoria's Strategy in Namibia." In *Namibia in Perspective*, edited by Gerhard H. K. Tötemeyer, Vezera Kandetu, and Wolfgang Werner, 27–35. Windhoek: Council of Churches in Namibia, 1987.

Gunn, Gillian. "The Angolan Economy: A Status Report." In *Angola, Mozambique[,] and the West*. The Washington Papers no. 130, edited by Helen Kitchen, 54–70. New York: Praeger; published with the Center for Strategic and International Studies, Washington, D.C., 1987.

———. "Post-Nkomati Mozambique." In *Angola, Mozambique[,] and the West*. The Washington Papers no. 130, edited by Helen Kitchen, 83–104. New York: Praeger; published with the Center for Strategic and International Studies, Washington, D.C., 1987.

Guriab, Theo-Ben. "The Genesis of the Namibian Constitution: The International and Regional Setting." In *Constitutional Democracy in Namibia: A Critical Analysis after Two Decades*, edited by Anton Bösl, Nico Horn and André du Pisani, 109–117. Windhoek: Macmillan Education Namibia, 2010.

Hamutenya, Hidipo L., and Gottfried H. Geingob. "African Nationalism in Namibia." In *Southern Africa in Perspective: Essays in Regional Politics*, edited by Christian P. Potholm and Richard Dale, 85–94 and 351–352. New York: The Free Press, 1972.

Heinecken. Lindy, and Donna Winslow. "The Human Terrain: The Need for Cultural Intelligence." In *South Africa and Contemporary Counterinsurgency: Roots, Practices, Prospects*, edited by Deane-Peter Baker and Evert Jordaan, 197–208. Claremont: University of Cape Town Press, 2010.

Holloway, Anne F. "Congressional Initiatives on South Africa." In *African Crisis Areas and U.S. Foreign Policy*, edited by Gerald J. Bender, James S. Coleman, and Richard L. Sklar, 89–94. Berkeley: University of California Press, 1985.

Hunter, Justine. "Dealing with the Past in Namibia: Getting the Right Balance between Justice and Sustainable Peace?" In *The Long Aftermath of War: Reconciliation and Transition in Namibia*. Freiburger Beiträge zu Entwicklung und Politik, 27, edited by André du Pisani, Reinhart Kössler, and William A. Lindeke, 403–433. Freiburg i. Br.: Arnold Bergstraesser-Institut, 2010.

———. "No Man's Land of Time: Reflections on the Politics of Memory and Forgetting in Namibia." In *Beyond the Border War: New Perspectives on Southern Africa's Late-Cold War Conflicts*, edited by Gary F. Baines and Peter Vale, 302–321. Pretoria: University of South Africa Press, 2008.

———. "Who Should Own the Land?: An Introduction." In *Who Should Own the Land?: Analysis and Views on Land Reform and the Land Question in Namibia and Southern Africa*, edited by Justine Hunter, 1–7. Windhoek: Konrad-Adenauer-Stiftung and Namibia Institute for Democracy, 2004.

"Introduction." In *Namibia: SWAPO Fights for Freedom*, edited by Liberation Support Movement, 9–19. Oakland, Calif.: Liberation Support Movement Information Center, 1978.

Jackson, Robert H. "The Weight of Ideas in Decolonization: Normative Change in International Relations." In *Ideas and Foreign Policy: Beliefs, Institutions, and Political Change*, edited by Judith Goldstein and Robert O. Keohane, 111–138. Ithaca, N.Y.: Cornell University Press, 1993.

Jaster, Robert S. "War and Diplomacy." In Robert S. Jaster, Moeletsi Mbeki, Morley Nkosi, and Michael Clough, *Changing Fortunes: War, Diplomacy, and Economics in Southern Africa*, 19–65 and 181–184. [New York]: Ford Foundation and Foreign Policy Association, 1992.

Kandetu, Vezera, "The Role of the Church in Namibia." In *Church and Liberation in Namibia*, edited by Peter Katjavivi, Per Frostin, and Kaire Mbuende, 207–214. London: Pluto Press, 1989.

Klotz, Audie J. "Making Sanctions Work: Comparative Lessons." In *How Sanctions Work*, edited by Neta C. Crawford and Audie J. Klotz, 264–282. New York: St. Martin's, 1999.

Kössler, Reinhart. "Genocide and Reparations: Dilemmas and Exigencies in Namibian-German Relations." In *The Long Aftermath of War: Reconciliation and Transition in Namibia*. Freiburger Beiträge zu Entwicklung und Politik, 27, edited by André du Pisani, Reinhart Kössler, and William A. Lindeke, 215–241. Freiburg i. Br.: Arnold Bergstraesser-Institut, 2010.

———. "Public Memory, Reconciliation[,] and the Aftermath of War: A Preliminary Framework with Special Reference to Namibia. " In *Re-examining Liberation in Namibia: Political Culture since Independence*, edited by Henning Melber, 99–112. Uppsala: Nordic Africa Institute, 2003.

———, and Henning Melber. "Political Culture and Civil Society: On the State of the Namibian State." In *Contemporary Namibia: The First Landmarks of a Post-*

Apartheid Society, edited by Ingolf Diener and Olivier Graefe, 147–160. Windhoek: Gamsberg Macmillan, 2001.

Kramer, Paul A. "Introduction: Decolonizing the History of the Philippine-American War." In, Leon Wolff, *Little Brown Brother: How the United States Purchased and Pacified the Philippine Islands at the Century's Turn*, [ix]-xviii. Francis Parkman Prize ed. New York: History Book Club, 2006.

Kruys, G[eorge] P. H. "Doctrine Development in the South African Armed Forces up to the 1980s." In *Selected Military Issues with Specific Reference to the Republic of South Africa*. Ad hoc publication no. 28, edited by M[ichael] Hough and L[ouis] du Plessis, 1–19. Pretoria: University of Pretoria Institute for Strategic Studies, 2001.

Lamb, Guy. "Militarising Politics and Development: The Case of Post-Independence Namibia." In *The Security-Development Nexus: Expressions of Sovereignty and Securitization in Southern Africa*, edited by Lars Buur, Steffen Jensen, and Finn Stepputat, 152–173. Uppsala: Nordic Africa Institute; Cape Town: Human Sciences Research Council Press, 2007.

———. "Putting Belligerents in Context: The Cases of Namibia and Angola." In *Civilians in War*, edited by Simon Chesterman, 25–39. Boulder, Colo: Lynne Rienner Publishers, 2001.

Lee, Richard. "The Gods Must Be Crazy, But the State Has a Plan: Government Policies towards the San in Namibia and Botswana." In *Namibia, 1984–1984: Readings on Namibia's History and Society*, edited by Brian Wood, 539–546. London: Namibia Support Committee in cooperation with the United Nations Institute for Namibia, Lusaka, 1988.

Louis, William R., and Ronald Robinson. "The United States and the Liquidation of [the] British Empire in Tropical Africa, 1941–1951." In *The Transfer of Power in Africa: Decolonization, 1940–1960*, edited by Prosser Gifford and William R. Louis, 31–55. New Haven: Yale University Press, 1982.

Low, Anthony. "The End of the British Empire in Africa." In *Decolonization and African Independence: The Transfers of Power, 1960–1980*, edited by Prosser Gifford and William R. Louis, 33–72. New Haven: Yale University Press, 1988.

Lubkemann, Stephen C. "Unsettling the Metropole: Race and Settler Reincorporation in Postcolonial Portugal." In *Settler Colonialism in the Twentieth Century: Projects, Practices, Legacies*, edited by Caroline Elkins and Susan Pedersen, 257–270. New York: Routledge, 2005.

MacDougall, Gay. "Implementation of the [Comprehensive] Anti-Apartheid Act of 1986." In *Sanctioning Apartheid*, edited by Robert E. Edgar, 19–56. Trenton, N.J.: Africa World Press, 1990.

Manwaring, Max G. "Toward an Understanding of Insurgency Wars: The Paradigm." In *Uncomfortable Wars: Toward a New Paradigm of Low Intensity Conflict*, edited by Max G. Manwaring, 19–28. Boulder, Colo.: Westview, 1991.

Maxwell, Kenneth R. "Portugal and Africa: The Last Empire." In *The Transfer of Power in Africa: Decolonization, 1940–1960*, edited by Prosser Gifford and William R. Louis, 337–385. New Haven: Yale University Press, 1982.

McMaster, H.R. "Preserving Soldiers' Moral Character in Counter-Insurgency Operations." In *Ethics Education for Irregular Warfare*, edited by Don Carrick, James Connelly, and Paul Robinson, 15–26. Burlington, Vt.: Ashgate, 2009.

Melber, Henning. "'Namibia, Land of the Brave': Selective Memories on War and Violence within Nation Building." In *Rethinking Resistance: Revolt and Violence in African History*, edited by Jon Abbink, Mirjam de Bruijn, and Klaas van Walraven, 305–327. Leiden: Koninklijke Brill, 2003.

———. "'Presidential Indispensability' in Namibia: Moving out of Office But Staying in Power?" In *Legacies of Power: Leadership Change and Former Presidents in African Politics*, edited by Roger Southall and Henning Melber, 98–119. Pretoria: Human Sciences Research Council Press, 2006.

———. "Public Sector and Fiscal Policy." In *Namibia: A Decade of Independence, 1990–2000*. NEPRU Publication no. 7, edited by Henning Melber, 87–108. Windhoek: The Namibian Economic Policy Research Unit, 2000.

Metsola, Lalli, and Henning Melber. "Namibia's Pariah Heroes: SWAPO Ex-Combatants between Liberation Gospel and Security Interests." In *The Security-Development Nexus: Expressions of Sovereignty and Securitization in Southern Africa*, edited by Lars Buur, Steffen Jensen, and Finn Stepputat, 85–105. Uppsala: Nordic Africa Institute; Cape Town: Human Sciences Research Council Press, 2007.

Minter, William. "An Unfinished Journey." In *No Easy Victories: African Liberation and American Activists over Half a Century, 1950–2000*, edited by William Minter, Gail Hovey, and Charles Cobb, Jr., 9–58. Trenton, N.J.: Africa World Press, 2008.

Nathan, Laurie. "'Marching to a Different Beat': The History of the End Conscription Campaign." In *Society at War: The Militarisation of South Africa*, edited by Jacklyn Cock and Laurie Nathan, 308–323. New York: St. Martin's, 1989.

Nolutshungu, Sam C. "South Africa and the Transfers of Power in Africa." In *Decolonization and African Independence: The Transfers of Power, 1960–1980*, edited by Prosser Gifford and William R. Louis, 477–503. New Haven: Yale University Press, 1988.

Nöthling, F. J. "Muddy Waters in the New World." In *History of the South African Department of Foreign Affairs, 1927–1993*, edited by Tom F. Wheeler, 389–415. Johannesburg: South African Institute of International Affairs, 2005.

———. "The Search for Defence Co-Operation." In *History of the South African Department of Foreign Affairs, 1927–1993*, edited by Tom F. Wheeler, 365–388. Johannesburg: The South African Institute of International Affairs, 2005.

———. "South Africa and Africa." In *History of the South African Department of Foreign Affairs, 1927–1993*, edited by Tom F. Wheeler, 253–278. Johannesburg: South African Institute of International Affairs, 2005.

———. "The South West Africa Dispute: 1948–1966." In *History of the South African Department of Foreign Affairs, 1927–1993*, edited by Tom F. Wheeler, 309–336. Johannesburg: The South African Institute of International Affairs, 2005.

Ohlson, Thomas, "The End of the Cold War and Conflict Resolution in Southern Africa." In *Sub-Saharan Africa: A Sub-Continent in Transition*, edited by Rukhsana A. Siddiqui, 233–258. Aldershot: Avebury, 1993.

Østbye, Eva H. "The Namibian Liberation Struggle: Direct Norwegian Support to SWAPO." In *Norway and*

National Liberation, edited by Torre L. Eriksen, 88–130. Uppsala: Nordic Africa Institute, 2000.

———. "Pioneering Local Activism: The Namibian Association of Norway," in *Norway and National Liberation*, edited by Torre L. Eriksen, 353–372. Uppsala: Nordic Africa Institute, 2000.

Panter-Brick, S. Keith. "La Francophonie with Special Reference to Educational Links and Language Problems." in *Decolonisation and After: The British and French Experience*. Studies in Commonwealth Politics and History no. 7, edited by W. H. Morris-Jones and Georges Fischer, 330–345. London: Frank Cass and Company, 1980.

"Paramilitary Shock Troops." *Resister* 37 (May 1985), as reproduced in *War and Resistance: Southern African Reports: The Struggle for Southern Africa as Documented by Resister Magazine*, edited by Gavin Cawthra, Gerald Kraak, and Gerald O'Sullivan, 114–117. London and Basingstoke: Macmillan, 1994.

Pedersen, Susan. "Settler Colonialism at the Bar of the League of Nations." In *Settler Colonialism in the Twentieth Century: Projects, Practices, Legacies*, edited by Caroline Elkins and Susan Pedersen, 113–134. New York and London: Routledge, 2005.

Philip, Kate. "The Private Sector and the Security Establishment." In *Society at War: The Militarisation of South Africa*, edited by Jacklyn Cock and Laurie Nathan, 202–216. New York: St. Martin's, 1989.

Posel, Deborah. "The Language of Domination, 1978–1983." In *The Politics of Race, Class, and Nationalism in Twentieth Century South Africa*, edited by Shula Marks and Stanley Trapido, 419–433 New York: Longman, 1987.

Prisk, Courtney E. "The Umbrella of Legitimacy." In *Uncomfortable Wars: Toward a New Paradigm of Low Intensity Conflict*, edited by Max G. Manwaring, 69–91, Boulder, Colo.: Westview, 1991.

Puchala, Donald J. "The United Nations and Ecosystem Issues: Institutionalizing the Global Interest." In *Politics in the United Nations System*, edited by Lawrence S. Finkelstein, 214–245. Durham, N.C.: Duke University Press, 1988.

Riggs, Robert E. "The United Nations and the Politics of Law." In *Politics in the United Nations System*, edited by Lawrence S. Finkelstein, 41–74. Durham, N.C.: Duke University Press, 1988.

Roberts, Alun R. "British Economic Involvement in South African-Occupied Namibia, 1845–1986." In *Allies in Apartheid: Western Capitalism in Occupied Namibia*, edited by Allan D. Cooper, 156–174. New York: St. Martin's, 1988.

Robinson, Roland. "Andrew Cohen and the Transfer of Power in Tropical Africa, 1940–1951." In *Decolonisation and After: The British and French Experience*. Studies in Commonwealth Politics and History, 50–72. London: Frank Cass & Co., 1980.

Rosenau, James N. "Introduction: Political Science in a Shrinking World." In *Linkage Politics: Essays on the Convergence of National and International Systems*, edited by James N. Rosenau, 1–17. New York: The Free Press, 1969.

Rotberg, Robert I. "Political and Economic Realities in a Time of Settlement." In *Namibia: Political; and Economic Prospects*, edited by Robert I. Rotberg, 29–40. Lexington, Mass.: Lexington Books, 1983.

Satchwell, Kathy. "The Power to Defend: An Analysis of Various Aspects of the Defence Act." In *Society at War:*

The Militarisation of South Africa, edited by Jacklyn Cock and Laurie Nathan, 40–50. New York: St. Martin's, 1989.

Saul, John S., and Colin Leys. "SWAPO: The Politics of Exile." In *Namibia's Liberation Struggle: The Two-Edged Sword*, by Colin Leys and John S. Saul with contributions from Susan Brown et al., 40–65. London: James Currey; Athens: Ohio University Press, 1995.

Saunders, Christopher C. "From Apartheid to Democracy in Namibia and South Africa: Some Comparisons." In Henning Melber and Christopher Saunders, *Transition in Southern Africa: Comparative Aspects: Two Lectures*, 5–16. Discussion Paper no. 10. Uppsala: Nordic Africa Institute, 2001.

———. "History and the Armed Struggle: From Anti-Colonial Propaganda to 'Patriotic History?'" In *Transitions in Namibia: Which Changes for Whom?*, edited by Henning Melber, 13–28. Uppsala: Nordic Africa Institute, 2007.

———. "Liberation and Democracy: A Critical Reading of Sam Nujoma's Autobiography." In *Re-examining Liberation in Namibia: Political Culture since Independence*, edited by Henning Melber, 87–98. Uppsala: Nordic Africa Institute, 2003.

———. "Transition in Namibia, 1989–1990 and the South African Case." In *Peace, Politics[,] and Violence in the New South Africa*, edited by Norman Etherton, 213–219. London: Hans Zell Publisher, 1992.

Schade, Klaus. "Poverty." In *Namibia: A Decade of Independence, 1990–2000*. NEPRU Publication no. 7, edited by Henning Melber, 111–124. Windhoek: The Namibian Economic Policy Research Unit, 2000.

Shubin, Vladmir. "Unsung Heroes: The Soviet Military and the Liberation of Southern Africa." In *Cold War in Southern Africa: White Power, Black Liberation*. Cold War History Series no. 24, edited by Sue Onslow, 154–176. New York: Routledge, 2009.

Sigg, Bernard W. "The Children of the Occupation and Colonial Ideology." In *The Algerian War and the French Army, 1954–1962*, edited by Martin S. Alexander, Martin Evans, and John F. V. Keiger, 211–221. Basingstoke, Hampshire, England: Palgrave Macmillan, 2002.

Silvester, Jeremy. "Beasts, Boundaries & Buildings: The Survival & Creation of Pastoral Economies in Southern Namibia, 1915–1935." In *Namibia under South African Rule: Mobility & Containment, 1915–46*, edited by Patricia Hayes, Jeremy Silvester, Marion Wallace, and Wolfram Hartmann, 95–116. Oxford: James Currey; Windhoek: Out of Africa; and Athens: Ohio University Press, 1998.

———, and Jan-Bart Gewald. "Footsteps and Tears: An Introduction to the Construction and Context of the 1918 'Blue Book.'" In Jeremy Silvester and Jan-Bart Gewald, *Words Cannot Be Found: German Colonial Rule in Namibia: An Annotated Reprint of the 1918 Blue Book*, xiii-xxxvii. Leiden: Koninklijke Brill, 2003.

Simon, David, and Richard Moorsom. "Namibia's Political Economy: A Contemporary Perspective." In *Namibia in Perspective*, edited by Gerhard H. K. Tötemeyer, Vezera Kandetu, and Wolfgang Werner, 82–101. Windhoek: Council of Churches in Namibia, 1987.

Simpson, Graeme. "The Politics and Economics of the Armaments Industry in South Africa." In *Society at War: The Militarisation of South Africa*, edited by Jacklyn Cock and Laurie Nathan, 217–231. New York: St. Martin's, 1989.

Singer, J. David. "The Level-of-Analysis Problem in International Relations." In *The International System: Theoretical Essays*, edited by Klaus Knorr and Sidney Verba, 77–92. Princeton: Princeton University Press, 1961.

Smith, Robert B. "Disaffection, Delegitimation, and Consequences: Aggregate Trends for World War II, Korea and Vietnam." In *Public Opinion and the Military Establishment*, edited by Charles C. Moskos, Jr., 221–251. Beverly Hills, Calif.: Sage Publications, 1971.

Smuts, David. "The Interim Government and Human Rights." In *Namibia in Perspective*, edited by Gerhard H. K. Tötemeyer, Vezera Kandetu, and Wolfgang Werner, 219–226. Windhoek: Council of Churches in Namibia, 1987.

Spiegel, Marianne A. "The Namibia Negotiations and the Problem of Neutrality." In *International Mediation in Theory and Practice*, edited by Saadia Touval and I. William Zartman, 111–139. SAIS Papers in International Affairs no. 6. Boulder, Colo.: Westview Press with the Foreign Policy Institute, School of Advanced International Studies, The Johns Hopkins University, 1985.

"Statement by Toivo Herman Ja Toivo Delivered in Open Court on February 1, 1968." In *Erosion of the Rule of Law in South Africa*, 55–60. Geneva: International Commission of Jurists, 1968.

Steenkamp, Philip. "The Churches." In *Namibia's Liberation Struggle: The Two-Edged Sword*, by Colin Leys and John S. Saul et al., 94–114. London: James Curry; Athens: Ohio University Press, 1995.

Steenkamp, Willem. "Politics of Power: The Border War." In *Southern Africa within the African Revolutionary Context: An Overview*, edited by Al. J. Venter, 183–223. Gibralter: Ashhanti Publishing, 1989.

Stoecker, Helmuth, and Peter Sebald. "Enemies of the Colonial Idea." In *Germans in the Tropics: Essays in German Colonial History*, edited by Arthur J. Knoll and Lewis H. Gann, 59–72. Westport, Conn: Greenwood, 1987.

Stora, Benjamin. "The 'Southern' World of the *Pieds Noirs*: References to and Representations of Europeans in Colonial Algeria." In *Settler Colonialism in the Twentieth Century: Projects, Practices, Legacies*, edited by Caroline Elkins and Susan Pedersen, 225–241. New York: Routledge, 2005.

Suret-Canale, Jean. "From Colonization to Independence in French Tropical Africa: The Economic Background." In *The Transfer of Power in Africa: Decolonization, 1940–1960*, edited by Prosser Gifford and William R. Louis, 445–481. New Haven: Yale University Press, 1982.

Tapscott, Chris. "Class Formation and Civil Society in Namibia." In *Contemporary Namibia: The First Landmarks of a Post-Apartheid Society*, edited by Ingolf Diener and Olivier Graefe, 307–325. Windhoek: Gamsberg Macmillan, 2001.

———. "War, Peace & Social Classes." In *Namibia's Liberation Struggle: The Two-Edged Sword*, by Colin Leys and John S. Saul with contributions from Susan Brown et al., 153–170. London: James Currey; Athens: Ohio University Press, 1995.

Thomas, Wolfgang H. "The Economy in Transition to Independence." In *Namibia: Political and Economic Prospects*, edited by Robert I. Rotberg, 41–91. Lexington, Mass.: Lexington Books, 1983.

Toase, Francis. "The South African Army: The Campaign in South West Africa/Namibia since 1966." In *Armed Forces and Modern Counter-Insurgency*, edited by Ian F.W. Beckett and John Pimlott, 190–221. London: Croom Helm, 1985.

Tötemeyer, Gerhard K. H. "The Interim Government and Its Rule: The Legitimacy Crisis." In *Namibia in Perspective*, edited by Gerhard H. K. Tötemeyer, Vezera Kandetu, and Wolfgang Werner, 54–68. Windhoek: Council of Churches in Namibia, 1987.

———. "The Legal Framework and Organisational Requirements." In *Elections in Namibia*, edited by Gerhard K.H. Tötemeyer, Arnold Wehmhömer, and Heribert Weiland, 13–80. Windhoek: Gamsberg Macmillan, 1996.

———, Vezera Kandetu, and Wolfgang Werner. "Introduction," In *Namibia in Perspective*, edited by Gerhard H. K. Tötemeyer, Vezera Kandetu, and Wolfgang Werner, 7–10. Windhoek: Council of Churches in Namibia, 1987.

van Wyk, At J. "South West Africa: Origin of a World Problem." In *History of the South African Department of Foreign Affairs, 1927–1993*, edited by Tom F. Wheeler. 197–221. Johannesburg: The South African Institute of International Affairs, 2005.

Venter, Al J. "The South African–Algerian Connection: Why Algeria?" In *Challenge: Southern Africa within the African Revolutionary Context: An Overview*, edited by Al J. Venter, 31–62. Gibralter: Ashanti Publishing, 1989.

Vermaak, Chris. "South West Africa: The Case for 'Namibia.'" In *The Silent War*, by Reg Shay and Chris Vermaak, 153–189. Salisbury: Galaxie Press, 1971.

Voipio, Rauha. "Contract Work through Ovambo Eyes." In *Namibia: The Last Colony*, edited by Reginald Green, Marja-Liisa Kiljunen, and Kimmo Kiljunen, 112–131. Harlow, England: Longman Group, 1981.

Walker, Eric A. "South Africa and the Empire." In *The Cambridge History of the British Empire. Volume VIII: South Africa, Rhodesia and the High Commission Territories*, edited by Eric A. Walker, 763–787. Second edition. Cambridge: Cambridge University Press, 1963.

Weaver, Tony. "The South African Defence Force in Namibia." In *Society at War: The Militarisation of South Africa*, edited by Jacklyn Cock and Laurie Nathan, 90–102. New York: St. Martin's, 1989.

Weiss, Thomas G., David Cortright. George A. Lopez, and Larry Minear. "Toward a Framework for Analysis." In *Political Gain and Civilian Pain: Humanitarian Impacts of Economic Sanctions*, edited by Thomas G. Weiss, David Cortright, George A. Lopez, and Larry Minear, 35–53. Lanham, Md.: Rowman & Littlefield, 1997.

Werner, Wolfgang. "Agriculture and Land." In *Namibia: A Decade of Independence, 1990–2000*, edited by Henning Melber, 29–48. NEPRU Publication no 7. Windhoek: Namibian Economic Policy Research Unit, 2000.

———. "Promoting Development among Farm Workers: Some Options for Namibia." In *Who Should Own the Land?: Analysis and Views on Land Reform and the Land Question in Namibia and Southern Africa*, edited by Justine Hunter, 19–45. Windhoek: Konrad-Adenauer-Stiftung and Namibia Institute for Democracy, 2004.

Wessels, André. "Afrikaners at War." In *The Boer War: Direction, Experience and Image*, edited by John Gooch, 73–106. London: Frank Cass, 2000.

Woldendorp, Jaap. "The Oil Embargo against South Africa: Effects and Loopholes." *Sanctioning Apartheid*, edited by Robert E. Edgar, 165–180. Trenton, N.J.: Africa World Press, 1990.

Wolfendale, Jessica. "Preventing Torture in Counter-Insurgency Operations." In *Ethics Education for Irregular Warfare*, edited by Don Carrick, James Connelly,

and Paul Robinson, 57–74. Farnham, Surrey, England: Ashgate, 2009.
Wolpe, Howard E. "The Dangers of Globalism." In *African Crisis Areas and U.S. Foreign Policy*, edited by Gerald J. Bender, James S. Coleman, and Richard L. Sklar, 284–290. Berkeley: University of California Press, 1985.
Young, M. Crawford. "The Colonial State and Post-Colonial Crisis." In *Decolonization and African Independence: The Transfer of Power, 1960–1980*, edited by Prosser Gifford and William R. Louis, 1–31. New Haven: Yale University Press, 1988.
Zeller, Joachim "Symbolic Politics: Notes on the German Colonial Culture of Remembrance." In *Genocide in German South-West Africa: The Colonial War of 1904–1908 and Its Aftermath*, edited by Jürgen Zimmerer and Joachim Zeller. Translated and introduced by Edward J. Neather, 231–251. Monmouth, Wales: The Merlin Press, 2003.

Articles in Journals and Yearbooks

Akindele, R. A. "Reflections on the Preoccupation and Conduct of African Diplomacy." *Journal of Modern African Studies* 14, no. 4 (December 1976): 557–576.
"Angolan, South West Freedom Movements to Collaborate." *Contact* 5, no. 16 (9 August 1962): 1.
Arts, Karin. "The Legal Status and Functioning of the United Nations Council of Namibia." *Leiden Journal of International Law* 2, no. 2 (November 1989): 194–208.
Baines, Gary F. "SADF Soldiers' Stories: Review Article." *Journal of Namibian Studies* 5 (2009): 7–25.
_____. "The Saga of South African POWs in Angola, 1975–82." *Scientia Militaria: South African Journal of Military Studies* 40, no. 2 (2012): 102–141.
_____. "South Africa's Vietnam?: Literary History and Cultural Memory of the Border War." *South African Historical Journal* 49 (November 2003): 172–192.
_____. "Vietnam Analogies and Metaphors: The Cultural Codification of South Africa's Border War." *Safundi: The Journal of South African and American Studies* 13, nos. 1–2 (January-April 2012): 73–90.
Barnard, Leo. "Die Gebeure by Cassinga, 4 Mei 1978: 'n Gevallestudie van die Probleme van 'n Militêre Historikus." *Historia* 41, no. 1 (May 1996): 88–99.
_____. "Die Suid-Afrikaanse Lugmag (SALM) se Optrede in die Teaters Angola en Rhodesië (circa 1966–1974) as Aanloop tot die Grensoorlog." *Journal for Contemporary History* 31, no. 3 (December 2006): 74–90.
_____. "The South African Air Force's Transport Aircraft: Acquisition and Utilisation during the Border War." *Journal for Contemporary History* 31, no. 3 (December 2006): 233–250.
Barratt, John. "The Outlook for Namibian Independence: Some Domestic Constraints." *International Affairs Bulletin* 7, no. 1 (1983): 14–24.
Beaumont, Roger. "Small Wars: Definitions and Dimensions." *The Annals of the American Academy of Social and Political Science* 541 (September 1995): 20–35.
Bell, Trevor. "The Impact of Sanctions on South Africa." *Journal of Contemporary African Studies* 12, no. 1 (1993): 1–28.
Bond, Patrick. "Can Reparations for Apartheid Profits Be Won in U.S. Courts?" *Africa Insight* 38, no. 2 (September 2008): 13–25.
Booysen, H. "Prisoner of War Status for South African Citizens or Persons Owing Allegiance to the State." *Strategic Review for Southern Africa* 10, no. 1 (May 1988): 91–105.
_____. "Terrorists, Prisoners of War, and South Africa." *South African Yearbook of International Law* 1 (1975): 14–45.
_____, and G. E. J. Stephan. "Decree No. 1 of the United Nations Council for South West Africa." *South African Yearbook of International Law* 1 (1975): 63–86.
Botha, Christo. "Internal Colonisation and Oppressed Minority?: The Dynamics of Relations between Germans and Afrikaners against the Background of Constructing a Colonial State in Namibia, 1884–1990." *Journal of Namibian Studies* 2 (2007): 7–50.
_____. "South Africa's Total Strategy in the Era of Cold War, Liberation Struggles[,] and the Uneven Transition to Democracy." *Journal of Namibian Studies* 4 (2008): 75–111.
Brzoska, Michael. "Arming South Africa in the Shadow of the UN Arms Embargo." *Defense Analysis* 7, no. 1 (March 1991): 21–38.
Burns, David. "Insurgency as a Struggle for Legitimation: The Case of Southern Africa." *Small Wars and Insurgencies* 5, no. 1 (Spring 1994): 29–62.
Cherry, Janet. "'Just War' and 'Just Means': Was the TRC Wrong about the ANC?" *Transformation* no. 42 (2000): 9–28.
Clark, Roger S. "The International League for Human Rights and South West Africa, 1947–1957: The Human Rights NGO as [a] Catalyst in the International Legal Process." *Human Rights Quarterly* 3, no. 4 (Fall 1981): 101–136.
Claude, Jr., Inis L. "Collective Legitimation as a Political Function of the United Nations." *International Organization* 20, no. 3 (Summer 1966): 367–379.
Coetzee, P. "'n Loopbaan vol Hoogtepunte." *Paratus: Official Magazine of the SADF* 28, no. 3 (March 1978): 6.
Cooper, Allan D. "The Institutionalization of Contract Labour in Namibia." *Journal of Southern African Studies* 25, no. 1 (March 1999): 121–138.
Crowder, Michael. "Tshekedi Khama, Smuts, and South West Africa." *Journal of Modern African Studies* 25, no. 1 (March 1987): 25–42.
Culverson, Donald R. "The Politics of the Anti-Apartheid Movement in the United States, 1969–1986." *Political Science Quarterly* 111, no. 1 (Spring 1996): 127–160.
Dale, Richard. "African Nationalism and Subnationalism in Namibia: The Conflict over Self-Determination, 1945–1971." *Canadian Review of Studies in Nationalism* 15, nos. 1–2 (1988): 25–32.
_____. "The Ambiguities of Self-Determination for South-West Africa, 1919–1939: A Concept or a Symbol of Decolonization?" *Plural Societies* 5, no. 1 (Spring 1974): 29–57.
_____. "A Comparative Reconsideration of the Namibian Bush War, 1966–89." *Small Wars and Insurgencies* 18, no. 2 (June 2007): 196–215.
_____. "Reconfiguring White Ethnic Power in Colonial Africa: The German Community in Namibia, 1923–50." *Nationalism & Ethnic Politics* 7, no. 2 (Summer 2001): 75–94.
_____. "The UN and African Decolonization: UNTAG in Namibia." *TransAfrica Forum* 8, no. 3 (Fall 1991): 31–48.

Dedering, Tilman. "Petitioning Geneva: Transnational Aspects of Protest and Resistance in South West Africa/Namibia after the First World War." *Journal of Southern African Studies* 35, no. 4 (December 2009): 785–801.

de Visser, Lieneke E. "Winning Hearts and Minds in the Namibian Border War." *Scientia Militaria: South African Journal of Military Studies* 39, no. 1 (2011): 85–100.

"Dirty War in Namibia," *Southern Africa Report* 1, no. 1 (June 1985): 12–13.

Dobell, Lauren. "Namibia's Wall of Silence." *Southern Africa Report* 11, no. 4 (July 1996): 30–33.

Dorning, W.A. "A Concise History of the South African Defence Force (1912–1987)." *Militaria: Official Professional Journal of the SADF* 17, no. 2 (1987): 1–23.

Dreyer, Ronald. "Dispute over Walvis Bay: Origins and Implications for Namibian Independence." *African Affairs* 83, no. 333 (February 1984): 497–510.

Dugard, John. "South West Africa and the 'Terrorist Trial.'" *American Journal of International Law* 64, no. 1 (January 1970): 19–41.

du Pisani, André. "Namibia: From Incorporation to Controlled Change." *Journal of Contemporary African Studies* 1, no. 2 (April 1982): 281–305.

———. "Namibia: The Political Economy of Transition." *South Africa International* 15, no. 3 (January 1985): 150–156.

———. "Namibia: The Quest for Legitimacy." *Politeia* 2, no. 1 (1983): 43–51.

du Plessis, T.A.P. "Die Ontwikkeling van die SWA Weermag." *Militaria: Official Professional Journal of the SADF* 13, no. 1 (1983): 28–34.

Dzinesa, Gwinyayi A. "Postconflict Disarmament, Demobilization, and Reintegration of Former Combatants in Southern Africa." *International Studies Perspectives* 8, no. 1 (February 2007): 73–89.

Ellis, Stephen. "The Historical Significance of South Africa's Third Force." *Journal of Southern African Studies* 24, no. 2 (June 1998): 261–299.

Emerson, Rupert. "Colonialism, Political Development, and the UN." *International Organization* 19, no. 3 (Summer 1965): 484–503.

Erasmus, Gerhard. "Mandates, Military Service and Multiple Choice." *South African Yearbook of International Law* 11 (1985–1986): 115–137.

Evans, Graham. "Walvis Bay: South Africa, Namibia[,] and the Question of Sovereignty." *International Affairs* 66, no. 3 (July 1990): 559–568.

Evans, Luther H. "Are 'C' Mandates Veiled Annexations?" *The Southwestern Political and Social Science Quarterly* 7, no. 4 (March 1927): 381–400.

Foltz, William J. "United States Policy toward Southern Africa: Economic and Strategic Constraints." *Political Science Quarterly* 92, no. 1 (Spring 1977): 47–64.

Gewald, Jan-Bart. "Who Killed Clemens Kapuuo?" *Journal of Southern African Studies* 30, no. 3 (September 2004): 559–576.

Gordon, Robert J. "Anthropology in the Service of Apartheid." *Southern Africa Report* 4, no. 3 (December 1988): 22–25.

———. "The Impact of the Second World War on Namibia." *Journal of Southern African Studies* 19, no. 1 (March 1993): 152–161.

Grundlingh, Albert M. "The King's Afrikaners?: Enlistment and Ethnic Identity in the Union of South Africa's Defence Force during the Second World War, 1939–45." *Journal of African History* 40, no. 3 (1999): 351–365.

Grundy, Kenneth W. "The Social Costs of Armed Struggle in Southern Africa." *Armed Forces and Society* 7, no. 3 (Spring 1981): 445–466.

Harpvoken, Kristian B. "Landmines in Southern Africa: Regional Initiatives for Clearance and Control." *Contemporary Security Policy* 18, no. 1 (April 1977): 83–108.

Harris, Verne, "'They Should Have Destroyed More': The Destruction of Public Records by the South African State in the Final Years of Apartheid." *Transformation* 42 (2000): 29–46.

Heitman, Helmoed-Römer. "Equipment of the Border War." *Journal for Contemporary History* 31, no. 3 (December 2006): 91–111.

Henk, Dan. "The Botswana Defense Force and the War against Poachers in Southern Africa." *Small Wars and Insurgencies* 16, no. 2 (June 2005): 170–191.

Henriksen, Thomas H. "Portugal in Africa: Comparative Notes on Counterinsurgency." *Orbis* 21, no. 2 (Summer 1977): 395–412.

Henshaw, Peter. "Britain and South Africa at the United Nations: 'South West Africa,' Treatment of Indians' and 'Race Conflict,' 1946–1961." *South African Historical Journal* 31 (November 1994): 80–102.

Hough, Michael. "'Legitimacy' and 'Recognition' in Revolutionary Warfare." Institute of Strategic Studies, University of Pretoria, *Strategic Review* (December 1984): 14–19.

Howard, Lise M. "UN Peace Implementation in Namibia: The Causes of Success." *International Peacekeeping* 9, no. 1 (Spring 2002): 99–132.

Hyslop, Jonathan. "The Invention of the Concentration Camp: Cuba, Southern Africa[,] and the Philippines, 1896–1907." *South African Historical Journal* 63, no. 2 (June 2011): 251–276.

Ibrahim, Azeem. "Conceptualisation of Guerrilla Warfare." *Small Wars and Insurgencies* 15, no. 3 (Winter 2004): 112–124.

"Information Newsletter: Meeting on South West Africa/Namibia in Geneva, 7–14 January 1981." Supplement to the *South Africa Digest*, 6 February 1981: [2]-[3].

Jackson, Robert H., and Carl G. Rosberg. "Why Africa's Weak States Persist: The Empirical and the Juridical in Statehood." *World Politics* 35, no. 1 (October 1982): 1–24.

Jaques, François. "The Decolonization of French-Speaking Territories in Africa as Reflected in the South African Press: A Case Study of Algeria and the Belgian Congo." *Journal of European Studies* 36, no. 1 (March 2006): 36–41.

Johnson, David. "The South West African Issue in International Law." *Optima* 11, no. 3 (September 1961): 118–124.

Johnston, Alexander M. "Self-Determination in Comparative Perspective: Northern Ireland and South Africa." *Politikon: The South African Journal of Political Science* 17, no. 2 (December 1990): 5–22.

Jordaan, Everet. "The Role of South African Armour in South West Africa/Namibia and Angola, 1975–1989." *Journal for Contemporary History* 31, no. 3 (December 2006): 161–186.

Karns, Margaret P. "Ad Hoc Multilateral Diplomacy: The United States, the Contact Group, and Namibia." *International Organization* 31, no. 1 (Winter 1987): 93–123.

Kay, David A. "The Impact of African States on the United Nations." *International Organization* 23, no. 1 (Winter 1969): 20–47.

Kebonanang, Boammaruri B. "The History of the Herero in Mahalapye, Central District: 1922–1984." *Botswana Notes and Records* 21 (1989): 43–60.

Kenton, Daniel R., and Roni du Preez. "Namibian-De Beers State-Firm Relations: Cooperation and Conflict." *Journal of Southern African Studies* 23, no. 4 (December 1997): 585–613.

Levy, Marc A. "Mediation of Prisoners' Dilemma Conflicts and the Importance of the Cooperation Threshold: The Case of Namibia." *Journal of Conflict Resolution* 29, no. 4 (December 1985): 581–603.

Leys, Colin, and John S. Saul. "Liberation with Democracy?: The Swapo Crisis of 1976." *Journal of Southern African Studies* 20, no. 1 (March 1994): 123–147.

Lomperis, Timothy. "Vietnam's Offspring: The Lesson of Legitimacy." *Conflict Quarterly* 6, no. 1 (Winter 1986): 18–33.

Lord, R[ichard] S. "SAAF Fighter Involvement in the Border War, 1965–1988." *Journal for Contemporary History* 31, no. 3 (December 2006): 251–266.

Louw, Chris. "Stryd Begin vir die Hart van 'n Nuwe Namibia." *Die Suid Afrikaan* 20 (April 1989): 10–18 and 25.

Lubbe, Henriëtte J. "The Myth of 'Black Peril': *Die Burger* and the 1929 Election." *South African Historical Journal* 37 (November 1997): 107–132.

Maechling, Jr., Charles. "Insurgency and Counterinsurgency: The Role of Strategic Theory." *Parameters: Journal of the U.S. Army War College* 14, no. 3 (Autumn 1984): 32–41.

Marks, Thomas A. "Counterinsurgency in the Age of Globalism." *Journal of Conflict Studies* 27, no. 1 (Summer 2007): 22–29.

McLaughlin, Peter. "Victims as Defenders: African Troops in the Rhodesian Defence System[,] 1890–1980. *Small Wars and Insurgencies* 2, no. 2 (August 1991): 240–275.

Meiring, G[eorg] L. "Current SWAPO Activity in South West Africa." Institute of Strategic Studies, University of Pretoria, *Strategic Review* (June 1985): 8–18.

Melber, Henning. "One Namibia, One Nation?: The Caprivi as Contested Territory." *Journal of Contemporary African Studies* 27, no. 4 (October 2009): 463–481.

Metz, Steven K. "Pretoria's 'Total Strategy' and Low-Intensity Warfare in Southern Africa." *Comparative Strategy* 6, no. 4 (1987): 437–469.

Mittelman, James H. "Collective Decolonisation and the U.N. Committee of 24." *Journal of Modern African Studies* 14, no. 1 (March 1976): 41–64.

Moore, Dermot M. "The South African Air Force in Korea: An Assessment." *Military History Journal* 6, no 3 (June 1984): 88–94.

Munger, Edwin S. "South-West Africa: Evolution or Revolution? (ESM-6–61)." *American Universities Field Staff Reports Service*, Central & Southern Africa Series, 9, no. 6 (July 1961): 1–[16].

"Namibia: Prisoner-of-War Status." *Focus on Political Repression in Southern Africa* 41 (July-August 1982): 1 and 4.

O'Brien, Kevin A. "Special Forces for Counter-Revolutionary Warfare: The South African Case." *Small Wars and Insurgencies* 12, no. 2 (Summer 2001): 79–109.

Osieke, Ebere. "Admission to Membership in International Organizations: The Case of Namibia." *The British Yearbook of International Law* 51 (1980): 189–229.

Pandya, Paresh. "Foreign Support to ZANU and ZANLA during the Rhodesian War." Institute of Strategic Studies, University of Pretoria, *Strategic Review* (November 1987): 1–31.

Pearson, Patrick "The Rehoboth Rebellion," *Working Papers in Southern African Studies* 2 (1981): 31–51.

"Police Strength in S.-W. Africa." *The Forum* 20 May 1939: 11.

Pomerance, Michla. "Methods of Self-Determination and the Argument of 'Primitiveness.'" *The Canadian Yearbook of International Law* 12 (1974): 38–66.

"POW Interlude in Angola." *Paratus: Official Magazine of the SADF* 29, no. 10 (October 1978): 10–12.

Powelson, John P. "The Balance Sheet on Multinational Corporations in Less Developed Countries." *Cultures et Développement*, 9, no. 3 (1977): 413–432.

Preston, Rosemary. "Integrating Fighters after War: Reflections on the Namibian Experience, 1989–1993." *Journal of Southern African Studies* 23, no. 3 (September 1997): 453–472.

"Prisoners of War." *Focus on Political Repression in Southern Africa* 42 (September-October 1982): 10.

Rheinallt Jones, John D. "The Director's Letter: The South West Africa Question." *Race Relations News* 8, no. 5 (May 1946): 37–39.

Roberts, Alun R. "Namibia: What They Didn't Tell Us." *Africa Report* 34, no. 4 (July-August 1989): 61–62.

Rodman, Kenneth A. "Public and Private Sanctions against South Africa." *Political Science Quarterly* 109, no. 2 (Summer 1994): 313–334.

Rogerson, Christian M. "A Future 'University of Namibia?': The Rôle of the United Nations Institute for Namibia." *Journal of Modern African Studies* 18, no. 4 (December 1980): 675–683.

"Die S.A. Polisiester vir Voortreflike Diens." *SARP* 7, no. 10 (August, 1971): 26–27.

"SADF Murder." *Focus on Political Repression in Southern Africa* 67 (November-December 1986): 10.

Saul, John S., and Colin Leys. "Lubango and After: 'Forgotten History' as Politics in Contemporary Namibia. *Journal of Southern African Studies* 29, no. 2 (June 2003): 335–353.

Saunders, Christopher C. "Michael Scott and Namibia." *African Historical Review* 39, no. 2 (December 2007): 25–40.

———. "Namibian Solidarity: British Support for Namibian Independence." *Journal of Southern African Studies* 35, no. 2 (June 2009): 437–454.

Saxena, S[uresh] C. "[The] Role of the U.N. Council for Namibia." *Africa Quarterly* 17, no. 3 (January 1978): 5–31.

Scholtz, Leopold. "The Namibian Border War: An Appraisal of the South African Strategy," *Scientia Militaria: South African Journal of Military Studies* 34, no. 1 (2006): 19–48.

———. "The Standard of Research on the Battle of Cuito Cuanavale, 1987–1988." *Scientia Militaria: South African Journal of Military Studies* 39, no. 1 (2011): 115–137.

Seegers, Annette. "If Only….The Ongoing Search for Method in Counter-Insurgency" (review article). *Journal of Contemporary African Studie*s 8–9, nos. 1–2 (1989–1990): 203–224.

Shafer, D. Michael. "The Unlearned Lessons of Counterinsurgency." *Political Science Quarterly* 103, no. 1 (Spring 1988): 57–80.

"The Shape of Things" (editorial). *The Nation* 163, no. 20 (16 November 1946): 541–543.

"Shifidi Lilling: Appeal Heard." *Focus on Political Repres-*

sion in *Southern Africa* 79 (November-December 1988): 3.
Shugart, Matthew S. "Guerrillas and Elections: An Institutionalist Perspective on the Costs of Conflict and Competition." *International Studies Quarterly* 36, no. 2 (June 1992): 121–152.
Simon, David. "Strategic Territory and Territorial Strategy: The Geopolitics of Walvis Bay's Reintegration into Namibia." *Political Geography* 15, no. 21 (April 1996): 193–219.
Smith, Tony. "A Comparative Study of French and British Decolonization." *Comparative Studies in Society and History* 20, no. 1 (January 1978): 70–102.
Sole, Donald. "South African Foreign Policy Assumptions and Objectives from Hertzog to De Klerk." *South African Journal of International Affairs* 2, no. 1 (Summer 1994): 104–113.
"Some Observations Regarding the Settlement Plan for Namibia." Institute for Strategic Studies, University of Pretoria, *Bulletin* 2/89 (March 1989): 1–11.
South African Defense Force. Military Information Bureau. "The War in SWA [South West Africa]/N[amibia]." Institute for Strategic Studies, University of Pretoria, *Bulletin*, 4/87 (24 September 1987): 1–11.
"South African Experiment." *The Economist* 151, no. 5387 (23 November 1946): 820–821.
"South Africa's Delegation to World Body." *South African Scope* (New York: South African Information Service), December 1974: 4–5.
Sparks, Donald L. "Namibia's Coastal and Marine Development Potential." *African Affairs* 83, no. 333 (October 1984): 477–496.
Starry, Donn A. "La Guerre Révolutionaire." *Military Review* 47, no. 2 (February 1967): 61–70.
Stultz, Newell M. "[The] Evolution of the United Nations Anti-Apartheid Regime." *Human Rights Quarterly* 13, no. 1 (February 1991): 1–23.
Sullivan, David, and Stephen Majeski. "A Methodology for the Study of Historical Counterfactuals." *International Studies Quarterly*, 42, no. 1 (March 1988): 79–108.
Suy, Erik "The Status of Observers in International Organizations." *Recueil des Cours: Collected Courses of the Hague Academy of International Law* 160 (1978, part 2): 75–180.
Tapscott, Chris. "Namibia: A Class Act?" *Southern African Report* 7, no. 2 (November 1991): 3–6.
"Treacherous Crossing: Namibian Independence Debacle." *Southern Africa Report* 5, no. 1 (July 1989): 15–17
van der Schiff, Christa. "Considerations of International Humanitarian Law in [the] Sentencing of Members of SWAPO – *S v Sagarius 1983 1 SA 833 (SWA)*." *South African Yearbook of International Law* 9 (1983): 112–116.
van Deventer, André, and Philip Nel, "The State and 'Die Volk' versus Communism, 1922–1941," *Politikon: The South African Journal of Political Science* 17, no. 2 (December 1990): 64–81.
Visser, Deon. "Marrying Sparta and Athens: The South African Military Academy and Task-Orientated Junior Officer Development in Peace and War, 1950–2001." *Journal for Contemporary History* 27, no. 3 (December 2002): 184–198.
Visser, Wessel. "The Production of Literature on the 'Red Peril' and 'Total Onslaught' in Twentieth-Century South Africa." *Historia* 49, no. 2 (November 2004): 105–128.
Vivelo, Frank R. "The Entry of the Herero into Botswana." *Botswana Notes and Records* 8 (1976): 39–46.
Weatherford, M. Stephen. "Measuring Political Legitimacy." *American Political Science Review* 86, no. 1 (March 1992): 149–166.
Welch, Jr., Richard E. "American Atrocities in the Philippines: The Indictment and the Response." *Pacific Historical Review* 43, no. 2 (May 1974): 233–253.
Werner, Wolfgang. "A Brief History of Land Dispossession in Namibia." *Journal of Southern African Studies* 19, no. 1 (March 1993): 135–146.
Wessels, André. "The South African Navy during the Years of Conflict in Southern Africa, 1966–1989." *Journal for Contemporary History* 31, no. 3 (December 2006): 283–303.
"What Prize [sic] Unity?" *South West Africa Today* (Dar es Salaam: SWAPO Information Service), no volume or number (June 1964), [1].
Wheeler, Douglas L. "African Elements in Portugal's Armies in Africa (1961–1974)." *Armed Forces and Society* 2, no. 2 (February 1976): 233–250.
Wright, Joanne. "PIRA [Provisional IRA] Propaganda: The Construction of Legitimacy," *Conflict Quarterly* 10, 3 (Summer 1990): 24–41

Conference and Other Papers

Baines, Gary F. "Perpetuating a Culture of Impunity: War Crimes, Indemnity[,] and Amnesia in Namibia and South Africa." Unpublished draft manuscript, dated 1 May 2012.
Cefkin, J. Leo. "International Legitimation and Southern Africa: Principles and Practice." Paper presented to the sixty-fourth annual meeting of the American Political Science Association, Washington, D.C., 2-7 September 1968.
Fourie, Deon F. S. "The Strategic Significance of South West Africa." Paper presented to the course South West Africa: Problems and Alternatives, Summer School, University of Cape Town, Rondebosch, 10–14 February 1975.
Gordon, Robert J. "Anthropology on High: The South West Africa Case at the World Court." Unpublished manuscript, dated 6 March 2000.
International Defence and Aid Fund for Southern Africa. Research, Information, and Publication Department. "Prisoners of War in Namibia: The Capture and Treatment of Combatants of the People's Liberation Army of Namibia (PLAN) and Other Prisoners-of-War." RI/COM II/002E. No. 010. International Conference in Solidarity with the Frontline States, Lisbon, 25–27 March 1983.
Sanders, Deborah A. "Problems and Prospects for the National Liberation Movement: The Dilemma of SWAPO in Namibia." Paper presented to the twenty-fifth annual meeting of the African Studies Association, Washington, D.C., 4–7 November 1983.
Sparks, Donald L. "Namibia's Economy at Independence." Paper presented to the twenty-third annual meeting of the African Studies Association, Philadelphia, 15–18 October 1980.
Tötemeyer, Gerhard K. H. "Bestuursontwikkelinge in Suidwes-Afrika sedert die Bestaan as Mandaatsgebied tot met die Odendaal-Verslag: 'n Oorsig." Paper presented to the course South West Africa: Problems and Alternatives, Summer School, University of Cape Town, Rondebosch, 10–14 February 1975.
Warwick, Rodney C. "The South African Military under Verwoerd: SADF Popularisation among the White Community, 1960–66." Paper presented to the biennial

conference of the South African Historical Society, Cape Town, 29 June 2005.

Theses and Dissertations

Addison, Graeme E. "Censorship of the Press in South Africa during the Angolan War: A Case Study in News Manipulation and Suppression." M.A. thesis, Rhodes University, 1980.

Alexander, Edward G. M. "The Cassinga Raid." M.A. thesis, University of South Africa, 2003.

Andersen, Ann-Charlotte. "Koevoet: A Brief History." B.A. (Hons.) thesis, University of Cape Town, 1997.

Ballard, Jr., Brook B. "South West Africa, 1945–50: Union Province or United Nations Trust Territory." M.A. thesis, University of Chicago, 1955.

Barnett, Baron F. "Southern African Student Exiles: The Function of Politics." Ph.D. dissertation, Yale University, 1969.

Bennett, Peter C. "South West Africa/Namibia Issues Related to Political Independence." M.A. thesis, University of Cape Town, 1983.

Biehl, Amy. "Chester Crocker and the Negotiations for Namibian Independence: The Role of the Individual in Recent American Foreign Policy." Senior thesis, Stanford University, 1989.

Bishop, Fred E. "Apartheid in Theory and Practice, 1948–1959." Senior thesis, Princeton University, 1961.

Boulter, Roger S. "F[rans] C[hristiaan] Erasmus and the Politics of South African Defence, 1948–1959." Ph.D. dissertation, Rhodes University, 1997.

Bradford, Robert L. "The Origin and Concession of the League of Nations Class 'C' Mandate for South West Africa and the Fulfillment of the Sacred Trust, 1919–1939." Ph.D. dissertation, Yale University, 1965.

Brüggeman, Bern. "The United Nations Council for Namibia with Especial Emphasis on Its Decree No. 1." LL.M. thesis, University of Cape Town, 1992.

Burger, Frederik J. "Teeninsurgensie in Namibië: Die Rol van die Polisie." M.A. thesis, University of South Africa, 1992.

Callister, Graeme. "Compliance, Compulsion[,] and Contest: Aspects of Military Conscription in South Africa, 1952–1992." M.A. thesis, Stellenbosch University, 2007.

Chang, King-yuh. "The United Nations and Decolonization, 1960–1968: The Role of the Committee of Twenty-Four." Ph.D. dissertation, Columbia University, 1971.

Correia, Paulo E. S. L. de F. "Political Relations between Portugal and South Africa from the End of the Second World War until 1974." D.Litt. et Phil. dissertation, University of Johannesburg, 2007.

Crocker, Sally E. "South West Africa: A Test Case for the International Trusteeship System of the United Nations." Senior honors thesis, Radcliffe College, 1954.

Dale, Richard. "The Evolution of the South West African Dispute before the United Nations, 1945–1950." Ph.D. dissertation, Princeton University, 1962.

Devraun, L. Joan D. "South African Foreign Relations with Angola, 1975–1988: A Structural Perspective." M.A. thesis, University of Cape Town, 1997.

Dowd, Herbert W. "Non-White Land and Labor Policies in South West Africa from 1918 to 1948." Ph.D. dissertation, Tufts University, The Fletcher School of Law and Diplomacy, 1954.

Eils, Robert C. "The German Colonial Scandals, 1890–1900." M.A. thesis, University of Wisconsin–Madison, 1977.

El-Said, Mahmoud F. "The United Nations and Namibia: Implications for Institutional Development of the Organization and the Creation of Norms of International Behavior." Ph.D. dissertation, City University of New York, 1986.

Fikeni, Somadoda. "Exile and Return: The Politics of Namibia's 'Returnees.'" M.A. thesis, Queen's University, 1992.

Fokkens, Andreas M. "The Role and Application of the Union Defence Force in the Suppression of Internal Unrest." M.Mil. thesis, Stellenbosch University, 2006.

Ford, Christopher. "South African Foreign Policy since 1965: The Cases of Rhodesia and Namibia." D.Phil. dissertation, University of Oxford, 1991.

Gaglione, Anthony G. "Anti-Colonialism and the South West Africa Case: A Study in Majoritarianism at the United Nations." Ph.D. dissertation, Rutgers University, 1971.

Geingob, Hage G. "State Formation in Namibia: Promoting Democracy and Good Governance." Ph.D. dissertation, University of Leeds, 2004.

Grofe, Jan. "Shadows of the Past: Chances and Problems for the Herero in Claiming Reparations from Multinationals for Past Human Rights Violations." LL.M. thesis, University of the Western Cape, 2002.

Jahanbani, Mansour E. "The Question of South-West Africa." M.A. thesis, Columbia University, 1956.

John, Nerys. "South African Intervention in the Angolan Civil War, 1975–1976: Motivations and Implications." M.A. thesis, University of Cape Town, 2002.

Jones, Robert E. "Anti-Colonialism at the United Nations: The Origin and Policy of the United Nations Special Committee on Colonialism, 1960–1967." Ph.D. dissertation, University of Notre Dame, 1974.

Kangas, Lari. "Namibian Democracy: Consolidated?" M.A. thesis, Stellenbosch University, 2006.

Kajavivi, Peter H. "The Rise of Nationalism in Namibia and Its International Dimensions." D.Phil. dissertation, University of Oxford, 1986.

Knight, Casimir S. B. "The British Churches and the Namibian Struggle." M.A. thesis, Queen's University, 1991.

Lamb, Guy. "Civil Supremacy of the Military in Namibia: An Evolutionary Perspective." M. Soc. Sci. thesis, University of Cape Town, 1998.

Livhuwani, Nengovhela J. "The Role Played by the People's Liberation Army of Namibia (PLAN) during the Namibian Struggle, 1978 to 1989." M.A. thesis, Rand Afrikaans University, 1999.

Makkawi, Khalil. "The Fourth Committee of the United Nations General Assembly." Ph.D. dissertation, Columbia University, 1968.

McCrary, Michael S. "Guerrilla Warfare in Namibia and Associated Implications for External Military Involvement." M.A. thesis, [U.S.] Naval Postgraduate School, 1979.

Mei, Ko-Wang. "The Theory and Practice of Modern Guerrilla Warfare." Ph.D. dissertation, Michigan State University, 1965.

Moukambi, Victor. "Relations between France and South Africa with Special Reference to Military Matters, 1960–1990." D.Phil. dissertation, Stellenbosch University, 2008.

Mukumbi wa Nyembo, Jules. "The Assistance Given to SWAPO by Certain African Countries and Organisations, 1960–1985." B.A. (Hons.) thesis, University of Cape Town, 2002.

Mushelenga, Samuel A.P. "Foreign Policy-Making in Namibia: The Dynamics of the Smallness of a State." M.A. thesis, University of South Africa, 2008.

Nathan, Laurence. "Force of Arms, Force of Conscience: A Study of the Militarisation, the Military, and the Anti-Apartheid War Resistance Movement in South Africa, 1970–1988." M.Phil. thesis, University of Bradford, 1990.

Phillips, Merran W. "The End Conscription Campaign, 1983–1988: A Study of White Extra-Parliamentary Opposition to Apartheid." M.A. thesis, University of South Africa, 2002.

Riveles, Susanne. "Human Rights as a Political Catalyst in South African Policy toward Namibia" Ph.D. dissertation, Howard University, 1991.

Schrank, Gilbert I. "German South West Africa: Social and Economic Aspects of Its History, 1884–1915." Ph.D. dissertation, New York University, 1974.

Schüring, Esther. "'History Obliges': The Real Motivations behind German Aid Flows in the Case of Namibia." M.A.L.D. thesis, Tufts University, Fletcher School of Law and Diplomacy, 2004.

Sieff, Michelle. "Reconciling Order and Justice?: Dealing with the Past in Post-Conflict States." Ph.D. dissertation, Columbia University, 2002.

Small, Alden C. "The United Nations and South West Africa: A Study in Parliamentary Diplomacy." Ph.D. dissertation, Tufts University, The Fletcher School of Law and Diplomacy, 1970.

Stone, David F. "Namibia 1979: Another Angola?" M.A. thesis [U.S.] Naval Postgraduate School, 1979.

Stumpf, Harry P. "South West Africa: The Question of Its Incorporation into the Union of South Africa." M.A. thesis, George Washington University, 1958.

van der Merwe, Paul S. "Die Ontwikkeling van Selfbestuur in Suidwes-Afrika, 1919–1960." M.A. thesis, University of South Africa, 1963.

van Wyk, Martha S. "The 1963 United States Arms Embargo against South Africa: Institution and Implementation." M.A. thesis, University of Pretoria, 1998.

———. "The 1977 United States Arms Embargo against South Africa: Institution and Implementation to 1997." D.Phil. dissertation, University of Pretoria, 2004.

Velthuizen, Andreas G. "Applying Military Force for Political Ends: South Africa in South-Western Africa, 1987–1988." M.A. thesis, University of South Africa, 1994.

Wallenkampf, Arnold V. "The Herero Rebellion in South West Africa, 1904–1906: A Study in German Colonialism." Ph.D. dissertation, University of California, Los Angeles, 1969.

Warwick, Rodney C. "White South Africa and Defence, 1960–1968: Militarization, Threat Perception, and Counter Strategies." Ph.D. dissertation, University of Cape Town, 2009.

Williams, Christian A. "Exile History: An Ethnography of the SWAPO Camps and the Namibian Nation." Ph.D. dissertation, University of Michigan, 2009.

Index

Abbas, Ferhat 112
Abernathy, David B. 3
Abrahams, Kenneth 84
Ad Hoc Committee on South West Africa 48
Addison, Graeme N. 66
Administrator-General of South West Africa 46, 82, 104, 106
Administrator of South West Africa 26, 38, 40–42, 46, 47, 50, 92
Advisory Council of South West Africa 26
advocacy networks 52
aerial photography/reconnaissance/surveillance 65, 78, 100
Afghanistan 103, 119, 126
Åfreds, Johanna 113
Africa Bureau 30
African Communications Project 108
African farm workers 117
African farmers 117
African majority rule 71, 127, 131
African majority-ruled states 128
African National Congress of South Africa 25, 59, 71, 79, 88, 101, 115
African protonationalism 33
African soldiers 125
African subnationalism 48
African Union 120
African veterans of Namibia 98
African workers 126
Afrikaner civil-military tradition 95
Afrikaner civil religion 17
Afrikaner community in Namibia 122
Afrikaner community in South Africa 98, 121, 122
Afrikaner diaspora in Namibia 71, 72
Afrikaner nationalism 20
Afrikaner political culture 96
Afro-American community 33, 34
Afro-Asian Conference 28
Afro-Asian Peoples Solidarity Organization 4

Ahtissaari, Martti 36, 82, 90, 106, 109
Al-Qaida 88
Alexander, Edward G. 105
Algeria 35, 38, 53, 70, 76, 84, 88, 99–101, 112, 115, 122, 126, 127
Algerian Liberation Front 97
Algerian War 15, 72, 97, 119
Alien Tort Claims Act 113, 114
Alkindele, R. A. 3
Allen, H. J. 40
American Council on African Affairs 34
American Indians 74
American lobbyists and public relations firms 52
Amporo, Edward 97
analytic reasoning 125
Anderson, George 20
Anglin, Douglas G. 90
Anglo-Boer Wars 95, 104, 122
Angola 4, 13, 14, 17, 23, 24, 35, 47–49, 55, 58, 60, 64–68, 71, 73, 77–83, 85, 86, 88–91, 94, 96, 100, 101, 104, 105, 107, 108, 115, 116, 119, 120, 122, 124, 126, 128, 130, 131
Angra Pequena 67
Ansprenger, Franz 55
anti-aircraft weaponry 65
anti-apartheid campaign 23
anti-apartheid movement 58, 61, 125
anti-apartheid non-governmental organizations 52, 57
anti-colonial actions 56
anti-colonial bloc 28
anti-colonial catchwords 28
anti-colonial ideas 28
anti-colonial mission 29
Anti-Colonial Resistance and the Liberation Struggle Project of Namibia 1
anti-colonial rhetoric 34, 56
anti-colonial slogans 28
anti-colonial states 28, 56

anti-colonial talents 28
anti-colonial themes 29
anti-colonialism 18, 31
anti-communism 34, 51, 52, 121, 129
anticipatory sovereignty 22
apartheid 4, 19, 31, 35, 38, 43, 45, 46, 59, 66, 69, 77, 95, 98, 96, 112, 114, 115, 130, 131; by proxy 35; war machine 54
Appeals Court of South Africa 97
armed decolonization 2, 15
armed forces: German 19; United States 126
armed insurgency 34
armed liberation struggle 2
armed liberation war 2
armed resistance/revolution 75
armed struggle 73
arms: boycotts/embargoes/sanctions 2, 63, 64, 67, 100, 131
Army of National Liberation of Algeria 53
Ashipala, Danger 85
atrocities 60, 74, 102
Auala, Leonard 30

Baines, Gary F. 3, 15, 60, 87, 104, 105
Ballard, Sebastian 76, 77
Bamangwato people 33
Bantustans 19, 21, 44, 86
Bar Council of Namibia 103
Barnard, Leo 60
Barnett, Baron F. 14
Barratt, John 31
Basarwa/Bushmen/San 96, 97, 103, 119, 127
bases 47, 60, 65, 71, 77, 78–84, 94, 101, 104, 106, 109, 118
Basson, Nico 108
Basson, Wouter 104
Batista, Fulgencio 78
Bauer, Gretchen 57
Beaufre, André 100–102
Beaumont, Roger 24

195

Bechuanaland Protectorate 33, 34, 47
Beckman, Ulla 61
Belasco, Amy 72
belated decolonization 1
Belgium 35
Bell, Trevor 4
Bellegrade, Dantès 50
Berat, Lynn 47, 55
Berlin airlift 51
Berridge, Geoffrey R. 51
Beukes, Jacobus 27
Binga, Eric 97
Bishop, Fred E. 38
black peril (*swart gevaar*) on German rule in South West Africa 121, 129
Blue Book 26, 103
Bonaparte, Napoleon 54
Bondelswart rebellion 50, 93
Bondelswarts group of Nama people 33
Bonus Army of the United States 119
border infiltration 100
border war 2
Boston massacre 33
Botha, Christo 109
Botha, Louis 26, 96
Botha, M.C. 44
Botha, Pieter W. 51, 72, 100, 121, 130
Botha, Pik 107
Botswana 17, 21, 30, 33, 37, 71, 74, 75, 78–80, 96, 122
Botswana Defense Force 97
Bradford, Robert L. 17
Branch, Daniel 122
Brazil 48, 115, 118
British Anti-Slavery Society 48
British Army Military Advisory Team 119
British Council of Churches 58, 104
Brüggeman, Bern 66
Buffer/perimeter territories/zone 51, 71, 100, 130
Bull, Hedley 25
Burns, David 16
Burundi 120
bush war 2, 72, 98

Cahama, Angola 65
Callister, Graeme 3, 126
Cambodia 120
Campbell, Horace 5
Canada 17, 50, 61, 66, 90, 98
Cape Province 19, 47, 67–69, 117
Cape Verde islands 60
Caprivi Zipfel or Strip 47, 71, 83, 88, 93, 96, 111
Carter, Gwendolen M. 37
Cassinga, Angola 60, 83, 100, 104, 105, 115
Castro, Fidel 78
Catholic Institute of International Relations 59
Cefkin, J. Leo 16
Central Intelligence Agency 88, 101

Chand, Prem 109
Cherry, Janet 59
Chile 68
China 75, 82, 84, 89, 115, 123
Chobe River 77
Church Action on Namibia 104
Churchill, Winston L.S. 39
civil liberties 17
civil service: of Germany 70; of Namibia 120; of South Africa 46, 127
Civilian Cooperation Bureau of South Africa 108, 109
Clapham, Christopher 25
Clark, Roger S. 27
Claude, Inis L., Jr. 16
Clayton, Anthony 85
Cold War 25, 52, 60, 63, 115, 124, 125, 129
Cole, Tony 4
collective decolonization 32
collective legitimation 16
colonial consensus 38
colonial guilt lie 39
colonial idea 15
colonial spoils 73
colonial wars 2
colonialism 1, 3, 28, 70, 129
Commission of Inquiry into South West Africa Affairs 48
Commissioner-General for the Indigenous Peoples of South West Africa 48, 49
Commonwealth of Nations 62, 63, 94, 114, 115
Commonwealth of Nations Secretariat 114
Communist Party of Namibia 51
competing narratives 113
competing national histories 113
conscience constituency 4
conscientious objection 95, 98
conscription 95, 97, 126
constitutive legitimacy 17, 18
constructive engagement 124
contestation over legitimacy 17
contiguous colonialism 126
contract labor 68, 69, 84
controlled change 45
conventional warfare 14, 90, 100, 105, 128
Cook, Al 59
Cooper, Allan D. 4
Copson, Raymond 24
Corporal's war 23
Cortright, David 3
Council of Churches in Namibia 57, 58
counterfactuals 123, 130
countergovernments 25
counterideology 5, 127, 129
counterinsurgency 1, 14, 24, 34, 59, 60, 64–66, 74, 83, 87, 93, 94, 96, 97, 100–103, 105, 106, 126, 128; doctrine 100, 102, 130; German campaign 100, 113; policy 126, 130

counter-narrative 113
counter-revolutionary warfare 102
counter-sanctions 53
counter-state 124, 130
Covenant of the League of Nations 39
Crawford, Neta C. 2, 4, 15, 39, 53, 121, 123
Crocker, Chester A. 79, 124
Cronje, Gillian 21
Cronje, Suzanne 21
cross-border operations 104, 105
cross-case comparisons 3
Cuba 1, 13, 14, 23, 65, 78–85, 87–90, 104, 105, 115, 122, 128
Cuito Cuanavale, Angola 65
culture of entitlement 120
culture of impunity 104
culture of secrecy 130
Culverson, Donald R. 4
cutline 83, 104

Dale, Richard 38
Davidson, Alex 111
Davies, Joanne E. 3, 125
death penalty 47, 88
de Beer, David 66
Declaration on Principles of International Law 87
Declaration on the Granting of Independence to Colonial Countries and Peoples 87
decolonization 1–5, 14, 15, 18, 25, 29, 31, 32, 35, 38, 41, 44–46, 56, 61, 70, 71, 94, 105, 117, 121–126, 128, 130
decolonization wars 2, 5, 113, 125, 127
Dedering, Tilman 27
Defense Act 97, 98, 104
de Gaulle, Charles 63
de Kok, Eugene 85
delayed decolonization 15
deligitimation/delegitimization 16, 25, 34, 35, 41, 42, 55
demilitarization 79–81
demobilization 106, 107, 119
democracy 111
Democratic Turnhalle Alliance of South West Africa 103, 107, 108
Denmark 60
deportation of missionaries from Namibia 57
destabilization 71, 122
destruction of church properties in Namibia 57
detainees 108
Deutsche Kolonial Gesellschaft für Süd-west Afrika 70
development brigades in Namibia 120
Development of Self-Government for Native Nations in South West Africa Bill 43, 44
Devraun, L. Joan D. 124
de Wet, Jannie 48, 49

Index

diamond mining 70
Dickens, Charles 112
diplomacy of shame 32
diplomatic isolation 130
diplomatic sanctions 53
dirty war 102
dissident 94
divine legitimacy 59
Dobell, Lauren 13, 14, 22, 28, 56, 85
dominant narrative 113
domino theory of international politics 71, 121
Drechsler, Horst 73
Dreyer, Johannes 94
Dreyer, Ronald 4, 14, 49
Drolsum, Nina 56
du Pisani, André 16, 38, 45, 70, 105
du Plessis, Abraham H. 70
du Plessis, Wentzel C. 50
du Preez, Roni L. 70
Durban Light Infantry 102
Dutch Reformed Church 95

East Germany 84–86, 89
economic isolation 130
economic sanctions 3, 14, 20, 23, 53, 54, 66, 69, 123
economic warfare 53
effective decolonization 3, 114
Egypt 75, 76, 84, 88
Eils, Robert C. 26
electronic surveillance 100
Elkins, Caroline 122
Emerson, Rupert 29
emigration 126, 127
empirical statehood 3, 25
End Conscription Campaign 98
Englebert, Pierre 17
English-speaking community in South Africa 122
Erichsen, Casper W. 30
Eritrea 120
ersatz diplomatic corps 28, 114
ersatz embassies 25
Escher, Alfred M. 45
Ethiopia 22, 27, 31, 44, 89, 120, 124, 129
European Economic Community 115
Evangelical Lutheran Church in Namibia (Rhenish Mission Church) 30
Evangelical Lutheran Ovambo-Kavango Church in Namibia 30
Evenson, John 59
Executive Outcomes 127
exile politics 16
external legitimacy 16
external sovereignty 47

Fall, Bernard B. 102
Finkelstein, Lawrence S. 16, 29, 34
Finland 60, 61, 111
Finnish Lutheran church 57
First World War 18, 26, 37, 67, 71, 92, 95, 96, 98, 103, 119

fishing and fish canneries 33, 68, 69, 118
flag independence 3
Foltz, William J. 51
Ford, Christopher A. 38, 124
foreign debt of Namibia cancellation 116, 117
Foster, Donald H. 103
Fourie, Deon 98
France 1, 16, 17, 35, 38, 53, 54, 63, 64, 66, 70, 72, 88, 97, 99–102, 112, 115, 119, 122, 123, 126, 127, 130
franchise 17
Frankel, Phillip H. 64
Franklin, Benjamin 35
Franklin, William 35
Fraser, C.A. 101
Frayne, Bruce 112
freedom ferry 77
freedom fighter 94
Freikorps 119
French National Assembly 99
Front Line States 17, 79
frontier war/warfare 2, 105
fuel rationing 66
fuel shortages 66
Fukuyama, Francis 16

Garoëb, Moses M. 115
garrison state 131
Garvey, Marcus 33, 34
Geingob, Hage G. 19, 36, 55, 107
Geldenhuys, Deon J. 3, 25, 66
Geldenhuys, Jannie 72, 101, 108
General Law Amendment Act 65
General Observer to the United Nations General Assembly 32, 54–56
Geneva conventions 87, 88
German citizens in Namibia 46, 127
German colonial policy 103
German Condor Legion 105
German military conduct/personnel/policy 30, 57, 92, 103
German National Socialism 50
German navy 70, 71
German officials 33
German policemen 92
German Reichstag 26
German residents of Namibia 33, 112
German *Schutztruppe* 113
German-speaking community/whites in Namibia 19, 27, 50, 92, 122, 127
German-speaking veterans in Namibia 119
German Third Reich 27, 50, 78
German Weimar Republic 26, 39, 70, 92, 112, 119
Germany 1, 14, 17, 19, 20, 29, 39, 57, 67, 73, 74, 85, 92, 93, 108, 112–116, 127, 128
Ghana 76, 79, 84, 108, 114, 124
G.I. Bill of Rights 119

Gifford, Prosser 128
globalist school of international politics 124, 125
Goldsworthy, David 27
Gordon, Robert J. 21, 103
Goulding, Marrack 82
government-in-waiting 22, 78
Governor General of South Africa 27
Gowaseb, Paulus 30
Great White Hoax 49
greater Ovamboland 48, 49
Grimal, Henri 3
Grofe, Jan 114
Groth, Siegfried 57, 58
Grundlingh, Albert 4
Grundy, Kenneth W. 3
Guernica, Spain 105
guerrillas 94, 122, 128; movement 125; warfare 54, 74–76, 79, 84, 86, 88–90, 101, 102, 105, 128
Guinea-Bissau 35, 60, 78
Gunn, Gillian 130
Gurirab, Theo-Ben 44, 115

Haggoy, Alf A. 102
Hahn, C.H.L. 40
Hailey, Lord 40
Haiti 27, 50
Hamaambo, Dimo 85
Hanyeko, Tobias 85
harkis 97
Harpvoken, Kristian B. 120
Heep, Uriah 112
Heitman, Helmoed-Römer 4
Hendrik Witbooi School 115
Henriksen, Thomas H. 3, 5, 127
Herero-Nama rebellion 73
Herero people 30, 32, 33, 73, 74, 113, 114, 128
Herero rebellion 30, 57
Heroes' Acre 113
Heroes' Day 73
Hertzog, James B.M. 26, 36, 50, 92
Heunis, Jan C. 56
Heywood, Annemarie 60
High Commission Territories 37, 41, 92, 122
high treason 47
Hirschman, Albert 33
Hitler, Adolf 92
Ho Chi Minh Trail 64, 89
Hochschild, Adam 74
Hofmeyr, Gysbert R. 38
Holsti, Kaveli J. 18
Hoogenhout, Petrus I. 41
Hooper, Jim 85
horizontal legitimacy 18
Horne, Alistair 15
Hosea Kutako School 115
Hough, Michael 16
Howard, Lise 82
Hübschle, Michaela 109
Hull, Isabel V. 57
Hume, Shirley 4
Hunter, Justine 2, 113

Huntington, Samuel P. 16–18
Hurd, Ian 17

Iceland 60
ideological legitimacy 17
impartiality clause/package 107, 108
imperialism 49
incorporation of Namibia into South Africa 33, 39–42, 50, 129
indemnity 103
independence, Namibia 31, 32, 39, 42, 45, 46, 50, 66, 75, 80, 81, 90, 122, 124, 125, 129; constitution 90
India 50, 109, 115
Indonesia 28
infiltration routes 71
insurgencies 4, 14–16, 73, 93, 103, 124, 125; warfare doctrine 77
interim government of South West Africa 72
internal desertion 125, 126
internal legitimacy 16
internal sovereignty 47
International Aid and Defense Fund for Southern Africa 59
International Court of Justice 13, 22, 27, 28, 30, 31, 34, 44, 47, 55, 66, 73, 97, 114, 123, 124, 129, 130
International Criminal Court 108
international legitimacy 16, 25, 74, 90, 106, 124
international monitoring/oversight 17, 39, 79
International Red Cross 87, 88
international solidarity lobbyists 57
international trusteeship system 48
Iraq 71, 72, 119, 126
Isle of Pines, Cuba 115
Israel 63, 122
Israel, Mark 57
Israeli Defense Force 101
Italo-Ethiopian War 49
Italy 36, 49, 63
Ivory Coast 120

Jabri, Vivienne 3
Jackson, Robert H. 3, 15, 25
Japan 27, 115
Jaster, Robert S. 121
Ja Toivo, Toivo Herman 112
Jeanson, Francis 53
John, Nerys 65, 66
Joint Nordic Program of Action against Apartheid 61
Jones, Johan 72
Jooste, Rina 85
Jowell, Kate 127
Jubilee South Africa 114
juridical statehood 3, 25
just war doctrine 59, 60

Kahimise, Rahimisa 79
Kangas, Lari 111
Kangumu, Bennett 111

Kapuuo, Clements 86
Karns, Margaret P. 56
Kauluma, James 57
Kaunda, Kenneth 85
Kay, David A. 124
Kempton, Daniel L. 70
Kennedy Administration 19
Kenya 35
Kenya Human Rights Commission 122
Kerina, Mburumba 28
Khama, Tshekedi 30, 33
Khapoya, Vincent B. 125
Khulumani Support Group 114
King George III 33
kith and kin politics 122
Klotz, Audie J. 4, 53
Koep, Peter 109
Koevoet 1, 64, 81, 82, 87, 89–91, 94, 102, 106, 107, 119, 127; veterans 119
Korean War 51, 96
Kosovo 120
Kössler, Reinhart 114
Kotjipati, Alfons 97
Kozlov, Aleksei 87
Kriger, Norma J. 82
Kuhangua, Jacob 75
Kutako, Hosea 30

labor-hire companies 118
labor unions 33
Lakota (Sioux) 74
Lamb, Guy 4, 14, 81, 84
land alienation 117
land distribution 20
land reform legislation 117
land tenure 21
landmines 24, 89, 120, 128
Lasswell, Harold D. 53
laws of war 84
Lawyers Committee for Civil Rights under Law 59
League of Nations 26, 27, 31, 33, 37, 39, 47–50, 93, 123, 128, 129; mandate 44, 46, 92, 97, 99, 126; mandate agreement 1, 22, 29, 57, 94, 114; mandated territories 22, 26, 28, 30, 31, 84; mandates reports 49, 50; mandates system 22, 26, 28, 36, 38, 39, 42, 50, 71; mandatory powers 27, 33, 46, 66
League of Nations Assembly 49
League of Nations Covenant 126
League of Nations Permanent Mandates Commission 22, 26, 27, 33, 34, 36, 38, 40, 47, 49, 50
legal decolonization 3, 114, 117
Legislative Assembly of South West Africa 26, 27, 40, 43
legitimacy 15–18, 23, 26, 32, 34, 37, 41, 46, 59, 60, 75, 76, 78, 80, 87, 88, 93, 97, 111, 123, 131; deficit 16; deflation 16; language 17; war 16
legitimating strategy 17

legitimation 4, 17, 23, 83
Lesotho 37, 122
leverage of legitimacy 29, 34
lexicon of obscurity 131
Leyveld, Joseph 43
Liberal Party of South Africa 71, 128
liberated areas/zones 77–79, 82, 128
liberation struggle 2
liberation theology 57
liberation war 2
Liberia 22, 27, 31, 40, 44, 124, 129
Liebenberg, Kat 108
Lijphart, Arend 70
linkage 80, 122
Lister, Gwen 109
Livhiwani, Nengovhela J 4
Lombard, Christo 109
Lombard, Hans J. 76
Lomperis, Timothy J. 16
London Agreement 26, 92
Lopez, George A. 3
Lord, Richard 85
Louis, William R. 26, 128
Louw, Eric 41, 48
Lubowski, Anton 108, 109
Luderitz Bay 67, 70
Ludorf, Joseph F. 47
Lush, David 112
Lutheran World Federation 58
Lutherans 58

Machtergreifung explanation 82
Maechling, Charles, Jr. 54
Malan, Daniel F. 19, 50, 51
Malan, Magnus 101, 109
Malaya 101
Malaysia 102
Mandela, Nelson 116, 117, 131
Manela, Erez 18
Mao Tse-tung 84, 85
Marcum, John A. 75
Marengo, Jakob 74
Marquard, Leo 71
Mau Mau insurgency 122
Maxwell, Kenneth R. 3
May, Theo 108
McCarthy, Joseph R. 34
McCuen, John J. 102
Meiring, Georg 101
Melber, Henning 111, 113, 119
Memmi, Albert 70
memory management 15, 113
memory politics 113
Metsola, Lalli 119
Michigan State University 1
migrant labor system 20–22, 33, 69, 84, 118
military: coups 16; resources 71; sanctions 61, 62, 64, 66, 123; supplies 74; training 74, 75
Minear, Larry 3
minerals 69
mining industry 69, 70, 118
Ministry of Foreign Affairs of Namibia 114

Ministry of Veterans Affairs of Namibia 120
missionaries: foreign 57, 58; German 38; German Protestant 57
Mittelman, James H. 3, 32, 117
Moorcraft, Paul L. 105
Moorsom, Richard 59
moral legitimacy 16, 57
Morengo, Jacob 85
Mosaka, Paul R. 124
Motinga, Ben 108
Mozambique 17, 24, 35, 71, 79, 89, 94, 100, 113, 122, 126, 130
Mudge, Dirk F. 46, 103
Mueshihange, Peter 85
Mugabe, Robert 82
Mukumbi wa Nyembo, Jules 124
multi-centric world 4
multinational/transnational corporations 14, 22, 31, 32, 64, 67, 69, 70, 114, 123, 125
Multi-Party Conference of South West Africa 72, 131
Munger, Edwin S. 79
mutiny 97, 125

Nama people 33, 74
Nama rebellion 30
Namibia Communications Center 30, 59
Namibia Day 73
Namibia Defense Force 4, 118
The Namibian (newspaper) 109
Namibian African People's Organization 14
Namibian archives 1, 41, 56
Namibian clergy 58
Namibian Constituent Assembly 18, 36, 45, 56, 69, 82, 90, 91, 106–108
Namibian Council of Churches 97
Namibian Defense Force 4, 89, 117–120; maritime wing 115, 118
Namibian detainees 58
Namibian Economic Policy Unit 59
Namibian foreign debt cancellation 116, 131
Namibian general election of 2009 51
Namibian National Assembly 51, 107
Namibian People's Army 75
Namibian People's Organization 14
Namibian Prayer Day 60
Namibian presidential election of 2009 51
Namibian War for/of Independence 1, 4, 13, 17, 23, 38, 46, 50, 55, 60, 72, 93, 96, 111, 115, 118, 120, 122, 123, 126
Nanyemba, Peter 85, 88
Nasser, Gamal 84
Nathanael, Keshii P. 76
National Front for the Liberation of Angola 49
National Liberation Front of Algeria 53, 101

National Party of South Africa 31, 41, 43, 45, 51, 96, 113
National Party of South West Africa 99
national reconciliation in Namibia 108, 112, 120
National Union for the Total Independence of Angola 49, 71, 85, 105
National Union for the Total Liberation of Angola 14, 79, 83
National Union of Namibian Workers 118
natural resources of Namibia 20, 22, 23, 66
Naudé, Willem C. 19
Netherlands 70
Neto, Agostinho 79
Neuberger, Benyamin 19, 26, 39
New York Accords 81
Niehaus, J.P. de M. 40
Nigeria 79, 84, 115
Non-Aligned Movement 4, 81
nongovernmental organizations 22, 57, 61, 124
non-self-governing territories 28, 31, 40
non-state actors 79
non-violence 61
Nordic Africa Institute 60
North Atlantic Treaty Organization 60, 63
North Korea 84
Northern Rhodesia 92
Norval, Morgan 102
Norway 26, 60, 61, 76
Nöthling, Frederik J. 51
Novick, Peter 16
Nujoma, Sam 14, 73, 76, 79, 81–84, 88, 116
Nye, Joseph, Jr. 14

Obozuwa, A. Ukiomoge 130
O'Brien, Kevin A. 94, 102
observer groups 40
Odendaal, Frans H. 48
Odendaal Plan/Report 43, 44, 48
Oermann, Nils O. 57
Office of Governmental Affairs of the Lutheran Council in the United States 52
oil embargo/sanctions 62, 65
Okavango River 83
oligopsony 21
O'Linn, Bryan 81, 113
Ongulumbashe 60, 73, 77, 78, 83, 84, 88, 93, 100, 101, 130
Operation Agree 108
Operation Blue Wildebeeste 93, 101
Operation *Dikmelk* 93
Operation 435 108
Operation Heyday 108
Operation Plan Olympus 93
Operation Reindeer 100, 104, 105
Operation Savannah 65, 66, 87
oral petitions 27, 32, 33

Organization of African Unity 17, 55, 75–77, 79, 90, 115, 125; Liberation Committee 55, 75, 84
Orwell, George 113, 119
other-determination 19, 26, 39
Ottawa Treaty 120
Ovambo people 21, 49, 74, 84
Ovamboland 21, 30, 42, 48, 49, 73, 76, 77, 85, 100, 103, 116
Ovamboland People's Organization 69
Ovenden, Keith 4
Oxford University 59

Palestine 53
Palme, Olaf 59
pan-African conference system 28
Pan-African Congresses 50
Pan Africanist Congress of South Africa 78, 79, 88
Papenfus, Johan 88
pariah regime 25
pariah states 25
Paris Peace Conference 39, 43
partisan warfare 54
partition of Namibia 48
Peled, Alom 100, 101
Pendleton, Wade C. 112
People's Armed Forces for the Liberation of Angola 80, 83, 85, 86, 88, 89, 128
People's Liberation Armed Force of Vietnam/Viet Cong 64
People's Liberation Army of Namibia 4, 24, 55, 60, 65, 71, 75–77, 79–91, 97, 99–103, 105–107, 119, 120, 124, 128, 130, 131; bases 60, 79, 80, 82, 83, 101; veterans 119, 120
performance legitimacy 17, 22, 28
petitioning the United Nations 27, 28, 30, 33, 34, 36, 48, 60, 75, 123, 129
petty apartheid 46
Philippines 3, 74, 78, 79, 86
Phillips, Merran W. 98, 126
Picasso, Pablo 105
Pirow, Oswald 51
plebiscite 19, 39–45, 48, 105, 130
police element of UNTAG 90
Police (South-West Africa) Act 92
Police Zone 86
political consolidation 18
political correctness 19
political fragmentation 18
political legitimacy 16
political mythology 17
political war 24
politics of hyperbole 32
politics of inequality 37
politics of legitimacy/legitimation 17, 87
politics of memory 2, 60, 112, 113
politics of shame 124
Pool, Ithiel de Sola 43
Popular Movement for the Liberation of Angola 49, 86

population resettlement 104
Portugal 1, 15, 20, 35, 60, 74, 78, 83, 85, 89, 95, 96, 101, 113, 122, 124–128
Posel, Deborah 16
post-traumatic stress disorder 119
Pottinger, Brian 101
Pretoria terrorism trial 34, 47
Pretorius, Phil 101
Prisk, Courtney E. 16
prisoners of war 30, 85, 87, 88
procedural legitimacy 17, 18
Progressive Party of South Africa 44, 76
prohibition of violence act of Botswana 77
protobargaining 34
pseudo operations 87
Public Service Commission of Namibia 114

quasi-diplomatic missions 28
quasi-states 25
Quebecquois 98

racial discrimination 50
racial equality 50
radio intercepts and monitoring 65, 93
RAND Corporation 2, 125
Rand revolt 51
Reagan, Ronald 124
realist school of international politics 124
realpolitik 125
rebel 94
Rebellion of 1914 95
referendum 39, 41, 46
refugees 78, 83, 84, 96, 104, 106, 124, 128; camps 60, 61, 104
regime legitimacy 17
regionalist school of international politics 124, 125
Rehoboth community 27, 33, 43
Rehoboth rebellion 50, 93
reinterpretation of legitimacy 17
relics of the Namibian war 112
reparations 69, 122
Republic of South Africa 20
Revolutionary Government of Angola in Exile 75
revolutionary war 54, 102
Rhenish Missionary Society 29
Rhodes Scholar 57, 122
Riggs, Robert E. 29
Roberto, Holden 75
Roberts, Alun R. 66
Rodman, Kenneth A. 4
Roosevelt, Theodore 32
Rosberg, Carl G. 3
Rosenau, James N. 22, 122
Rotberg, Robert I. 38
Royal Military Academy 85
Royal Navy 63, 70, 94
Ruppel, Hartmut 109
rural poverty 117
Russia 1

sabotage 86
Sabotage Act 65
sacred trust of civilization 50, 129
Salazar, Antonio de Oliveira 35
sanctions 49, 53–55, 59, 61, 63, 64, 65
Santcross, Nick 76, 77
Saunders, Christopher C. 4, 27, 51, 113
Saunders, Cliff 73, 83
Saxena, Suresh C. 4, 123
Schamberger, Paul 68
Schmokel, Wolfe W. 26
Scholtz, Leopold 85, 98, 106, 123
Schrire, Robert 38, 50
Schüring, Esther 127
Scott, Michael 27, 28, 30, 57
Sebald, Peter 26
securocrats 121, 131
Seegers, Annette 105, 130
self-determination 15, 17–20, 30–32, 39, 40, 42–45, 48, 50, 87, 111, 130
self-government 18, 19, 26, 43
Selous Scouts of Southern Rhodesia 101, 102
semi-conventional warfare 105
separate development 17, 19–21, 43–45, 48, 49, 86, 103, 112, 121, 130
settler colony 26
shadow embassies 25
shadow government 22, 23, 78, 90
Shafer, D. Michael 130
Shain, Yossi 15, 16, 18, 23
Sharpeville, South Africa 114
Shepherd, George W., Jr. 4
Shipanga, Andreas 58, 84
Shuuya, Leonard P. 76
Silvermine center 100
Simonstown Agreement 94
Singer, J. David 15
Singham, A.W. 4
skilled white workers 126
small scale wars 2
small wars 13, 24
Smith, Tony 3, 38, 96
Smuts, Jan C. 19, 26, 37–41, 50, 51, 92, 94, 98, 99, 129
Snyman, P.H.R. 4
Social Democratic Party of Germany 26
socially accepted narratives 113
socially accepted national narrative[s] 113
Socio-Economic Integration for Ex-Combatants in Namibia 120
soft targets 87
solidarity organizations 30, 57, 58, 67, 90, 124
solidarity workers 61
South Africa Foundation 52, 130
South African Air Force 23, 51, 64, 65, 78, 85, 93, 94, 101, 104, 131
South African archives 1, 56, 116
South African armaments industry 64, 131

South African Army College 101
South African Broadcasting Corporation 85
South African Cape Corps 96
South African Catholic Bishops' Conference 59
South African coal 62
South African Council of Churches 59
South African defense budget 64
South African Defense Force 1, 4, 15, 24, 54, 55, 60, 62, 63, 65, 66, 71, 72, 78, 80, 81, 83–90, 93–106, 108, 109, 115, 116, 119, 120, 122, 127, 130, 131; civic action program 103; conscript combat deaths 95; ethnology unit 103; military training 95; reserve and mobilization structure 95; reserve duty 95, 96
South African Defense Force Military Intelligence 58, 98, 107–109
South African Department of External Affairs 50
South African foreign service 50
South African general elections: (1929) 121; (1948) 43, 45, 95
South African High Commission in London 50
South African House of Assembly 22, 27, 41, 44, 56, 70, 99
South African Institute of International Affairs 31
South African Institute of Race Relations 40
South African Military Academy 101
South African Minister of Justice 103
South African Native Military Corps 84
South African Native Representative Council 124
South African Navy 63, 94, 100
South African Parliament 27, 35, 44, 46, 47, 64, 68, 94, 99
South African Permanent Mission to the United Nations 35
South African Police 54, 55, 64, 66, 73, 76, 78, 82, 83, 85, 87, 90, 92–95, 100–102
South African President 103
South African railway network 62
South African Senate 22, 27, 38, 99
South African Special Account 64
South African Special Forces 101
South African State Information Office 50
South African State President 27
South African State Security Council 68
South African Truth and Reconciliation Commission 59, 107
South Vietnam 88
South West Africa Affairs Act 68

South West Africa Affairs Amendment Act 99
South West Africa Liberation Army 75, 76
South West Africa National Union 75–77, 84
South West Africa Native Labor Association 21
South West Africa Protection Unit 86
South West Africa Territorial Force 4, 24, 80, 81, 88–91, 97, 99, 100, 106, 109, 119, 127; combat fatalities 99; veterans 119
South West African People's Organization 1, 3, 14, 15, 18, 22–24, 26, 28, 30, 32, 44–47, 51, 53–61, 64, 68, 69, 73–85, 87–91, 97, 102–104, 107, 108, 112–115, 117, 124, 128, 130; defense headquarters 85; diplomatic corps 59; membership dues 54; military council 85; secretary of defense 85
South West African People's Organization Youth League 76
South West African Police 1, 106, 128
Southern Rhodesia 15, 35, 37, 65, 80, 89, 92, 94, 95, 97, 100, 101, 104, 125–127, 130
Southern Rhodesian Special Air Service 101
sovereignty 4, 18, 22, 23, 46, 47, 97
Soviet Consulate in South Africa 51
Soviet spies 52, 87
Soviet Union 61, 65, 79, 82, 84, 87, 89, 115, 123
Soviet weaponry 52
Sovik, Martin A. 52
Spain 54, 79, 104
Spanish Civil War 105
Sparks, Donald L. 70
Special Representative of the United Nations Secretary General 36, 82, 90, 106
spirit mediums 58
spiritual scramble for Africa 29
Srivastava, Rachna 2
state-centric view 4
state legitimacy 57
Stellenbosch University 45
Stevenson, Adlai 63
Stiff, Peter 85, 87, 93, 106, 107
Stoecker, Helmut 26
Strand, Per 51
subnational sanctions 66
subsistence agriculture 21
Sudan 120
Sudetenland 92
supply routes 71
Suppression of Communism Act 51
Supreme Court of South West Africa 88, 97
Suret-Canale, Jean 2
suspended sovereignty 22

Suzman, Helen 76
Swakopmund 67, 70
Swanepoel, Theunis J. 78, 100
swart gevaar 121, 129
Swaziland 37, 122
Sweden 26, 59, 60, 76, 108, 112, 115
Swedish International Development Authority 111
Switzerland 45, 108, 112
symbolic arsenals 15, 23
symbolic warfare 31
symbols 15, 17, 130; manipulation 129, 131

Taliban 88
talk and thump 130, 131
Talmon, Stefan 75
Tamarakin, Mordechai 14, 16
Tanzania 17, 75–77, 79, 84, 88
taxation 21, 53, 70
technology transfer 63, 64
territorial apartheid 43
territorial fragmentation 48, 49
territorial integrity 19, 48, 68, 111
territorial legitimacy 17, 18
territorial waters of Namibia 117
terrorism 47, 93
Terrorism Act/Bill 47, 76
Theodoli, Marquis 36
theological heresy 59
Third World 13, 16, 22, 25, 129
Thomas, Wolfgang H. 127
Thompson, J.H. 85
Thompson, Robert 102
Thörn, Håkon 4
Thornberry, Cedric 81
Timo Line of Namibia 104
Togoland 70
Toivo Ya Toivo, Herman 112
Torreguitar, Elena 3
torture 76, 88, 100–103, 119
total onslaught policy 51, 102, 121, 130
total strategy 102, 130
Tötemeyer, Gerhard 45, 109
traditional agriculture 21
Transkei 19, 40, 49, 79
transnational anti-apartheid: groups 125; support network 53
transnational business firms 4
transnational issues 14
Treaty of Paris 79
Treaty of Versailles 50, 68
trust territories 31
trusteeship 31
Tuhadeleni, Eliaser 34, 47, 59, 76, 100, 112
turkey shoot 81
Turnhalle Conference 45, 46
Typhoon 85

unacceptable political objective 130
União das Populações de Angola 75
Union Defense Force 93, 96, 98; white women volunteers 96

Union of South Africa 20
United Kingdom 2, 17, 20, 33–35, 37–39, 41, 43, 47, 48, 50, 52, 58–60, 63, 66, 67, 70, 71, 74–76, 85, 92, 94, 95, 98, 100–102, 104, 108, 114, 115, 122, 123, 125
United National South West Party 40
United Nations 13, 16–18, 23, 25–29, 32–34, 38–44, 48–50, 55–57, 59–61, 63, 67–69, 79–82, 97, 99, 104, 107–109, 115, 117, 120, 122–125, 129, 130
United Nations Angola Verification Mission 106
United Nations Charter 29, 31, 39, 63
United Nations Commissioner for Namibia 58
United Nations Committee on South West Africa 75, 123
United Nations Conference on International Organization 31
United Nations Council for Namibia 22, 23, 55, 66–68, 88, 90, 114; decree no. 1 66
United Nations Council for South West Africa 36
United Nations Department of Peacekeeping Operations 90
United Nations financial data/flows/support 67, 107
United Nations Fund for Namibia 36, 56
United Nations General Assembly 1, 13, 14, 18, 19, 22, 27, 29, 31, 32, 34–36, 39–44, 47, 48, 50, 54–56, 67, 68, 74, 87, 90, 97, 107, 113, 115, 123, 128–130
United Nations General Assembly Fourth (Trusteeship) Committee 27, 28, 34, 56
United Nations General Assembly resolutions 13, 18, 22, 29, 31, 32, 34, 41, 54, 56, 66, 87, 123, 124
United Nations Good Offices Committee 48
United Nations Institute for Namibia 34, 36, 123
United Nations Secretariat 79
United Nations Secretary-General 43, 45, 79, 81, 107
United Nations Secretary-General's Special Representative in Namibia 36, 82, 106
United Nations Security Council 32, 34, 35, 44, 47, 54, 55, 63, 68, 69, 81, 82, 84, 87, 90, 107, 115, 122–124, 129, 130; resolutions 13, 32, 45, 66, 69, 105
United Nations Transition Assistance Group 36, 42, 45, 80–82, 90, 105, 106, 107, 109; military component 106, 107, 109
United Nations Trust Territory 31, 38, 75
United Nations trusteeship system

18, 28, 38, 42; system visiting missions 36
United Nations Undersecretary-General for Peacekeeping 82
United Party of South Africa 41, 44
United States 2, 17–20, 33, 35, 38, 48, 50, 52, 59, 61, 63, 64, 66, 67, 72, 74, 79, 82, 88, 95–97, 101–103, 105, 113–115, 119, 123–126, 130
United States Army 101–103
United States Army Command and General Staff College 101
United States Army Special Warfare School 101
United States Coast Guard 118
United States Congress 66, 125
United States Coordinating Committee on Multilateral Export Controls 63
United States Defense Intelligence Agency 64
United States House of Representatives 52, 58
United States House of Representatives Committee on Foreign Affairs Africa Subcommittee 106, 107
United States Marine Corps 13, 24, 102
United States military 78, 101, 118, 120, 126
United States Naval Postgraduate School 126
United States Naval War College 52
United States Navy 103
United States Senate 52
United States Supreme Court 69
United States veterans 119, 120
University of London 59
University of Namibia 4, 109
Unlawful Organizations Act 59
urban guerrilla warfare 86
Uys, Stanley 127

vagrancy laws 21
van der Merwe, Paul S. 99
van der Mescht, Johan 85, 87
van der Waals, Kaas 101
van der Westhuizen, Christi 127
van Wyk, Frederik 108
Vedder, Heinrich 38
Vergau, Hans-Joachim 3
vertical legitimacy 18
Verwoerd, Hendrik F. 43, 112
Veterans for Victory 98
vicarious representation 27
Viet Cong 64, 86
Viet Minh 64, 65, 78
Vietnam 78, 86, 89, 96, 101, 102, 104, 119, 126
Vietnam War 61, 64, 95, 96, 121
Viljoen, Constand 102
Volcano 85
voluntary arms embargo 63
Vorster, B.J. 30, 44, 45, 47, 68, 73, 85, 87

Waldheim, Kurt 45
Walvis Bay 19, 47, 67–69, 71, 93, 99, 111, 115, 117, 118, 131
Walvis Bay Administration Proclamation 68
war costs 71, 72
war of independence 2
war of national liberation 87
wars of decolonization 2
Warwick, Rodney C. 99
Wasserman, Gary 37
Watson, Adam 25
weapons transport system 65
Weatherford, Jack 74
Weiss, Thomas G. 3
West Germany 66, 112
West New Guinea 70
Western Contact Group 17, 66, 69, 79, 117
white community: of Namibia 21, 31, 40, 43, 46, 49, 68, 97, 99, 112, 116, 120, 127, 131; of South Africa 20, 97, 98, 127, 130
white dominance/minority rule/paramountcy/power/privilege/supremacy 12, 32, 33, 38, 43, 45, 50–52, 71, 98, 103, 112, 121, 122
white electorate: of Namibia 46, 50; of South Africa 50
white farmers of Namibia 116, 117
white farming areas of Namibia 128
white minority 126
white minority regimes 55
white settler diaspora 122
white veterans of Namibia 98, 119
Williams, Christian A. 105, 113
Williams, David 73
Wilson, Woodrow 18, 39, 43
winning hearts and minds 59, 102, 103
Winter, Colin 58
within-case analysis 3
World War II 1, 19, 20, 25, 27, 33, 35, 37, 50, 51, 68, 70, 78, 84, 93, 95, 96, 98, 102, 119, 121, 122, 124, 125, 128
Wright, Joanne 16
Wright, Quincy 22
written petitions 27

Yale University 59
Yati Strip of Namibia 104
Young, M. Crawford 3
Yu Chi Chan Club 84
Yugoslavia 84

Zaire 75
Zambezi River 77
Zambia 17, 36, 55, 75, 77, 78, 80, 83, 85, 86, 88, 89, 104, 105, 112, 115, 119
Zambian Defense Force 89
Zartman, I. William 3, 16, 54, 126
Zimbabwe 14, 17, 23, 37, 57, 58, 71, 76, 80, 82, 86, 101, 112, 115, 120
Zimbabwe African National Liberation Army 76
Zimbabwe African National Union 76
Zimbabwe African People's Union 76
Zimbabwe National Army 86
Zimbabwe People's Revolutionary Army 76
Zuijdwijk, Ton J.M. 27

www.ingramcontent.com/pod-product-compliance
Lightning Source LLC
Chambersburg PA
CBHW081556300426
44116CB00015B/2903